The African Experience

The African Experience

An Introduction

Fourth Edition

VINCENT B. **KHAPOYA**

Professor Emeritus
Oakland University

Boston   Columbus   Indianapolis   New York   San Francisco   Upper Saddle River   Amsterdam
Cape Town   Dubai   London   Madrid   Milan   Munich   Paris   Montreal   Toronto   Delhi
Mexico City   São Paulo   Sydney   Hong Kong   Seoul   Singapore   Taipei   Tokyo

Senior Acquisitions Editor: Vikram Mukhija
Editorial Assistants: Isabel Schwab, Beverly Fong
Executive Marketing Manager: Wendy Gordon
Full Service Project Management and Composition: Moganambigai Sundaramurthy/
   Integra Software Services, Pvt. Ltd.
Cover Design Manager: Jayne Conte
Cover Designer: Karen Noferi
Cover Illustration/Photo: Hugh Sitton/Corbis
Production Manager: Fran Russello
Printer and Binder: Courier Companies, Inc.

Library of Congress Cataloging-in-Publication Data
Khapoya, Vincent B.
   The African experience : an introduction / Vincent B. Khapoya.—4th ed.
      p. cm.
   Includes bibliographical references and index.
   ISBN 978-0-205-85171-3 (alk. paper)
   1. Africa—History. I. Title.
   DT20.K47 2013
   960—dc23

                                        2011047946

1 2 3 4 5 6 7 8 9 10—CRW—12 11 10 09

ISBN-10:   0-205-85171-1
ISBN-13: 978-0-205-85171-3

Izzat, Aman Cabral, and Aisha K. Robinson

BRIEF CONTENTS

CONTENTS

CHAPTER 4
Colonialism and the African Experience   99

PREFACE

The fourth edition of this book comes out at a critical juncture, not only for Africa, but for the world community as a whole. I am pleased to be able to update the book and to reflect on some of the changes that have occurred since the third edition was published only two years ago. When I first began to teach an introductory course on Africa, for nearly twenty years, I could not find a textbook that presented Africa in its totality. There were edited books, compilations of chapters written by eight or ten authors, from different disciplines in the humanities and the social sciences. Despite the best efforts of the editors to maintain thematic coherence, my students continued to complain about the unevenness of the material they were reading, in both style and content. I then decided to write this book to meet the need for a text that shows how culture, history, politics, and European imperialism have interacted to produce an Africa that is much more complex and dynamic. In the paragraphs that follow, I will briefly discuss the features of the book, what is new in this edition, and provide summaries of the chapters.

NEW TO THIS EDITION

1. Chapter 1, "The Continent and Its People," has been updated with the most recent demographic data in Table 1.1 and includes information on Africa's newest nation: the Republic of South Sudan, which came into being on July 9, 2011. Table 1.2 on languages spoken in African countries has also been updated.

2. With regard to the use of violence to subjugate Africans who were resisting colonization, additional evidence of German brutality is provided in the form of a recent admission by the German government that what the German soldiers did to the Nama and Herero people in Namibia could probably be described as genocide and the German government was prepared to apologize, but would not consider paying reparations to the descendants of the 65,000 Africans killed by German soldiers.

3. Additional discussion of the "Arab Spring," in North Africa and Yemen, a term being used to refer to the people's uprisings in the form of mass demonstrations which have brought down the governments of Tunisia, Egypt, and Libya, all now being ruled by interim

governments while they decide on the next steps. The future of Libya, ruled autocratically by Muammar Qaddafi for 42 years does not bode well for the country. Qaddafi was the only dictator to die defending his regime. Now, as in so many African countries to the south, when the revolutions should have given people a sense of one destiny, Libyans are killing one another in disturbingly large numbers under the guise of "tribal" loyalties.

4. An update on the **African Union (AU)**, founded in 2002 with high hopes of being more successful and more forceful in articulating and protecting African interests. So far, the AU is struggling financially to maintain troops in Darfur, refuses to declare the killings in Darfur as genocide, and decided to recognize the interim national council in Libya as the legal representative of the Libyan people only after Qaddafi was captured and killed. I can't even begin to talk about Africa's newest country, the Republic of South Sudan, which came into being on July 9, 2011. After more than thirty years of war, and only six months of existence as a sovereign nation, the armed militias are slaughtering people to settle old "tribal" scores. The new government is unable to intervene, the AU peace keepers are not instituted to fight. They are afraid that if they intervene to protect civilians, they might make things worse. The AU, indeed, has its work cut out for it.

FEATURES

The book assumes no prior knowledge of Africa. It also does not confine itself to sub-Saharan Africa, so-called Black Africa. Hence, it takes the student from the geography of the continent—physical, political, and demographic—to the linguistic classification of the more than 800 major languages spoken on the continent. This is followed by a presentation of traditional institutions and customs, the precolonial history of Africa, the scramble for imperial control of the Africans by European powers. The depth of the colonial experience is illustrated by the fact that only two states (out of the current fifty-four independent nations) were never formally colonized: Ethiopia and Liberia. The introduction of the concept of the "civilizing mission" is an attempt to explore the cultural reasons for European colonization of Africa and to raise the question, "What did the Europeans expect a civilized African to be like once they were done with their mission?" African nationalism, which was a response to colonialism, is discussed, as well as the attainment of independence, beginning in the early 1950s. The last three chapters deal with the choices made by the first generation of African leaders in trying to create new nations out of their new sovereign states and to raise the living standards of their people. The first three decades of independence were probably wasted as African leaders experimented with one-party systems and government-controlled (or socialist) economies. With prodding from international institutions like the World Bank and IMF and from major aid donors, African countries have embarked on free-market economies. They have also opened up more democratic space. There are now nearly a dozen countries in Africa—Ghana, Botswana, South Africa, Namibia, to name four examples—which meet standards of democracy. The book concludes with an examination of the role that Africa has played on the world stage, the African Union (formed in 2002 to replace the Organization of African Unity), the African leaders' efforts to take care of their own problems and lessen their dependence on the United States and European countries.

Chapter 1, in the first half, introduces the African continent in terms of geography and demography. Statistics pertaining to population and gross national income (GNI) per person have been updated to 2011. The second half treats in some detail the diversity and convergence of African people in the cultural and linguistic patterns and discusses the problem of referring to African culture groups as "tribes." There is an emphasis on norms, values, and historical experience as key variables that define people who they are rather than as labels called tribes.

Chapter 2 describes the main traditional cultural forms and institutions found in Africa. The stress is on those forms that are shared in such matters as kinship, marriage, socialization, including initiation rites. Four types of nonkinship groups are explored. The reader will realize that I depart from usual convention of textbook writing by narrating in the first person what the rites of passage meant to me. Since I was not merely an observer, but a participant, why not personalize the experience? Reader reaction has been uniformly positive.

Chapter 3 is an interpretive essay on African history, which attempts to place Africa at the center rather than the periphery of major world historical happenings. It treats such things as state building, alliance formation, and the rise and decline of various kingdoms, and examines several pieces of archeological evidence which disprove Western myths about the marginality of African history. In this edition, this chapter was only edited for style.

Chapter 4 is a discussion of the African experience under European colonial rule. Reasons for colonization, "the civilizing missions" of the various European powers (France, Britain, and Portugal), and colonial policies and administrative styles are analyzed. For this edition, I have included new material on the colonial policy and practices of the Germans in Namibia, as well as the dismal record of Belgian colonial rule in the present Democratic Republic of Congo. The chapter concludes with an assessment of colonial rule.

Chapter 5 examines the successful African resistance to colonial rule and the role played by external forces and internal factors in that resistance.

Chapter 6 takes a hard look at the first thirty years of African independence, the challenges facing this first generation of leaders, their dalliance with socialist economies and one-party systems, resulting in repressive governments, economic stagnation, and increased economic and security dependency on former colonial powers.

Chapter 7 is a detailed discussion of the struggle for democracy and free markets which has been going on for the past two decades and a half. Behind the push for democracy and free markets were the World Bank and IMF and Western aid donors like the United States and Britain. Some of the key issues addressed in this chapter are these: When and how did the Africans realize that earlier experiments had not been successful and were not likely to work for the future? What other forces, internal or external, have been central to this struggle for political transparency and economic self-sufficiency? How has the struggle faired? Who have been the gainers and the losers and why?

Chapter 8, the final chapter, is an analysis of the role that Africa has played on the world stage. The influence of the cold war is stressed, properly so, as are the contributions that African states collectively have made in keeping on the world agenda issues of vital importance to them and in sensitizing the world community to matters of human rights and racism which never got much attention when the world was being run almost exclusively by Western nations. This chapter has been updated to include information on the African Union (AU), formed in 2002 to replace the Organization of African Unity (OAU) (a compromise organization founded in 1963). The hope was that the AU would be more effective in addressing security issues on the continent, but the crises in Darfur, Sudan, and in Zimbabwe are proof that, despite a new enlightened AU charter, without commitment of resources, the AU is not going to be any more successful than its predecessor.

SUPPLEMENTS

Pearson is pleased to offer several resources to qualified adopters of *The African Experience* and their students that will make teaching and learning from this book even more effective and enjoyable.

MySearchLab

For over ten years, instructors and students have reported achieving better results and better grades when a Pearson MyLab has been integrated into the course. MySearchLab provides engaging experiences that personalize learning, and comes from a trusted partner with educational expertise and a deep commitment to helping students and instructors achieve their goals. It contains writing, grammar, and research tools and access to a variety of academic journals, census data, Associated Press newsfeeds, and discipline-specific readings that help you hone your writing and research skills. To order MySearchLab with the print text, use ISBN 0-205-20860-6.

Passport

Choose the resources you want from MyPoliSciLab and put links to them into your course management system. If there is assessment associated with those resources, it also can be uploaded, allowing the results to feed directly into your course management system's gradebook. With MyPoliSciLab assets like videos, mapping exercises, *Financial Times* newsfeeds, current events quizzes, politics blog, and much more, Passport is available for any Pearson political science book. To order Passport with the print text, use ISBN 0-205-23160-8.

ACKNOWLEDGMENTS

This book has benefited from contributions from many people. Professor James D. Graham and I have worked closely together in the African Studies Program for the entire time I have been at Oakland University. Jim is a historian whose appreciation of the African experience is profound and his enthusiasm for sharing that experience with his students and colleagues infectious. It was for that reason that I asked him to contribute an interpretive chapter on African history (Chapter 3). For this chapter, for the editorial contributions which he made to the first edition of the text, and for his friendship, I am deeply grateful.

This edition also benefited a great deal from the careful review by Keith A. Gottschalk, senior lecturer in political studies at the University of the Western Cape (UWC). In response to my inquiry if I could spend my sabbatical leave in South Africa while undertaking research on identity issues among the "Coloureds" in the new South Africa, Keith, who was then head of the Department of Political Studies at UWC, enthusiastically offered to host me at his institution from January to June 2007. I was able to return the favor when Paul Kubicek, then chair of the Political Science Department at Oakland University, and I wrote a proposal to the Fulbright Committee. Keith was able to spend a full academic year (2009–2010) as a Fulbright Scholar at Oakland University. I am grateful to him for his time, optimism, and infectious fascination with the world of ideas. Without Professor Kubicek's support and involvement, Keith would not have won the Fulbright fellowship.

The four reviewers of the manuscript of the fourth edition did a wonderful job of pointing out the strengths and weaknesses of the book and made many suggestions. They include Tom Dolan, Columbus State

University; Charles Hartwig, Arkansas State University; Michael Nwanze, Howard University; and Donald Williams, Western New England College. This book is a better product because of them. I thank them sincerely.

The patience of my editors at Pearson, Vikram Mukhija and Beverly Fong, and their colleagues was severely tested as I struggled to complete the revisions while trying to cope with health issues. I appreciate their patience, professionalism, encouragement, and support.

Finally, I would like to thank my wife, Izzy, for her love and encouragement. This is as much my book as hers. In continuing gratitude, I once again dedicate this book to my wife and our adult children.

Despite all the assistance, I alone am responsible for any errors of fact or interpretation.

VINCENT B. KHAPOYA
PROFESSOR EMERITUS
OAKLAND UNIVERSITY, ROCHESTER, MICHIGAN

The African Experience

Africa: The Continent and Its People

Africa is not one country. It's a continent: the second
largest continent. Not only is it vast, but it also overwhelms
the rest of the world in the diversity of its people, the
complexity of its cultures, the majesty of its geography,
the abundance of its resources, and the resiliency
and vivacity of its people.

INTRODUCTION

People writing about Africa customarily begin with a brief reference to how little Africa is known among Americans. Unlike European powers, the United States never had colonies in Africa, although Liberia (in West Africa) was founded in 1847 by freed African slaves from the United States, and the U.S. government has maintained special ties with Liberia from then until now. Since the early 1960s, when dozens of African colonies became independent nations, public ignorance in the United States about Africa has declined markedly. Air travel between Africa and America has increased since then, and American television has reported on a wide range of African problems—from severe drought and famine throughout the Sahel and the Horn to political crises in Libya, Nigeria, and Rwanda. Educated Americans now realize that countries such as Egypt, which had formerly (and mistakenly) been regarded exclusively as part of the Middle East (Asia Minor), are actually located in Africa.

The United States has long been a favorite destination of Africans in search of higher education. During the early years of Africa's independence, tens of thousands of African students traveled to the United States to further their education. The presence of these students made it possible for many educated Americans to meet Africans from different parts of the continent and to show some appreciation for the diversity of the African

1

continent and its people. As the struggle for racial justice and equality in America has involved increasing numbers of African Americans, traditional civil rights organizations like the National Association for the Advancement of Colored People (NAACP) and the National Urban League have joined efforts with such lobbying groups as Africa Action (formerly the American Committee on Africa) and TransAfrica Forum in seeking actively to influence U.S. government policies toward Africa. Although Africa accounts for the smallest proportion of new American immigrants, nevertheless more African students and visitors are choosing to live permanently in the United States, thereby helping to expand Americans' familiarity with Africa.

Despite such developments and the fact that media coverage of events in independent Africa has improved significantly since colonial times (before 1960), many Americans do not fully appreciate the physical size and ethnic diversity of the African continent. Living in such a huge country as the United States, Americans tend to view Africa as a single country rather than as a continent that includes over fifty different countries; they even assume that it is as easy to travel from Cameroon to Tanzania as it is to drive from Colorado to Tennessee. For instance, it is not uncommon for an American to ask an African visitor from Nigeria whether he knows someone from Senegal or Zambia. This chapter introduces some of the geographic, demographic, and cultural-linguistic diversity in Africa, so that American students can begin to understand the incredible complexity and richness of Africa's various landscapes and cultures.

GEOGRAPHY

Africa is indeed a very large place, the world's second largest continent. Its land area is 30 million square kilometers, stretching nearly 8,000 kilometers from Cape Town (South Africa) to Cairo (Egypt) and more than 5,000 kilometers from Dakar (Senegal) to Mogadishu (Somalia). It is nearly three and one half times the size of continental United States. The political geography of this huge continent consists of fifty-four modern nations, including island republics off its coasts. With the exception of Western Sahara, unilaterally and forcefully annexed by Morocco when Spain suddenly relinquished its colonial control in 1976, these African countries are independent states with their own political institutions, leaders, ideologies, and identities. All these countries belong to a continental forum called the African Union (formerly the Organization of African Unity, OAU), which is permanently headquartered in Addis Ababa, the capital of Ethiopia. South Africa was admitted into the organization only in 1994 after being excluded for more than thirty years because its white minority government had constitutionally denied full rights of citizenship to its nonwhite majority. Each of these African nations—except for a handful of states like Somalia, Swaziland,

Lesotho, and Botswana—is multilingual. Nigeria, for instance, encompasses more than 300 different language groups (probably more than any other nation), Tanzania has more than 100, Kenya has more than 40, and so on.

Geographically, Africa has been described as a vast plateau and is the most tropical of all continents, lying astride the equator and extending almost equal distances toward both north and south of the equator. Dominating the northern third of the continent is the world's largest desert—the vast Sahara Desert. Africa's most significant geological features—the highest and lowest elevations, largest lakes, and source of the world's longest river, formed by unique patterns of "drift" between the African, Somali, and Arabian continental plates—lie along East Africa's Great Rift Valley, the earth's deepest continental crevice. One end of the Great Rift Valley follows the Red Sea northward from Lake Assai (Ethiopia) to the Dead Sea (Palestine); southward,

MAP 1.1

Africa: Political Map

Source: Adapted from *Africa Report,* African American Institute of New York, 1964.

along the rift between the African and Somali continental plates, lie Africa's highest mountains and largest lakes. Whereas Lake Assai lies many hundreds of meters *below* sea level, such long-extinct volcanoes as Mt. Kilimanjaro (5,900 meters or 19,340 ft.) and Mt. Kenya (5,200 meters or 17,040 ft.) rise hundreds of meters higher than the highest peaks in the continental United States. Many mountain ranges throughout the continent (e.g., Ethiopian, Drakensberg, Cameroon, and Atlas Mountains) include peaks between 3,000 and 4,900 feet and support dense populations living in various ecozones between 3,000 and 8,000 feet above sea level. Many of Africa's plateaus and highlands have provided sustenance (and in some cases, refuge) for some of the continent's densest and most productive populations.

Other dense and productive populations in Africa have settled along the shores of the continent's freshwater lakes and rivers, as well as along parts of its tropical coastlines. Africa's great lakes—including Lake Victoria (the world's second largest freshwater lake, after Lake Superior), Lakes Tanganyika and Malawi (among the four deepest and eighth largest in the world), Lakes Turkana, Nakuru, and Rukwa—lie on the floor of the Great Rift Valley, while shallower lakes like Chad and Bangweulu (or the Okavango Swamp) have served as life-giving water catchments for nearby savanna (or rolling grassland) regions elsewhere in the continent. On a continent where deserts have been expanding and savannas have been becoming drier, not just during past decades but in past millennia, Africa's river systems (like her lakes) have also been crucial to people's growth and survival.

Beginning with ancient Egyptian and Cushitic civilizations several thousand years ago, the Nile River Valley has provided the vital water needed to sustain large populations along the only fertile strip that cuts across the entire Sahara Desert. The longest river on earth (more than 6,400 kilometers), the historic Nile originates from Lake Victoria-Nyanza and derives two-thirds of its waters from the Ethiopian Highlands before plunging over several cataracts downriver (northward) into the rich Nile Delta on the Mediterranean Sea. In modern times, the Lower (northern) Nile has become an important source of hydroelectric power, as well as vital irrigation water, to the Egyptians and the Sudanese who benefit from the electricity generated at the Aswan Dam. Much further upstream (southward) and beyond the Sudd marshlands of southern Sudan, the Ugandans and the Kenyans "plug in" to smaller hydroelectric projects at Nalubaale Dam (formerly called the Owen Falls Dam) and Kiira Dam, both near Jinja (Uganda).

Flowing from Lake Bangweulu in central Africa and draining the entire Congo tropical rain forest into the Atlantic Ocean is the world's tenth longest (and second most voluminous) river—the Congo (over 4,300 kilometers)—which is fed by large tributaries such as the Ubangui, Kasai, and Cuango Rivers. Hydroelectric projects around cataracts near Kinshasa in the Democratic Republic of Congo provide electricity for nearby modernizing cities. Also from central Africa, flowing eastward into the Indian Ocean at the southern end of Africa's Great Rift Valley is the Zambezi River (about

2,600 kilometers) where the Kariba and Cabora Bassa Dams have harnessed much hydroelectric power (creating, as elsewhere, large new reservoirs), even while preserving Africa's most famous single cataract—the beautiful and wondrous Victoria Falls (called Mosi la Tunya in the local Bemba language). Over in West Africa, where the Sahara Desert has been perceptibly expanding southward into the dry savannas of the Sahel during recent decades, the Niger River (about 4,800 kilometers) has long been regarded as a "lifeline" to the tens of millions of people it serves in about a half dozen nations but especially in Niger and Mali. Along with its major tributary (the Benue River) and such other prominent West African rivers as the Senegal, the Gambia, and the Volta (where the continent's first major hydroelectric dam was built in Ghana), the Niger's waters are collected by interior highlands and plateaus.

The Sahara Desert, which is nearly as large as the continental United States and still growing, engulfs much of the northern third of Africa. The Namib and Kalahari Deserts of southern Africa cover much of modern Namibia and Botswana, and Africa's Horn (especially in eastern Ethiopia, northeastern Kenya, and Somalia) is rapidly devolving from dry savanna into desert proper. Other than such vast and thinly populated deserts and particular areas of densely populated mountain terrain, river valleys or deltas, lake basins, and fertile coastal strips, much of rural Africa is characterized by scattered villages of farmers and herders living on savannas. Less than 10 percent of the continent's landscape, contrary to popular imagination, can be classified as tropical rainforest or "jungle." In so far as "jungle" still exists, it is mostly found in the Congo drainage basin (which is lightly populated). Most tropical rainforest on the coastlines are now used for farming, fishing, lumbering, and city life. It can be seen that African people have adapted to countless different, and challenging, local environments. Even now, San hunters-gatherers have been forced to adapt their traditional lifestyles to harsh living conditions on the edge of the Namib and Kalahari Deserts. Nuer and Dinka cattle keepers persist in following intricate traditional patterns of transhumance in the Sudd marshes amid prolonged civil war in the Sudan. Fulani herders and Bozo fishers, despite recent decades of severe drought and famine in the Sahel, continue to practice their traditional patterns of cattle husbandry and canoecraft, while coexisting and trading with local farmers. Africans living in such vastly different local circumstances have naturally developed different customs and lifestyles, although communities that survive today *primarily* as hunters-gatherers, herders, or fishers are very few compared to the vast majority of African farming communities (where hunting, gathering, fishing, and/or herding may be seen as supplemental activities).

Especially in humid tropical rainforests, lake basins, or river valleys, untold varieties of insects and bacteria abound, including many species unknown in more temperate climates. Africans living in areas so rich in life have also had to cope with the lethal varieties of illness that abound in tropical climates.[1] As of 2008, it was estimated that over 300 million people in the tropics (including Africa) suffered from malaria (which kills

MAP 1.2

Africa: Physical Map

Source: Drawn by James D. Graham and Vincent B. Khapoya.

nearly 2.7 million people annually and is caused by a parasite carried by the anopheles mosquito), 300 million suffered from schistosomiasis, also known as *Bilharzia*, a debilitating illness carried by freshwater snails, and another 130,000 (in 1995) suffered from guinea worm disease, carried by water fleas. It was estimated that 5 million children die each year in the tropics of diarrheal illness, 2 million die of tropical fevers, and 1.5 million from measles. There are estimated to be 18 million cases of onchocerciasis (river blindness) in West Africa, more than 66 million cases of trypanosomiasis (sleeping sickness) mainly in East and central Africa, and 90 million cases of filariasis, a debilitating worm illness, throughout the continent. Trypanosomiasis also severely affects domestic animals, thereby impeding the development of animal husbandry. Tuberculosis and polio, which have been virtually eradicated from much of the world, are still killing Africans, particularly in urban areas. Since 1980, the AIDS virus has spread rapidly across central Africa, from Kinshasa (Democratic Republic of Congo) to Nairobi (Kenya) and Dar-es-Salaam (Tanzania), through the use of unclean syringes and contaminated blood transfusions as well as unsafe sex, leading some experts to estimate that 10 percent of the babies in central Africa are now being born with the AIDS virus. Thus, the very abundance of life generated in Africa's humid ecozones, in all these ways, has led to the proliferation of organisms that carry deadly or debilitating illnesses. In the case of malaria, Africa's major "killer" illness, many Africans have used leaves from the neem tree as an antidote, while some coastal peoples have inherited a sickle-cell trait in their bloodstreams as a protective adaptation against lethal doses of malaria. When Americans study Africa, they should remember that people living in humid tropical environments have to confront a much wider variety of life forms—and life-threatening illnesses—on a daily basis than do those living in temperate climates such as those of North America, Europe, or Japan.

DEMOGRAPHY (Relates to Ecology)

The Population Reference Bureau in Washington estimates that in 2011 Africa was host to nearly 1.05 billion people. Compared to other continents, Africa is not terribly crowded, with a population density of only about 32 people per square kilometer. This compares with 72 in Europe, 93 in Asia, 14 in North America, and 33 in South America. However, when one considers the continent's high population growth rate (about twice that of the rest of the world), the vast arid and semiarid regions, and the diminishing supplies of arable land, there are serious grounds for concern about Africa's future capacity to feed its own people.

As in other continents, pockets of population density in Africa have emerged in various rural areas because of favorable local climates, freshwater supplies, cultivable land, or useful minerals. Africa's largest current concentrations of people have historically expanded along the shores of interior rivers and lakes, as well as in well-watered highland areas—near river deltas or mouths—and in Mediterranean strips along some of Africa's coastlines. Although most of Africa's interior geography was unknown to Europeans until the nineteenth century, its shorelines were more accurately mapped 300 years earlier by European explorers, traders, slave-raiders, and pirates. Many centuries before then, Africans along the Mediterranean Sea, the Red Sea, and the Indian Ocean coasts were intermediaries between diverse interior trade routes and long-established seagoing commerce.

Africa's Mediterranean coastal climate supports densely settled agricultural populations, especially in the Maghreb (north of the Atlas Mountains in Morocco, Algeria, and Tunisia) and the Nile River Delta. The Maghreb has a Mediterranean climate (also typical of the coastal foothills and plains near the extreme southwestern portion of South Africa), which is both well-watered and temperate. A rich variety of foods and wines have traditionally been raised there that the Maghreb was long ago known as "the breadbasket" of Rome's ancient Mediterranean empire. By turning desert into productive farmland through irrigation along the lower (northern) Nile Valley, most people living in both ancient and modern Egypt and Sudan (about one eighth of Africa's current total population) have long been able to raise nutritional fruits, grains, and vegetables, as well as livestock. Population along the Nile Valley, the Nile Delta, and the Maghreb coast, as indicated earlier, is quite densely settled.

Much of the West African coast, between the Senegal and Congo Rivers, is also densely populated—especially near the rich alluvial soils of the Niger River Delta and the mouths of other West African rivers. The dominant coastal vegetation (where a few valuable hardwood trees still stand) is tropical rain forest. Between what remains of this coastal rain forest and the vast reaches of the Western Sahara lie the rolling grasslands of the West African Sahel. Prior to the beginnings of European colonialism about a century ago, these West African savannas supported some of the continent's largest and most famous cities, kingdoms, and empires. After the colonial conquest, and with the deterioration of the more fragile savanna ecosystems during the past few decades, a frightening process of dessication (drying up or desertification) has forced many hundreds of thousands to leave their dried-up lands. West Africa's highland areas and plateaux, from the Futa Jalon eastward to the Cameroon Mountains, have continued to support sizable local population densities with more patterns of regular rainfall. The continent's largest remaining tropical rain forest, the central interior drained by the Congo River and its tributaries, is relatively lightly populated except near cities (primarily due to the fragile nature of rainforest soils, which are subjected to constant heavy rains and to being "leached" of their nutrients).

From the East African Horn southward to the Zambezi River, tropical rain forests are limited primarily to coastal or lowland areas (including the Lake Victoria-Nyanza Basin), although lower elevations in the Horn are usually arid. Most of the East African mountain ranges and peaks, however, attract more than adequate rainfall on some very good soils. Highland populations living on the more fertile hillsides of these Rift Valley mountains are among the most densely settled peoples in East Africa. From the Rift Valley savannas of central Kenya and Tanzania to the central savannas drained by the Zambezi River to the south, large numbers of East Africans have traditionally practiced "shifting cultivation" and/or herding; these lifestyles have encouraged much contact and local trade among these plateau peoples. Today, considerable numbers of East African herders and mixed farmers continue to live in scattered settlements, depending primarily on irregular rainfall for their water needs. Meanwhile, dwindling numbers of herders eke out their daily existence on the dessicated former savannas of the Horn. East Africa's densest populations live in its fertile highlands, population centers along its lake and ocean coasts, and savanna towns.

South of the Zambezi River lies the region of southern Africa, where patterns of population density parallel those discussed above. Density is lowest on the Namib and Kalahari Deserts, where dwindling numbers of San hunters and gatherers persist in maintaining some semblance of their ancient lifestyles. Large villages and towns are scattered among the rural plateaus and savannas of modern Angola, Zimbabwe, Mozambique, and northern South Africa, while the densest populations of this region inhabit the areas which have summer rainfall to the south and east of the Drakensberg Mountains as well as the most productive highlands and river valley areas. Modern cities like Johannesburg and Bulawayo have grown up around mineral deposits. Except for European immigrants (Afrikaners and British) and small remnants of the region's original Khoisan inhabitants, the vast majority of southern Africans have traditionally spoken Bantu languages, practiced farming and herding, and developed complex cultures and civilizations that reflected local differences as well as generally similar values.

Off the coast of southeastern Africa in the Indian Ocean lies the world's fourth largest island, Madagascar, as well as a number of smaller island nations such as Seychelles, Comoros, and Mauritius. Together with Cape Verde Islands in the Atlantic Ocean, these are among Africa's most densely populated countries. As Table 1.1 indicates, Africa's smallest nation-states (in geographical area) are often among its most densely populated.

There are wide variations in population density both *within* these African nations and *between* them. In addition to particular ecozones favored by peoples within each country (e.g., the Nile Valley in Egypt and Sudan), the populations of modern cities have expanded dramatically since World War II. Although two-thirds of Africans still live in the countryside, high rates of rural-to-urban migration have been documented throughout the continent, leading to urban unemployment and overcrowding. In both the countryside and the cities, Africa's population is growing at an alarming rate. At the continent's current population growth rate of about 2.4 percent a year, the number of Africans has already hit the 1 billion mark by the year 2011. Indeed, the Population Reference Bureau projects the African population to be 1.4 billion by the year 2025 and 2.3 billion by the year 2050. Mortality rates for African children—74 per 1,000 live births—compared to 44 for the world and 5 for the industrialized countries are among the highest in the world, yet more African children now survive due to modest increases in local availability of vaccines, antibiotics, and clean water. Because the cities and the most productive rural lands of Africa are already overpopulated and so much of the remaining land is arid, it seems to many

TABLE 1.1

Area, Population, and Population Density of African Nations in Descending Order of Population (2011)

Country	Area (in square kilometers)	Population (in millions)	Density (people/sq. km)
Nigeria	913,070	162.3	176
Ethiopia	1,091,509	87.1	79
Egypt	989,850	82.6	83
Congo, Democratic	2,317,699	67.8	29
Republic of	1,206,897	50.5	41
South Africa			
Tanzania	934,139	46.2	49
Kenya	573,647	41.6	72
Algeria	2,354,153	36.0	15
Uganda	238,249	34.5	143
Morocco	441,377	32.3	72
Sudan	1,864,215	31.1	17
Ghana	235,773	25.0	143
Mozambique	792,305	23.1	29
Côte d'Ivoire	318,725	22.6	70
Madagascar	792,305	21.3	36
Cameroon	469,934	20.1	42
Angola	1,232,259	19.6	16
Burkina Faso	270,828	17.0	62
Niger	1,252,323	16.1	13
Malawi	117,107	15.9	134
Mali	1,225,825	15.4	12
Zambia	743,892	13.5	18
Senegal	194,442	12.8	65
Zimbabwe	386,235	12.1	31
Chad	1,269,128	11.5	9
Rwanda	26,035	10.9	415
Tunisia	151,715	10.7	65
Guinea	243,013	10.2	42
Burundi	27,507	10.2	367
Somalia	630,275	9.9	16
Benin	111,316	9.1	81
South Sudan	619,745	8.3	13
Libya	1,739,159	6.4	4
Eritrea	116,237	5.9	51
Togo	56,133	5.8	103

(continued)

TABLE 1.1 (CONTINUED)

Country	Area (in square kilometers)	Population (in millions)	Density (people/sq. km)
Sierra Leone	70,909	5.4	75
Central African	615,764	5.0	8
Republic Congo	338,038	4.1	29
Republic ofLiberia	110,080	4.1	37
Mauritania	1,013,642	3.5	3
Namibia	814,743	2.3	3
Lesotho	29,998	2.2	72
Botswana	574,991	2.0	3
Gambia, The	11,169	1.8	157
Guinea-Bissau	35,702	1.6	45
Gabon	264,568	1.5	6
Mauritius	2,017	1.3	630
Swaziland	17,160	1.2	69
Djibouti	22,932	0.9	39
Reunion	2,481	0.9	341
The Comoros	2,204	0.8	813
Equatorial Guinea	27,725	0.7	26
Cape Verde	3,983	0.5	123
Western Sahara	249,201	0.5	2
Mayotte	371	0.2	563
SãoTomé and Principe	952	0.2	187
Seychelles	445	0.1	194

Source: 2011 World Population Data Sheet (Washington, DC: Population Reference Bureau, Inc., 2011). For South Sudan, which became an independent state on July 9, 2011, see http://en.wikipedia.org/wiki/South_Sudan, accessed on August 11, 2011.

outsiders (if not to many Africans) that Africa's high population growth rate will have to decline if the continent is to become self-reliant in sustaining its people's health and improving their material lives.

LANGUAGE AND CULTURE

As African families settled and expanded in different ecozones during past millennia and throughout the continent, they developed somewhat different customs and vocabularies to order and explain their lives. During centuries of interaction, descendants of original settlers and subsequent immigrants to different localities developed cultures and languages that distinguished their particular lifestyles from those of their neighbors (who may have lived in different ecozones or organized their communities according to different ancestral traditions). Anthropologists and linguists alike have argued that "language" and "culture" are virtually the same. Each culture or subculture is most fully described in the particular language or dialect which characterizes it; each language or dialect most intricately names and reflects its particular culture or subculture. It is helpful, when studying the similarities and differences between African peoples, to adopt such a perspective. In this text, a group's common elements of language and culture are seen as being most significant in identifying different "peoples" or ethnic groups sharing common language and culture. As elsewhere in the modern world, African ethnicity has many variants and undergoes much redefinition through time, yet one's home "people" (whom one grows up with, knows, or is related to through extended networks of kinship groups) remains a significant point of reference for most Africans today.

One of the most common (and often offensive) questions that Americans sometimes ask a newly introduced African in this country is, "Oh, you are from Africa; what tribe are you from?" Not only do many Africans regard the connotation of the word "tribe" (along with words like "primitive," "superstitious," and "natives") as derogatory, but most Africanist scholars have also come to regard the denotation of the word "tribe" as both imprecise and misleading. Jan Vansina, who pioneered the rigorous collection and analysis of Africa's rich oral traditions a few decades ago, observed that (1) social groupings in tropical Africa have increased and decreased dramatically (in both population size and geographical area) over time, and (2) the static connotation of the word "tribe" cannot possibly reflect the intricacies of these ever-changing relationships. Ironically, because the term "tribe" was popularized by colonial authorities in Africa and by Western scholars writing about Africa, it is still retained (at least for administrative and political purposes) by many independent African nations. These nations identify people by "tribe" in tax records and birth certificates and on identification cards.

Some of the problems of describing African peoples as "tribes" were summarized by David Wiley and Marylee Crofts:

> Unfortunately, the term is a bad word to describe African societies. Even worse, it carries the connotation of uncivilized, dangerous, uncontrolled, superstitious human beings unlike ourselves.... The word "tribe" has been used by scholars from the West to describe people living in smaller societies with less material technology than our own. Thus "tribes" are found in North America, Southeast Asia, ancient Israel, the hills and deserts of the Middle East, and, most of all, in Africa.
>
> However, we can find no definition in the scholarly literature of anthropology that really describes these societies. Some say that tribespeople have a common ancestor, others believe that tribes have a common language; some say persons who live under a chieftain are tribal; others say tribes share a common government or common culture. In fact, when we look at the societies of Africa, we find none of these definitions fits all of the societies that existed before colonial rule...

For these reasons, scholars prefer to discard the term "tribe" because it is misleading and creates an image of an inferior and sub-human people. In fact, Africa's small scale societies are much like the clans of Scotland or the villages of Ireland and Wales whose people are not called "tribal." More appropriate terms are societies, ethnicities, classes or simply the name of the people such as the Yoruba or the Lunda.[2]

People familiar with names such as Hausa, Yoruba, and Ibo (the three largest and best-known peoples of modern Nigeria) or the Kikuyu, Luo, Kalenjin, and Luhya (of Kenya) understand that these indigenous peoples can be distinguished from others by virtue of their different languages, kinship systems, rituals, and traditions. The larger groups of these peoples are often comprised of many subcultures, each speaking its own dialect and maintaining its own traditions. The Hausa peoples of Nigeria, for instance, are comprised of many subcultures, such as the Daurawa, the Gobir, and the Kanawa. Such subcultures, among the Hausa and elsewhere, will often identify themselves as though they were distinct ethnic groups, even fighting fiercely against neighboring and related subcultures.

Africanist scholars have come to regard the concept of "race" as even less accurate than the term "tribe" in distinguishing peoples. Back in 1930, C. G. Seligman's book *The Races of Africa* culminated more than a century of European scholars' efforts to classify Africans, and others in our world, in terms of skin color as well as physical traits like head form, nose form, hair type, lips, and so on. Since Linneaus (a famous eighteenth-century Swedish botanist) classified the four "races" of humankind as being distinguishable (and ordered divinely in the "Great Chain of Being") by white, yellow, red, and black skin colors, other European and American scientists have attempted to prove that skin color (genetically related only to eye and hair color) could positively be correlated to head size, intelligence, language complexity, civilization, and so on. Despite all their efforts to establish such implausible correlations, these scholars (including America's William Shockley, who spent the last two decades of his life trying to correlate skin color with IQ scores) have been unable to prove any of their hypotheses.

Seligman, for example, attributed the development of great civilizations throughout African history mostly to the long-term emigration of light-skinned "Hamites" from the ancient Middle East, because he (and other colonialist scholars) could not admit that the dark-skinned "negroid race" could have developed such remarkable civilizations as ancient Cush and Axum or medieval Mali and Songhay. This "hamitic hypothesis" was widely accepted and taught during colonial times, until Joseph Greenberg (another American scholar) published *The Classification of African Languages* in 1956. Greenberg and other historical linguists have thoroughly exposed the flawed assumptions of Seligman's hypothesis and suggested that Hamites were a mere fiction, a confused intermixing of obscurely known physical characteristics with inaccurate linguistic-cultural data. Scholars have subsequently demonstrated not only that culture and civilization had nothing to do with people's skin color but also that the more than 800 languages currently spoken in Africa can be related to one another in only four major language families. Language differences, based on Greenberg's original classifications, have indeed become the Africanist's primary tool in trying to differentiate, classify, or compare and contrast the various cultures and peoples of Africa (see Table 1.2).

TABLE 1.2

Selected Major Languages Spoken in African Countries

Country	Languages Spoken
Algeria	Arabic (official), French, Tamasight (Berber)
Angola	Portuguese (official), Umbundu, Kimbundu, Kikongo, Chokwe-Lunda
Benin	French (official), Fon-Ewe, Yoruba, Bariba, Ge, Dendi
Botswana	English (official), SeTswana, Shona
Burkina Faso	French (official), Mossi, Dyula, Mandé, Senufo, Fulani
Burundi	French (official), Kirundi (official), Swahili
Cameroon	French (official), English (official), Fulani, Bamileke, Bulu, Ewondo, Kirdi, Douala
Cape Verde	Portuguese (official), Crioulo (Creole)
Central African Republic	French (official), Banda, Baya, Sangho (lingua franca)
Chad	French (official), Arabic, Sara, Kirdi, Sangho, Wadai, Tubu
Comoros	French (official), Arabic, Comoran-Swahili
Congo	French (official), Kikongo, Teke, M'bochi, Lingala, 'Mbete, Sanga
Congo, Democratic Republic of	French (official), Lingala, Swahili, Kikongo, Tshiluba
Djibouti	French (official), Arabic, Somali, Afar
Egypt	Arabic (official), English
Equatorial Guinea	Spanish (official), French, Fang, Bubi
Eritrea	Arabic (official), English, Tigrinya, Tigre
Ethiopia	Amharic (official), Oromo, Tigrinya, Somali
Gabon	French (official), Fang, Bateke, Eshira, Mbete, Kota
Gambia	English (official), Mandingo, Fulani, Wolof, Soninke
Ghana	English (official), Twi, Ewe, Ga, Hausa
Guinea	French (official), Malinke, Poular, Sousou
Guinea-Bissau	Portuguese (official), Balante, Crioulo, Fulani, Mandinga
Ivory Coast	French (official), Akan, Kru, Mandé, Senufo, Dioula, Abidji
Kenya	English (official), Swahili (official), Kikuyu, Luo, Luhya, Kamba, Kalenjin

(continued)

TABLE 1.2 (CONTINUED)

Country	Languages Spoken
Lesotho	English (official), SeSotho, Xhosa, Zulu
Liberia	English (official), Kpelle, Mano, Kru-Bassa, Krahn
Libya	Arabic (official), Tamazight (Berber)
Madagascar	French (official), Malagasy
Malawi	English (official), Chichewa, Lomwe, Ngoni, Yao
Mali	French (official), Bambara, Fulani, Malinké, Senufo
Mauritania	French (official), Arabic, Sarakole, Fulani, Wolof
Mauritius	English (official), Creole, Hindi, Urdu, Tamil
Morocco	French and Arabic (both official), Tamazight (Berber)
Mozambique	Portuguese (official), Makua-Lomwe, Swahili, Chichewa, Shona, Tsonga
Namibia	English (official), Afrikaans (official), Oshivambo, Herero, Kavango, Nama-Dama (Khoisan), German.
Niger	French (official), Hausa, Songhai, Fulani, Kanuri, Tuareg
Nigeria	English (official), Hausa, Yoruba, Ibo, Tiv, Kanuri
Reunion	French (official), Creole
Rwanda	French (official), Kinyarwanda, Swahili
São Tomé and Principe	Portuguese (official)
Senegal	French (official), Wolof, Pulaar, Serer, Mandé
Seychelles	French (official), English, Creole
Sierra Leone	English (official), Creole, Temne, Mendé, Mandé, Krio, Fanti
Somalia	Somali (official), Arabic, Swahili, English, Italian
South Africa	11 official languages: English, Afrikaans, Zulu, Xhosa, Sotho, Swati, Tswana, Pedi, Ndebele, Venda, Tsonga
Sudan	Arabic (official), Dinka, Acholi, Ta, Lango, English
Swaziland	English (official), SiSwati, Sesotho, isiZulu
Tanzania	Swahili (official), English, Sukuma, Nyamwezi, Chagga
Togo	French (official), Hausa, Ewe, Kabre, Moba, Kotocoli, Dagomba
Tunisia	Arabic (official), French (official)
Uganda	English (official), Luganda, Lusoga, Runyankole, Rutoro, Acholi, Swahili, Lango
Western Sahara	Arabic (official), Spanish, Tuareg, dialects of Tamazight
Zambia	English (official), Bemba, Nyanja, Barotse, Lunda, Lozi
Zimbabwe	English (official), Shona, IsiNdebele, Nyanja

Source: Donald George Morrison, Robert C. Mitchell, and John N. Paden. *Black Africa: A Comparative Handbook,* 2nd Edition (New York: Paragon House, 1989). Helpful suggestions from Keith Gottschalk of the University of the Western Cape, a Fulbright Scholar-in-Residence at Oakland University, 2009–2010.

Greenberg's successors in historical linguistics have developed some intriguing data (and hypotheses) through the application of rigorous methods of lexicostatistics (and glottochronology) to present-day African languages. Through such methods, it has been possible to determine how closely the basic vocabularies of any two languages are related and to estimate approximately when such language groups may have originally separated and begun to develop different dialects. Through lexicostatistics, historical linguists have subsequently modified and elaborated on Greenberg's original model of African language families—adding newly researched languages, rearranging language subfamilies, and renaming the four major families.

For this text, it is sufficient to designate the major families (and a few significant subfamilies) of African languages in Greenberg's original terms. The four major language families that he first identified were Afro-Asiatic, Niger–Congo, Nilo-Saharan, and Khoisan (or Click). Except for Afrikaans (an amalgam of Dutch, French, and German now spoken by the so-called Coloureds and about 2 million white South Africans who also call themselves "Afrikaners"), Malagasy (a Malayo-Polynesian derivative spoken on the large Indian Ocean island of Madagascar) and other European languages (English, French, Portuguese, Spanish, Italian, and German), or local creole adaptations, all the many hundreds of languages and thousands of dialects now spoken on the continent are historically related to one of these four basic language families.

The Khoisan languages (including Khoi and San subfamilies) are currently spoken only by isolated groups of hunters and gatherers living on marginal lands in southern and central Africa. The distinctive "clicks" of Khoisan languages seem to have survived from very early speech patterns, and some of these click sounds have been incorporated into neighboring languages like Xhosa and Zulu (in South Africa). A much larger present-day language family, but still considerably less widespread than the other two dominant language families of modern Africa, is what Greenberg called the Nilo-Saharan. Several subfamilies and dozens of different modern languages with Nilo-Saharan roots have been researched and recorded among peoples now living in the area bounded by Lake Chad and the Nile River, the Sahara Desert, and Lake Victoria. Sometimes referred to as Nilotes, such cattle-keeping peoples as the Luo and Maasai, the Nuer and Dinka are linguistically related to one another.

Africa's most widespread language family (which includes many hundreds of languages spoken throughout the southern two-thirds of the continent) is the one Greenberg named Niger–Congo. He originally identified a dozen Niger–Congo subfamilies, including the populous Mande and Kwa subfamilies of West Africa and the most extensive language subfamily in all of Africa—Bantu. Historians have debated when, why, and where the remarkable expansion of Bantu-speaking peoples started ever since

Greenberg estimated that about 400 different languages now spoken south of the Sahara have Bantu origins. These hundreds of Bantu languages apparently began differentiating from one another within the past 3,000 years or so (according to the estimates of glottochronologists). Consequently, many Bantu-speaking peoples, especially those bordering on each other, have similarities in vocabulary and in culture. The most widely spoken Bantu language, which has become somewhat of a lingua franca in East and central Africa, is Kiswahili. Throughout the past millennium, east coast Swahili city states have incorporated different words from Arabic, Asian, and European immigrants into their Bantu-based language, broadening their perspectives and helping to expand their international commerce.

The most widely spoken language in the northern third of Africa is Arabic, which (along with the Hebrew) is classified as part of the Semitic subfamily. Together with four other subfamilies, Semitic languages are classified as part of Greenberg's Afro-Asiatic family. Glottochronologists have hypothesized that an original Afro-Asiatic mother tongue existed about 10,000 years ago, probably somewhere near the confluence of the Blue Nile and the White Nile, before the original speakers of Semitic, ancient Egyptian, Cushitic, Berber, and Chadic subfamilies separated and began to disperse in different directions. As the ancient Egyptians went north, Berbers and Chadic (including Hausa) speakers moved westward, Cushitic (including Amharic, Somali, and Galla) speakers inhabited Africa's Horn, and the ancestors of ancient Semites moved into what is now known as the Middle East. In ancient times, these various descendants of Afro-Asiatic speakers built the first great cities and civilizations. Today, the descendants of those ancient subfamilies vary widely in language, skin color, and local traditions, although Arabic (the language of Islam) is widely understood throughout northern Africa and the Middle East.

Because language is so closely associated with culture, it would follow that African peoples have developed more than 800 distinctive cultures (corresponding to their languages) that not only differ from each other (as their languages differ) but also share many common characteristics and values. For example, the Nuer, Dinka, Maasai, and Luo (all of whom, as noted, speak related Nilotic languages) have similar traditions associated with cattle herding, initiation and age grades, even though their particular rituals, traditions, and lifestyles vary considerably according to their local circumstances.

This chapter has only introduced some dimensions of diversity in the African experience. In the following chapters, examples are drawn from different cultures and ecozones to illustrate some common, cross-cultural continuities in African customs, values, and experiences. The very different kinds of ecozones with correspondingly different population densities, the many hundreds of distinctive languages and cultures, and the many dozens of modern nation-states found in Africa provide some indication of what size, variety, and complexity exists on the continent. It is strongly recommended that readers of this text spend some time studying Africa's physical and political geography (as depicted in the maps in the preceding sections of this chapter), as well as the demographic data (Table 1.1) and language/culture list (Table 1.2 on p. 14). In addition, please refer back to Tables 1.1 and 1.2 while reading this text, so as to reaffirm constantly the specific different circumstances in which various African peoples live throughout the continent.

NOTES

1. Figures pertaining to various tropical diseases were obtained from the following websites in October 2008: www.malaria.org/wheredoesitoccur.html, www.astdhpphe.org/infect/guinea.html, www.emedicine.com/med/topic1667.html, and www.micro.msb.ac.uk.
2. David Wiley and Marylee Crofts, *The Third World: AFRICA* (Guilford, CT: Dushkin Publishing Group, 1984), pp. 63–65.

African Traditional Institutions

"I am because you are." An African defines himself or herself by the group—the word "tribe" is still inaccurately used—to which he/she belongs. "Communalism" or "collectivism" is a term which captures the essence of this traditional value. It served the Africans well in the past. Is it a curse in the twenty-first century?

INTRODUCTION

Most non-African scholars of Africa tend to emphasize the heterogeneity of the African continent and to imply not only that the differences that exist outweigh the values and institutions that Africans share in common but also that these differences are somehow unbridgeable. Certainly, differences do exist. They are readily discernible in levels of economic development and in the multiplicity of languages.

Nigeria and Kenya are more economically developed than Somalia and Chad. Botswana and Senegal have enjoyed reasonable political stability, whereas Somalia and the Central African Republic have continually experienced painful civil strife. African countries have different languages, ideologies, and political traditions. Indeed, the languages of Europe—English, French, Portuguese, and Spanish—continue to be used by African countries that were colonized by the respective European nations. The adoption of European languages as official languages is due to the fact that African states are politically unable to decide which of their own indigenous languages should be adopted nationally. When attempts have been broached to launch an indigenous language as the official language of a country, serious national conflict has often loomed on the horizon, hampering national debate of the matter. In adopting nine African languages as official languages in addition to the two—English and Afrikaans—which have been used for decades, South Africa is a trailblazer on the language issue.

A wide ideological spectrum is represented among African states. There have been genuine Marxist states in the past, such as Ethiopia under Mengistu Haile Mariam, the Republic of the Congo under Marien Ngouabi, and Benin under Mathieu Kerekou. Monarchists in Uganda yearn for the return of traditional kingdoms that were dismantled soon after Britain granted Uganda independence under the leadership of Apollo Milton Obote. There are reigning monarchs in Swaziland, Lesotho, and Morocco with varying constitutional powers. At one time, it was fashionable for African leaders to claim that they were socialists. Most of them, of course, were not. Until communism and its socialist systems began to crumble in Eastern Europe in the late 1980s, those African states that would fit the label of "socialist" included Ghana and Congo. Kenya and Côte d'Ivoire were, for years, clearly among the continent's conservative proponents of the free market. Still other countries such as Zambia, Zimbabwe, and Algeria followed fairly complicated models perhaps best referred to as mixed economies.

Relationships between individual African countries and the European nations that colonized them vary in closeness. It is well known, for example, that French-speaking African states maintain closer ties with France than do the English-speaking countries with Britain. (This will be explored in more detail when the African colonial experience is analyzed.) These differences not only play a role in discussions of important issues pertaining to Africa but also have led some students of Africa to assert that African states have more in common with their former colonial masters than with each other.

This chapter seeks first to discuss in some detail those values, institutions, and characteristics that African people and their countries have in common. Second, it examines their differences, how those differences arose, and the way in which they influence not only the interactions among African countries but also their internal politics.

Some of the values shared by Africans are not very easily measured. They have to do with how Africans psychologically feel toward these values and identify with one another. When, upon graduating from high school, I first ventured out of my native Kenya to visit Tanzania, an affinity with the Tanzanian people put me at ease. The fact that I could speak Swahili to ordinary Tanzanians helped a great deal. I discovered that there was no new social protocol to learn. That was certainly not the case when, in search of higher education, I came to North America where social traditions are vastly different.

This racial or cultural affinity exhibits itself in interesting ways. One afternoon many years ago, while strolling downtown Ayr on the west coast of Scotland, I saw a black man waving wildly at me from across the street. I stopped. When he crossed the street and walked over to me, he said he could just tell from a distance that I was African. He said there were no other Africans in Ayr and he was dying to talk to "a brother." The gentleman was from Nigeria. We talked as though we had known each other for years. Ndabaningi Sithole of Zimbabwe describes a similar incident that occurred in 1955 while he was on his way to the United States:

> When I was in Naples [Italy] in February 1955, on my way to the United States, I startled six of my white missionary friends when I suddenly ordered our taxi-driver to stop.
>
>   "What is the matter, Ndaba?" the Reverend John Marsh asked me.
>
>   "There is a friend of mine over there," and no sooner had I said that than I banged the door of the taxi behind me and hurried across the street to see my friend who also had seen me. We just fell into each other's arms. I was so happy to see him. He was so happy to see me. The only word I could understand from him was "'Somalia," and when I reciprocated this with "Rhodesia," he apparently understood me, and cried, "Africa." I repeated, "Yes, Africa." We shook hands again and indicated by gestures that we were well and that Africa was going up, up, up. We shook our heads that it was no longer going down, down, down. I bade him goodbye. I had to hurry back to our taxi which I had unceremoniously stopped and which was impatiently waiting for my return.
>
>   "What was that, Ndaba?" the Reverend John Marsh asked.
>
>   "I don't know except that he's an African like me," I said.
>
>   "But we thought he was a friend of yours!" the Reverend John Marsh cried with surprise.
>
>   "Oh, yes, he is, although I have never met him before."[1]

Sithole then goes on to explain the episode, in almost spiritual terms:

> What had happened was this. For four weeks I had not seen a black face. I had been completely lost in this vast ocean of white faces. When suddenly a black face appeared in this vast ocean of white faces, "consciousness of kind" seized me and gave me wings and I flew across the street, and there united with my own kind, and in spite of the language difficulty between us, my heart and his throbbed in unison. We communicated the warmth of our hearts to each other.[2]

When I first went overseas and found myself among non-Africans, I felt that I had to learn new cultural basics almost from scratch. What was the appropriate greeting? What kinds of questions could one ask at dinner? What topics were proper for conversation, which ones were not? The casual advice I had been given—when you are in America, avoid talking about politics, sex, or religion in polite company—was not entirely unfounded. What was the family structure like? How were young people expected to relate to older people or to people of the opposite sex, and so on? In traditional Africa, a casual greeting such as the American "hi" would be considered rude or impolite. The normal greeting is long; one is expected to inquire about the other's health, home, family, crops, and so on. One does not call people older than oneself by their first names. Old people are treated with a great deal of respect. It is the custom for a dinner guest to compliment the host or hostess for an excellent meal after the meal has been eaten rather than before or during the meal. I very quickly discovered that when I did not say how delicious the meal was or even how wonderful it looked, my American hosts assumed I wasn't enjoying myself or did not like the meal. The fact that I was eating or had eaten with relish did not convey my appreciation adequately. It was important that I say it. Cultural values and social norms such as these, along with spiritual values and family structure, are shared by Africans across the continent. Upon arrival in the United States, when, for the first time, I met Africans from outside East Africa, I was surprised to discover how much alike we all were.

Cultural values are powerful and have come into play when Africans have collectively come under attack. In 1985, during a United Nations Conference on Women held in Nairobi, Kenya, women from outside Africa wanted to talk about polygyny, the custom of men having multiple wives, which non-African women saw as a mark of oppression of African women. Some of them also had an agenda of their own: a discussion on sexual orientation with hopes of convincing the world community that same-sex intimacy was merely an alternative lifestyle. The African women, on the contrary, considered same-sex intimacy a perversion rather than an alternative lifestyle, and certainly not a topic worthy of discussion at an international conference. Clearly, there was a clash of cultures. It is true that many African women do not like polygyny. However, they do not see it as an issue that requires the intervention of their sisters worldwide. A compromise was struck. Neither polygyny nor sexual orientation would be topics for discussion at the conference. Female circumcision, widely condemned by the African women themselves and seen as a totally unnecessary sexual incapacitation of women, was discussed at the conference. To date, the Republic of South Africa is the only African country which guarantees in its constitution the basic political and civil liberties to all of its people without regard to sexual orientation. Enforcement, however, is lax. Beyond the cultural commonalities, the experiences of slavery and colonization have created for Africans a shared history of suffering, pain, and alienation that further serves to bring them together.

Let us begin with a discussion of social groups, which, after all, form the basic building blocks of any society. We have already discussed the much larger groups characterized by a common language and certain cultural practices. These groups go by names such as Igbo, Yoruba, Ewe, and Baganda. But what is the immediate reference group for an individual African? In Africa, as in much of the less industrialized world, there are three types of fundamental social groups: those based on kinship; those based on other criteria such as age, skill, or craftsmanship; and those based on residence or locality.

KINSHIP

A kinship relationship is one that binds individuals through either birth or marriage. Blood relationships are called *consanguine* relationships and those based on marriage are called *affilial*. Consanguine relationships pertain to one's ancestry or descent and how it is determined through generations. There are four basic ways by which descent is determined. The most common method is to trace descent through one's father and other male ancestors. This is called *patrilineal descent*. The second type of descent, *the matrilineal descent*, entails tracing descent through male relatives on one's mother's side. When a group traces its descent through one side only, namely, either the father's or the mother's, we say that the group has *a unilineal descent* system. The vast majority of African societies use patrilineal descent. The third type of descent, called *duolineal or bilineal*, is established through both parents. People in the United States normally trace their descent duolineally, although they usually take their father's family name. The last type, *bilateral descent*, involves tracing one's ancestors through both sets of grandparents, that is, both sides of one's father and mother. Bilateral descent, which is rather difficult to track in any event, is used in some form by the Hausa people of Nigeria.[3]

Descent is important in African societies because it determines such matters as inheritance, identity, the identity of a child born into a marriage (or outside marriage, for that matter), and even the location of a new home for a newly married couple. In Kenya, both Luo and Luhya peoples have patrilineal descent systems. For instance, if a Luo man married a Luhya woman, the child born in that marriage would be identified as a member of the Luo community. Under patrilineal descent systems, boys have inheritance rights; girls do not, unless they are specifically willed property by their father. In matrilineal descent systems, such as the Akan people of Ghana, children inherit property from their maternal uncle, not from their father. One of the changes taking place in Africa today is that as more people intermarry, their children are beginning to have dual identities, to refer themselves as belonging to both their parents' ethnic groups. They are becoming what I call "hyphenated" Africans. However, inheritance rights are not likely to be affected by this dual ethnic identity for some time to come.

Lines of descent are called lineages, and many African groups have been known to trace their lineage to a common ancestor. Two or more lineages that can trace their lines to a common ancestor then constitute a clan. When a clan becomes too large, when a portion of it is relocated, or when a powerful member of a clan, for political or other reasons, decides to break away, taking new followers with him, then new divisions often occur giving rise to new clans. This process of mutation permits a detailed knowledge of the lineage that cements the relationships in the first place.

The second type of kinship is based on marriage, an institution of prime importance in all human societies. In Africa, due perhaps to agrarian economies and the collective ethic of the communities, marriage acquires probably a far greater societal significance than in modern Western societies. When asked why people get married, an individual in a Western society is likely to answer that people get married for love and for the need to share their lives with someone special. An African is likely to respond that people get married because it is a vital social tradition, because they want a family and children. Marriage is intimately linked to reproduction, to having children, to the very survival of the community. And having children is an important contribution that each individual is expected to make to his/her society. Society recognizes that contribution by elevating the status of a married person above that of an unmarried one.

Marriage is also conceived as a relationship between two extended families rather than just between a man and a woman. The family's stake in marriage is never fully emphasized until something goes wrong with the marriage, at which point it becomes everyone's business to try to save the marriage and to prevail on the couple to stay in the marriage. This social idea of marriage is universal in Africa and has been passed on from generation to generation. Moreover, traditionally marriages used to be arranged by family elders. That is changing now. Relatively few marriages are still being arranged, and only in remote rural areas, away from the seductive influence of the cities or towns. Young people themselves now prefer to choose their own future mates, although it is expected that they will seek their parents' permission, and most of them do so. The community still gets involved during the preliminary phases when arrangements have to be made regarding the actual marriage ceremony and the transfer of property called bridewealth. The bridewealth, in the form of cattle, goats, sheep, and/or money is transferred from the family of the groom to that of the bride. Bridewealth has often been called brideprice, but the latter term connotes the purchasing of a bride which is not an accurate reflection of the true meaning of the custom. Dowry, as a gift to the bride from her own family, is quite rare. In most African communities, the transfer of property, often occurring in installments rather than just at one time, seals the legality and validity of the marriage. In a few cases in the past, when the prospective groom was too poor to afford the bridewealth suggested, he spent several years working for his future father-in-law as a form of payment. This form of labor was also referred to as bridewealth. Among the !Kung people in southern Africa, the newly married couple stayed with the bride's family, during which time the groom worked for his in-laws. When the bride service was completed, usually after several years, the couple then went to live with the groom's community.

There appear to be four reasons for the existence of bridewealth. First, it is an expression of gratitude by the groom's family to the bride's family for their having raised a wife for the groom. Second, it compensates the woman's family for the loss of her labor as she leaves her own family to join her new husband's. Third, in keeping with patrilineal societies, it guarantees the rights of the man and his family group over the children to be born in the marriage. Finally, it serves to strengthen the marriage and the relationship between the two families and the two communities involved. Custom dictated that should the marriage fail, some of the property was to be returned to the groom's family, depending on the number of the children in the marriage. In practice, however, the bridewealth was spent soon after it was paid. It was often used to pay for the bridewealth of the wives of the bride's brothers or for the educational costs of the bride's siblings, or it was invested in other ways. As one can well imagine, if the wealth had been spent, as was almost always the case, there was a great deal of pressure from the woman's family on the couple contemplating a breakup to stay married.

What about *love*? Do Africans ever fall in love, or marry for love? Yes indeed, they do. African folklore is full of romantic tales. African music is replete with songs about broken hearts and lovers' laments. Some Americans may be familiar with a Swahili song titled "Malaika," meaning "angel" sung by the South African singer Miriam Makeba. It is a lament by a man in love with a beautiful woman. He wishes very much that he could marry her but does not have the bridewealth to do so. Ample research by anthropologists shows that love indeed is important in decisions pertaining to intimacy and marriage. As Gibbs states in his discussion of betrothal among the Kpelle people of Liberia,

> A man who wishes to marry will present his *sweetheart* (my italics) with a *weli sen* (love token), such as twenty-five or forty cents in coin or a bracelet, saying, for example, "I love you, I want you to be my wife." She will then present this to her parents, asking their permission to marry the suitor. If they assent, the man will follow this up by presenting them with a small sum of money, the *iyeei na sen* ("something from your hand") which affirms the honorableness of his intentions.[4]

Elopement was fairly common in many traditional African societies. There were several reasons for its occurrence, one of which was the possibility of having to pay a lower bridewealth. But in the majority of cases, the eloping couple were young people who had met at a dance or had been introduced by friends, "fallen in love" and decided to run off and get married. In some cases, the elopement was an act of defiance against objections from parents or the community to the courtship. My parents eloped after my father rejected the woman who had been picked for him by his own parents. Public displays of love and affection such as kissing and handholding are frowned upon by Africans. Needless to say, this is changing in modern Africa. In a broader sense, love and affection are viewed in terms of commitment, respect, and caring for the needs of those close to you and an affirmation of your responsibility toward your spouse and children. It is not so much an exclusive attraction and affection between two individuals.

Moreover, Western social norms require and expect sexual fidelity on the part of both partners in marriage. African norms do not, although Christianity espouses it. Some African men, for religious and pragmatic reasons, observe fidelity, but many do not. Indeed, as the incidence of polygyny declines in Africa and urbanization increases, with men leaving their villages to find paid work in towns, extramarital liaisons appear to be taking the place of formal marriages. As Kayongo-Male and Onyango observe, "Many men may be keeping women in towns without going through formal ceremonies and without informing the wife of these relationships."[5] Not surprisingly, the patriarchal nature of African societies and the existence of bridewealth are presumed to give men absolute control over the women's sexual activities. African men, therefore, are possessive about their wives and expect them to be sexually faithful. Moreover, sexual indiscretions on the part of the woman, if and when discovered, were grounds for divorce or at least required the woman's family to be assessed some compensatory damages to be paid to the man.

There is a definite caring and a palpable fondness between partners in African marriages. There is a widely shared view that this thing called "love" is a feeling that grows and is nurtured over time. One cannot simply fall out of love just as he/she cannot simply fall in love. As time goes on, the married couple become good and dear friends, partners, coworkers, each with clearly delineated responsibilities and behavior. Due to the lack of public, physical displays of affection and the absence of a strict code of sexual fidelity, some Western observers have asserted that there is no love involved in marriages or in intimate relationships between African men and women. For example, in a book, long on racial stereotypes but woefully short on insight or understanding, David Lamb glibly writes, "In the cities, sexual morals are looser, but affection between men and women is only rarely displayed or expressed. You will *never* (my italics) see a young couple in East Africa exchanging touches or simply sitting in a restaurant, looking at each other. Africans skip the preliminaries known in the West; where a European couple might kiss, the Africans copulate."[6] Such an assertion is simply wrong and grossly ethnocentric. It makes one wonder if David Lamb did not go to Africa simply to confirm what he already believed about African people.

FORMS OF MARRIAGE

As the foregoing discussion suggests, polygamy is found virtually in all African societies. Polygamy can be either polygyny (in which one man has two or more wives) or polyandry (in which there is one wife and two or more husbands). Polygyny is practiced in Africa, while polyandry is not. It should be stated that the vast majority of marriages in Africa are monogamous. The practice of polygyny varies greatly in Africa. It is virtually nonexistent in Tunisia, which outlawed the practice, whereas in Nigeria about 30 percent of marriages are polygynous. Current research on polygamy covering Benin, Chad, Congo, Gabon, Ghana, Kenya, Mali, Niger, Senegal, Tanzania, Togo, and the Democratic Republic of Congo show that the proportion of polygyny ranges from 20.4 to 36.4 percent, with the average number of wives in polygynous marriages found to be two.[7]

Western social scientists feel uneasy when trying to explain the origins of polygyny in African societies. They seem to think that monogamy is so natural and polygyny is or should be considered an aberration or another one of those African social contrivances created to oppress African women. It should be noted that African societies have not been the only ones in the world to practice polygyny. Biblical communities were polygynous. Modern Muslim societies still allow a man to marry up to four wives under certain conditions if he can support them adequately. Marriage customs, like other customs, were instituted for a reason, to meet a need. There are many reasons why polygyny was permitted in African societies. The first reason springs from the social stability provided by people having families. Marriage was seen as being socially desirable. Everyone was expected to get married since it was important for the community as a whole. Unfortunately, it was not always possible for everyone to have a spouse. There were not enough men to go around. The surplus of marriageable women over men meant that the only way every woman would be assured of a husband was if the men were permitted to have more than one wife. The shortage of men was created by higher mortality rates of male infants. Those males who survived the hazardous infant years faced further diminution in numbers when, as young candidates for initiation, they engaged in extremely danger-ous tests to prove their readiness for manhood. Such exercises consisted of raiding neighboring communities for cattle or going on hunting expeditions for lions or leopards. The communities that were raided fought ferociously to protect their property, often killing some of the attackers. Young men who survived these initiation rites continued to sustain high mortality rates through frequent armed conflicts.

The second reason for polygyny is economic. Agrarian societies require a large number of field hands to contribute to the economic well-being of the community, to work on the farms, to look after cattle, and to perform other chores. It was, therefore, necessary for men to have large families. The surest way to have large families was for men to have more than one wife. Research among the Yoruba people of Nigeria showed that polygyny increased considerably during the colonial period when the British introduced cocoa as a cash crop. More wives and children were needed to assist the men in ensuring a plentiful, or at least an adequate, economic production.

The third reason was rooted in the high mortality rates, especially for male children. Having large families provided a hedge against unforeseen and, all too frequently, inevitable losses of children due to disease. In my own family's experience, my father had only one sibling—a brother—even though his mother bore twelve children. Ten of them died in infancy. One of my grandfather's other wives also bore more than ten children, but only three survived. A generation or so later, my own mother had a dozen children and only seven of us survived. Of the first seven children born to my parents between 1941 and 1952, only two survived. All of the five born after 1952 survived. The birth of my younger siblings coincided with the improvement in the standard of living of my family and the availability of rudimentary modern health care in Kenya. Those of my generation can point to many African women who lost most of the children they bore. Fortunately, modern medicine has brought cures to children's maladies, and though many African children continue to die in far larger numbers than anywhere else in the world—infant mortality rate of Africa is 74 deaths per 1,000 live births versus the world average of 44—the survival rates are high enough to result in rapid population increases in many countries. Family planning has now become a real public policy issue for African governments as they try to moderate population growth, so they could provide for their people's needs in health care, education, housing, and other areas.

Fourth, permitting men to have more than one wife made it possible for a widow and her children to be looked after. When a married man died, his brother was often expected to assume responsibility for his widow and her orphaned children.[8] If the surviving brother or cousin happened to be married, then the widow became a second or third wife. If he was not married, he could still inherit his relative's widow, but custom allowed him to marry a young woman, never married before, if he so chose. In the absence of government-sponsored foster-care homes for children or of opportunities for women to support themselves, it made ample sense for society to expect, indeed to require, that a widow and her orphaned children be cared of by the immediate male relatives of the woman's late husband.

The fifth reason pertains to the absolute necessity in African traditions for a man to have an heir, especially a male heir to carry on the family name. If a married woman turned out to be barren, her husband technically would be justified in divorcing her. However, divorce was always discouraged for two important reasons: a woman's family may not be able to return the bridewealth, and the woman's own social and economic situation would be devastated. Generally speaking, traditional African societies, with few exceptions, gave no inheritance rights to women. A divorced woman, therefore, literally had nowhere to go unless she could be taken in by her parents if they were still alive or by her male relatives if they were kind enough. A man whose wife could not have children was allowed to marry another woman to try for an heir. Hence, men married additional wives in order to produce the number of heirs they wanted. Moreover, the more heirs a man had, the higher was his social status. Among the Tswana and Zulu people of southern Africa, the family of the barren woman would sometimes provide the woman's younger sister to bear children for her. If a younger woman could not be provided, then the bridewealth must be returned. Among the Zulu people, it was common for a man not to send the barren woman away even after he got the bridewealth back. He often might simply "use the returned marriage-cattle [bridewealth] to obtain a wife whom he puts 'into the house' of his barren wife to bear children for her."[9] In what seems like a variation of African *machismo*, it was widely felt that if a couple could not have children, it was the woman's fault—it was because the woman was barren. The man could not possibly be infertile! So, he could marry another woman and almost always did. What, then, if nothing happened with the second wife, suggesting perhaps that the man might be at fault? Could she have another husband? Not exactly; she was not allowed a second husband. Instead, some arrangement was made so that the woman could be impregnated by the husband's brother or some such close relative. An heir would then be produced bearing the name of the husband. The Zulu people, in fact, traditionally allowed an infertile, or even an impotent, man to marry and have his relatives produce heirs for him to carry on the family name.

The sixth reason is that large families were so successful economically that the practice of polygyny became associated with wealth and social prestige. The custom persists even today in Africa, though infant mortality rates have declined significantly and African society is no longer entirely agrarian and children have to be in school rather than on the farm contributing to the family's economy. Prominent politicians, traditional leaders, and wealthy individuals continue to maintain two, three, or even four households. When these people can maintain their large families in conspicuous comfort, the practice acquires prestige and status. Moreover, some men have been able to use polygyny as a way of establishing additional economic units in the larger extended family that can generate a lot of wealth. Consider an example of a Kenyan politician that I happen to know, who was a well-to-do individual to begin with. He had a good education and had worked in the colonial civil service. He has four wives. The first wife, who did not have a modern education, lived on and cultivated a small traditional farm that this man had inherited from his father. The second wife, who was educated, lived on and managed a second farm, which was large and modern and was located in what used to be called "The White Highlands" of Kenya. The third wife ran a large store in another town. The fourth wife was a school teacher in the capital city. This man, in effect, had four economic units all bringing in income or generating wealth. It is easy to see how polygyny and the resultant multiple households are equated to economic success and a high social status. However, when a shortcut to prestige is attempted by an individual who has not got the means to support several households, results are often disastrous, with a poor man burdened with children from several wives that he cannot adequately provide for.

The final reason for polygyny may be related to another common African custom that prohibited sexual intimacy between a man and his wife who had given birth. Sexual activity did not resume until the child was weaned, which normally lasted two to three years. Among the Yoruba people of Nigeria, in fact, as soon as a woman discovered that she was pregnant, she would stop having sexual relations with her husband. In some cases, especially in the early years of her marriage, she would go to her parents' home to deliver the baby and be cared for by her own mother for some time before returning to her own home. Some groups in East Africa thought that sexual intercourse with a nursing mother spoiled the mother's milk and endangered the child's health. In practical terms, for a man with just one wife, this prohibition, accompanied possibly by a long separation, meant a two or three-year forced abstinence, a circumstance not easily to be endured. Polygyny seemed to provide an acceptable solution. Indeed, Daryll Forde, in his study of the Yako people of Nigeria, made precisely the same observation: "There is a particular inducement to take a second wife very shortly after the first if the latter has borne a child, for a child is normally suckled for two years during which intercourse between the parents is forbidden. In such a situation the second wife is often a previously unmarried girl."[10] Anthropologists have also found that this system of sexual abstinence during the nursing period helped to space the children apart every two to three years, which meant a lower fertility rate for women. Monogamy and the use of bottle-feeding—instead of breast-feeding—have resulted in more and more women who do not use family planning methods to have children as frequently as every fifteen months, thus helping to raise the average fertility rate in Africa which in 2011 hovered around 4.7 compared to a world average of 2.5.

This custom is likely to decline in the future. The cost of raising children continues to climb as more men enter the wage sector and move to the cities or urban areas, where housing is designed for smaller (nuclear) families rather than extended families found in the rural areas and where children cannot be put to work to contribute to the family's economy at an early age. Indeed, as societies, in general, become more mobile, as more people embrace Christian tenets pertaining to monogamy and, perhaps more importantly, as more women are empowered educationally and economically and, therefore, able to choose not to be involved in polygynous marriages, one can see the incidence of plural marriages diminishing even further.

The prevalence of HIV/AIDS in Africa, where the infection rate in 2009 was about seven times that of the United States—4.3 percent versus 0.6 percent—is forcing Africans to take a serious look at the practice of "wife inheritance." Adherence to this custom has increased the death rate due to HIV/AIDS as men taking over their sisters-in-law whose husbands died of AIDS have themselves become infected and died.

Anthropologists have given specific terms to different forms of polygyny. For example, when a man marries his wife's sister, as in the Tswana and Zulu examples provided, that marriage is referred to as sororate. When a man "inherits" his dead brother's or other male relative's widow, for reasons already discussed, that marriage is called levirate. It is worth noting that there is a variation of the levirate marriage found among the Akamba of Kenya, in which when a man who is already married dies without issue, a close male relative takes over his widow and produces a male heir with her who takes the name of the dead man in order to continue the family line.

There is an unusual marriage form called "surrogate" or "woman-to-woman" marriage. In this kind of marriage, practiced among the Zulu as well as the Nuer of Sudan and the Akamba of Kenya, a woman unable to have children "gives bridewealth for and marries a woman, over whom and whose offspring she has full control, delegating to a male genitor the duties of procreation."[11] The male genitor is decided upon by either of the two women, depending upon local custom. This kind of relationship traditionally had no sexual connotations whatsoever for the women involved. It simply made it possible for the barren woman to secure her relationship to her husband by having another woman have children for her. In other African societies, this practice could be employed by a woman who was not barren but wanted time to pursue important traditionally male occupations such as being a political leader or a diviner. Surrogate marriages can also occur in a situation in which a man dies leaving only daughters and no son. The eldest daughter then uses the man's cattle to marry a wife or two for her father to produce sons for him.[12]

Another marriage form, called a ghost marriage, is also found among the Nuer people of Sudan and the Zulus. If a young man, an only heir of his family, dies when he has attained a marriageable age but before he has actually married, thereby depriving his family of an heir, a marriage is conducted between a woman and his ghost—hence, the term "ghost marriage." The bride then is impregnated by the dead man's relative. The offspring carries the name of the dead person, thereby restoring the family line.

There are other marriage forms that are not formalized through ceremonies or the transfer of bridewealth. These are called trial marriages and cohabitations.[13] A trial marriage is a relationship in which the couple who actually intend to get married decide to live together for a while to see if they are compatible and really like each other. Cohabitation, by contrast, is a relationship in which there is no such explicit intention of future marriage. Most of the urban liaisons one finds these days are probably of the latter variety. Children from these relationships, so long as their paternity is acknowledged by the man, enjoy the same inheritance rights as other children.

All the marriage forms are taken very seriously, "enforced by ancestral wrath" and stem "from the importance of continuing the agnatic [patrilineal] line."[14]

NONKINSHIP GROUPS

As we have seen, kinship certainly is the most basic factor underlying the formation of social groups. Other important factors that we will now turn our attention to are age, skills, and residence.

Age grades are almost a universal feature of traditional African societies. An age grade is a social organization composed of several age sets. An age set is a collection of males living in a village who are nearly of the same age, having been either born within a few years of each other or initiated into the set during special ceremonies. Among the Afikpo (a subgroup of the Ibo people of Nigeria), for instance, an age set was formed by young men initiated into the set at childhood. Among the Tiriki (a subgroup of the Abaluhya [Luhya] in western Kenya), the initiation occurred during the circumcision ceremonies when the young men were at puberty. Each age grade has specific functions assigned to it in society. In a study of the Afikpo, Phoebe Ottenberg identified four age grades and their basic functions as follows: the young grade was composed of young men who enforced the social rules of society and acted like the police; the junior grade consisted of married men whose task was mostly administrative; the middle grade was made up of yet older men who performed both legislative and adjudicative functions; and, lastly, the senior grade, consisting of very old men whose function was largely advisory.[15] The role of old people will be discussed in some detail shortly. Ottenberg says that those in the senior category were often called "retired," and even though they were usually treated deferentially due to their old age, they were "sometimes referred to as 'half dead.'"[16]

Among the Tiriki people of western Kenya, young men were initiated into adulthood during circumcision.[17] The rites were held every four to five years. There were seven age-groups, each age-group spanning a fifteen-year period. Moreover, each age-group passed through four discrete age grades: warriors, elder warriors, judicial elders, and ritual elders. This process was cyclical so that each age-group was being reinstated with new initiates every 105 years. The best way to explain age-groups and their relationship to age grades is to use the analogy of the traditional American college class system. Young people entering college in 1997 may be called the class of 2001 to show when they will graduate. While in college, however, they must go through four grades as freshman, sophomore, junior, and senior. While people in college may be identified by the year they entered college or graduated from it, among the Tiriki people, individuals in each age-group were identified by their initiation during a fifteen-year span. Because the initiation rites are held once every four or five years, each age-group will receive new members from three or four initiations. There were specific tasks assigned to each age grade. The primary task of the warriors was to guard and protect their land. The reputation established in this category remained with the group throughout their lives. The elder warriors' tasks were not as clearly spelled out as the others; however, they performed administrative functions such as presiding over post-funeral meetings to settle property claims, initiating compromises in conflicts, and seeking the advice of elders when in doubt. They also served as messengers between elders of different ethnic groups. The judicial elders performed most of the functions that in modern systems would entail adjudication, such as settling land and bridewealth disputes and mediating assault and accidental injuries. They also conducted initiation rites and ensured that shrine observances were carried out properly. Ritual elders carried out spiritual functions often acting as mediums or diviners. Their advice was sought in a wide variety of matters. Senior elders, few as they were, acted largely as advisers and were not as deeply involved in the daily activities of the community.

The picture of the age-groups that is given above is one that existed before the massive changes induced by colonization and the advent of Christianity. Age-groups still exist, but only nominally. Initiation rites are still being carried out, although they have been modified considerably. And now, instead of young men spending their time training as warriors to defend their communities, many go to school. After graduating from school, they go on for further education or to look for jobs in towns away from home. As many rituals are abandoned in favor of Christian practices, some of the elders have lost a few of their functions along with the prestige that those functions earned them. Some duties (such as mediating land disputes) are still decided on the basis of local customs and handled by the judicial elders, but these days younger persons with modern education may also be involved in those decision-making activities. Moreover, there is currently a certain amount of paperwork and record-keeping that is expected by centralized government bureaucracies. These clerical tasks require modern education.

This discussion of age-groups would be incomplete without some mention of deep reverence that is universally shown toward older folks in Africa. Old folks are very much respected. They are regarded as wise, experienced, and knowledgeable. They have made their contributions to their communities and now, in their old age, it is the communities' turn to recognize and honor them. Old people then have performed several important functions. They governed in formal ways as chiefs, kings, or councilors. They presided over family rituals and religious ceremonies. They interpreted traditions and folklore and helped pass them on to younger generations. They looked after small children while the younger and physically more able members of the family worked in the fields. They mediated conflicts within families and between clans. They were consulted in choosing mates for young people, and old women would often act as go-betweens in marriage negotiations. They served as judges in land disputes. And finally, they personified the link between the past and the present. It is understandable, then, why people in African societies, in general, even today, do not approach old age with the kind of trepidation evident in industrial societies.

As suggested earlier, skills form another basis of social organization in Africa. Such organizations are normally called guilds, or craft guilds. This phenomenon, of course, is not limited to Africa, and other societies, elsewhere, attach different social values to certain occupations. Occupations rated high socially are usually financially better rewarded. Members of craft guilds have special skills that are needed by society. Skills are acquired through long rigorous training and tend to be passed on from parents to their children. In some African societies, craft guilds were numerous, well-organized, and highly specialized; in others, they were few and not so specialized. An example of the former can be found among the Hausa of Nigeria who had more than thirty craft guilds including those of hunters, fishers, builders, blacksmiths, and musicians.[18] Among the Swazi people of southern Africa, on the contrary, guilds were not as strong, and specialization tended to be diffuse, with some individuals able to perform more than one specialized function.[19] In areas where craft guilds existed, they monitored their members' activities, regulated their behavior, and promoted their interests.

Medicine people were highly regarded for their healing abilities. Individuals who performed initiation rites enjoyed high social status. Oral historians, musicians, and poets also had a high social standing. Rain makers were valued for their magical powers to bring rain. Mediums (cf ritual elders) were respected for their ability to maintain contact with ancestral spirits and to facilitate communication with the spirit world. Chiefs and kings, as one might expect, were highly respected, in fact so much so that, even today, obedience and elaborate rituals of deference to those in authority seem deeply embedded in African political culture, which in turn feeds the highly personalized rule so prevalent in Africa. Village people regularly paid visits to leaders bearing gifts. Leaders not only performed the normal political governing functions but also adjudicated interpersonal and intracommunity conflicts.

Changes continue to occur in African societies. Many of these organizations are being eclipsed by modern government. Mediums are not as important as they used to be, although they are still being consulted even by modern politicians and others who are influential and wealthy and fearful of losing their social standing through circumstances beyond their control. Traditional medicine people are still active and are used to help cure a number of maladies for which modern cures have not been found. Countries like Nigeria and Kenya are making attempts to integrate traditional medicine and modern medicine. It is not easy. Many of these special abilities were guarded secretly to pass onto appropriate heirs, but this important knowledge of herbs and medicines should not be lost to present generations. Blacksmiths have lost some of their luster because modern technology allows the easy manufacture of items that previously could be made only by these people (in a much longer time span). Old people who derived so much status from performing initiation rites, for example, now face the prospect of a diminished status as young parents, who believe in circumcision more as a cosmetic procedure rather than as a true rite of passage, take their boys to modern hospitals for the operation. As I shall explain later, there is considerable resistance to the practice of female circumcision, even in Africa. This means that the prestige enjoyed by the old women who traditionally performed this rite is threatened in the near future.

There are other important social organizations in Africa called secret societies that perform a variety of functions deemed vital to the community as a whole. There are both men's and women's secret societies, although men's societies are better known and have been studied more by Western scholars. To join a secret society, one must meet certain criteria and subject oneself to a series of sometimes lengthy initiation rituals. As the name of the organizations suggests, one must swear to absolute secrecy on the society's belief codes and rituals. Normally secret societies are ethnically based, but the larger ones may cut across ethnic groups and villages. Secret societies range from small village-based groups to large well-known groups, such as the Poro society found among the Mende people of Sierra Leone and the Kpelle people of Liberia and the Ogboni society of the Yoruba people in Nigeria. According to Gibbs, the Poro society is headed by the Grand Master, who always is masked when he appears in public and has his body completely covered. He disguises his voice when he speaks. The society's meetings are held at night in secret locations. When the Grand Master visits villages, special music is played to warn women and nonmembers either to stay indoors or face serious consequences if they should happen to see him.[20] Not much research on secret societies exists, but existing research shows that "Men's [secret] societies, in particular, had important judicial functions, helping to settle disputes between lineages, sometimes ordering punishments and seeing them carried out by its junior members wearing masks to conceal their identity—and to emphasize the spiritual basis of their authority."[21] Men and women who belong to these societies regard each other as sisters and brothers.

It is suspected that secret society officials such as those of Poro play a dual sacred–secular role. In their social control functions, they are able to mete out punishment for violations of social rules while also deflecting any resentment that might come from the people to the supernatural as represented by the masks that they wear. Nowadays, small women's secret societies which continue to exist assist their members in many ways such as sharing business ideas, helping with marriage or funeral expenses, and providing critical emotional support to one another in time of need.

There are also many social organizations found today in traditional African villages that function as worker cooperatives. They tend to be informal, are village-based, and consist of ten to fifty people who assist their members with farmwork or business enterprises. They are sometimes referred to as local or residence groups. They normally go in rotation to each member's farms or plots. They are occupied during the planting, weeding, and harvest times. In my own society, these residence-based workers' cooperatives were most likely to consist of women, although sometimes men joined. People were not paid for the work they did. Gibbs explains in reference to the Kpelle people of Liberia who had a very strong system of such work cooperatives:

> A day with a good *kuu* [as a cooperative work group is known in the Mande-Kpelle language] is a day of hard work. But it is a day of pleasure as well, for the farmer-member who is host for the day provides a large meal for the long break at noon ... Sometimes a musical group provides continuous rhythmic accompaniment, and a *kuu* with marked *espri de corps* may even outfit itself with costumes for the bits of dancing that go with cutting bush or sowing rice.[22]

THE INDIVIDUAL IN AFRICAN SOCIETIES

African societies are collectivist societies. The group is paramount, and the group's interests clearly supersede those of the individual. A person defines his/her identity in terms of belonging to a group. Everyone belongs and is responsible to a group. For instance, when a person commits an offense against another person, the offense reflects badly not just on the individual offender but on his group as well. His group is therefore held accountable, and the matter is handled by the elders of his group. Reparations, if any are demanded, are made to the group of the aggrieved person, not necessarily to the aggrieved individual. If a murder is committed, and punishment against the murderer is not considered fair or commensurate, the victim's group may seek to avenge the murder by killing a member, any member, of the group of the murderer. Perceiving an individual as part of a corporate group— clan, ethnic group, or family—serves as a powerful deterrent to social transgressions. As will be explained later, religious beliefs also reflect this basic orientation of subordinating individual interests to those of society. Because belonging to a group is prized above anything else, banishment from the community serves as a very harsh punishment indeed.

Like most social values, the collectivist ethos so prevalent in Africa arose out of a supreme need for group survival. For societies that eked out a living from the soil, that hunted and gathered, or that appeared always to live at the mercy of diseases, vagaries of weather, and high mortality rates, survival was very much dependent on people living together, working the soil together, sharing tasks, and protecting and comforting each other in a variety of groups such as those we have just discussed. To be banished from one's group, for any reason, was to have one's life hang in the balance, to be at high risk. One simply could not survive on one's own. There were notable modifications to the dominant collectivist ethos; the Ibos of Nigeria, the Baganda of Uganda, and the Kpelle of Liberia, to name a few, traditionally had ethos that stressed individual autonomy and fulfillment within and between social groups.

With the economic and social changes now taking place in Africa, the collectivist ethos is being eroded. When it is now possible for an individual to move to a city and find the means to support himself and his immediate family, thereby becoming autonomous and possibly self-sufficient, the group is no longer able to exercise the degree of social control on him that it once did. And because adjudication functions once performed by judicial elders or "wise old men" are gradually being taken over by modern courts employing elements of European law, individuals are becoming increasingly accountable to themselves and not to their primary groups.

Individuals in African societies, as is already clear from the preceding discussion, go through distinct life stages (called age grades, after initiation): infancy, childhood, young adulthood, mature adulthood, and if you will, elderhood. The transition from one stage to another is marked by a special ritual or ceremony and is occasion for community celebration.

When a baby is born, a special ceremony is called for. Babies are prized. They affirm the community, provide hope for the future, and bestow pride on the parents. During the ceremony, a special name is given and the baby becomes a member of the community in a formal sense. Due to the high infant mortality rates that African societies used to face, families often waited, sometimes as long as two years to be sure of the infant's long-term survival, before inducting the child into the family. The name was carefully chosen to convey good fortune, to commemorate a revered ancestor, or to reflect the parents' sense of gratitude or pride. In almost every case, the child was taken to the mother's relatives to be introduced to them. The childhood experience in Africa used to be extremely comforting and nurturing. As Maquet says,

> The African child is born Black but becomes African ... For the first months of his life—and often for more than a year—the African baby is in constant physical contact with his mother. She carries him, often skin to skin, on her hip or her back; she gives him the breast whenever he is hungry ... This constant contact with the mother, the source of warmth, food and comfort, gives the young African a much greater sense of security than the Western child enjoys, alone in his crib, fed on schedule and, if he is bottle-fed, in amounts determined by impersonal formulas ...
>
> When this child is weaned—very late by Western standards—and he can get around independently, his human horizon broadens more rapidly than that of the European or American child. The latter is still confined with his nuclear family: father, mother, brothers and sisters.

Relationships with relatives by blood and marriage are not very close, and, besides, relatives usually live some distance away. The African child has only to take a few steps in his village to visit several people who can substitute for his father, mother, brothers and sisters, and they will treat him accordingly. Thus the child has many homes in his village, and he is simultaneously giver and receiver of widespread attention.[23]

The entry of a young person into adulthood is marked by an initiation ceremony. Initiation is prevalent in Africa. Its form, however, varies from group to group. In many ethnic groups across the continent, such as the Luhya and the Kikuyu (Kenya), the Zulu (South Africa), the Ibo (Nigeria), and the Gisu (Uganda), to name a few examples, initiation for boys was characterized by circumcision between the age of twelve and eighteen. The Hausa of Nigeria and the Somali people in eastern Africa practice circumcision, but not as an initiation rite, preferring instead to use marriage as the rite of passage into adulthood. Some groups, including the Hausa and the Somali, practice female circumcision as well, but this custom is not practiced by a majority of Africans. Cicatrization, skin scarification, or tattooing of the face or the upper torso are examples of initiation rites for both boys and girls in parts of West Africa. Still others favor the removal of certain teeth as a form of initiation. The custom of female genital cutting (FGC) is under attack both by some Africans themselves and human rights activists and feminists outside the continent—for obvious reasons that we'll discuss in a moment. Different groups have different explanations for the origin of the female cut, a surgical procedure that varies in its severity, but involves, in its less radical form, the removal of the clitoris. The Dogon people of Mali, for instance, believe that every child is born both male and female. The penile foreskin on the boy represents "femaleness," whereas the clitoris represents "maleness." Both accessories must be removed during initiation for the boys to be completely "male," and the girls to be completely "female," so as to be considered a full member of the community and ready for the adult responsibility of marriage. "Only at puberty, after circumcision or excision, does the child become a full member of society, having rid himself of his dual sexual nature."[24] A woman who refuses to submit to the rites does not have a legitimate status in the community, and no man would want to marry her. Similarly, a man who is not, or refuses to be, circumcised has no social standing in the community and cannot get married or have children.

Another explanation for the custom cites the long-standing male dominance over women. In most African societies, men controlled all levers of power and asserted exclusive rights over women. Men also believed that women had a higher sexual drive than men and feared that if men went to war leaving their womenfolk behind in the villages, the women would seek the sexual intimacy of other men. The custom of FGC was instituted, therefore, to curb the women's supposed excessive sexual desires. It most likely interfered with their capacity for sexual pleasure. The men, however, knew that the procedure did not significantly impair their ability to enjoy sex or the women's capacity to have children. This is one of the explanations often cited by feminists in their opposition to the custom.

FGC has been under attack by Christian missionaries as a barbaric custom from the time they arrived in Africa to begin proselytizing. The Africans have always resisted any attempts to ban the custom. In Kenya, even Jomo Kenyatta, a Western-educated nationalist, who became the first president of Kenya, sided with his people, the Kikuyu, when he argued that the cut was an essential element of the religious and cultural heritage of his people. He suggested that to forbid Africans to practice this rite was to destroy their culture and, therefore, their identity as a people. Western critics have also pointed out that FGC sexually incapacitates women. At any rate, it is primarily for religious and cultural reasons that governments in Africa have been slow in outlawing the practice. Twenty-eight African countries have outlawed the practice, although enforcement has been extremely lax.

Beyond the philosophical explanations, there is a strong practical case to be made against FGC. There is little doubt that the custom sexually incapacitates women, although this point has not been, and is not likely to be, publicly made by African women opposed to the practice. Another point against FGC—and this is the one that is most often made by Africans opposed to the practice—is that it severely imperils women's health due to the fact that it is almost always carried out under unsanitary conditions. Those women who survive the operation and any concomitant infections are left with scar tissue that makes subsequent childbirth extremely risky. In fact, in Kenya, European missionaries detected a very high death rate among Kikuyu women resulting from childbirth. It had never occurred to the Kikuyu people that the scar tissue might be the cause of these deaths. They responded, like most Africans elsewhere, by thinking that perhaps these misfortunes were due to the wrath of ancestral spirits. Despite appropriate offerings in appeasement to the ancestors, the problem persisted. When the practice of FGC declined, the death rate associated with delivery declined as well. Finally, FGC is unduly painful and unnecessary. To traumatize young women simply for the sake of preserving an ancient rite, or for the sake of protecting the status of the old women who perform this procedure, is too high a price to pay.

Before we leave the subject of initiation, as someone who underwent this process in its true form, I want to say a few words as to what the male initiation rites mean to a young man who goes through them.

1. Initiation marks a time when a person officially becomes an adult. The actual removal of the foreskin symbolizes separation from childhood in much the same way that a newly born baby is separated from its mother by cutting the umbilical cord.

2. Initiation represents the only time when formal instruction takes place. The instruction covers the basic knowledge of your community, its roots, its heroes, its life-sustaining myths, values, and taboos, and the basic responsibilities of adulthood. The candidate is told that from that moment on, he/she is an adult, able to get married, and fully responsible for certain actions.

3. Initiation enhances the self-esteem of the young person and establishes his/her position among peers. The physical pain that the young initiate is expected to endure without flinching is designed to prepare him for the hardships and pain of adult life. As John Mbiti says, "Endurance of physical and emotional pain is a great virtue among Akamba people (of Kenya), as indeed it is among other Africans, since life in Africa is surrounded by much pain from one source or another."[25]

4. It is a source of immense pride for the family when it is successfully done. In some ethnic groups, the young man's father's position in his age grade is elevated.

5. It is a mark of group identity. The differences in the form of the ritual tell other people where you come from, what group you belong to, and what is special about you.

6. There is much stress on the sexual identity of the young initiates. The rites may very well enhance "sexual imprinting," thereby lessening the confusion in sexual identity so often mentioned in the Western world.

7. Initiation represents a time of renewal and affirmation for the community.

Initiation rites are very elaborate, generally speaking, and include invocations of ancestral spirits. This point is highlighted in a detailed study by Victor Turner about initiation rites of the Gisu people in Uganda. During the fourth and final phase of the preparations for the rites, Turner says,

> The maximal lineage elders clean out the sacred groves of patrilineal ancestors, rebuild shrines in them, and sacrifice a chicken and a beer. The grandfathers of the novices ... make similar sacrifices to the ancestors in their own ... compounds. Each novice then goes to his mother's brother to ask formal permission to be circumcised and to receive the blessings of the ancestors.[26]

Mbiti also points out that the shedding of blood into the ground binds the initiate mystically to the ancestral spirits who are "living" in the ground. In the case of the Bukusu (a subgroup of the Luhya), at the precise moment of the circumcision, the father of the initiate stands on top of the hut to invite the participation of the ancestral spirits and to ask for their help. Often temporary shrines are erected to honor the dead grandparents of the initiate. The rejoicing and showering of the initiate with presents of money and animals demonstrate this sense of community and the welcoming into it of the young person as a new adult.

In most African groups, after initiation into adulthood, the individual does not undergo any other important milestone until he/she gets married. Among the Masaai of East Africa, however, initiation is a simple transition to a warrior status, a stage that is marked by a great deal of training and development in individual military and athletic skills and the learning of the traditional ways of the community.

Relationships among the warriors formed at this stage tend to be strong and to last a lifetime. Sexual activity is condoned, indeed expected and even encouraged, between the warriors and the uninitiated pubescent girls. Leaders emerge at this point. The period of warriorship lasts several years after which a simpler rite involving the shaving off of all of their hair signals their entry into adulthood. Angela Fisher says that the shaving of the warrior's head, which is performed by his mother, is "a traumatic event during which the man, overcome with emotion, often trembles, weeps and foams at the mouth. The loss of his hair, which has not been cut at all during his warriorship, signifies the end of the most enjoyable and privileged years of his life."[27] Many of them begin to prepare for marriage and the responsibilities of raising, protecting, and providing for a family. The next stage is marked by marriage followed by another one when the person becomes a parent. The process culminates with the elder being inducted into a council of elders.

FAMILY LIFE AND SOCIALIZATION
Family Life

Having discussed social groups and the place of the individual in those groups, let us turn our attention now to the family structure. The extended family system is the most prevalent family system in Africa. It is a larger family structure and includes more blood relatives than the basic nuclear family of the Western world. In the United States, the modal family membership is one or two parents and children. Because of the high divorce rate in the United States, one now finds an increasing incidence of step-families, made up of previously divorced parents and their children from earlier marriages. Even in step-families, the composition is basically the same: parents and their children. In traditional African families, however, there were three or more generations of relatives: grandparents, uncles, aunts, nephews, and nieces all living in proximity and working together for the common good. The extended family system seemed to fit nicely into the communal life patterns also.

In Africa, large families are highly valued. Studies in Nigeria show that even today, the ideal family size is four to six children. Children are prized because they perpetuate the family name and the social values and norms handed down by ancestors. Children belong to the parents as well as to the community of relatives. The kind of parental possessiveness toward children that one finds in the community is rare in the Western world. It was quite common for children to be sent to live with relatives in other villages for years without parents having not to worry about how the children were being raised. The lack of worry is, in itself, an illustration of the harmony and consistency in cultural values. In the past, this practice of sending children to live with other relatives may also have served to strengthen kinship bonds. These days the practice is becoming a matter of necessity as relatives with too many children seek the help of better-off relatives or those with fewer children in sharing the burden of taking care of their children.

In traditional Africa, work was gender-based. The men performed certain tasks such as building homes, blacksmithing, carving wood objects, fishing, weaving fishing nets, hunting, working the land especially with ox-drawn plows, protecting the homesteads, making political decisions for the community, and adjudicating conflicts. The women worked on the farm and did all the household chores—cooking, taking care of the children, fetching water and firewood, and cleaning the house. They also weaved baskets and made pots. In pastoral groups like the Fulani of West Africa or the Somali of East Africa, taking care of domestic animals would be the men's responsibility, while keeping the animal sheds clean would be the women's job. There were variations, of course, among different groups. For example, among the Hausa people of West Africa, men did most of the farming—clearing, burning, planting, and weeding—but during harvest time, the women helped out. Among the Maasai of East Africa, women built their huts and learned how to defend them when the men were gone on hunting expeditions.

Socialization

Socialization is a universal process. It allows society's values to be inculcated among the young through formal training and education. Without it, most societies would not have the sense of continuity and persistence that is so vital. Much of traditional Africa did not have schools and classrooms for teaching values and culture. Young people learned by doing and by observing their peers and older people. The emphasis by the older members of the community was on those skills and values that were designated for boys or girls and judged essential for the survival of the community as a distinct group. Young girls learned household chores, such as carrying water from the well, fetching firewood, cooking, and cleaning the house, by observing and helping their mothers and grandmothers. Any special crafts like pottery, weaving, and cloth making were taught by women to their daughters. The boys likewise learned hunting, house building, and tool-making from their fathers and older male relatives. The family was therefore an important socializing agent.

In communal societies, children began contributing to the family's welfare much earlier than in more developed societies. One of the very first tasks that children learn is taking care of their younger siblings. Kids begin baby-sitting from about the age of four or five, while adults work on the farm. Many of the parent functions such as toilet-training are taught to youngsters by other youngsters. These are tasks which, in Western societies, have turned out to be extremely challenging to adults and have spawned a plethora of lively "how-to" books. For some reason, kids seem to learn faster from other kids than from impatient adults. Youngsters teach their peers by doing. In some communities, formal structures like age sets or younger people's unstructured organizations helped in the transmission of community values and what was expected of every member of the community. The basic values shared by the community were rarely questioned. Peers were, therefore, a second important socializing agent.

Young people were seldom confronted with ideas that contradicted what their parents and elders wanted them to know. Barring disasters like floods, famines, and epidemics, which were beyond the control of mere mortals, life was predictable and unchanging. That is no longer the case. With industrialization, education, urbanization, and increased mobility, young people are beginning to meet people from other parts of their own countries or from abroad. Their horizons are broadening. Inevitably, their values and views are beginning to be challenged.

Many people have heard that African societies take care of their older people better than Western societies do. The extended family system makes it easier to look after grandparents. The deference given to old people also means that grandparents need not fear being pushed to the sidelines of their families' lives. They can age with dignity, surrounded by caring family members. Because old people are respected for their age and wisdom (which is presumed to come with age), they had many things to do. One of those things was to spend a large amount of time with small children. This is where their role as socializing agents was really highlighted. While adults and young adults worked in the field, old people stayed at home and looked after the youngsters. The earliest memories of my childhood, when I was about five or six, are those of my paternal grandfather taking me and my girl-cousin to herd cattle with him. He was extremely fond of my cousin, who was named after his mother. He always called her by his mother's name and swore that she had all the wonderful qualities of his deceased mother. In any case, grandparents were riveting storytellers, patient playmates (unlike parents), and interested listeners. One learned a great deal from them about the old times, about past struggles and challenges of the community, about those rare qualities and strengths that made one's family so special. I have always attributed to my grandfather whatever personal strengths I have exhibited in dealing with an array of adverse and difficult times in my life. He instilled in me a very strong sense of self-esteem. He explained our customs and traditions and how well they had served us. He told inspiring stories about our great heroes and legends. He spoke about the intention of the European colonizers to destroy our way of life, how they despised us Africans, and how we must not be broken as a people. I took all this to heart. In the majority of African societies, grandchildren had a very close and relaxed relationship with their grandparents that permitted them to tease and kid each other. Anthropologists have characterized this relationship as "a joking relationship." In the context of this relationship of familiarity, the children felt free to discuss any problem or to seek advice on any matter that they would not do with their parents, with whom they had a more structured relationship. Besides the grandparents, the children could maintain "joking relationships" with maternal uncles or paternal aunts, relatives that normally did not stay in the same compound as part of the extended family.

The fourth and last socializing agent is the initiation ritual. As described earlier, it is during initiation that what might be characterized as formal instruction actually occurs. As I recall from my own experience, it was during the latter part of the rites, just before the "coming out" ceremony that the male elders of the community sat down with young initiates and went over the basics, the triumphs and the failures of the clan (mostly the triumphs, rarely the failures, unless they happened to be incidents of great suffering and tragedy that eventually were overcome), and the major responsibilities expected of an adult. For ethnic groups that practiced clitoridectomy, this formal instruction was conducted by female elders. In the old days, the initiation itself would have been preceded by a series of tests to determine a young person's readiness for this gruelling and painful rite of passage. In those ethnic groups, like mine, where circumcision was the specific rite of passage, the test would have been to lead a dangerous hunt for a lion or a leopard, or to raid a neighboring village for cattle.

As is the case with so many other African traditions, initiation rites too are in the process of change. Many parents are having their children circumcised in a hospital at a much earlier age or even at infancy. The initiation rites performed in the villages are taking a much shorter time as many initiates have to return to school after only four weeks of recess. The kind of bonding, so important in later life, that occurs during the four- or five-month period preceding the "coming out" ceremony is no longer possible. People in villages still talk about age sets, and new initiates will be told what age set and the corresponding age grade they belong to, but age sets do not do much together anymore. There is considerable opposition to clitoridectomy by younger and more educated parents. As mentioned earlier, Kenya is the only African country to have outlawed the practice officially. However, the ban is resisted in the remote areas of the country, since the custom is considered so central to the culture. The government is reluctant to prosecute those who violate the ban. Instead, public health officials are encouraging parents to take their young girls to government clinics where a much less severe version of clitoridectomy (involving simply a small cut of the tip of the clitoris) is performed to meet the spirit of the rites.

TRADITIONAL RELIGIOUS BELIEFS

Religion, which Durkheim defined as a set of beliefs and practices related to sacred things that unites adherents into a single moral community, is as old as human society itself. Religion deals with those basic questions that human beings have been grappling with from the very beginning. Where did we come from? How did the universe and all the things in it come about? What forces out there influence our lives? Why are we here? What is our purpose, our mission, in this life? What happens to us when we die?

Africans are a deeply spiritual people, yet the least understood facet of African life probably has to do with their religious traditions and beliefs. Foreign missionaries who went to Africa became obsessively interested in ancestral spirits and spirits in general as though that was all there was to African spirituality. Since these missionaries went to Africa with the purpose of converting Africans to Christianity, they did not feel duty bound to learn much about Africans' spiritual values and heritage. Scholars of religion, in addition, could have done better than they did in trying to understand African religion so they could explain it to the rest of the world. However, since these scholars were themselves mostly Christians, it was difficult for most of them to step out of their own religious mind-sets and explore various religious traditions in Africa. They overlooked the parallels in religious superstitions between angels, for example, and ancestral spirits. Today, negative and misleading terms still abound in reference to African religious traditions. When reporting on a military coup in some African country, American newspapers will run that country's profile and use terms like "animism" or "paganism" to characterize the religious practices of that country. What amazes me as an African who was educated in Christian mission schools is the parallels that exist between the traditional religious beliefs of Africans (as I saw them celebrated by my grandfather when I was growing up) and the religious rituals I observed in school and church.

A serious analysis of any religion must recognize that religious beliefs are determined by social and cultural conditions of a people, the physical environment in which they live, their past experiences, and their collective needs and goals as a people. There are universal manifestations of religious behavior that one finds in Africa as a whole and that any observer would have to take into account, including a belief in a supernatural being or supernatural forces, a belief in the existence of one or more deities or gods, prayer or specific words that one is supposed to use when one is addressing these deities or supernatural forces, certain body movements such as kneeling, prostrating oneself, or dancing that are required in the course of directing prayer to these supernatural forces, some kind of sacred code, sacred objects designed to bring good fortune when handled properly or misfortune when misused, sacrifices or feasts held to mark certain important occasions, and groves, shrines, or monuments.

What follows is not, by any means, a detailed analysis of African religious traditions. It is basically an overview, the limited purpose of which is to lay out the salient features of religious thinking and practice in Africa, pointing out certain rituals and ideas that are common to the more established religions elsewhere with which most of us are familiar.

Belief in God

The vast majority of Africans traditionally believed in the concept of God, of a Supreme Being, who created the universe and everything in it. There are quite a few variations; the Ibo and the Yoruba people of Nigeria, for example, believe in a Supreme Being who is assisted by smaller deities. The Yoruba have the idea of an Almighty God, whom they gave the name *Olorun*. This Supreme Being is assisted by lesser deities called *orishas*. Every orisha, each one of whom had a name, was responsible for a specific function among the humans. The orishas were God's assistants who looked after God's creation. There was the God of Rain, the God of Fertility, the God of the Forest, the God of the Sea, and so on. When the rains had not come for a long time and the people were threatened with a severe drought and famine, they would pray to the God of Rain. When the women were not producing enough children for the community, the people prayed to the God of Fertility to make the womenfolk more fertile so that they would give the community more children. When hunters went hunting, prayers would be said to the special deity to look after the hunters and to ensure that their hunts were bountiful. When fishers set out to sea, the God of the Sea was invoked to provide safety and a good catch to the men.

The Kipsigis (a subgroup of the Kalenjin people) of Kenya also believed in one God (called *Asis* or *Asista*). Robert Manners says that because the Kipsigis used many names to refer to God, some scholars assumed that there were many Gods, when most probably the terms referred to a variety of functions or activities that *Asis* performed.[28] Manners also suggests that the Kipsigis were not terribly religious in terms of holding many formal religious meetings, but when their community faced a crisis, special appeals were then made. However, spirit mediums played a far more pervasive role in the lives of the Kipsigis community. According to Jomo Kenyatta, the first president of Kenya and author of *Facing Mount Kenya* (an excellent study of the Kikuyu people),

> The Gikuyu believes in one God, *Ngai*, the Creator and giver of all things. He has no father, mother, or companion of any kind. His work is done

in solitude. He loves and hates people according to their behavior. The Creator lives in the sky, but has temporary homes on earth, situated on mountains, where he may rest during his visits. The visits are made with a view to his carrying out a kind of "general inspection," and to bring blessings and punishments to the people.[29]

The universe that God created is composed of two parts, or perhaps three: the heavens (where God lives, and also where the stars, the sun, the moon, and the sky are), the earth (which is full of such things as people, plants, mountains, or rivers), and probably the underworld (where some spirits may reside). Man is the main link between the universe and God. This universe is orderly; there may be at least four main levels at which this order is maintained:

1. The natural level, governed by the laws of nature, as revealed to us, for instance, through science.
2. The moral level, which consists of a moral code, laws, and doctrines given by God that people are required to obey so as to have harmony and peace in their societies. In most societies, these laws are revealed to the people through prophets, or "wise men," and passed on down through generations or through some vision. The moral code spells out for the people what is right or wrong, and what is evil or righteous.
3. The religious level that refers to man-made institutions, such as churches, temples, and shrines, whose duty is to advise people to live their lives as God wants them. Institutions fashion rules pertaining to rewards one receives for being good and proper punishment for failing to obey the edicts. The great variety of denominations in various religions can be attributable to institutional differences based on varying interpretations of basic doctrines.
4. Finally, the mystical level, which deals mainly with magic and witchcraft, powers given to certain individuals and spirits to communicate with supernatural forces. Individuals who have mystical powers are able to see the departed, to receive premonitions of coming events and disasters, and to carry out "miracles" or "wonders" which other people normally are unable to do.[30]

Most groups even have their own myths or legends of how the universe came to be, how the creation occurred, or how their own community originated. One of the more interesting "creation myths" is offered by the Abaluhya people of western Kenya. It deserves to be quoted extensively, if not for anything else, at least for the fascinating parallel it offers with the Biblical story. This is how it goes:

> The world was created by *Wele Xakaba,* the granter or giver of all things. Before he created the whole world with everything in it, he made his own abode, heaven. To prevent heaven from falling in, he supported it all

round with pillars just as the roof of a round *hut* is propped up by pillars. Wele Xakaba created heaven alone, without the assistance of anyone else. In a miraculous way, *Wele Xakaba* then created his two assistants, *wele muxobe* and *wele murumwa.*

Heaven, being the dwelling-house of God and his two assistants, is said to be always bright (i.e., during day and night). Is a place of everlasting scintillation. God created it like lightning and in a mysterious way. Also, the substance of which heaven is made is a mystery.

After God created heaven, he decided to put certain things in it. First he made the moon and put it in the sky, and then he created the sun ...

After having created the sun and the moon, God made clouds and put them into the sky. He then created a big rooster from which lightning originates. This rooster *(engoxo enjahi)* is of reddish color and lives among the clouds. Whenever it shakes its wings there is lightning, and whenever it crows there is thunder.

God also created the stars to assist the sun and the moon ...

Next, God created both air and "cold air." It is this cold air which makes some of the water in the sky form into hailstones *(kamarara or amatjina).*

After God created heaven and everything in it, he wondered where his two assistants, *wele muxobe* and *wele murumwa,* and all the other things he had made could do their work. He therefore, decided to create the earth. Again, he did so in a mysterious way, providing the earth with mountains, valleys and larger depressions.

Having created the sun and given it the power of resplendence, he asked himself, "For whom will the sun shine?" This led to God's decision to create the first man. The Vugusu believe that the first man was called Mwambu. Because God had created him so that he could talk and see, he needed someone to whom he could talk. God therefore created the first woman, called, Sela, to be Mwambu's partner ...

After God had provided the surface of the earth with water, he created all plants. He then said to himself that all those plants were useless unless there was something to eat them. So animals, birds and other creatures living in the water, on the surface of the earth, and in the soil were created....

God completed the whole work of creation in six days [sic]. On the seventh day he rested because it was a bad day. The Vugusu have all sorts of beliefs and taboos *(gimisilu)* referring to this day and the number seven.[31]

There were, of course, many concepts of God in Africa, for the simple reason that "in each locality, the concept of God usually takes its emphasis and complexion from the sociological structure and climate. It is necessary to understand the variations in the sociological patterns in order to see clearly the reason for certain emphasis and tendencies."[32] Some African groups had an anthropomorphic image of God and used human terms to describe who God was. Some described God in masculine terms, others used feminine terms, yet for others, God did not have any specific image at all. He was part of everything he created. This strong belief in God, in a supernatural being, was often ignored by foreigners.

Belief in Spirits

A second attribute of African religious thinking consists of the idea of spirits. Spirits are a life force but have no concrete physical form. John Mbiti has divided African spirits into two types: nature spirits and human spirits. Nature spirits are associated with certain natural objects or forces in the sky or on the earth. Examples of sky objects are the moon, the sun, the sky, rain, and wind. Examples of earth objects are forests, hills, mountains, and metals. Again, one finds interesting differences among different groups. For example, some groups will recognize the spirits associated with the sky like the moon and rain, but not earth objects like mountains and rivers. The point here is that these differences are mediated by culture and experience. Different communities need different answers to the basic spiritual or religious questions posed at the beginning of the chapter. Human spirits are those of people who have died. Most of these people are relatives who died either in the distant past or more recently. Another way of putting what I just stated is that living things have spirits within them. When living things die, however, the spirits continue to exist. You cannot see a spirit, just as you cannot see God. In the film *Atumpan*, on the talking drums of Ghana, a group of Africans set out to the forest to find the right kind of tree to cut down and use for carving a ceremonial drum. The drum is needed for the very special occasion of enstooling a new chief. The enstoolment is planned to coincide with the celebration of the harvest, known as the *Odai* festival. Before the chosen tree is felled, a brief ritual is held during which a libation is poured on the tree. The spirit of the tree is told that the tree is going to be cut down for the making of a drum for the ceremony, and that those assembled are asking the spirit of the tree to continue to reside in the tree and to make their chief fertile and to give him a long life and a long reign. It is the notion that living things have spirits that gave rise to the rather pejorative term "animism," which is often applied to traditional African religious thinking.

Belief in Ancestors

A third attribute of African religions has to do with the important place held by ancestral spirits, since the African community is defined as being made up of the dead as well as the living. When a person dies, he/she becomes a spirit with extra attributes that make him/her more powerful than living human beings. The spirits of the dead continue to reside in the community and are actively involved in the life of the community. As spirits, they act as intermediaries between God and those still alive. No African ritual fails to include ancestral spirits; they are always called upon to help in time of need. The role that the ancestral spirits play is really no different from the role played by (guardian) angels and patron saints in Catholic doctrine, for instance. Bad spirits, on the other hand, can also be harnessed, but only to do harm or evil, and hence the term "witchcraft." In some African groups, malevolent spirits were those of bad people who died. In other groups, spirits can be either good or bad, depending upon what they are called upon to do by witches or sorcerers or how upset they are at not being honored or at being excluded by their community. An example from the Bukusu might be a case in which a new initiate bled unconscious following circumcision and was at the point of death. A medium was quickly consulted. Her verdict was that the initiate's father had forgotten to build a shrine to his late father (the initiate's grandfather), and the spirit of the boy's grandfather was sending a message of unhappiness by causing the boy to bleed profusely. A shrine was quickly put up and a small sacrifice made to appease the grandfather's spirit. To be sure that the crisis was not fatal, a local health assistant who worked in a government clinic and moonlighted on weekends as a doctor was called in to try to stop the bleeding and dress the boy's wound, which he succeeded in doing.

Among the Lele people of the Democratic Republic of Congo, it was found that the spirits were a separate entity who were created by God. The spirits were very much feared because of the magical and curative powers they held. This notion of spirits is very much in keeping with Christian thinking which holds that human beings do not simply disappear when they die; they become spirits and are either rewarded or punished according to whether they lived their lives in conformity with the laws of God as interpreted by churches and their high priests. In many African communities, the concept of community is much broader than the Western societies; in addition to the living, it includes the dead, for example, the spirits of the dead relatives or ancestors, and those yet to be born. Celebrations note this at all times and rituals have to take into account the nonliving.

Religion as a Way of Life

A fourth attribute is related to the fact that Africans *live* their faith. Their lives are not compartmentalized in the way life tends to be in the Western world. Religion is not something that is simply practiced at one time on a given day in a certain building or place. This is not a criticism of religious life in the West; it is merely a description of how Africans order their lives. John Mbiti has put it eloquently this way:

> Because traditional religions permeate all the departments of life, there is no formal distinction between the sacred and the secular, between the religious and the non-religious, between the spiritual and the material areas of life. Wherever the African is, there is his religion: he carries it to the fields where he is sowing seeds or harvesting a new crop; he takes it with him to the beer party or to attend a funeral ceremony ... Although many African languages do not have a word for religion as such, it nevertheless accompanies the individual from long before his birth to long after his physical death. Through modern change these traditional religions cannot remain intact, but they are by no means extinct. In times of crisis they often come to the surface, or people revert to them in secret.[33]

African religious symbolism was often misunderstood by foreigners. A few examples will drive home the point. A cow is a very important animal to the Nuer. Cattle are the center of the people's economic, social, and political existence. They permeate the Nuer culture. People will often form attachments to their cattle, composing poems about their favorite animals. To the Nuer, the cow represented economic and emotional security, without which life lost much of its meaning. The behavior exhibited toward these animals does not and should not mean that the animals are worshipped or regarded as having divine attributes.

To the Mbuti people of the Democratic Republic of Congo, the forest is pivotal to their lives. As Colin Turnbull says,

> When a [Mbuti] child is born, ... it is bathed in water mixed with the juice of a forest vine, it is clothed with a circlet around the waist, decorated with one or two small pieces of pierced wood and with similar circlets around the wrists, and it is an object of pride and interest and concern to every member of the band. The vine circlets, the juice, and the wooden ornaments are not only for decoration, but place the child in this way always in physical contact with the physical forest, which as well as being the protector is the life-giver.[34]

For a Mbuti person, it made ample sense to compose poems and songs in praise of the forest as concrete evidence of God's providence.

Finally, to the Kikuyu people, Mount Kenya was a sacred mountain. They always faced it when they prayed, asking their ancestors for help. Foreigners assumed that the Kikuyu people were praying to an inanimate object, the mountain, when, in fact, the mountain was nothing but a symbol—in much the same way that the crucifix that a Christian wears or the statues in front of which I knelt in church as a young Catholic boy were not God but simply symbolic representations of God, or the Virgin Mary, or Jesus.

POLITICS AND GOVERNMENT IN TRADITIONAL AFRICA

Much has been written about politics in Africa before colonization. Most of these works have been case studies conducted by political anthropologists. As one might expect, given the size of Africa, there are many types of political systems, ranging from small chiefdoms, in which everyone was related to everyone else (and therefore power and authority were based on kinship), to huge empires such as those discussed in Chapter 3.

One generalization that can be made about precolonial Africa is that there were essentially two types of political systems: states and "stateless" societies. States were organized structurally in much the same way as modern states. Bureaucracies carried out certain functions such as collecting taxes, supervising ceremonies, entertaining dignitaries, and compelling people to do what the kings or chiefs wanted them to do. The "stateless" societies, on the other hand, were politically decentralized entities, had no bureaucracies to speak of, and tended to be based on kinship (i.e., lineage systems and extended families). In these kinds of decentralized systems, social groups that we discussed earlier, like age sets and secret societies, played a very strong role in maintaining order and discipline and harnessing the resources of the community for collective goals. The vast majority of Africans, before the advent of Europeans, lived in "stateless" societies. This does not mean that "stateless" societies did not have politics. In fact, they did.

David Apter sought successfully to develop a theory of political change and to delineate why some African countries, in the face of colonial intrusion, were able to change faster or less painfully than others.[35] To do so, he established a comparative scheme of African traditional political systems based on two key concepts: values and authority patterns. He identified two kinds of values and, borrowing Parsonian terms, labeled them as instrumental and consummatory. Instrumental values were those that permitted the adoption of new ideas and techniques on the basis of their utility in producing a given desired result. Consummatory values, on the other hand, were those that were meant to affirm the cultural integrity of the community. They often linked new ideas to the ultimate spiritual ends of the community and were discarded if they were seen to clash with spiritual needs. Most new ideas were considered threatening to the social order. Apter then turned his attention to authority and again identified three kinds of authority patterns: segmental, hierarchical, and pyramidal. In the following sections, I define these three types of political systems and give illustrations of each. Two of the examples are segmental systems, or "stateless" societies, one example is a hierarchical system, and the last example is pyramidal.

Segmental Systems

A segmental system is a decentralized system, a "stateless" society in which power is diffuse and shared. Such a society is ruled by elders, members of an age set or council chosen from different lineages; it does not have a powerful political figure. The Nuer of Sudan, the Kikuyu of Kenya, and the Ibo people of Nigeria are examples of segmental systems often cited, but their values were not all the same; the Nuer had consummatory values, and were, therefore, extremely resistant to change, whereas the Kikuyu and the Ibo were instrumental in their value structure and, therefore, quite adaptable to change.

Kenyatta begins his discussion of government among the Kikuyu by suggesting that, according to legend, Kikuyu people were originally ruled by a tyrant, who was subsequently overthrown by his subjects because they were opposed to tyranny. A new government was then formed. A council was created to which every village in the land occupied by the Kikuyu people appointed a representative. A constitution was drawn up containing guidelines as to how the leaders were to exercise their authority. New rules in the constitution guaranteed the freedom of the people to acquire land and work under family ownership and provided for election of elders to the governing council. Leaders pledged their efforts to unify the entire Kikuyu nation. A new army was recruited from among the warriors. Taxation was introduced to provide resources for tribal ceremonies and festivals. New criteria for those aspiring to leadership positions were enunciated and included the requirement that leaders must be married. Procedures for resolving or adjudicating conflicts were put into place. Kenyatta says that when these rules were promulgated, a special ceremony was held to codify them into law. The new system was heavily influenced by the age grades, such as the warriors and the elders and by other organized groups. It was a democratic system. The administrative functions of government were performed by the age-grade associations. They enforced morality, collected taxes, and watched over the property of the village.

According to Uchendu, among the Ibos of Nigeria, each village was regarded as autonomous in matters affecting it. The village was segmented into lineages, and each lineage was further subdivided into sublineages. A lineage occupied a certain area that was divided into compounds. Within each compound were several households. The compound, the lineage, and the village each had a head. Indeed, politics and government at the village level were "an exercise in direct democracy."[36] The political structure at the village level included a legislative assembly. What we might call interest groups like secret societies, priestly associations, title societies, and age-grade associations played important roles. The legislative assembly held open-air meetings at which extensive discussions took place, much like town hall meetings in early New England in the United States. Everyone was free to contribute to the debate, after which the elders (of the legislative assembly) retreated to a separate meeting to consider all the views presented and to reach a wise decision, usually by consensus. The elders were men of high standing and prestige, respected for their wisdom, and trusted to consider all the views presented at the open-air meetings. The decision reached was then declared law only after it was given "a ritual binder" by one of the holy men, to be sure that it was in keeping with custom and tradition. Compound heads were responsible for fully informing everyone in their compounds about new laws so promulgated.

Hierarchical Systems

The hierarchical system was a highly centralized political system presided over by a very powerful king and served by an efficient bureaucracy or a military machine. The king, paramount chief, or military commander had subordinates, who exercised whatever power they had entirely at the discretion of the person at the top. The Baganda people of the Buganda kingdom in Uganda and the Fon people of Benin provide excellent examples of the hierarchical system, although, again in this case, these two groups exhibited different values; the Baganda had instrumental values, whereas the Fon had consummatory value systems.

In David Apter's matrix, Buganda would be classified as a hierarchical system with instrumental values. It was highly centralized with a strong bureaucracy and an extremely powerful king called a *kabaka*. Because the structure was so tight and centralized, Buganda was never really colonized by the British. Instead the British entered into a series of treaties and agreements that preserved the power of the king of Buganda, who was coopted into the colonial administrative structure under a policy known as "indirect rule." The *kabaka* was offered "protection" by the British, in exchange for allowing the British to pursue their imperial dreams in eastern Africa. In Chapter 4, we shall discuss various colonial policies in some detail. The *kabaka* was assisted by a prime minister called a *Katikkiro* and a parliament called the *Lukiiko*. The king was so powerful that, if he wished, he could ignore the advice of both the *Katikkiro* and the *Lukiiko*, although there was some risk in doing so. For example, there was always some jealousy among the princes; the *Katikkiro* could condone or even encourage plots against the king by other princes interested in becoming king. Moreover, the *kabaka* did not become king through automatic succession as one would expect in a monarchy. He was elected from among the princes, that is, the men whose father or grandfather had been a *kabaka*. If the reigning *kabaka* picked an heir apparent, his preference was not held to be binding. The criteria considered in selecting a new king were the personality of the prince, his personal reputation, and the degree of support he enjoyed among the senior chiefs in the kingdom. The mother and sisters of the king, who had formal titles of their own, were believed to be influential with the king, but did not have any formal power.

Buganda was divided into counties, subcounties, and villages. Each of these units was headed by a chief, each of whom was appointed by the king and was responsible to the chief above him. The chiefs maintained law and order, public works such as road maintenance, maintaining the shrines and groves of the ancestors as well as the compounds of the other chiefs above them and of the king, drawing water, and protecting villages against dangerous animals. Tax collectors were appointed by the king, but they were assisted in their task by the chiefs who kept a small portion of the taxes collected in their areas. Although the king was all-powerful, he was not always completely sure of the support of his subjects. For that reason, he came to rely on another group of men called the *batongole* who, technically, were people who supplied the king with provisions. In time, many of them were incorporated into the chiefly system and ended up serving as village chiefs, the first key link between the king and his people.

Pyramidal Systems

A pyramidal system is one that consists of different levels of segmental groupings that are not entirely autonomous; the groups were usually based on kinship and each one had a chief, a paramount chief, or a king. The levels of a pyramidal system are based on some sort of seniority; the chiefs of higher levels have the right to intervene in the affairs of the lower levels, if necessary. The chiefs of the lower levels are expected to show appropriate deference to those above. As one might expect, a pyramidal system is characterized by substantial conflict and by frequent alliances among the different groups and different levels. The Yoruba people, among the most urbanized Africans, provide a good example of a pyramidal system.

The Yoruba system of government was as complex as their religious traditions. Western Nigeria, the traditional home of the Yoruba, had many kingdoms. What follows is a description of Yoruba government distilled from Peter Lloyd's account of the kingdom of Ado.[37] Each kingdom was headed by a king, called *Ewe* or *oba,* depending on the size of the kingdom. It is considered important that every town have a king or an oba. It is through the king and his considerable wealth and splendor that a town shows itself to the outside world. The oba is praised lavishly to the extent that some people have thought of him as having divine powers. For instance, the king rarely appears in public; when he does, he is "heavily veiled" and surrounded by many attendants and servants. He cannot be seen eating in public. People often prostrate before him to show their respect and deference. He has many wives; in fact, he can claim any unmarried woman in the kingdom as his wife. A new king is installed in a ceremony that is majestic and elaborate and includes mystical elements.

The king was assisted by a council of senior chiefs, who make the executive decisions and have those decisions given royal assent by the king. There were three grades of chiefs: the *Ihare*, the *Ijoye*, and the *Elegbe*. The *Ihare* consisted of senior chiefs who work directly with the king. They were mostly hereditary chiefs although the king had the power to bestow the *Ihare* title to his subjects, if he so wished. The *Ijoye* grade had only a few senior chiefs and appeared to consist of mostly administrative cadres. The *Elegbe* grade was closely associated with the age grades.

The king and his council were sovereign. They maintained law and order, settled disputes among lineages, especially over land, and saw that the kingdom prospered. There was some opportunity for people to express their opinions at meetings, although this was not done very often. The junior chiefs would pass these views on to the senior chiefs, who would, at their discretion, share them with the king. Decisions made by the council were carried out by the junior chiefs, the *Ijohe* and the *Elegbe*. Public works were carried out by the age grades and defense by the warriors recruited from among the age grades. Revenue for the government came from levies and tributes provided in the form of free labor, palm oil, livestock, and food crops for festivals and other ritual ceremonies, judicial fines and fees, charges collected for bestowing titles, and any property seized during occasional wars with neighboring groups.

Besides the main town, where the king, or Ewe resided, there were smaller towns. Their structures were very similar to that of the main city. The ruler of a smaller town within the kingdom governed without a council and was, of course, subordinate to the king. In many cases, he owed his position to the king, who had the authority to choose heads of towns. The senior chiefs of the king's on behalf of the king council were responsible for the government of the smaller towns.

The Yoruba kingdom, as a pyramidal system, consisted of several levels. The top level was run by an Ewe, assisted by senior chiefs. The second level of government, found in smaller towns, was run by a ruler or an oba, assisted by lesser chiefs, all of whom were subordinate to the king. There was a third level, at the village level, which was dominated by lineage heads, appointed also by the chiefs above them. Yoruba kingdoms, understandably, were dynamic systems characterized by alliances, conflicts, and rivalries among the lineages and between the obas and chiefs as they struggled for power and influence.

NOTES

1. Ndabaningi Sithole, *African Nationalism*, 2nd Edition (New York: Oxford University Press, 1968), pp. 67–68.
2. Ibid., p. 68.
3. M. G. Smith, "The Hausa of Northern Nigeria," in James L. Gibbs, Jr., ed., *Peoples of Africa* (New York: Holt, Rinehart & Winston, 1965), p. 148.
4. James L. Gibbs, Jr., "The Kpelle of Liberia," in James L. Gibbs, Jr., ed., *Peoples of Africa* (New York: Holt, Rinehart & Winston, 1965), p. 210.
5. Diane Kayongo-Male and Philista Onyango, *The Sociology of the African Family* (New York: Longman, 1984), p. 9.
6. David Lamb, *The Africans* (New York: Vintage Books, Random House, 1984), p. 37.
7. Diane Kayongo-Male and Philista Onyango, *The Sociology of the African Family*, p. 8.
8. Isaac Schapera, "Kinship and Marriage Among the Tswana," in A. R. Radcliffe-Brown and Daryll Forde, eds., *African Systems of Kinship and Marriage* (New York: Oxford University Press, 1965), p. 149.
9. Max Gluckman, "Kinship and Marriage Among the Lozi of Northern Rhodesia and the Zulu of Natal," in A. R. Radcliffe-Brown and Daryll Forde, eds., *African Systems of Kinship and Marriage* (New York: Oxford University Press, 1965), p. 185.
10. Daryll Forde, "Double Descent Among the Yako," in A. R. Radcliffe-Brown and Daryll Forde, eds., *African Systems of Kinship and Marriage* (New York: Oxford University Press, 1965), p. 290.
11. Diane Kayongo-Male and Philista Onyango, *The Sociology of the African Family*, p. 7.
12. Max Gluckman, "Kinship and Marriage Among the Lozi of Northern Rhodesia and the Zulu of Natal," p. 184.
13. James L. Gibbs, Jr., "The Kpelle of Liberia," p. 211.
14. Max Gluckman, "Kinship and Marriage Among the Lozi of Northern Rhodesia and the Zulu of Natal," p. 184.
15. Phoebe Ottenberg, "The Afikpo Ibo of Eastern Nigeria," in James L. Gibbs, Jr., ed., *Peoples of Africa* (New York: Holt, Rinehart & Winston, 1965), pp. 15–16.
16. Ibid., p. 17.
17. Walter H. Sangree, "The Bantu Tiriki of Western Kenya," in James L. Gibbs, Jr., ed., *Peoples of Africa* (New York: Holt, Rinehart & Winston, 1965), pp. 41–79.
18. M. G. Smith, "The Hausa of Northern Nigeria," pp. 124–125.
19. Hilda Kuper, "The Swazi of Swaziland," in James L. Gibbs, Jr., ed., *Peoples of Africa* (New York: Holt, Rinehart & Winston, 1965), pp. 495–496.
20. James L. Gibbs, Jr., "The Kpelle of Liberia," *op. cit.*
21. Paul Bohannnan and Philip Curtin, *Africa and Africans* (Prospect Heights, IL: Waveland Press, 1988), p. 152.
22. James L. Gibbs, Jr., "The Kpelle of Liberia," p. 223.
23. Jacques Maquet, *Africanity: The Cultural Unity of Black Africa* (New York: Oxford University Press, 1972), pp. 55–56.
24. Angela Fisher, *Africa Adorned* (London: Collins, 1984), p. 109.

25. John Mbiti, *Introduction to African Religion* (London: Heinemann Educational Books, 1979), p. 161.

26. Victor Turner, "Symbolization and Patterning in the Circumcision Rites of Two Bantu-Speaking Societies," in Mary Douglas and Phyllis M. Kaberry, eds., *Man in Africa* (New York: Anchor Books, Doubleday, 1971), p. 238.

27. Angela Fisher, *Africa Adorned,* p. 27.

28. Robert A. Manners, "The Kipsigis of Kenya: Culture Change in a 'Model' East African Tribe," in Julian H. Steward, ed., *Contemporary Change in Traditional Societies,* Vol. I (Urbana, IL: University of Illinois Press, 1967), p. 270.

29. Jomo Kenyatta, *Facing Mt. Kenya* (New York: Vintage Books, Random House, 1965), p. 225

30. John Mbiti, *African Religions and Philosophy* (Garden City, NY: Anchor Books, Doubleday & Co., 1970), pp. 36–37.

31. Gunter Wagner, "The Abaluyia of Kavirondo (Kenya)," in Daryll Forde, ed., *African Worlds* (New York: Oxford University Press, 1968), pp. 28–30.

32. E. Bolaji Idowu, *African Traditional Religion* (Maryknoll, NY: Orbis Books, 1975), p. 148.

33. John Mbiti, *Introduction to African Religion,* pp. 2–3.

34. Colin Turnbull, *The Forest People* (New York: Doubleday Books, 1965), p. 305.

35. David E. Apter, *The Politics of Modernization* (Chicago: University of Chicago Press, 1965), pp. 1–42.

36. Victor C. Uchendu, *The Igbo of Southeast Nigeria* (New York: Holt, Rinehart & Winston, 1965), pp. 40–41.

37. P. C. Lloyd, "The Yoruba of Nigeria," in James L. Gibbs, Jr., ed., *Peoples of Africa* (New York: Holt, Rinehart & Winston, 1965), pp. 567–573.

Political Development in Historic Africa

JAMES D. GRAHAM

Is it true that Africa had no history as one Oxford University professor declared in a speech in 1963? He said perhaps in the future, there will be African history, but for now, there is only the history of Europeans in Africa. Yet a few years ago, a cover story in a U.S. weekly magazine could unabashedly aver, "We are all Africans." As we reflect on the professor's assertion, we might also ask, "Is Egypt an African country?"

INTRODUCTION

Since the African continent includes a wide diversity of cultures, languages, and ecological zones, its history reflects this diversity. This chapter recognizes such diversity by introducing readers to a wide-ranging, widely known variety of historic African leaders, nations, and state policies in selected regional and chronological contexts prior to 1900. The section of this chapter devoted to early modern Africa is unusually brief; on the other hand, particular details of political culture are more fully outlined for ancient Egypt, medieval Ethiopia, Mali, and Songhay or nineteenth-century Igbo (Ibo), Yoruba, and Asante (Ashanti) than for other historic states. Because of the succinct, if not dense, writing style mandated by the challenge of consolidating such massive subject matter into a forty-page chapter, readers might be well-advised to study selectively herein (only a few pages, or civilizations, at a time). They might want to read more slowly than usual, allowing their imaginations to roam beyond particular phrases or sentences into distant times and places of historic Africa. In any case, Africa's long and complex history provides abundant examples of ways in which people from different regions established and maintained large-scale governments over time. These structures enabled Africans from different families and localities to join together, through confederacies or conquests, in order to build large and complex states in different times and places prior to 1900. Amid all the diverse and particular details, African political systems developed or changed in different ways during different historical epochs (even during the disruptions that accompanied the Atlantic slave trade)— until the historic development of African statesmanship was *interrupted* by imperial Europe's infamous "Scramble for Africa" (*c.* 1880–1900). During the first half of the twentieth century, under European colonial laws and policy initiatives, Africans were forced to live and work in the unfamiliar and severely restrictive political systems of colonial rule (see Chapter 4). Beginning in most African regions around 1880, and lasting in many regions beyond 1960, the colonial period interrupted the political life of Africans as never before; they were effectively removed from international political history, divested of domestic political power, and substantially excluded from colonial decision making.

Despite the systematic removal of Africans from any substantive decision-making power during European colonial rule (*c.* 1900–1960), and despite the persistent conflicts and crises that have continued to impede African development since colonial times (*c.* 1960–present), historic Africa occupies a central position in our world. Africa has been called the most central of all continents geographically, with the majority of its landmass and population concentrated in the tropics (immediately north and south of the equator) and its Great Rift Valley being the earth's most visible topographical feature (when viewed from the moon). East Africa's Great Rift Valley has provided more opportunities for modern archaeologists to dig deeper into the early development of human beings than any other place. Since most of the documented prehistory of humankind took place in or near the Great Rift Valley, many scholars have argued that Africa was the original home of our earliest human ancestors. It is widely recognized that ancient Egypt (in the northern part of Africa's Nile River Valley) developed the world's earliest grand-scale civilization. It is also known that medieval African empires supplied large exports of gold to medieval Eurasian civilizations. African history, so central to the early development of human beings, ancient civilizations, and medieval commerce in our world's history, has nonetheless been disregarded in Eurocentric studies. As late as the 1960s, a renowned British historian even maintained that Africa had no history. By that time, however, new kinds of historical techniques and data made it possible for Africans and Africanists (affiliated with new universities in independent African nations) to seriously begin reclaiming the rich African past. Historians like J. A.

Rogers, Cheikh Anta Diop, and Basil Davidson had already begun to reassert the primacy of African civilizations in the ancient world by 1960. Around that time, archaeological reports from Louis and Mary Leakey hypothesized that the prehistoric ancestors of all human beings first evolved in the Great Rift Valley; linguists following Joseph Greenberg and Malcolm Guthrie developed techniques for indicating ancient historical connections between different African language families; and historians after Jan Vansina developed increasingly rigorous techniques for collecting, transcribing, and evaluating different kinds of oral traditions from medieval African kingdoms. D. T. Niane's *Sundiata: An Epic of Old Mali* and J. A. Egharevba's *Short History of Benin* are examples of such traditions which have been transcribed, after having been passed along orally through many generations of trained court historians, contributing immensely to our current understanding of important events and leaders in those parts of historic Africa. By carefully analyzing such transcribed oral traditions, in conjunction with various written sources and ethnographies, African and Africanist scholars have continued to expand our current knowledge of Africa's rich historical heritage.

By the 1970s, the accumulation of historical, archaeological, linguistic, and ethnographic evidence about the African past had given rise to a new generation of Afrocentric historians (as exemplified by Walter Rodney and Joseph Harris), who reacted against older Eurocentric perspectives by arguing that Africans originated and developed many of the arts and techniques of ancient civilizations. Some contemporary Afrocentric historians (like Molefe Asante and Martin Bernal) have been criticized for exaggerating Africa's contributions to world history (in opposition to Eurocentric historians, who have continued to deny or marginalize such contributions). With respect to some Afrocentric claims about the superiority of historic "black" civilizations, in opposition to Eurocentric notions of "white" superiority, it is wise to note that both "black" and "white" are artificial categories which perpetuate overly simplistic racialist thinking rather than advancing more detailed historical analysis. In any case, today's Americans would do well to realize that African nations have not always been so relatively underdeveloped, destitute, and dependent as they are today. Africa's long and distinguished history affords many examples of successful political consolidation and multiethnic cooperation, and this chapter focuses primarily on such themes.

Since much history is particularist analyzing the unique qualities of specific regions, people, and time periods, this introduction to the history of Africa provides illustrative examples of how African leaders and people succeeded in building effective large-scale governments in specific times and places. While such specific data are central to any historical analysis, broader hypotheses about historical trends and tendencies also inform the writing of any historical synthesis.

Some general themes which emerge from this synthesis of African political history are as follows:

1. People from different communities and chiefdoms sometimes joined together through confederation or conquest, for purposes of commerce or defense, to develop kingdoms.
2. Those living in the jurisdiction of such confederations or kingdoms found that the breadth and complexity (scale) of their political consciousness increased.

FIGURE 3.1

Prehistoric and Ancient Africa

Source: Map drawn by James D. Graham.

3. Large-scale empires sometimes "rose" out of such kingdoms by expanding through military or diplomatic leadership, but they invariably "fell" (fragmenting into their component parts) at some later time.
4. Large-scale empires usually recognized the legitimacy and autonomy of local kings or chiefs.
5. The political traditions of such local communities usually remained vital and resilient, even during serious disruptions when the bureaucratic traditions of imperial civilizations were abandoned or destroyed.

These general historical tendencies have been illustrated through the specific examples of political development emphasized in this chapter, and it is helpful to keep these general themes in mind while reading about the various particularities of Africa's historical heritage.

The following historical synthesis is designed to provide some minimal information about the political history of African civilizations prior to colonial times. While it does not include all such civilizations and presents some of them in more detail than others, this chapter places important "basic facts" about Africa's political development (prior to 1900) into appropriate historical contexts. These historical contexts include four conventional periods—ancient, medieval, early modern, and nineteenth-century history. In prehistoric times (before the beginnings of written records), there were no known civilizations (in which people lived in cities); but early hunters and gatherers gradually developed those physical, mental, technical, cultural, *and* political qualities that later enabled ancient human beings to build cities and create large and complex systems of governance. The deepest roots of African history, if not of all humankind, are most fully revealed by the archaeological excavations undertaken in the prehistoric Great Rift Valley, which is where this introduction to historic Africa begins.

PREHISTORIC AFRICA

During the early prehistory of Africa, the Rift Valley ancestors of modern human beings gradually evolved and developed hunting-gathering bands over many hundreds of millennia. Toward the end of this prehistoric development, during neolithic times (the past 10,000 years or so), some of these nomadic bands began to settle more permanently in villages (initially in the Nile River Valley) to develop the political foundations of ancient civilization. Archaeologists throughout the world, who previously had unearthed skeletal remains of prehistoric Neanderthal, Cro-Magnon, Java, and Peking "man" at different sites in Eurasia, were astounded by Louis Leakey's discovery of Zinjanthropos, a 2-million-year-old tool-making hominid in the Rift Valley's Olduvai Gorge in 1959. Since then, other archaeological findings in the Great Rift Valley (including a 3,500,000-year-old Ethiopian girl named "Lucy," discovered in 1974) have focused much international attention on interpreting different ways in which early tool-making hominids in the Rift Valley may have evolved into human beings.

Drawing also from recent research on primate behavior, archaeologists have sought to explain how these hominids might have become so differentiated from other primates as to have evolved into the ancestors of modern human beings. Initial findings from current research in microbiology indicate that the early hominid ancestors of modern human beings diverged from the ancestors of other Rift Valley primates (like chimpanzees, gorillas, and extinct species of australopithecines) between 4 and 8 million years ago. Contemporary research on living primates in the Great Rift Valley, pioneered by Jane Goodall, has revealed that chimpanzees and gorillas currently live there in small bands that gather and share food in ways not unlike early prehistoric hominids may have done.

Taken as a whole, recent research in prehistoric Africa suggests enough evidence for evolutionary theorists to hypothesize the following:

1. Early hominids had become differentiated from other primates by developing larger brains and bipedalism (walking on two feet) by about three and a half million years ago.
2. Further adaptation and "natural selection" processes led to the evolution of *Homo habilis* hunter-gatherers who were developing linguistic and tool-making skills by about 2 million years ago.
3. Continued developments in brain size, upright posture, manual dexterity and hand-axe technology helped more advanced *Homo erectus* hunter-gatherers to migrate from Africa into Eurasia more than 1 million years ago and subsequently.
4. More precisely differentiated brains and hands developed in archaic *Homo sapiens* (like Neanderthal) and reached fruition in modern *Homo sapiens* (including Cro-Magnon hunter-gatherers) during the past 200,000 years.

Evolutionary theory, in short, suggests that small bands of hunters and gatherers may have migrated from Africa to inhabit Eurasia, gradually adapting to very different environmental conditions there, throughout prehistoric times.

During all the long millennia of human evolution and development in early prehistoric Africa (and elsewhere), human beings seem to have lived in small hunting-gathering bands that sought to achieve some balance or harmony with one another and with nature. Such small bands (from 15 to 40 people each) seem to have arranged their working tasks so that men hunted wild animals and women gathered wild nuts, berries, roots, and grains. They probably found much to eat in Africa's diverse tropical environments, which were thinly populated but often teeming with abundant varieties of wild life and vegetation. Contemporary hunting and gathering bands in southern Africa (where some still exist and continue to adapt along the outer margins of modern civilization) have been found to practice a kind of direct democracy. Controversial decisions are made by consensus through group discussions, during which men and women both have ample opportunity to contribute and be heard, and each band chooses a prominent person to represent them in negotiating with outsiders. Although prehistoric hunters and gatherers may have arranged their political lives quite differently from contemporary hunting-gathering bands studied by modern anthropologists, it is clear that they nevertheless succeeded in developing viable ways of resolving their conflicts and coexisting with their local environments. Cave paintings from prehistoric times (within the past 30,000 years) suggest that the immediate ancestors of neolithic Africans valued such guiding principals as mutual aid, cooperation, and respect for life. From the time of the early hominids like *Zinjanthropos* through the gradual emergence of modern *Homo sapiens* (during the past 200,000 years), small bands of prehistoric hunter-gatherers gradually developed the tools and techniques, language arts, and community values which made it possible for their ancient descendents to domesticate some species of plants and animals, establish more permanent homes and villages, and develop broader political communities.

By 6200 B.C.E., some of Africa's prehistoric hunting-gathering bands had begun to settle permanently along the banks of the Nile River, cultivating domesticated grains and breeding domesticated livestock. During the neolithic "revolution" in late prehistoric times, semipermanent villages developed more structured political arrangements through ties of kinship and co-residency. As these early farmers and villagers first increased their mastery over the rich soils and animal life of the Nile Valley, their populations and food production multiplied. By 4000 B.C.E., they produced enough food to send their surpluses as "tribute" to local or regional politico-religious leaders. As local farming villages in the Nile Valley continued to grow, unilineal descent systems developed as a means of defining each person's family lineage and rights of residency. In politics and religion (which were usually connected), the "small traditions" of different Nile Valley communities began to blend together around more general myths of common origin ("great traditions"), even as local ties remained primary. Different villages came to recognize their common interests in coordinating the irrigation of their riverside farms, and broadening community linkages led (by about 3500 B.C.E.) to the development of two large confederated kingdoms called Upper and Lower Egypt. Thus, gradual increases in the scale of political development in the late-prehistoric Nile Valley—from small nomadic hunting-gathering bands to large settled farming villages and regional confederations—both preceded and made possible the creation of history's earliest large-scale national government in the united kingdoms of ancient Egypt.

ANCIENT AFRICA

The Kingdoms of Egypt

It was in the united kingdoms of Egypt that ancient Africa's contributions to the development of early civilization are best documented and most well known. Without more extensive indigenous written records, the political histories of other ancient African civilizations (e.g., Kush–Meroe, Axum, Carthage, Mauritania, Jenne, and Nok) remain fragmentary. The grand scale and extraordinary longevity of ancient Egyptian civilization, on the other hand, are well known and much admired even today—so much so that many contemporary Afrocentrists, following research published by Cheikh Anta Diop in the 1950s, argue that Egypt was a "black" civilization. In fact, contrary to many Hollywood portrayals of ancient Egyptians, there is no reason to think that Egypt's ancient population was ever fair-skinned or "white." Many historians today disagree with Cheikh Anta Diop's translation of *Kmt* (the name of ancient Egypt) as "land of the blacks," however, because *Kmt* could also mean "the land of black [Nile Valley] soils," in opposition to the *Dsrt* ("redness") of surrounding desert lands. Modern scientists hypothesize that different skin pigmentations reflect different amounts of dark melanin and keratin particles in people's underskin (properly regulating the skin's intake of sun rays), according to their relative distance away from the direct sunshine of the tropics. It seems reasonable to assume, then, that northern Egyptians (living in a temperate Mediterranean climate) had somewhat lighter skin coloring than their southern neighbors (who lived in or near the tropics). The artificial categorization of widely different shades of skin color in ancient Egypt as either "black" or "white," therefore, is both inexact and misleading. Ancient Egyptians had many different shades of skin color, from very light brown (or "olive-color") Mediterranean-type skins to very dark Nubian-type skins. Whatever their shade of skin pigmentation, however, ancient Egyptians lived in Africa, and their renowned ancient civilization was African.

Under the rule of divine pharaohs, The Old Kingdom of ancient Egypt (*c.* 3100–2180 B.C.E.) developed Africa's earliest large-scale political economy, blending local and regional traditions, economic activities, religious beliefs, and political power into one Nile Valley nation. This blending of local differences did not radically alter the various political traditions of local village life, except insofar as villagers were subsequently expected to render tribute and loyalty to the central authority embodied by their pharaohs. Such tribute and loyalty were usually forthcoming, partly because the pharaohs of Egypt's Old Kingdom were commonly regarded by their people as gods. These pharaohs were identified with the gods Horus (in life) and Osiris (in death) and were thought to maintain *Maat* (order) by balancing the life forces of order and chaos in nature—most starkly represented to them by ordered life in the black, fertile Nile Valley and the chaos of existence in the red, arid Sahara Desert. Pharaohs reputedly ruled over their united kingdoms by virtue of their place within a royal matrilineage that is said to have traced its ancestry back to an original mother, Isis (the divine sister-wife of Osiris and mother of Horus). The powerful energy of the sun (represented by Horus), combined with various local myths about primeval struggles (wherein Isis resurrected Osiris, who fathered Horus), contributed to the widespread belief that a single pharaoh could best mediate between all ancient Egyptians and their creator god Re (symbolized by the sun). Because of their sincere religious belief in the divinity of their pharaohs, Egyptians in the Old Kingdom rendered enough tribute in labor and food to support the building of massive pyramids and other public works, as well as to maintain large and specialized state bureaucracies. The earliest of ancient Egypt's architectural masterpieces, now known as the step pyramid, was designed by Imhotep (*c.* 2600 B.C.E.) in honor of Pharaoh Zoser, whom he served. In addition to his considerable and creative skills as an architect, Imhotep is widely remembered for his ancient studies in astronomy, medicine, mathematics, and philosophy; one of his best-known proverbs, handed down through the ages, is said to have been "Eat, drink and be merry, for tomorrow we shall die." The Great Pyramid at Giza (481 feet high, 755 feet on each side at the base) was constructed for Pharaoh Khufu (*c.* 2500 B.C.E.). It is now estimated that Egyptian subjects cut, hauled, and carefully fit together more than two and a half million 5,000-pound blocks of limestone rock for over twenty years to erect this massive, powerful, and enduring monument. Such awe-inspiring monuments attest to a more complex and widespread political and religious system than had ever existed previously, a system so successful that it still excites our imagination today.

Central authority in Egypt's Old Kingdom gradually fragmented, and it "fell" during what is now called the First Intermediate Period (*c.* 2180–2080 B.C.E.), as regional political centers (or nomes) regained their autonomy under local ruling families. When centralized state authority was again reestablished in the Nile Valley during the "rise" of the Middle Kingdom (*c.* 2080–1640 B.C.E.), living pharaohs were no longer considered by their people to be divine, even though ordinary Egyptians continued to render tribute and loyalty to them. In Egypt's Middle Kingdom, commerce and construction revived, the first secular literature began to circulate in Nile Valley towns, and some pharaohs launched military expeditions against foreign nations (like Cush, to the south). After about 400 years of developing and maintaining an effective large-scale government over a reunited Nile Valley, Egypt's Middle Kingdom was conquered by Hyksos invaders (using horse-chariots). Thereafter, central authority again fragmented, and local autonomy again surfaced in what came to be known as the Second Intermediate Period (*c.* 1640–1570 B.C.E.).

After ancient Egypt's Second Intermediate Period, regional leaders from Upper Egypt reimposed centralized authority in the entire Nile Valley, establishing ancient Egypt's New Kingdom or Empire (*c.* 1570–1090 B.C.E.). A succession of warrior pharaohs reunited the ancient Egyptian nation, invaded and conquered other ancient civilizations in Cush, Libya, Palestine, and elsewhere, and established the earliest multinational empire in ancient Africa. Produce and labor from conquered peoples were demanded by Egypt's imperial armies. Skilled artisans and workers were recruited from different nations to work for their conquerors, in rendering their labor as tribute to Egypt's pharaohs. The finest workers in Egypt's empire were brought to their capital city of Thebes as slaves to help build and decorate such religious temples as Karnak and Luxor, as well as the elaborate passageways and chambers of tombs in their Valley of the Kings, or to serve as soldiers.

Although Egypt's New Kingdom expanded to become an empire under military leadership, its most widely known pharaohs now are those who sought to develop commerce, communications, construction, and the arts. One such noted pharaoh was Queen Hatshepsut, thought to be a descendant of Isis, who ruled as coregent during the reigns of three imperial pharaohs (*c.* 1500 B.C.E.) and who is now remembered as the most successful female ruler in ancient Africa. Ruling as a pharaoh (i.e., as a man) for about twenty years, she is particularly known for expanding Egypt's sea commerce southward into the land of Punt (modern-day Somalia) and also for the unique architecture of her terraced, rock-carved mortuary temple. Another famous ruler in the New Kingdom, who still commands much worldwide admiration, took the name of Akhenaten when he became pharaoh (*c.* 1375 B.C.E.). Proclaiming the revolutionary idea that there was only one God, Akhenaten mobilized Egypt's tributary labor to build an exemplary new city worthy of this God and wrote beautiful poems to honor him. Akhenaten is also known for promoting "classical" standards in ancient artwork, as typified by the famous sculpted head of his wife Nefertiti. But his visionary ideas were not shared by most other politico-religious leaders, and his reforms were soon undone. By the time that Tutankhamon became pharaoh (*c.* 1345 B.C.E.), Akhenaten's monotheistic doctrines and new capital city had been abandoned. Tutankhamon (known to us as "King Tut") ruled only a short time, but he remains well known today because of the uniquely abundant treasures recovered from his burial tomb in the Valley of the Kings. Construction, commerce, and communication in Egypt's New Kingdom or Empire reached fruition under Pharaoh Ramses II (*c.* 1290–1220 B.C.E.), who devoted most of his sixty-seven-year reign to maintaining peace, expanding international trade, and undertaking extensive building projects (including large statues and temples) throughout the Nile Valley. Successor pharaohs continued to rule the New Kingdom of ancient Egypt until the time of Ramses XII (*c.* 1100 B.C.E.), although they gradually lost political authority over outlying peoples in their Empire. After 1100 B.C.E., the New Kingdom itself began to fragment. Various local and regional leaders in the Nile Valley no longer rendered tribute or professed loyalty to Egypt's pharaohs; and central authority in Thebes again gave way to local autonomy in various towns and regions along the Nile.

Ancient Egyptians were the first people in recorded history to develop such a large-scale national kingdom and multinational empire. Because Egypt's early history is documented relatively well, it stands alone among ancient African civilizations as being indicative of the early development of large-scale governments. In studying ancient Egypt, it is possible to imagine how farming lineages along the Nile Valley may have first joined together as villages, then in the regional confederations of Upper and Lower Egypt, prior to unifying under the central authority of divine pharaohs in the Old Kingdom (c. 3100–2180 B.C.E.). It is also possible to understand how the pharaoh's strong central authority eventually fragmented into local autonomy, later to reemerge, and subsequently to fragment again during the two Intermediate Periods, which have come to be seen as punctuating the rise and fall of Egypt's Middle Kingdom (c. 2080–1640 B.C.E.). Egypt's New Kingdom (c. 1570–1090 B.C.E.) rose again, this time to become a multinational empire through the conquest of foreign nations; yet it also eventually fell when neither the conquered peoples nor those of Egypt's Nile Valley continued to render tribute and loyalty to central authorities in Thebes. In the case of ancient Egypt, as in subsequent instances where central authorities in kingdoms and empires have attempted to rule over locally autonomous villages or regions, the "rise and fall" of large-scale governments reflect alternating periods of unification (consolidation) and disunity (fragmentation). Not only because Egypt merits special treatment in any history of ancient times but also because its historical development is illustrative of broad historical processes to be noted throughout this chapter, Egypt's early political history has been particularly emphasized in this section.

Many of the political traditions of early Egyptian civilization, nurtured by the Nile Valley's enduring local traditions, continued to develop up until the Roman conquest, around the time of Christ. The succession of foreign conquerors who came to rule Egypt, during the millennium between the fall of the New Kingdom (c. 1090 B.C.E.) and the beginnings of Roman imperial rule (c. 30 B.C.E.), includes some of the most famous names in ancient history. Libyans under Shoshenk were the first outsiders to conquer and rule in Thebes (c. 950 B.C.E.); Piankhy later led the Cushites in conquering the entire Nile Valley (c. 750 B.C.E.); Sennacherib's Assyrians invaded Egypt almost a century later (c. 660 B.C.E.), with new iron-tipped weapons—driving the Cushites southward. Assyrian rulers in Egypt were subsequently defeated and absorbed by Nebuchadnezzar's ancient Babylonian Empire; then, powerful Persian armies of Cyrus subsequently defeated the Babylonians and proceeded to rule the Nile Valley for almost two centuries (*c.* 525–332 B.C.E.). By 330 B.C.E., Alexander the Great of Greece had gained control of Lower Egypt, establishing the city of Alexandria as a major political and commercial center in his vast empire. After his death, Greek rulers named Ptolemy (I–XII) continued to rule Alexandria for three centuries, until the Roman conquest. Although the Ptolemies used their political authority to exact tribute (in produce and skilled labor) from Egyptians, they generally continued to promote the development of international commerce, culture, and communications in Alexandria, which grew to become the largest and most dynamic of all cities in the ancient Mediterranean area.

Alexandria continued to thrive after Caesar Augustus (Octavian) established Roman imperial authority there (*c.* 30 B.C.E.). Queen Cleopatra VII, who had sought to maintain some vestiges of Egyptian political autonomy through negotiating with early Roman rulers (Julius Caesar and Mark Anthony) committed suicide, rather than face the public humiliation that Octavian had planned for her in Rome. Thereafter, imperial Roman law and religion were imposed on Egyptians, until the fourth century, when Emperor Constantine declared official tolerance toward all religions (*c.* 313), convened the first ecumenical Christian Council (to try to establish official church doctrine) at Nicea (325), and subsequently moved Rome's imperial capital to the city of Byzantium (the site of modern Istanbul), which he renamed and rebuilt as Constantinople (330). Orthodox Christianity became the official imperial religion under the reign of Emperor Theodosius I (379–395). He and succeeding rulers of the eastern Roman (later Byzantine) Empire persecuted Christian "heretics" throughout Egypt; orthodox Christians destroyed or defaced ancient temples and burned valuable ancient manuscripts associated with Egypt's "pagan" past.

Other Ancient African Civilizations

While Egypt occupied the best-documented role in ancient political development, other African civilizations also established their own systems of governance during ancient times. The stone buildings, ciphered inscriptions, and, after 600 B.C.E., extensive ironworks in ancient Kush–Meroe (*c.* 2000 B.C.E.–350) provide glimpses of the rise and fall of large-scale governments to the south of Egypt, but the ancient traditions of government there were largely abandoned after the fall of Meroe (*c.* 350). Sophisticated terracotta sculptures from ancient Nok and Jenne (*c.* 500 B.C.E.–200) suggest that refined civilizations also existed long ago near the Niger River. Ancient trade routes across the Sahara linked early Niger River civilizations to Mauritania and to Carthage's lucrative commercial empire in northwest Africa (*c.* 600–150 B.C.E.) and excited the envy of Rome's early rulers. In the midst of a century of commercial sea wars fought between Carthage and ancient Rome, Hannibal made his famous long march across European mountain ranges to wage extended war on the very outskirts of Rome itself (*c.* 218–202 B.C.E.). Toward the end of these Carthaginian wars, Roman ships and soldiers attacked, looted, burned, and completely destroyed the ancient city of Carthage, imposing what has come to be known as an uncompromising "Carthaginian Peace" on the inhabitants. Even after laying waste to the city of Carthage, Roman imperial rule did not destroy the continuing development of various local traditions; other ancient cities emerged as agricultural production increased. These new cities traded southward for gold into the Sudanic kingdoms of Ghana and Takrur. Along Africa's Red Sea coasts, on the other hand, ancient written references to international commerce date back to the Queen of Punt (*c.* 1500 B.C.E.) and to Makeda, the fabled Queen of Sheba (*c.* 950 B.C.E.). The ancient Ethiopian kingdom of Axum (*c.* 200 B.C.E.–700) actively participated in Red Sea commerce for many centuries, while Greek Ptolomies and Roman emperors ruled in Egypt. Later, Axum's King Ezana (*c.* 350) established direct linkages with the Alexandrian Church, proclaiming Coptic Christianity to be the official imperial religion of Axum. Even though he and his successors did not manage to convert all Ethiopians (including Jewish Falashas) to Christianity, King Ezana did establish ancient foundations for the development of continuing religious and political ties between Alexandria's Coptic Christian patriarch and Axum's bishops, monks, and kings. Ancient Axum's Christianity survived as an official state religion for 1600 years (*c.* 350–1975) in Ethiopia. The ancient traditions associated with government ideologies in Nok, Jenne, and Mauritania, however, have not yet been clearly documented—nor have their relations with other ancient West African kingdoms that later evolved in Ghana and Takrur (*c.* 400). The imperial traditions in Egyptian and Carthaginian politics and ideology were substantially destroyed or undermined during Roman and Byzantine rule (*c.* 30 B.C.E.–640) and the later expansion of Islam (*c.* 640–710). Ancient governing principles in Kush–Meroe were also undermined by Christian ideologies (beginning in the sixth century) and later Islamic conquests. Various local traditions that had nurtured these ancient civilizations continued to develop, however, sustaining vital regional communities through which medieval Africans could later consolidate new kingdoms and empires.

MEDIEVAL AFRICA

As with civilizations in ancient times, historical tendencies toward political consolidation and political fragmentation continued to mark the "rise and fall" of kingdoms and empires in medieval Africa. Medieval African leaders continued attempting to balance the ongoing traditions of local and regional autonomy with their people's developing needs to confederate or consolidate into large-scale kingdoms and empires—often for purposes of trade or defense. In the centuries following 622, the first year of

Muslim calendar, the historical Age of Islam (*c.* 640–1600) took root and became an important catalyst for political development in medieval African civilizations. Expanding rapidly from the ancient trade city of Mecca, Muslims inspired by the Prophet Muhammad (a man, not a god) conquered or converted most of Egypt and the Maghreb by the early 700s—establishing religious principles of governance that decisively displaced most remnants of ancient and Christian ideologies throughout North Africa. Muslims, those who practice the teachings of Islam, believed that one God (Allah) called on them to live moral lives in accordance with the teachings of the holy Koran (their written scriptures). Muslims have also been called on to make *hajj* (a holy pilgrimage to Mecca) if possible, and to undertake *jihad* (holy war against nonbelievers or corrupt Muslim rulers) when necessary. The most renowned of Africa's medieval civilizations (including the empires of Mali, Songhay, and Morocco) rose to the highest stages of their international influence with medieval Islam as their imperial religion. On the other hand, many medieval African kingdoms and empires developed indigenous political ideologies based on regional customs and beliefs, while Christianity remained the official state religion in the Abysinnian kingdom of medieval Ethiopia.

About 1150 in Ethiopia, some four centuries after the fragmentation of ancient Axum, the first of a new line of emperors (known as the Zagwe dynasty) began to reunite various local kings and Christian monasteries under a single ruler, "King of kings." In 1270, the Zagwe Empire was taken over by a new dynasty of Christian Abysinnian rulers, who claimed royal authority by virtue of being direct descendants of ancient Israel's King Solomon and the Queen of Sheba (Makeda)—they claimed to be of the Davidic lineage, like Christ. The new Solomonic kings were confirmed in office by Christian monks, some of whom also compiled an extensive genealogical document called the *Kebra Nagast* (Glory of Kings) that served as both a written constitution and an historical chronicle for Abysinnia's Solomonic dynasty. Abysinnia's medieval Solomonic kings and bishops maintained their ancient religious ties with Alexandria's Coptic Christians and coexisted peacefully with neighboring Islamic governments in Egypt and in the Funj Sultanate. Beginning with Amda Syon (1314–1334), however, medieval Abysinnia's Christian kings waged war against their Muslim neighbors along the Red Sea coasts for control of commercial access. King Zara Yakob (*c.* 1434–1464) conquered some of the coastal lowlands and extended Abysinnian rule over much of the Ethiopian Highlands, establishing a militant Christian empire in which informants, secret police, and grand inquisitors could identify, arrest, and execute non-Christians. During the last years of a prolonged regency by Abysinnia's Empress Helena (1487–1522), a dynamic coastal leader named Ahmed Gran acquired muskets from Turkish Ottoman Muslims and declared a holy war against Christian Abysinnia. For about twenty years, Ahmed

Gran's coastal Muslims fought against Christians of the interior and conquered much of highland Abysinnia. By 1542, however, musketeers from Abysinnia's new Portuguese allies (who had initiated diplomatic relations in 1520) killed Ahmed Gran and helped Abysinnian Christians to reclaim many of their interior kingdoms. Christian Abysinnia then reunited under Solomonic emperors, who succeeded in reaffirming ties of tribute and loyalty with local kings in the highlands. By 1608, doctrinal differences between Portugal's Roman Catholic missionaries and Abysinnia's Christian bishops became so divisive that the Portuguese were told to leave Ethiopia. Solomonic emperors continued to exercise some political authority over various small kingdoms in the Ethiopian Highlands for almost another century thereafter, until regional kings became virtually autonomous around 1700.

Emerging international linkages between North African Muslims, meanwhile, actively promoted the expansion of new Islamic civilizations in medieval Egypt and the Maghreb. In 969, Muslims from the Maghreb conquered Egypt and established the Fatimid dynasty in Cairo (c. 970–1170), where they founded Al Azhar, the Western world's first modern university. When Fatimid rule in Egypt was threatened by European Roman Catholic Crusaders (c. 1170), however, it was Egypt's professional soldiers or *mamluks* who rallied behind their leader Saladin—defeating the Crusaders and establishing a new Mamluk dynasty in Cairo (1171–1517). Meanwhile, the Almoravids of Mauritania established a new Islamic empire in the Maghreb (c. 1090–1150). Their successors, known as the Almohads (c. 1150–1250), unified the entire Maghreb and southern Iberia into an Islamic empire that produced some of the most advanced architecture and scientific thought in early medieval times. As the Almohad Empire fragmented into different autonomous regions during the 1200s, cities like Tripoli, Tunis, Algiers, Tangier, Marrakesh, and Seville developed as regional urban centers of autonomous governments in the core areas of modern Libya, Tunisia, Algeria, Morocco, and Granada. In 1517, Turkish Muslims using muskets defeated the Mamluk military rulers of Egypt and incorporated the entire Nile Valley (southward to the Funj Sultanate of Nubia) as a province of the new Ottoman Empire. Libya, Tunisia, and Algeria were later incorporated into the Ottoman Empire as provinces, where (as in Egypt) Ottoman viceroys (*pashas*) officially governed and indigenous leaders (*beys*) retained much informal political influence. The Ottoman imperial armies never conquered Granada (which was absorbed by Christian Spain in 1492) or Morocco, where the prominent Sa'idi clan established a nationwide military confederation during the early 1500s. Morocco's national army repelled a major Portuguese invasion in 1578, after which their commander and king Ahmad al-Mansur (1578–1603) sent his best-trained musketeers southward to gain control over the lucrative commerce in the western Sudan—which was then dominated by the empire of medieval Songhay.

The medieval trans-Saharan trade in gold, which had originated in ancient times along the southern fringes of Mauritania, increased substantially as medieval Mediterranean civilizations in Iberia and Italy, as well as in the Maghreb and Egypt, increasingly used West African gold exports to underwrite their commercial expansion. Before reaching the Maghreb and Mediterranean civilizations, however, gold production and commerce had first to be organized in the western Sudan. This was a broad savanna zone stretching all across Africa, roughly between 10° and 20° north latitude—from the Senegal River to Lake Chad and eastward through the modern nation-state of Sudan. The earliest written reference to a western Sudanic civilization in what was called "the land of gold," from the 700s, mentioned the Mande-speaking (Soninke) kingdom of Ghana, around the twin cities of Kumbi (the political capital) and Saleh (the commercial center) in what were then farming and grazing lands in the savanna between the Niger and Senegal Rivers. Subsequent written sources portrayed Ghana's early medieval kings as living in great pomp and splendor, controlling a vast army and taking in much tribute and profit from the trans-Saharan gold trade. By about 1050, when other western Sudanic kingdoms had developed in Takrur (on the Senegal River), Songhay (on the northern bend of the Niger River), and Kanem (on the northern shores of Lake Chad), the kingdom of Ghana had expanded to become the largest medieval Sudanic empire. In Takrur, Islamic purifiers called Almoravids joined together to rebel against Ghana's imperial rule, defeated Ghana's armies in a jihad and broke up their empire (1076); then they moved northward to conquer and rule over a famous medieval empire in the Maghreb and southern Spain. Afterward, Ghana's Soninke kings were unable to reconstitute their fallen empire, although they and other Mande-speaking ruling families continued to exercise political authority in their regional kingdoms. During the next century and a half, local autonomy prevailed among different communities and kingdoms in the western Sudan.

As international demand for gold increased along with regional conflicts during the early 1200s, the autonomous Mande-speaking (Malinke) kingdom of Mali emerged along the upper Niger River as the center of a new imperial confederation, which eventually grew to more than twice the size of Ghana's earlier empire. Starting as a regional confederation based on initial alliances between Malinke kings (*mansas*), Mali subsequently rose to become the most famous empire in the medieval western Sudan (*c.* 1230–1430). The founding hero of Mali's medieval empire was Sundiata (1235–1255) who, according to the oral traditions transcribed by D. T. Niane, was born without the use of his legs; however, he miraculously started to walk at age seven. It is said he grew to become a healthy and powerful prince in the royal Keita clan, developed a strong confederation of Malinke mansas, led this confederation's warriors to victory over an allegedly evil Sosso king named Sumanguru (1235), and expanded the Mali confederation into an empire through further conquests. About thirty years after Sundiata's death, an outstanding army commander named Sakura (not of royal descent) seized control of Mali's imperial government and conquered even more territory in the western Sudan, before relinquishing authority again to Sundiata's descendants. One of these, Abubakari II, was said to have launched Mali's first trans-Atlantic voyages in the early 1300s, almost two centuries before Christopher Columbus sailed along the same Atlantic currents. The most famous of all Sundiata's descendants, however, was Mansa Musa (1312–1337), who attempted to consolidate Mali's imperial authority by encouraging the growth of Islam as an imperial religion (even though he was careful not to interfere with local religious practices in Mali's subordinate kingdoms and communities). During his well-known hajj to Mecca (1324–1325), Mansa Musa was recognized as the Islamic caliph of West Africa, and he impressed the international merchants in Cairo by distributing gold so freely as to drive down its market value. Mansa Musa arranged to have Sudanese Islamic scholars trained in the Maghreb, and he recruited other learned men from Cairo so they could teach Muslim students in West African centers of scholarship (theology and law) like those in medieval Jenne or Timbuktu. Under the rule of Mansa Musa and his brother Mansa Sulayman (1341–1360), many such commercial cities flourished in the western Sudan, and new sources of gold (from Akan country to the south) underwrote the steady expansion of Mali's trans-Saharan trade. Even as Islam provided some basis for developing a common imperial ideology in Mali's cities and among merchants, it failed to attract the genuine loyalties of most people living in various rural communities and subordinate kingdoms throughout the empire. By about 1430, when Muslim merchants in Timbuktu successfully refused to render tribute to Mali's rulers, the empire had begun to disintegrate. Its armies were no longer powerful enough to collect tribute or enforce imperial authority in outlying provinces; and locally autonomous kingdoms again asserted their independence.

The autonomous medieval kingdom of Songhay, founded around the trading town of Gao (c. 1000), broke away from Mali and subsequently arose to become the third grand empire in the medieval western Sudan (c. 1464–1591). Songhay's founding emperor Sunni Ali (1464–1492) used large war canoes and war cavalry to support his army's conquests of the entire Niger Bend, including the rich city-states of Timbuktu and Jenne. He established imperial authority northward into the Sahara in order to control international trade routes and valuable deposits of rock salt (which was mined and cut into large blocks to be traded for gold). Following his death, one of his army generals, or *askias,* named Muhammad Toure (a Soninke by birth), overthrew the legitimate heir. Subsequently, Askia Muhammad Toure embarked on a hajj to Mecca (c. 1496) and returned to wage jihad against non-Muslims, conquer new territories, and rule over Songhay's expanded empire as caliph of West Africa. Under Askia Muhammad's authority (1493–1528), Songhay rose to become one of the medieval world's largest multinational empires. Some of the Islamic world's most respected scholars taught at the Sankore center of higher learning in Timbuktu during these times. A papal emissary (named Leo Africanus) wrote that there were "many doctors, judges, priests and other learned men" who lived in Timbuktu, where "various manuscripts and written books" were imported from the Maghreb and "sold for more money than any other merchandise." Noting that the Songhay government in Timbuktu had "a magnificent and well furnished court" and that the city's inhabitants were "exceedingly rich," Leo Africanus also observed that there were "a great store of men and women slaves" in Songhay (as there had been in medieval Mali). Different categories of slaves (originally war captives) cultivated fields, constructed adobe buildings and mosques, acted as porters, or served as soldiers and officials in the imperial government. Some of the latter rose through government and military bureaucracies, by virtue of meritorious work, to achieve high positions of administrative responsibility—as, indeed, did Muhammad Toure, when he rose by military merit to become a general, then emperor, in Songhay. As emperor of Songhay during its "golden age," Askia Muhammad (known as Askia the Great) was an excellent administrator who established effective central supervision over near and distant provincial governors. He was a devout Muslim who tolerated a wide range of religious diversity within his empire. He also reformed Songhay's imperial government so that merit (rather than birth) became the principal criterion for advancement in government bureaucracies. Eventually, after he became blind and was deposed (1528), Songhay's trans-Saharan trade declined. This was partly due to increased competition from European sea traders along West Africa's Atlantic coast, which undercut the trans-Saharan gold trade, and partly due to the increasing competitiveness of Hausa and Bornu trans-Saharan commerce in the central Sudan. After the severe political crises that Songhay emperors faced during the 1580s (including succession disputes, rebellions, and civil war), their imperial army was decisively defeated by Morocco's elite musketeers at the Battle of Tondibi in 1591.

The fall of Songhay's vast empire, coupled with Morocco's subsequent failure to reestablish imperial authority in the western Sudan, illustrates the historical tendency of large-scale, multinational empires to break up, or fragment, into separate communities and kingdoms over time. Thus, the three largest empires of medieval western Sudan (not altogether unlike the three successive kingdoms of ancient Egypt) rose and fell even as the small traditions of community life generally continued to develop. While many of the grand traditions of imperial commerce and culture in medieval western Sudan have faded into history, Islamic practices continued to remain strong in Sudanic cities and among merchants. By the late 1400s, leaders living near the Akan gold fields (in the rain forests to the south of medieval Mali and Songhay) had begun to sell to the Portuguese along the Atlantic "Gold Coast," rather than to Mande-speaking merchants from the western Sudan. This created new patterns of international commerce in West Africa during the 1500s. As Akan gold came to be increasingly exported through Portuguese and other European fortresses along West Africa's Gold Coast, the volume of Songhay's trans-Saharan gold trade gradually declined. Even before the fall of Songhay's empire, however, the major centers of trans-Saharan trade had shifted from western to central Sudan.

From the Niger River Bend to the east of Lake Chad, Hausa city-states and the Kanuri Empire of Kanem–Bornu had developed trade-oriented Islamic civilizations in medieval Africa's central Sudan. In what is now northern Nigeria, a number of Hausa city-states—including Gobir and Katsina (northern trading centers), Kano (where dyed cotton fabrics and "Moroccan" leather goods were manufactured for export), Zaria (a southern center of slave-raiding), and others—developed during medieval times. War captives (slaves) built and maintained extensive walls around these cities and surrounding farms because the medieval Hausa city-states had to fight (against imperial armies from Songhay and Bornu, Saharan nomads to the north, non-Muslim communities to their south, and other Hausa city-states) in order to maintain their commercial competitiveness and political independence. Directly to the east of Hausaland, meanwhile, the medieval kingdom of Kanem had originally been established by the Sefawa dynasty of conquering Kanuri horsemen (c. 900), at the southern terminus of the shortest and most central of all trans-Saharan trade routes—the one between Lake Chad and Tripoli. Kanem's founding emperor (a contemporary of Mali's Sundiata) was Mai Dunama Dibbalemi (c. 1220–1248), who conquered various farming communities around Lake Chad and declared Islamic law to be the basis of medieval Kanem's imperial authority there. Replenishing his supply of Arabian horses (from Tripoli) by capturing non-Muslims and trading them northward as slaves, Dunama Dibbalemi and his successors established far-reaching commercial and religious ties with the medieval Islamic world. After local rebellions caused Kanem's rulers to move southward into Bornu (c. 1400), Kanuri horsemen continued to wage jihad against non-Muslim farmers unless the latter agreed to pay tribute. By the mid-1500s, after reestablishing their authority in Kanem as well as in Bornu, Sefawa sultans began to import Turkish muskets and military advisors from the new Ottoman rulers in Tripoli, reasserting their imperial authority around Lake Chad and northward into the Sahara. The most renowned ruler of this reconstituted empire of Kanem–Bornu, Mai Idris Alooma (1580–1617), is remembered as a devout and militant Muslim who conducted relentless armed raids against non-Muslims to the south. He also defeated and collected tribute from some Hausa city-states to the west, conquered much of the Fezzan region in modern Libya, established close diplomatic relations with Ottoman rulers in Tripoli and Cairo, and attracted trans-Saharan commerce away from the empire of Songhay. The sultans of Kanem–Bornu continued to rule over a loosely confederated empire and to control much of the continuing trans-Saharan trade (in horses, guns, salt, and slaves) until the 1750s, when local Saharan leaders refused to pay tribute and the empire began to fragment.

Medieval civilizations "rose and fell" throughout the tropical rain forests and savanna woodlands of West Africa's coasts and hinterlands during medieval times. In coastal hinterlands near the mouths of such rivers as the Senegal, Volta, Niger, and Congo, various kingdoms and city-states developed as important centers of medieval commerce and civilization—long before Portuguese sea explorers first "discovered" them (c. 1440–1490). On Goree Island, near the mouth of the Senegal River, and at the Elmina fortress near the mouth of the Volta River, early Portuguese explorers and sea captains traded directly for West African gold, as well as for slaves. Near the Lower Niger River, the Yoruba city-state of Ife, which produced some of the world's finest examples of classically sculpted bronze heads, was ruled by kings who were believed to be direct descendants of a divine mythical ancestor named Odudua (whose other descendants were thought to have founded other Yoruba city-states, after Ife). Some of the city-states founded by these putative descendants of Odudua developed into medieval kingdoms, and then into empires. The Yoruba kingdom of Oyo, for instance, developed an effective horse cavalry in the savanna woodlands which enabled its rulers (*alafins*) to conquer other Yoruba city-states during the late 1500s and to establish some of the enduring traditions in government that supported Oyo's loosely confederated empire (c. 1550–1830). The medieval kings (*obas*) of Benin near the Niger River Delta were also thought to be direct descendants of Odudua, although their language (Edo) is different from Yoruba. The obas of Benin gradually consolidated local farming and fishing communities into a large rain forest kingdom (c. 1220–1440), after which this kingdom expanded to become a famous coastal empire (c. 1440–1550). Benin's medieval empire was created by Oba Ewuare (c. 1440–1480), who was remembered in oral traditions as having "conquered 201 towns and villages" by the time Portuguese sea explorers first arrived (1473). Further south along the western sea coasts near the mouth of the Congo River, early Portuguese explorers also visited the confederated kingdom of Kongo where, as in Benin, Portuguese emissaries immediately sought to establish diplomatic relations. In Kongo, Portuguese advisors helped a Christian convert from the royal lineage to become King Affonso I (1506–1543). He, in turn, protested against Portuguese slave traders who were creating disorder and divisions within and around his confederated kingdom.

Despite heartfelt written protests by Kongo's King Affonso I to his "brother king" in Portugal and the refusal of Benin's obas to supply large numbers of slaves, Portuguese demand for West African war captives increased. By the 1520s, Portuguese ships had begun transporting West African slaves across the Atlantic Ocean—inaugurating the long and destructive epoch in which various European naval powers conducted the infamous Atlantic slave trade (c. 1520–1870). By 1600, many coastal cities (like Lagos, Bonny, or Loango) traded directly with European slave ships, obtained guns in return for war captives, refused to render tribute to higher authorities, and asserted their independence from kingdoms like Benin and Kongo. The Kingdom of Benin remained intact even as much of its empire dissolved during the late 1500s. While the Kongo kingdom itself broke up, their Mbundu neighbors to the south consolidated under military kings or *ngolas* (c. 1500) and then expanded through raids for war captives in the hinterlands of the Portuguese fortress and seaport at Luanda. These ngolas fought prolonged and persistent wars of resistance against Portuguese troops based in Luanda from the 1570s onward and throughout the reign of their warrior-queen Nzinga (1624–1663). All along the West African coast and hinterlands (from modern Senegal to modern Angola), medieval states like Benin and Kongo fragmented, while new military states among the Yoruba and Mbundu expanded. Atlantic coastal commercial ports (like Goree, Elmina, Lagos, Bonny, Loango, and Luanda) also grew. From the beginnings of the Atlantic slave trade in the 1500s, then, various West African communities and kingdoms responded and adapted in different ways to the challenges posed by new and growing European demand for war captives.

During medieval times (c. 1000–1600), different Bantu-speaking states in Central African savannas lived beyond the immediate range of coastal trade. They thrived on internal African trade around local copper, iron, or gold resources, and the leaders of their ruling lineages—usually descended from a founding hero—drew their political authority from shared regional beliefs and traditions. Near central Africa's copper belt, for example, the ruling lineages of medieval Luba and Lunda kingdoms were thought to be direct descendants of the heroic Ilunga (a legendary hunter and "magician").

In the Luba federated kingdom (which emerged and expanded during the 1300s), powerful kings appointed provincial governors to rule over local leaders. The Lunda kingdom (which developed during the 1500s), on the other hand, was more of a confederation, where local leaders were both entitled and empowered in state politics. During the late 1500s, titled Lunda leaders moved eastward to the frontiers of Mbundu territory to establish a military kingdom in Kasanje, where they incorporated local people as citizens of their new state. By 1600, the Lunda kingdom itself began to grow into a confederated empire, creating the kinds of broad political ties that encouraged the further growth of international trade. Well to the south of central Africa's copper belt, meanwhile, the Shona kingdom of medieval Zimbabwe was producing gold for international commerce as early as 1000. As Indian Ocean sea trade increased along with international demand for gold, medieval Zimbabwe flourished (c. 1250–1450). Zimbabwe's massive stone ruins, extensive craft work, and imported luxury items (from as far away as China) have provided archaeologists and historians with material evidence of the splendor in which the medieval rulers of Zimbabwe lived. During the 1400s, however, the people of Zimbabwe gradually stopped providing the tribute in food and labor that had sustained the luxurious existence of their kings. The neighboring kingdom of Mutapa (whose military rulers were known as *mwene mutapas*) began to attack and conquer the outlying provinces of Zimbabwe. The Mutapa empire (c. 1480–1680) withstood attacks by Portuguese military invaders during the 1570s and continued to develop until it was conquered and absorbed by new military leaders (*changamires*) of the early modern Rozwi dynasty in the 1680s.

In medieval East Africa, titled royal lineages also consolidated Bantu-speaking kingdoms near Africa's Great Lakes region (c. 1450–1650), while independent Swahili city-states along the Indian Ocean coasts emerged as important centers of international commerce and Islamic culture (c.1000–1500). To the south of Lake Nyasa (Malawi) and east of the Lunda and Mutapa empires, various Bantu-speaking communities consolidated into Maravi kingdoms under royal lineages of entitled *kalongas* during the 1400s. They grew through participating in the international ivory, gold, and copper trade, and eventually joined together to establish a military empire (c. 1600–1650) in the hinterlands of Mozambique Island. Meanwhile, Luo pastoralists from the north defeated and displaced indigenous Bantu-speaking rulers in the fertile highlands of the northern Lakes Region (between Lakes Tanganyika and Victoria-Nyanza) during the 1500s. Here, different pastoral clans began to consolidate indigenous farming communities into federated kingdoms, such as Bunyoro and Buganda (ruled by the royal Bito clan) or Rwanda and Burundi (ruled by a Tutsi caste). In these interlacustrine kingdoms, where banana and plantain trees provided regular supplies of food without much tending, patron–client relationships (in which owners of cattle would rent their use to those without cattle) grew to sustain powerful centralized governments—far away from any direct coastal commercial influences. The fortunes of coastal Swahili city-states, on the other hand, paralleled the rise and fall of commerce on East Africa's Indian Ocean coasts (which had been known to ancient merchants as Azania and was known in medieval times as the land of Zanj). From about 1000 to 1200, Swahili Muslims of the Shirazi clan, who first established an East African base in Mogadishu (modern Somalia), expanded southward to set up commercial outposts along the coast—including Mombasa, Zanzibar, Kilwa, Mozambique, and Sofala. Because of its position as the southernmost seaport to which Arab, Persian, or Indian ships could sail (because of prevailing wind patterns), Kilwa emerged as the wealthiest and most powerful of the medieval Swahili city-states (*c.* 1200–1500). While Kilwa was at the center of East Africa's export trade in gold and ivory, Shirazi sultans and Muslim merchants built splendid coral-rock residences there. During that time, urban middle classes specialized in various manufactures, trade, or government work, while surrounding non-Muslim farmers were sometimes put to work as slaves on large agricultural estates near cities. After Vasco da Gama's pioneering European sea voyage into the Indian Ocean (1498), however, fleets of armed Portuguese warships came to bombard and loot the medieval Swahili city-states (*c.* 1503–1528). Later they returned to build the large stone fortresses which established their military presence along the East African coast in Mozambique and Mombasa. By 1600, Portuguese fortresses and fleets had substantially disrupted the medieval sea trade along East African coasts, just as their armed ships and fortresses (at Goree, Elmina, and Luanda) had disrupted earlier patterns of political consolidation and commercial growth along West African coasts— posing new challenges to African communities and kingdoms in the hinterlands and interior.

EARLY MODERN AFRICA

In conjunction with the Turkish Ottoman conquest of Africa's Mediterranean and Red Sea shores, Portugal's sixteenth-century expansion along Africa's Atlantic and Indian Ocean coasts introduced new weapons and new demands for war captives throughout the continent. Different communities and kingdoms adapted differently to these new supplies of guns and demands for war captives, as Spanish, Dutch, British, French, German, Scandinavian, and Arab armed ships joined the Portuguese in demanding ever-increasing numbers of African youths for the growing international slave trade during Africa's "early modern" period (*c.* 1600–1800). During this period, the gold, sugar, tobacco, and cotton produced by African slaves in the Americas contributed toward making more capital available for Europe's "commercial revolution" in banking, corporate stock arrangements, insurance, and investment houses. All of this, in turn, helped to underwrite European expansion in overseas trade, colonization, and both its scientific and industrial "revolutions." Because the productive labor of more than 12 million West African war captives, and several million others from other parts of Africa, was lost to continental development during the international slave trade (*c.* 1440–1870), historian Walter Rodney has argued that the historical processes of development in early modern Europe were complementary to concurrent historical processes of underdevelopment in early modern Africa. Thus, the beginnings of underdevelopment in early modern Africa can be seen, historically, as part of the same process as the beginnings of development in early modern Europe—as "two sides of the same coin."

The escalating international slave trade in early modern Africa disrupted previous patterns of political and economic growth, even though many of the historic traditions of medieval African politics and ideology continued to guide various adaptations and initiatives undertaken by different indigenous governments. Although Kilwa and other Swahili city-states of medieval East Africa were laid waste by sixteenth-century Portuguese invaders, Omani Arab navies allied with local Swahili leaders to eject the Portuguese from all of East Africa north of Mozambique by the early 1700s. After 1750, French merchant ships opened up new large-scale demands for East African war captives to work as slaves on island plantations in the Indian Ocean. Both Omani and Portuguese demands also increased as the Indian Ocean slave trade expanded (*c.* 1750–1870), and coastal or island cities like Mombasa, Kilwa, Zanzibar, and Mozambique further broadened their interior trading networks. Most of the medieval states of central Africa similarly found themselves increasingly drawn into international commerce during early modern times. From about 1600 to 1800, for instance, such interlacustrine kingdoms as Buganda steadily expanded through northward and westward trade linkages, as well as through southward and eastward contacts with independent Nyamwezi traders. In southern Africa, the Maravi Empire first expanded and then fragmented (after 1650), surrendering commercial hegemony in southeast Africa to independent Yao traders. The Mutapa rulers of medieval Zimbabwe were defeated and displaced by a new Changamire military dynasty (*c.* 1680s). Lunda emperors (*mwata yamuos and kazembes*) and Kasanje kings in Angola came to dominate much of the transcontinental trade in central Africa, while complex commercial confederations also developed through the Congo River Basin.

In West Africa, strong commercial-military states like Oyo, Dahomey, and Asante expanded, and dozens of commercial city-states like Lagos, Bonny, and Calabar (in modern Nigeria) grew up along the sea coasts. Meanwhile, as medieval empires like Benin and Kongo lost control over their outlying provinces, their kings sustained power within smaller, more culturally integral regions. As the western Sudan's trans-Saharan gold trade further diminished, Songhay's medieval empire fragmented into smaller kingdoms. Different Hausa city-states expanded commercially and Sudanic sultanates from Kanem–Bornu (near Lake Chad) to Funj (along the Nile River) continued to wage jihad against their non-Muslim southern neighbors.

In early modern North Africa, meanwhile, Morocco retained its national independence under Sa'idi rulers while provincial pashas and local leaders in Egypt and the Maghreb periodically asserted some degree of regional autonomy from the distant overrule of Turkish Ottoman emperors. The medieval Christian empire of Abysinnia continued to collect tribute in many outlying provinces during the 1600s. As gradual Oromo expansion from the south challenged central Christian authority, however, Abysinnia's Amharic rulers split off into a multitude of smaller kingdoms, where Solomonic royal traditions continued to sustain the regional authority of many an autonomous Christian king (*ras*). Throughout early modern Africa (*c.* 1600–1800), in short, different communities and kingdoms sought to preserve their local traditions and community life while also developing new regional and religious linkages to justify confederation. Both despite and because of escalating demand for war captives in different regions, some early modern African kingdoms or empires fragmented, while others adapted to changing commercial and military circumstances. In the latter case, early modern Africans developed new international commercial ties and new kinds of regional, religious, and military confederations in order to address the changing requirements for continued political survival that they were to face during the nineteenth century.

NINETEENTH-CENTURY AFRICA

As early modern African states continued to develop, and trade between coastal cities and interior regions expanded throughout the continent, various African peoples established political confederations based on religious ideology, commercial linkages, and/or military authority. Such confederations were often committed to modernizing trends—for example, establishing broader nationalist ideologies, promoting literacy and advancement by merit, expanding both regional and international commerce, and undertaking significant administrative and military reforms. However, such modernizing trends were *interrupted* by Europe's "Scramble for Africa" (*c.* 1880–1900). Notable developments in Africa's nineteenth-century political and economic systems coincided historically with even more dramatic and profound changes that took place in Western Europe and North America during their nineteenth-century industrial "revolutions." The first half of Africa's nineteenth-century history continued to be significantly disrupted by international commerce in slaves, even as new Euro-American markets also began to demand large imports of such African-based commodities as palm oil, cotton, peanuts, and ivory. By mid-century, European merchants realized that Africans could produce such valuable exports more efficiently (and humanely) by working in their own countries than by working as slaves in the Americas. Thus, Europeans sought to increase "legitimate" trade in natural products and to decrease their demand for slave labor from Africa. From 1880 to 1900, however, most modernizing African states were unable to resist the steel gunboats, breech-loading rifles, artillery, and Maxim guns that fully industrialized European powers introduced during that time. While modernizing African nations developed different kinds of central authority during the nineteenth century, changing European demands—from captive slaves to natural commodities to colonial conquests—continued to disrupt, and ultimately interrupted, ongoing processes of political development in precolonial Africa.

North Africa (*c.* 1800–1900)

Along the Mediterranean coast of Islamic North Africa in the early 1800s, central authority in both the crumbling Turkish Ottoman Empire and the independent Sultanate of Morocco had come to depend on the cooperation of local leaders. Urban-based North African merchants, commerce raiders ("pirates"), and prominent families supported Ottoman provincial rulers or pashas, maintaining an outward semblance of Ottoman authority. Napoleon's French armies were temporarily able to occupy Egypt (1798–1801), and distant presidents of the young United States declared and fought naval wars against the Pasha of Tripoli (1801–1805) and the Dey of Algiers (1815). The first famous modernizing leader in North Africa during these times, ironically, was himself an Ottoman military commander—but one who was born of an Egyptian mother and identified with Egyptian nationalism—Muhammad Ali (1805–1848). Toward his goal of modernizing Egypt's national army, Muhammad Ali established Egypt's first secular schools, engineering and medical colleges, modern printing presses, and government-operated textile and munitions factories. His modernized armies waged successful wars against Wahabi reformers in Arabia and the Ottoman provinces of Syria and Palestine as well as conquering the Funj Sultanate in the 1820s. Egyptian rulers after Muhammad Ali continued his policies of borrowing foreign capital for expensive modernization projects, such as the building of the Suez Canal (completed in 1869). Foreign debts, however, eventually forced Egypt's rulers to submit to French and British "advisors," which in turn led Egyptian nationalist troops to take over their government and expel foreign advisors (1881). British troops then invaded Egypt using Maxim guns and established a colonial protectorate there (1882).

France, meanwhile, had attacked and colonized Algiers as early as 1830. For the next forty years, French armies fought costly military campaigns, originally against nationalist modernizer Abd al-Qadir (*d.* 1847), to suppress Algerian resistance to colonization. By the 1870s, French settlers in Algeria had accumulated enough land, wealth, and political power to become classified as full "citizens" of French Algeria, electing deputies to France's National Assembly. Indigenous Arabic and Berber-speaking Algerians, on the other hand, were classified as "subjects," with no such representation and no rights of citizenship. By 1900, Algeria had become the model of a "settler colony," where 500,000 French settlers (13 percent of Algeria's total population) enjoyed full rights and privileges of French citizenship, while most of Algeria's indigenous "subjects" enjoyed no such rights or privileges. French forces also colonized Tunisia in 1881. France and Britain effectively prevented one another from colonizing Libya, where Ottoman rulers remained in power until the Italian conquest of 1911–1912. Because different European powers had interests in Morocco, and because Sultan Mulai Hassan (1875–1894) was quite adept at playing European powers against one another as well as in reconciling various local differences, the loosely confederated independent Sultanate of Morocco also managed to avoid being colonized until 1912—when it was divided between France and Spain. Thus, despite all the efforts of North Africa's nationalist leaders, Europe's modern armies and navies were able to establish imperial control over all of North Africa's Mediterranean coast.

The African Sudan (*c.* 1800–1900)

Just as external intervention by industrialized European powers interrupted historical tendencies toward national development in North Africa, it also arrested such tendencies among indigenous confederations in nineteenth-century Sudanic states lying along the southern fringes of the Sahara Desert. Trans-Saharan trade routes continued to be controlled by various Islamic city-states and empires in the broad savannas south of the Sahara during most of the nineteenth century—until their development was interrupted by Europe's "scramble" to claim colonies there. Characteristically, large-scale confederations in the nineteenth-century Sudan were established by militant Muslim brotherhoods often following a moral leader in holy war and often seeking to reform existing governmental institutions by enforcing Islamic law.

Although such reformist movements had arisen during the previous century among Muslim communities near the Senegal River, it was in the Hausa city-states of the central Sudan that the influential Qadiriya movement took root, beginning in about 1775. After a Qadiriya cleric named Usuman dan Fodio and his Fulani followers fled northward from the Gobir city-state, in order to avoid being prosecuted by Hausa authorities there, they later returned to wage jihad against Gobir's Hausa rulers. After capturing Gobir (1804–1808), they instituted a new moral order, attracted followers from elsewhere, and eventually established an imperial capital city at Sokoto. Rebels and reformers in other Hausa city-states, usually led by Fulani clerics and herders, took inspiration from this example, sought recognition and received blessings from Usuman dan Fodio, and declared jihad against corrupt ruling classes throughout the central Sudan. After Usuman dan Fodio died (1817), his brother Abdullahi and son Muhammad Bello ruled over a large and loosely confederated empire that came to be known as the Sultanate of Sokoto. Sultans of Sokoto exercised wide-ranging religious and political influence throughout northern Nigeria, even after being conquered by British colonial armies in 1904.

Introduced elsewhere in the central Sudan by Fulani clerics, the Qadiriya movement spread beyond Hausa city-states. It spread from Hausaland to the east where, in 1808, jihad was declared against the corrupt rulers of Bornu, giving rise to a powerful counterreform movement. The counterreformers were led by a Kanuri cleric named Laminu el Kanemi, who initially supported the ruling Sefawa dynasty but eventually established his own heirs as successors in Kanem–Bornu. To the south of Hausaland, in 1817,

Fulani clerics and herders in the northern Yoruba city-state of Ilorin supported that province's rebellion against the crumbling imperial authority of Oyo. They eventually established Islamic rule in Ilorin, contributing directly to the eventual dissolution of the Oyo Empire. To the west of Hausaland, in 1819, a Quadiriya cleric named Hamad Bari led a jihad that established the reformed Mande Sultanate of Masina (1821–1862) along the upper Niger River. Another influential Islamic leader, a Tukolor cleric who took the name El Hadj Umar after his lengthy pilgrimage to Mecca, lived and studied for many years in the sultanates of the central Sudan—at the courts of El Kanemi, Muhammad Bello, and Hamad Bari (as well as in Cairo and Mecca)—before returning to his home along the upper Senegal River. There, during the 1840s, he introduced the new Tijaniya order and preached about a simple, direct relationship between Muslim individuals and Allah. From 1852 to 1864, El Hadj Umar led jihads that both converted and confederated many of the rural savanna peoples of the western Sudan.

Although El Hadj Umar's Tijaniya Empire was contested among provincial emirs after his death in 1864, one of his sons named Ahmadu Seku eventually succeeded in reuniting most of his father's imperial provinces. Ahmadu signed a treaty with invading French armies in 1881, which proved to be his undoing. This treaty with the French undermined his imperial authority, led him to reject possibilities of allying with other Africans against French colonization, and ultimately resulted in his defeat and deposition by French colonizers (1893). To the south of Ahmadu's confederation, a Mandinka trader named Samori Toure (1875–1898) also made use of Tijaniya brotherhoods to help create the last multinational empire in the precolonial western Sudan. As a modernizer and a nationalist, Samori developed innovative military tactics, adopted Islam as a unifying ideology, promoted schools and literacy, developed centralized administrative structures and industrial workshops, and sought alliances with other West African leaders in fighting against French invaders. Samori Toure established two successive multinational confederations, which fought effectively against French armies before he was captured in 1898.

Large-scale Islamic empires also developed throughout the nineteenth century in the eastern Sudan. The Sultan of Darfur lost his longstanding authority over some important eastern trans-Saharan trade routes during the 1840s, after which the Sultanate of Wadai allied with Libya's Sanusiya brotherhood to develop trans-Saharan linkages between Lake Chad and Tripoli. Eastern trans-Saharan trade was based primarily on exchanging non-Muslim African slaves and ivory for advanced firearms from the Ottoman Empire or from Red Sea and Persian Gulf slave markets. One of the leaders among the well-armed slave traders of Africa's eastern Sudan was Rabih Zubayr (1879–1900) who created a mobile army that conquered Darfur, Wadai, and Bornu before surrendering to French forces in 1900. Even further east, in the Egyptian province of Funj, a Muslim cleric named

Muhammad Ahmed proclaimed himself to be the *Mahdi* (messiah). In 1881, he declared holy war against Egypt's "infidel" government in Sudan, which was then headed by British governor-general Charles Gordon. The Mahdi rallied militant Sudanese Muslims to defeat the Anglo-Egyptian army and to kill Gordon at Khartoum, before he himself died (1885). The Mahdi's successor Khalifa Abdullah then ruled over a large Islamic confederation in the eastern Sudan until 1898, when Anglo-Egyptian armies killed 11,000 of his troops at the Battle of Omdurman and claimed Abdullah's empire as their colony. Before European expansion, the reforming zeal introduced by various Islamic brotherhoods proved to be instrumental in developing broader cultural, commercial, and political linkages throughout Africa's Sudan. Nonetheless, historical tendencies toward political centralization in the Sudan were, as elsewhere in Africa, interrupted by invading British and French armies in the late nineteenth century.

West Africa (*c.* 1800–1900)

Europe's "scramble" for influence and control over West Africa's coastal political economies started earlier than elsewhere in tropical Africa. By the early 1800s, after three centuries of an ever-expanding Atlantic slave trade along West African coasts, large numbers of city-states had emerged and were led by African, European, and Afro-European merchants who represented rival commercial interests. Usually in direct competition with one another, such city-states were often less likely to merge into large-scale nations. Particularly around the Kasanje kingdom of Angola and the disintegrating Oyo Empire of Yorubaland, the Atlantic slave trade actively continued into the 1850s. Meanwhile, "legitimate" trade in such natural products as palm oil, cocoa, cotton, and groundnuts also got underway. Even as nineteenth-century European explorers began charting the rivers and internal resources of what they called the "Dark Continent," Christian missionaries were settling and establishing church schools throughout West Africa. Such European missionaries, increasingly supported by modernizing industrialists at home (who recognized that market incentives could induce more worker productivity than slave labor), wrote to denounce the horrors of the Atlantic slave trade. As industrializing Europe generated new demands for commodities produced in Africa, leaders in West Africa's coastal city-states gradually turned away from slave-raiding and toward the production of "legitimate" commodities for export. So thoroughly did this change in West African commerce take place, for instance, that Nigeria's former "Slave Coast" became known to European merchants as the "Oil Rivers," because of the rapid changeover to large-scale production of palm oil (*c.* 1810–1850). Such new international market trends, away from slave trading toward commodity production and legitimate trade, were reinforced by the increasing activities of British naval squadrons which, after

1808, were authorized to interdict slave ships and to rescue African captives aboard such ships.

Many such rescued captives were then disembarked at Freetown in Sierra Leone, Britain's first West African colony (founded in 1787, as a home for freed slaves), where some attended Christian schools, assimilated European values, and even graduated as clergy from Fourah Bay College (after 1827). In 1822, Monrovia was founded as a similar settlement by free African Americans who later, in 1847, established the independent Republic of Liberia. Through policies of assimilation, indirect rule, one-party government, and submission to U.S. control over national finances (1912), Americo-Liberians avoided being colonized by European powers. Such urban settlements as Freetown and Monrovia, however, were only a few of the countless modernizing cities that grew up along Africa's nineteenth-century Atlantic coast. Nineteenth-century urban West Africans developed international legal perspectives, up-to-date commercial techniques, Christian schools and hospitals, and forward-looking civic leadership. Whether they traded in slaves, commodity exports, or both, nineteenth-century life in such coastal cities as Luanda, Loango, Duala, Calabar, Bonny, Lagos, Ouidah, Accra, Conakry, or Dakar was dynamic. These coastal city-states, in turn, were linked through the development of broader cultural and commercial ties with confederations in their respective hinterlands—among the Mbundu and Ovimbundu, the Tyo and Ngala, the Fang, the Efik and Ibo, the Yoruba, the Fon, the Akan, the Mandinka, or the Wolof. Even though Portuguese and Spanish slave traders continued to operate along West African coasts until mid-century, British and French merchants and missionaries enlisted government support in their campaigns to promote legitimate trade and to establish Christianity in West Africa.

The European "scramble" to claim West African colonies, it is often said, began when Belgium's King Leopold established a Congo Free State, which sought to rule over the massive Congo River Basin in 1879. During the early 1880s, the French and Portuguese established counterclaims around the mouth of the Congo River, Germany claimed three different strips of West Africa's coast, Britain consolidated its commercial interests around the Niger River Delta and elsewhere, and French armed forces were dispatched from Senegal into the western Sudan. These competing European nations met at the Berlin West Africa Conference of 1884–1885 in order to coordinate further plans and procedures for the conquest and partitioning of Africa—so that new European colonies could be formally established there. An introductory chapter like this cannot convey all the varied circumstances in which nineteenth-century West African cities and confederations sought to resist and/or negotiate with invading European colonists (c. 1880–1900). Focusing instead on the immediate coastal hinterlands of nineteenth-century West Africa, Ibo villages and Yoruba city-states (in modern Nigeria), as well as the kingdoms of the Asante confederation (in modern Ghana), illustrate how three important West African nations developed during the nineteenth century.

The Ibo (Igbo) nation had no large-scale system of political confederation, as had the Yoruba and Asante, but formal structures of power existed in each Ibo village or town. Such local power structures were often based on membership in titled or secret societies, and local Ibo communities were informally linked through the nationwide influence of religious and commercial "oracles" called *Arochukwu* and *Agbala*. The western Ibo, living in cities like Aboh and Onitsha near the Niger River, developed relations with Ibo commercial houses in the delta and maintained some of the royal offices originally introduced to them by the medieval obas of Benin. The eastern Ijo, living in trading villages or towns like Aro, developed commercial relations with the coastal city of Calabar, where Efik secret societies ruled by representing Calabar's wealthy merchant families and the talented upwardly mobile traders, businessmen, and estate managers who worked for them. The central Ibo, living in villages north of the Ibibio coastal city of Bonny, produced such forceful individuals as Alali (*c.* 1830–1861) and Jaja of Opobo (1869–1887), both of whom rose from the status of "slave" to become prominent leaders of the Pepple commercial house. As able, adaptable, and competitive businessmen, nineteenth-century Ibo and their coastal neighbors (the Ijo, Efik, and Ibibio) took much initiative in transforming their regional economy from the slave trade to the legitimate trade in palm oil. Local Ibo leaders both established and shifted their commercial and political confederacies during these times, in accordance with what they perceived as being the interests of their own communities. The principle of local autonomy remained paramount to the Ibo, who achieved much success in developing commercial and cultural networks and organizations that linked different Ibo communities together (often with their coastal neighbors). Until the 1880s, the Ibo were a developing African nation that functioned effectively without joining together politically to form a centralized state government. Because of their decentralized political confederacies, it took the British many decades to conquer Iboland. By the 1880s, when British missionaries had expanded from their initial outposts in Onitsha and Calabar into central Iboland, and British coastal merchants had been absorbed by Sir George Goldie's Royal Niger Company, the British began their piecemeal conquest of different Ibo communities. After arresting Jaja of Opobo (1887), whose powerful trading confederacy challenged the interests of Britain's Royal Niger Company, British armies and government officials began to move into the interior of Iboland. Some Ibo villages submitted to British forces, as did the fictional village of Umuofia in Chinua Achebe's famous historical novel *Things Fall Apart,* while others resisted. Even though a major British expedition attacked and destroyed the Arochukwu oracle in 1902, different Ibo villages continued to resist British colonial authority until the Aba Women's War in 1929.

To the west of the Lower Niger River, several Yoruba kingdoms had created a centralized military and commercial confederation called the Oyo Empire (c. 1550–1830). The rulers of the core kingdoms of the united Oyo confederation were thought to have been descended from Odudua, the ancestor god of the Yoruba. The cavalries of the core kingdoms of Oyo conquered and incorporated many other Yoruba city-states and collected tribute from such neighboring kingdoms as Dahomey and Nupe during the 1700s. By the early 1800s, however, conflicts between the Oyo emperor (*alafin*) and the hereditary kings (*obas*) of the core city-states, who comprised an independent executive council (*oyo mesi*), had considerably weakened central authority—even as the Oyo Empire began to lose control over outlying kingdoms and city-states. Nupe and Ilorin, which developed stronger Islamic ties with the emerging Sokoto Sultanate to their north, broke away from Oyo. So did Dahomey and Lagos, which developed stronger commercial ties with Europeans along the Atlantic coast. Shortly after reformist Muslim flag-bearers from Sokoto helped to overthrow Oyo's central authority in Ilorin, Oyo's tributary kingdom in Dahomey also revolted (1818). Thereafter, other Yoruba city-states sought and fought for local autonomy. After the Battle of Oshogbo (1835), which the Oyo army lost to the cavalries of Muslim reformers from Ilorin, the people of Oyo migrated southward. Subsequently, Yoruba kingdoms both allied and fought with one another—absorbing many refugees from Oyo and elsewhere—and built large-walled cities (like Ibadan and Abeokuta) to provide protection for their citizens. These Yoruba wars supplied many captives who were exported across the Atlantic, at least until the 1850s, when British gunboats directly intervened to stop slave trading in the port city of Lagos, and British missionaries living in Abeokuta began to promote local production and exports in palm oil. Even after palm oil had supplanted war captives as Yorubaland's leading export, Lagos was bombarded, conquered, and claimed as a British Protectorate (1862). By the 1860s, such educated Yoruba leaders as S. A. Crowther, who became the Anglican Bishop of West Africa in 1864, and J. W. Johnson, who helped to formulate the modern constitution that governed Abeokuta during 1865–1872, had returned from Sierra Leone to help build a new forward-looking Yoruba nation. Meanwhile, the powerful city-state of Ibadan attempted to conquer its neighbors and to reestablish some sort of broad central authority throughout Yorubaland. Since different Yoruba kingdoms fought against Ibadan's military expansionism (c. 1860–1890), Yorubaland remained divided when British troops from Lagos launched their Yoruba Campaign in 1892. Because of these divisions, and also because modern British weapons had such overwhelming firepower and accuracy, most Yoruba city-states accepted treaties that imposed British terms of colonial "protection" on them.

To the west of the Yoruba and directly inland from some two dozen European stone fortresses along the Gold Coast, several Akan kingdoms had (as in Oyo) confederated, conquered, and consolidated an extensive eighteenth-century empire. The original Asante (Ashanti) Confederation, established by seven clans near the city of Kumasi, united around the symbolic Golden Stool of their ruler (*asantehene*). This confederation expanded through the diplomacy and conquests of Osei Tutu and Opoku Ware (*c.* 1690–1750), and its leaders had already undertaken steps toward modernizing their confederated empire before 1800. During the early years of the nineteenth century, Osei Bonsu (1801–1824) further implemented such modernization policies—both in administration (e.g., promoting advancement by merit) and in commerce (e.g., supporting the development of state enterprise through investment). He also espoused a clear vision of Akan nationalism, based on encouraging all Akan kingdoms to join together in order to resist European penetration. Osei Bonsu and his successors led Asante's imperial armies in a series of seven wars against coastal Fante kingdoms allied with British forces, which decisively defeated Asante armies in 1874. British control over Fante commerce, meanwhile, grew by virtue of treaties that increasingly conceded commercial jurisdiction to British consuls at the Cape Coast fortress, until Britain annexed Fante territories into their new Gold Coast Colony (1874). By this time, various Fante peoples had joined together in a constitutionally based confederation. Historian A. Adu Boahen describes the Fante confederation as "very progressive, modern, and farsighted" in its plans to construct roads and to promote agriculture, commerce, industry, and education through "self-help and self-reliance."[1] In addition to disregarding this modern Fante constitution, British imperial armies also invaded Asanteland, burned the city of Kumasi, and broke the Asante confederation apart. By the 1890s, however, a new Asantehene named Prempeh I (1888–1896) had reunited the original Asante kingdoms and was once again assimilating outlying provinces into a new Asante confederation. After diligently seeking to negotiate with the British (sending dispatches and delegates to London), Prempeh I welcomed a British armed delegation to Kumasi in 1896. But the British arrested and deported him (rather than negotiating) in order to prevent a reunited Asante nation from emerging on the northern border of their Gold Coast Colony. In 1900, when the British governor of the Gold Coast demanded the surrender of Asante's historic symbol of national confederation and unity (the Golden Stool of Osei Tutu), Queen Mother Yaa Asantewaa led the core Asante clans in laying siege to the British governor (trapped in Kumasi), until imperial reinforcements arrived. Thereafter, Asanteland was officially annexed into Britain's Gold Coast Colony. As with the Ibo, Yoruba, and Asante of West Africa, many other nineteenth-century African nations (each with its own particular history) were consciously modernizing their various political economies—through developing new products and linkages in international trade as well as new regional confederacies, national confederations, or written constitutions—until such indigenous modernizing tendencies were interrupted by European colonial conquests.

East Africa (*c.* 1800–1900)

There was also much movement toward political consolidation and broader commercial linkages throughout East Africa, from the Limpopo River to Ethiopian Highlands, during the early and middle nineteenth century. Ngoni leaders from South Africa moved northward across the Limpopo River, conquered locally autonomous chiefdoms or communities, and incorporated them into large-scale military states—for example, as Soshangane organized the Gaza kingdom (in Mozambique) after 1821, or as Milikazi incorporated Shona chiefdoms into a Ndebele kingdom (in Zimbabwe) after 1838. The Lunda *kazembes* of central Africa's copper belt (in modern Zambia and Democratic Republic of Congo) developed a wide-ranging commercial network that integrated long-distance trade routes that connected Africa's Atlantic and Indian Ocean coastal trading systems. As the coastal city-states that handled overseas trade in southeast Africa remained under control of Portuguese garrisons and settlements in Mozambique, more interior trade from central Africa moved toward independent Swahili city-states like Kilwa, Bagamoyo, and Mombasa.

The Omani Sultan Sayyid Said (1806–1854) controlled powerful navies that dominated the sea traffic of the East African coasts during the early 1800s. After conquering Mombasa (1838), Sayyid Said moved his royal court from Oman to the island of Zanzibar, where he and his successors established a commercial emporium that attracted trade from the coastal Swahili city-states between Kilwa and Mombasa—and ultimately throughout the interior of east and central Africa. Because Zanzibar became such an important commercial center in an age of rapidly expanding international demand for East African ivory, it became an international port of call during the mid-nineteenth century. Despite British naval and diplomatic pressure, Omani rulers in Zanzibar also profited from a lively international slave trade, channeling captives from East Africa's interior to work on Zanzibar's clove plantations and coastal coconut estates, or on the sugar plantations of Indian Ocean islands. The major caravan routes that connected coastal commerce in nineteenth-century Zanzibar with interior trade networks had first been developed by Bantu-speaking peoples as the Yao, who operated long-distance trade routes from beyond Lake Nyasa to Kilwa; the Nyamwezi, whose trading networks extended from the upper Congo River eastward to Bagamoyo; and the Kamba, whose traders regularly traveled between Lake Victoria and Mombasa. This commerce attracted Swahili and Arab merchants (as well as Indian financiers) to these caravan routes until the 1880s—when the Swahili city-states had reasserted their independence from Zanzibar and when modern European gunboats and armies came to establish their colonial claims in East Africa. By this time, new nationalist confederacies led by Abushiri and Bwana Heri arose among the central Swahili and offered determined resistance, before submitting to German invaders (1888–1891).

Even before Zanzibar and Swahili traders began to dominate international commerce along interior caravan routes (*c.* 1850), large-scale kingdoms and confederations were developing throughout East Africa. By 1800, complex, highly stratified states had developed in East Africa's fertile interlacustrine region where, as historian Walter Rodney argues, federated kingdoms like Rwanda and Buganda achieved an advanced "state and sense of national consciousness" because they had remained "free to develop relatively unaffected by alien influence and certainly free from direct ravages of slave trading."[2] Further north in the Ethiopian Highlands, Emperors Theodore and John (1854–1889) succeeded in reestablishing a strong national confederation among many local kingdoms in Christian Ethiopia. Throughout the southern Great Rift Valley, there were significant movements toward the development of regional confederations during mid-century, until such developments were interrupted by European colonial conquests in the 1890s. In southeastern Africa, nineteenth-century Ngoni military kingdoms were also conquered by colonial armies in the 1890s, as Cecil Rhodes' British South Africa Company established control over King Lobengula's Ndebele federation and Portuguese armies conquered the Gaza kingdom. Aside from Portuguese garrisons in Mozambique and international commercial interests on Zanzibar, Europeans did not begin to explore or evangelize in most of East Africa until about 1850, and European armies did not begin to penetrate the interior until the 1890s. By that time, the Germans and the British had agreed to partition East Africa between themselves and to conquer or "pacify" those regions not already claimed by Portugal (Mozambique) or by Belgium's King Leopold (Democratic Republic of Congo). The impact of Europe's "scramble" for East African colonies seemed doubly significant because it was accompanied by a rinderpest virus that spread so rapidly during the 1890s that it killed 80–90 percent of East Africa's cattle. Throughout the Great Rift Valley, massive losses of livestock intensified the devastation wrought by invading colonial armies, marking a clear interruption of earlier tendencies toward economic and political development in East Africa.

In the Great Rift Valley (of modern Tanzania) during the mid-nineteenth century, the Ngoni warriors of King Zwangendaba (*d.* 1848) split apart and began to introduce "total warfare." Their devastating raids on Rift Valley communities between Lakes Malawi and Tanganyika brought some of these Ngoni warriors into contact with a notable Nyamwezi leader named Mirambo, near the commercial city of Tabora. Mirambo (1860–1884) incorporated Ngoni warriors within his own Nyamwezi age regiments and armed them with muskets obtained from coastal trade. By combining Ngoni military organization with imported firearms, Mirambo became so successful in conquering and confederating Nyamwezi and other Rift Valley chiefs (*ntemis*) that he was described by explorer Henry M. Stanley as "the Napoleon of central Africa." Mid-century Nyamwezi commerce, largely based on trading ivory and slaves for imported firearms and other products from Zanzibar, was first described in detail by British explorer Richard Burton in 1857. Several years later, Dr. David Livingstone established a mission station on the northern shores of Lake Nyasa (now lake Malawi), to the south of Mirambo's military-commercial confederation, and began writing plaintive reports to British Christians about the daily devastations of slave-raiding in East Africa. In response to these and other reports, the British increased their naval and diplomatic pressure on the Sultan of Zanzibar to abolish slave trading in East Africa (1873–1876). Under Mirambo's leadership, Nyamwezi commercial and military influence extended deep into central Africa, to the west of Lake Tanganyika. A Nyamwezi trader named Msiri (*c.* 1860–1891), for example, used his commercial contacts in Tabora to import guns and to gain control over the Lunda Kazembes of central Africa's copper belt. A Swahili ally of Mirambo named Tippu Tib (*c.* 1874–1890) also expanded his elephant-hunting and slave-raiding activities along the upper Congo River (in modern Democratic Republic of Congo), where he introduced Kiswahili as the language of international trade.

> In the eastern Rift Valley highlands (also in modern Tanzania), the mid-century arms trade, the demand for slaves and ivory, the presence of caravans and ... the development of notables [leaders] and standing armies, all had an enormous impact [on regional development], but the effect on centralized authority was not uniform. In some places, powerful chiefs fell; in others centralized rule emerged stronger than ever before.[3]

As an example of how central authority in a mid-century highland state disintegrated, historian Steven Feierman has shown how the Shambaa "had developed an orderly, prosperous and peaceful kingdom" after which they "broke up into a great many embattled chiefdoms, each seeking its own ties with traders, and each selling slaves to outsiders."[4] Further south, meanwhile, highland Hehe and Bena chiefdoms merged into larger scale confederations, especially under Hehe military leadership during the 1870s and 1880s. Their renowned leader Mkwawa (1880–1898) continued to wage a determined guerrilla struggle against well-armed German colonial armies until he was betrayed, surrounded by German soldiers, and killed himself (rather than surrender). In Mkwawa's case, as with other such nationalist leaders in East Africa during the 1890s, Europeans were able to enlist Swahili troops and other Africans to fight with them. Thus, their invading armies were able to "divide and conquer" East Africa's developing political confederations. Later in German East Africa, the Maji Maji Rebellion (1905–1907) brought the warriors of many different communities and chiefdoms (southeast of Kilwa) into a massive nationalist confederacy designed to rid their country of colonial rule. However, German officers and their Swahili troops retaliated brutally, and more than 75,000 died from the hunger induced by their scorched-earth tactics.

In the northern Rift Valley of modern Kenya meanwhile, shifting confederacies of autonomous Kikuyu (Gikuyu) and Maasai communities as well as Luo and Luhya chiefdoms increasingly developed commercial linkages with Kamba and Swahili traders, who passed through their lands along the Mombasa–Buganda caravan route. During the rinderpest epidemic of the 1890s, British imperial armies undertook piecemeal conquests (or "pacification") of colonial Kenya, with the aid of Swahili soldiers, but active local resistance continued in different regions until 1920. In the powerful federated kingdom of Buganda, the royal family and followers of Kabaka Mutesa (*c.* 1858–1884) also became deeply divided—among Muslims with ties to Zanzibar or the Egyptian Sudan, Protestants with ties to Britain, and Roman Catholics with ties to France—in the late nineteenth century. Religious persecutions and palace politics continually undermined the *kabaka's* authority after 1876, and matters only worsened when Mutesa died. In 1894, a Protestant faction in Buganda (backed by British forces) gained control over state power. Six years later, Buganda's leaders formalized an alliance with British colonial officials, granting Buganda's Protestant elites a great deal of administrative authority over internal affairs in the British Protectorate of Uganda.

In the northeast "horn" of Africa, coastal hinterlands were inhabited by autonomous Somali clans, and the interior regions of Ethiopia contained a multitude of diverse communities or kingdoms (including Christians, Muslims, Jews, Amhara, Oromo, and others)—all of which allied or competed with one another in various shifting confederacies. In Somalia, the largest and most effective confederacy of clans was led by Said Muhammad (1895–1920), who brought together a coalition that continued to resist colonial authority in British, French, and Italian Somaliland, as well as in Ethiopia's Ogaden region, into the 1920s. In the nineteenth-century imperial confederation of Ethiopia, on the other hand, Menelik II (1889–1912) was so successful in modernizing his national army that Ethiopians were able to repel Italian invaders (1890s) and avoid being colonized. Building on the earlier reestablishment of central authority in Ethiopia's highlands under Emperors Theodore and John (1854–1889), Menelik II exploited European rivalries skillfully enough to gain international diplomatic support and to arm his soldiers with up-to-date weapons. He also promoted literacy and modern infrastructure, building the foundations for a permanent capital in Addis Ababa and a centralized government in Ethiopia. Remarkably successful in his efforts to unite, modernize, conquer, and consolidate Ethiopia during the European "scramble," Menelik II did not contest the British, French, and Italian colonization of coasts and hinterlands in neighboring Somalia and Eritrea. Primarily because of the diplomatic and military leadership of Menelik II, Ethiopia's nineteenth-century political independence was not interrupted by the imposition of European colonial rule.

CONCLUSIONS

The continuing development of political confederacies, confederations, and federations throughout African history was never so widely and drastically interrupted by external intervention as during the last decades of the nineteenth century. European colonialism undermined the legacies of nineteenth-century African development by denying Africans sovereignty over their own lands, by establishing entirely new principles of colonial authority, and by restructuring Africa's internal and international commerce. During the last decades of the nineteenth century, historical African tendencies toward national confederations (which sought to balance local autonomy with central authority) were interrupted by the wholesale invasion of modern gunboats and armies from Europe. Prior to the European "scramble," as we have seen, nineteenth-century Africans were developing more modern approaches to nation-building, military and educational systems, commercial transactions, and international relations. New international linkages were forged through nineteenth-century Islamic brotherhoods in North Africa and the Sudan, explored through high-level diplomacy by leaders like Prempeh I or Menelik II, and articulated as new Pan-African perspectives by such West African intellectuals as Dr. J. A. Horton (Gold Coast) and E. W. Blyden (Liberia). On the eve of colonialism, as historian Jan Vansina has written, economic and social development accompanied political consolidation throughout nineteenth-century Africa:

> Long-distance trade had completely reorganized the social landscape, with virtually all of equatorial Africa falling within the scope of one of three trade networks [oriented toward the Mediterranean Atlantic and Indian Ocean coasts].... All this brought into existence new cultural patterns, marked most forcefully by the spread of linguae francae. Above all, the reorganization of trade created new social patterns everywhere, the old aristocracies (both in status and in lineage systems) gave way. Everywhere, achieved status replaced ascribed status, with wealth becoming the prime criterion marking achievement.[5]

The gradual ending of the international slave trade and corresponding developments in new kinds of legitimate trade throughout the continent, by 1850, had begun to open new possibilities for Africans to broaden their commercial interests and to modernize their different regional and national confederacies, confederations, and federations. Europe's "Scramble for Africa," however, decisively interrupted such significant developments.

In concluding this brief synthesis of historical trends or themes in Africa's political heritage, it seems appropriate to reflect on the persistence of local autonomy in African community life, as providing different foundations on which various kingdoms and empires have been built. Throughout their history, Africans have been able to preserve and develop many of their local traditions and rituals (along with their particular languages and dialects) successfully—in part because they were able to maintain a fair degree of local autonomy. Wherever local networks of elders continued to supervise a community's ongoing processes of adaptation and change, local beliefs and traditions could be substantially preserved over long periods of time. Africa's historic tendency toward preserving local autonomy gave rise to incredible richness and variety in African political culture. Their wealth of cultural diversity, as Pan-Africanist E. W. Blyden pointed out in the 1880s, could be seen as "the spiritual conservatory of the world." The grace and profundity of diverse human expression in the arts and religions of historic African nations, indeed, have inspired alternative perceptions in modernist art and world music, as well as in such international religions as Islam and Christianity. As kingdoms and empires expanded, consolidated, and later fragmented over past millennia, many of the cultural traditions associated with local community life endured.

During the scramble for Africa (*c.* 1880–1900), European missionaries, colonial armies, officials, businessmen, and settlers invaded different African nations. European colonialism in Africa interrupted important continuities in the development of large-scale political economies throughout the continent. Because of their racialist attitudes, colonial administrators often pursued policies that totally disregarded African interests or opinions—policies that removed colonized Africans as active participants in shaping their own history. Put succinctly, in the words of historian Joseph Harris,

> The establishment of European colonial rule in Africa placed ultimate
> power in the hands of aliens who came from a cultural background
> that traditionally had denigrated African people. Thus the dominant
> long-range force became the colonial state that emphasized modern forms
> of ... bureaucratic rule. Indigenous political and economic structures lost
> their legitimacy and authority.[6]

Even as nineteenth-century Africans were building more productive economies and broader national identities, European colonization ended such trends and interrupted the ongoing continuities in African political development. Large-scale kingdoms and empires (organized around military, religious, commercial, and kinship linkages) have been based on enduring principles of cooperation and local autonomy throughout historic Africa. Today, such historic confederacies, confederations, and federations could well provide models for the development of effective and responsive governmental systems in the multinational states of independent Africa.

NOTES

1. A. Adu Boahen, *African Perspectives on Colonialism* (Baltimore, MD: The Johns Hopkins University Press, 1989), pp. 11–12.
2. Walter Rodney, *How Europe Underdeveloped Africa* (Washington, DC: Howard University Press, 1981), pp. 124, 128.
3. Philip Curtin, Steven Feierman, Leonard Thompson, and Jan Vansina, *African History* (Boston: Little, Brown and Company, 1978), pp. 406–407.
4. Ibid., p. 407.
5. Ibid., pp. 442–443.
6. Joseph E. Harris, *Africans and Their History* (New York: Penguin Books, Inc., 1987), p. 206.

Colonialism and the African Experience

Virtually everything that has gone wrong in Africa since the advent of independence has been blamed on the legacies of colonialism. Is that fair? Virtually all colonial powers had "colonial missions." What were these missions and why were they apparently such a disaster? Did any good come out of the African "colonial experience"?

INTRODUCTION

Colonization of Africa by European countries was a monumental milestone in the development of Africa. The Africans consider the impact of colonization on them to be perhaps the most important factor in understanding the present condition of the African continent and of the African people. Therefore, a close scrutiny of the phenomenon of colonialism is necessary to appreciate the degree to which it influenced not only the economic and political development of Africa but also the African people's perception of themselves.

This chapter focuses on the major European colonial powers in Africa. It will begin by comparing and contrasting in some detail the racial attitudes of the British, the French, and the Portuguese, proceeds to discuss their respective political administrative styles in their colonies and their economic policies and practices, and concludes with some assessment of the effect of all these factors on the political and economic evolution of African countries.

The two largest colonial powers in Africa were France and Britain, both of which controlled two-thirds of Africa before World War I and more than 70 percent after the war (see Table 4.1). The period from the mid-1800s to the early 1900s marked the zenith of imperial rule in Africa. The formalization of colonial rule was accomplished at the

TABLE 4.1

European Control of Africa

Imperial Power	Period	
	Pre-World War I (percent)	Post-World War I (percent)
France	36	37
Britain	30	34
Belgium	8	8
Germany	8	0
Italy	7	7
Portugal	7	7
Uncolonized	4	7
Total	100	100

Berlin Conference of 1884–1885 when all the European powers met and partitioned Africa, recognizing each other's share of the continent. The conference was called to reach agreement on imperial boundaries so as to avoid any future conflict among European powers. Following World War I, Germany, as a defeated power, was deprived of all her colonial possessions, which were parceled out to the victorious allies as trust territories under the League of Nations' mandate system. Tanganyika (which is the mainland portion of Tanzania) went to Britain. Rwanda and Burundi, which together with Tanganyika formed what was then called German East Africa, went to Belgium. Cameroon was split into two, a small southwestern portion going to Britain and the remainder to France. Namibia, then known as South West Africa, was assigned to South Africa as a sort of trophy for South Africa having fought in the war on the side of the Allied powers. Togo, then called Togoland, became a French trust territory, but a small sliver along its western border went to Britain, which governed it together with Ghana.

REASONS FOR EUROPE'S INTEREST IN AFRICA

Before looking into the nature of colonialism in Africa, let's turn our attention to the key question: Why was Europe interested in Africa in the first place? One scholar of Portuguese imperial history has suggested that the Portuguese were moved by "a crusading zeal, the desire for Guinea gold, the quest for [the mythical Christian kingdom of] Prester John, and the search of spices."[1] Another scholar suggested Prince Henry's penchant for hazardous travel abroad, real thirst for adventure in the name of acquiring knowledge. For our purpose here, however, Ali Mazrui's three broad reasons for European exploration of the African continent, which later led to colonization, provide a good starting point.[2] The first reason has to do with the need to gather scientific knowledge about the unknown. Africa, then referred to as the "Dark Continent," provided just the right kind of challenge. It held a lot of mystery for European explorers, who traveled and observed and recorded what they saw. Many of the early explorers of Africa were geographers and scientists who were beckoned by the mysteries and exotic qualities of this new land. Expeditions of people like Samuel Baker, Joseph Thompson, Richard Burton, John Speke, and others in the nineteenth century, conducted in the name of science and knowledge, served to attract Europeans to Africa. They "discovered" rivers, lakes, and mountains. They studied the African people and wrote about them. Of Prince Henry's exploratory expeditions, including those to Africa, a historian has written, "While Henry directed exploratory activities, he placed high value on the collection of geographical knowledge and rewarded his captains 'in proportion to the efforts they had made to carry the boundaries of knowledge farther,' thus keeping them intent on the work of exploration."[3] Without revisiting the debate as to what the Europeans meant by claiming to have "discovered" Africa's rivers and lakes, which the Africans had known and sailed and fished from all along, and without belaboring the often extremely racist and distorted descriptions of African societies that they purveyed, it will suffice to say that the writings of some of these foreign travelers increased knowledge of Africa in their own countries and ultimately helped Africans to know their continent better.

The second reason stemmed from European ethnocentrism or racism, itself rooted partly in Western Christianity. Implicit in the Christian doctrine (as well as in Islam, I might add) is the requirement that followers of the faith spread the gospel (or the Koran) to others and win converts. Since much of Africa followed their own traditional religious beliefs, Europeans felt that there was a definite need to proselytize and convert Africans to Christianity. In the early years of both Christianity and Islam, evangelical work was often carried out with military campaigns. Later, other methods of persuasion were applied. Missionaries were dispatched to Africa. They set up health clinics, schools, and social service centers. They treated the sick and taught people how to stay healthy. They taught European languages to Africans, who in turn assisted missionaries in translating the Bible into African languages to help disseminate Christian doctrines. Individuals like Dr. David Livingstone were able to combine missionary activities with extensive scientific research and geographic investigations. To this day, Africa remains a favorite destination for missionaries.

The third reason was based on imperialism, the desire by European patriots to contribute to their country's grandeur by laying claim to other countries in distant lands. Imperial Germany's Karl Peters' adventures secured Tanganyika for his kaiser. Britain's Cecil John Rhodes' exploits yielded a huge chunk of central Africa for his king. Henry Morton Stanley's expeditions to Africa paved the way for the Belgians' King Leopold to acquire the Congo—which he ironically named "The Congo Free State." And Portugal's Prince Henry and others who followed founded an early Portuguese empire in the Indian Ocean, *Estado da India,* "the first Portuguese global empire, upon which the sun never set."[4]

The three reasons mentioned earlier are not mutually exclusive; indeed, they are very much interrelated. For example, scientific information collected by geographers was often evaluated by European governments to determine if a certain area was worth laying claim to. If the information collected suggested that a given area had a pleasant climate, friendly people, evidence of natural resources, or good prospects for lucrative trade, then plans were laid down for a government-financed expeditionary force. Frequently, the explorers themselves could not resist the temptation of greed and amassed large amounts of wealth or precious cargo. Often, exploratory trips were sponsored and subsidized directly by European governments or government-chartered learned organizations such as the Royal Geographical Society. In other cases, when missionaries or other explorers encountered hostility or when their lives were in danger (as happened, for instance, to Bishop Hannington, who encountered religious resistance in Uganda and was eventually murdered on orders of a local king), foreign troops were dispatched promptly either to punish the groups involved or to protect other foreign nationals. When foreign troops came in, they invariably stayed and, on short order, colonization expeditions arrived.

After colonial rule was established, the missionaries and the colonial authorities forged a very close working relationship. In most of colonial Africa, schools were staffed and run by missionaries but subsidized in varying degrees by colonial governments, whose interest in missionary education was simply to ensure that enough Africans were educated to meet the limited need for semiskilled workers in colonial bureaucracies. The missionaries had total control over the religious curriculum. Mission schools taught that the European presence in Africa was to benefit the African people and to uplift them from a state of barbarism. African customs were discouraged. African languages were banned in mission schools. African heritage was ridiculed and suppressed. The goal was to give Africans a new identity by requiring them to use new, Christian names. As I recall from my colonial school days, an African student who was proud of his African name and insisted on using it risked being severely punished or even expelled. In many ways, Western religion instilled submissiveness by stressing that life on earth was temporary and best used for preparing for eternal life. To qualify for eternal life, one was taught to exercise Christian virtues of forgiveness, submissiveness, and patience. Humiliation and suffering, such as were being endured by Africans during colonialism, were thought to be ennobling and spiritually cleansing. The relationship between the missions and the colonial governments was truly a symbiotic one.

There is no question that Africans took to Western education with zeal. The little education that they got opened their minds and provided them with practical and intellectual skills they never had before. With some Western education, an African had a chance at a lifestyle that up to that time he or she could only read about in Western school textbooks. There was a tremendous demand for education that was far beyond the ability of the missions to provide. Despite this, colonial education very often alienated young people from their own culture and undermined traditional authority. Gradually, African people began to acquiesce to colonial rule and to surrender the elements of their culture and traditions. Moreover, missionary intentions were not entirely limited to spiritual matters. There is a saying, attributed to Jomo Kenyatta, the first president of Kenya, that has been repeated quite often and carries some truth. It goes something like this: When Europeans came to Africa, they had the Bible and the African had the land. They gave the Bible to the African and told him to hold it in his hand, close his eyes, and pray. When the African opened his eyes, he had the Bible and the European had his land. In the Congo, it was the missions that undertook the campaign to transform—they used the term "civilize"—the African into an imitation black European. It is easy to see why the role of Christian missionaries in Africa has been assailed by many writers and social scientists as having abetted and aided colonial oppression and exploitation.

IMPERIALISM IN AFRICA: THE RATIONALE

Why were the Europeans so keen to acquire colonies and empires in Africa? Three reasons stand out and these can be categorized as political/strategic, cultural, and economic. The political motivation has to do with the political rivalry among European states for dominance in the international system of the eighteenth century. These states believed that colonial possessions conferred prestige and status. Even today, one can argue that possessions and wealth still bestow a great deal of status on those who have them. Large countries still compete for influence among small states. The competition between the United States and the former Soviet Union in the so-called Third World in the Cold War era rested in part on the drive for leadership and dominance in world affairs. Interventions during the past forty years in Vietnam (by the United States) and in Afghanistan (by the former Soviet Union) had as much to do with assisting an ally as projecting the interventionists' power and hoping to acquire clients in the process. The nearly unilateral invasion of Iraq by the United States in 2003 against the advice of the United Nations Security Council and European allies such as Germany and France is reminiscent of imperial behavior of the past. Acquiring an empire was a shortcut to a world power status. Just imagine the pride and the psychological self-importance felt by tiny Belgium in acquiring the Democratic Republic of Congo, a country nearly ninety times the size of Belgium. Or take the case of Britain which, at the zenith of its imperial power, controlled, in Africa alone, an area that was more than forty times its own size.

Beyond the psychological satisfaction of being a great power, acquisition of a colony also provided a large reservoir of manpower to be drawn upon in time of war. It is reported, for example, that during World War I—"the war," according to President Woodrow Wilson, "to make the world safe for democracy"—nearly 1 million soldiers of African descent fought on the side of the Allied powers. In World War II, about 2 million Africans—and 1 million African Americans—served, again, on the side of those who were fighting against tyranny and oppression. All told, the possession of huge colonies provided manpower that held out the promise of imperial powers getting richer and growing stronger by being able to wage successful military campaigns anywhere in the world.

There was one more geopolitical advantage to holding certain areas in Africa during armed conflict. For instance, at the beginning of the nineteenth century, Britain decided to seize the southern tip of South Africa in order to have a tactical advantage in its war against France. By controlling the Cape of Good Hope, Britain was able to effectively conduct naval operations against France in both the Indian and Atlantic Oceans. The Strait of Gibraltar, the small entrance into the western Mediterranean Sea, was the scene of intense military campaigns in World War II as the combatants sought to control it. Whoever controlled the straits gained access to certain areas, which could influence military outcomes of conflicts taking place in those areas. There are other areas of the world that have been scenes of strategic confrontations between imperial powers, such as the Straits of Magellan at the tip of South America, the Straits of Malacca in the Indonesian Islands, the Suez Canal, and the Panama Canal. Strategic security was one of the reasons behind colonization but, after certain areas had been claimed, it became necessary to protect them not only against their rightful owners but also against other rival imperial powers.

The cultural reason for colonization was deeply rooted in the ethnocentrism and cultural arrogance of the European people, who regarded anyone different as being culturally inferior. In the case of the Africans, because they were not technologically advanced or their achievements were not written and therefore not known to the rest of the world, the Europeans felt that it was their duty to "civilize" and "uplift" the African people. In a language that was used by those who sought to cast colonization in the most favorable light, Perham asserts that this role "saw the interests of the ruled as equal, if not indeed superior, to those of the rulers."[5] Once the decision to acquire colonies had been made, it was up to the poets, writers, and intellectuals to provide the moral and philosophical justification for colonialism. And to the challenge they rose! The famous phrase "the white man's burden," used by Rudyard Kipling in his equally renowned poem of the same name, vividly captures the sense of divine mission that was to characterize Europe's forceful entry into Africa. Kipling urges the West:

> Take up the White Man's Burden-
>   Send forth the best ye breed-
> Go bind your sons to exile
>   To serve your captives' need;
>   To wait in heavy harness,
>   On fluttered folk and wild-
> Your new-caught, sullen peoples,
>   Half-devil and half-child.

An eloquent example of "the white man's burden" is contained in a speech delivered in the U.S. Senate at the turn of this century by Senator Henry Cabot Lodge, an exponent of U.S. expansion in the Caribbean and the Pacific. In deliberations in the U.S. Senate on the Philippines following the ouster of Spain, Senator Lodge declared,

> If the arguments which have been offered against our taking the Philippine Islands because we have not the consent of the inhabitants be just, then our whole past record of expansion is a crime [sic]. I do not think that we violated in that record the principles of the Declaration of Independence. On the contrary, I think we spread them over regions where they were unknown... .[6]

The Senator continued,

> The next argument of the opponents of the Republican policy is that we are denying self-government to the Filipinos. Our reply to that is that to give independent self-government at once, as we understand it, to a people who have no just conception of it and no fitness for it, is to dower them with a curse instead of a blessing. To do this would be entirely to arrest their progress instead of advancing them on the road to the liberty and free government which we wish them to achieve and enjoy. This conten-tion rests of course on the proposition that the Filipinos are not today in the least fitted for self-government, as we understand it.[7]

Why did Senator Lodge feel that the United States was the best equipped to carry out this role in the Philippines? The answer is contained in the following paragraph:

> All our vast growth and expansion have been due to the spirit of our race, and have been guided by the instinct of the American people, which in all great crises have proved wiser than any reasoning. This mighty movement westward, building up a nation and conquering a continent as it swept along, has not been the work of chance or accident which brought us to

the Pacific and which has now carried us across the great ocean even to the shores of Asia, to the very edge of the cradle of the Aryans, whence our far distant ancestors started on the march which has since girdled the world.[8]

The British, the French, the Portuguese, and the Belgians may not have articulated their role in Africa in the same terms and perhaps not as eloquently as the American senator, but they nonetheless felt the same way when they embarked on their imperial adventure in Africa. It was their "manifest destiny" to take over Africa; not to respond to this special calling would have been a betrayal of that special, unique quality that had made them great.

The economic motivation for colonization has probably received the greatest amount of attention from scholars and thinkers. Early literature on colonization is replete with references to the vast resources and markets represented by Africa and the economic benefits that would accrue to the European powers by opening up the African continent. However, it was V. I. Lenin who, in his classic *Imperialism: The Highest State of Capitalism,* most systematically articulated the economic rationale for the extension of imperial rule to the Third World. Lenin and other scholars since then argued that European countries sought to colonize African states in response to the inherent demands of capitalist economies, which not only needed natural resources with which to fuel the industrial revolutions in their own countries but also sought to exploit the plentiful cheap labor. As the European economies expanded, captive markets in the Third World became necessary for disposing of surplus goods. Suffice it to say that the desire for wealth, trade, resources, and cheap labor did motivate European expansion into Africa and other parts of the Third World. Some revisionist historians have suggested that colonization was not all that economically lucrative to colonial powers. Later in this chapter, however, we explore more fully the economic practices of the major European colonizers.

RACE AND EUROPEAN COLONIZERS: "THE CIVILIZING MISSIONS"

Europe justified its colonization of Africa on grounds that it was its moral duty to "uplift" Africans from their primitive state. Ample evidence suggests that all European powers did not think much of Africans or African culture and history. Writings by Europeans who visited Africa before the actual colonization show views of individuals determined to look at Africa through their cultural prisms and conclude that Africans were backward and uncivilized. Preoccupation with skin color and other physical traits as measures of "civilization" was strong and consistent. Europeans, therefore, felt that colonization was right and that they had a mission "to civilize" Africans. How did they conceptionalize that mission? How were they going to execute it? What type of person did they expect to see once their mission in Africa was accomplished? Answers to these fundamental questions will reveal interesting contrasts among the European colonizers and, in so doing, tell us what their racial attitudes and the assumptions underlying their "civilizing mission" were, providing insights into how they defined themselves as British, French, Portuguese, or Belgian.

The British Mission

In most of the British colonies, the indigenous people and the British were segregated. Social institutions like schools, recreational facilities, and hospitals were maintained for different racial groups. In places like East Africa, principally Kenya, where significant Asian, Arabic (Islamic), and European communities settled, there were separate facilities for each of those groups, the best facilities, of course, being reserved for Europeans. There were Asian schools, European schools, African schools, and at the coast, Arab or Muslim schools. Transportation was often broken down into first class, second class, and third class. The separate schools were often racially designated, as were hospitals and bathrooms in public buildings. Transportation, for example, buses and trains, was not racially designated, but the use of higher fares and local custom made sure that Africans kept their place—in third-class coaches. Residences were segregated, with Africans in the cities confined in "African locations" with conspicuously crowded and inferior housing. As is well known, attempts were made to codify into law racial segregation in areas with substantial British settlers such as in Kenya, Zimbabwe, and South Africa.

Grudgingly, the British would allow a well-to-do African to purchase a house in a predominantly white area or to ride a first-class compartment if he did not share it with a European, but in general, they did not envisage a situation in which an African might be "uplifted" to the level that he or she might be considered the social equal of a British. It can be conceded that in a very general sort of way, the British tried to convert Africans into British ladies and gentlemen. Indeed, the British were very pleased to point to an "uplifted African" who affected British manners, but they did not consider such an African a social equal in the same way that the French did. It was obvious that an African who could read or use mechanical tools was more productive than one who could not, but it was unthinkable that an African could be educated to a level of social equality with a British person. Governors in British colonies often spoke of Africans eventually exercising political power in their countries, but clearly not as political partners with the British. Political power could be exercised by the Africans only over other Africans. In Kenya, Zimbabwe, and South Africa, where the whites constituted, respectively, 1 percent, 5 percent, and 15 percent of the population, the British granted a great deal of political responsibility to colonial governments, and the whites in the colonies insisted on dominating the Africans, not sharing power with them proportionately or even equally. In the course of British colonialism, not a single thought was given to the Africans (or other Third World people colonized by the British, for that matter) ever being represented in the British legislature. To have African representation in the British parliament (even under the pretext of training them in parliamentary government) would have suggested political and perhaps racial equality, an idea whose time would not come. Clearly, the only way someone could be as good as a British person was to have been born one. An African could acquire British culture, and many did, but never the ancestry to go with it. The British notion of what constituted "Britishness," therefore, was based *both* on ancestry and on culture.

The French Mission

Similarly, the French looked down on the Africans and on African culture. They had a social policy to buttress their colonial rule in Africa, known as "the assimilation policy." This policy was based on the very laudable revolutionary ideal of human equality, but only under French suzerainty.

> Thus the French, when confronted with people they considered barbarians, believed it their mission to convert them into Frenchmen. This implied a fundamental acceptance of their potential human equality, but a total dismissal of African culture as of any value. Africans were considered to be a people without any history, without any civilization worthy of the name, constantly at war with one another and fortunate to have been put in touch with the fruits of French civilization.[9]

Obviously, the French were in Africa to "civilize" and to remake the African in their own image. The policy of assimilation required an educational system that would transform Africans into French people. A lieutenant governor of Senegal in 1902 was quoted as telling African students at a local school,

> The French language is the language of the entire world, and you are not an educated or distinguished person, whatever your race, unless you know how to speak French ... To speak French, my young friends, is to think in French ... it is to be something more than an ordinary man, it is to be associated with the nobility and destiny of our country ... Love France with all your strength because she loves you well.[10]

Since educational opportunities were extremely limited in French colonies, only a few Africans actually qualified for full rights as French citizens. Nevertheless, after World War II, following reforms that conferred French citizenship on Africans, the acculturated Africans, living in cities in Senegal, Ivory Coast, Guinea, and elsewhere in the French empire do not recall having to use separate bathrooms, being sent to separate schools, having to sit on the opposite side of the aisle in the church, being forced to ride in separate train compartments, having to drink from separate fountains, or even having to endure the humiliation of signs reading: "Africans Only," "Europeans Only," or "Africans and Dogs Not Allowed." This is not to say that racial indignities were completely absent in French colonies. It is merely to say that when Africans became acculturated into French culture, they were included in the French community in a manner that the British in their own colonies would not have considered doing. It is this degree of acceptance of acculturated Africans that gave rise to the view that the French were "color-blind," not racist. Moreover, after 1946, Africans could participate in French political affairs at three levels: in their own countries (such as Senegal, Guinea, Cameroon), in their federated regions (such as French West Africa or Equatorial Africa), or in the metropolitan French political system. French social practice with respect to the Africans suggests that the French considered culture rather than racial ancestry as the fundamental ingredient of "Frenchness."

The French and the British Contrasted: Senghor and Khama

The British and the French can perhaps most vividly be contrasted by looking at the way they treated two Africans from their respective colonies: Léopold Sédar Senghor (1906–2001) of Senegal, a French colony in West Africa and Seretse Khama (1921–1980) of Botswana, a British colony in southern Africa. Senghor was the product of the best circumstances that French colonial rule had to offer. He was born into a well-to-do African Catholic merchant family, went to good French mission schools in Senegal, and proceeded to the Sorbonne in France where he graduated in philosophy and literature. Senghor lived in France for many years and later joined politics as a member of France's Socialist Party, rising to become a member of the National Assembly representing Senegal. Senghor also represented France for a year at UNESCO and served as a minister in a couple of French governments in the late 1940s. When Senghor retired from the presidency of Senegal in 1980, he chose to live in France until his death in 2001. Senghor's experience, as you will soon see, was quite different from that of his counterpart in a British colony. Seretse Khama, on the other hand, was the son of the king—Sekgoma II—of the Bamangwato people, the largest subgroup of the Tswana people in what used to be called Bechuanaland (now Botswana). His father died when Khama was less than five years of age. Khama's uncle, Tshekedi Khama, became a regent until Khama could assume the throne later. The young Khama went to mission schools in Botswana, then on to a black college at Fort Hare, and to a segregated University of the Witwatersrand in South Africa. Later, he proceeded to Oxford University in England to study law, politics, and economics and became a lawyer.

In a real sense, both Senghor and Khama were deeply acculturated with European values of their respective colonial powers, and both were products of the finest institutions of higher learning in their respective metropoles. Senghor wrote a great deal in his essays and poems about his dual identity as a Frenchman and an African. France, however, was not devoid of racism. Indeed, his experience in France led him to articulate a philosophy of negritude, by which he and his fellow black intellectuals asserted the inherent worth of "blackness." In any event, both Senghor and Khama met and fell in love with and decided to marry white women. Senghor's marriage to a white woman caused no ripple, no negative excitement at all in France. His fellow deputies in the French National Assembly and the French public reacted to his marriage positively. It was as though the French had expected all along that Senghor, as a fine self-respecting Frenchman, albeit with African ancestry, would marry a French woman. It is striking that in most of Senghor's biographies, no special point is made of his marriage to a white French woman.

On the other hand, Khama's marriage to an English woman was received with utter dismay by the British government. His uncle, the regent, also objected vigorously and had, in fact, tried unsuccessfully to stop the marriage from taking place in the first place. Paraphrasing the reasons for Tshekedi Khama's refusal to accept his nephew's marriage, Michael Dutfield writes,

> Seretse was turning his back on the duties and obligations to which he had been born. In Bamangwato custom, to marry without your father's permission was a serious offense. If you were the chief-to-be, to marry without the tribe's permission struck at the foundations of government. In the hotbed of tribal politics, the marriage of the chief was a principal instrument in forging alliances, breaking up power blocs and helping to ensure the future of the tribe. The Bamangwato had a right to decide who their future queen would be. European monarchs had never been able to marry just as they pleased.[11]

The British public was both intrigued by the very vociferous opposition to the marriage displayed by Seretse's uncle in Botswana and put off by the unusual nature of the marriage. As Dutfield explains, "Blacks, in 1948, were, in most people's eyes, both inferior and slightly mysterious. They were certainly not the sort of people that white girls should marry."[12] Seretse returned to Botswana where, in a specially convened traditional assembly, his people voted to accept him as their leader and to welcome his white wife into the community as their future queen. The British government would not allow Seretse to be installed on the throne. Dutfield vividly describes the strong opposition expressed to the marriage by the governments of South Africa and Southern Rhodesia (now Zimbabwe)—both countries then committed to racial segregation and white supremacy—which saw this mixed marriage between a future black leader of a neighboring country and a white woman as a dangerous precedent. The British government acquiesced to these two countries to protect its highly valued relationship with them and planned to do so in a manner that would not look racial. In actual fact, Britain's official attitude to the marriage went beyond a simple act of disapproval by one government in solidarity with its allies. The British set up a commission ostensibly to investigate whether Khama was fit to be a leader of his people (but really to raise questions about his sanity for marrying a white woman). They enticed him to London, where he was told he would not be allowed to return to Botswana, but would, instead, be sent into exile in order to prevent him from assuming his traditional role as king. The official reason given was that the best interests of his people would not be served by his assumption of office. The interests were never defined. The government publicly—but rather disingenuously—denied that his marriage to a white woman had anything to do with the ignominious manner in which he was being treated. He was allowed back into Botswana six years later, in 1956, only after he renounced his right to "the throne." Returning to Botswana with his wife as "private persons," Khama founded the Bechuanaland Democratic Party, which won elections that were held when Botswana was granted independence by Britain. Khama became the first president of Botswana in 1966 and was shortly thereafter knighted by the Queen of England. Nevertheless, it is fair to conclude that even though Khama was of "royal" blood and had an Oxford University education, the British could never accept him as a social equal. His marriage to a white woman had been regarded as an act of racial impudence on his part. The contrast in the way Senghor and Khama were treated illustrates the perceptual difference on race between the French and the British. The French were prepared to and did accept Senghor as a black Frenchman, whereas the British, through their government, could not bring themselves to think of Khama as a social equal, let alone a black Briton.

Fanon's Theory of French Racism

It is clear to see why the French were always considered the most enlightened of imperial masters. But were they? A further look as to how truly enlightened the French were is provided by Frantz Fanon, a black psychiatrist, who was born on the West Indian island of Martinique. Fanon says that as a product of rather comfortable family circumstances in Martinique, he grew up thinking and believing that he was French until he went to France to study medicine specializing in psychiatry. France was in the process of putting down an Algerian armed struggle for independence. Fanon was extremely curious as to why French people, whom he believed to be so enlightened, would be so violently opposed to the demand of the Algerian people for freedom and for their own self-government. The outright disdain and racism shown by French people toward the Algerians shocked him. There was also a lot of hatred toward African and Arab people living in France. Some of the antagonism toward Arabs undoubtedly must have had some relationship to the rising death toll inflicted on French troops by Algerian rebels. The French people were also frustrated that the Algerian war was dragging on for so long. In any event, as evidence of French racism became more obvious, many black people began to assert their identity as people of color and to affirm their worth as human beings.

Fanon seems to have been shocked by the very strong French reaction to declarations by prominent literary figures like Aime Cesaire that they were proud of their black heritage. The French wondered how anyone could be proud of being black.[13] Nevertheless, Fanon's observations led him to theorize that the French were in fact just as racist as the other European powers in accepting colonized people, people of color, only when they gave up their cultural identity—when, as it were, they committed cultural suicide. He felt that the French had shown no racial tolerance at all toward Africans or Arabs who chose to retain their culture and heritage. He argued that what had been characterized as French tolerance was really nothing but a form of French self-love. The French, he concluded, accepted the colonized people only to the degree that the latter reflected French culture, values, and traditions. In that sense, then, the French were as contemptuous and destructive of the traditional ways of the African people as the British, the Portuguese, or the Belgians. Additional evidence that the French were not as color-blind as widely believed can be found in Ousmane Sembene's classic novel *God's Bits of Wood*, based on the building of the railroad across the vast expanse of what was known as French West Africa. The attitudes of the French foremen toward the African railroad workers were laced with racism, brutality, and callousness found among other colonial masters.

The Portuguese Mission

The Portuguese were ethnocentric, some would say racist, toward Africans. They too had a "civilizing mission" in Africa. However, their concept of what constituted a Portuguese was a combination of the ideas of both the French and the English. It included both ancestry and culture. A key element of the Portuguese social policy in Africa (as elsewhere in their empire such as in Brazil) was the condoning and promotion of the mingling of cultures and races through marriage and cohabitation. This process was mostly one-way, involving Portuguese men and African women. There was much abuse in this system, especially as far as African women were concerned. Most of the unions were never made legal. Without the force of law, most Portuguese fathers refused to accept responsibility for their biracial children. The consequence was that these children of interracial liaisons did not have the strong identification with Portuguese society that this practice was supposed to instill. As one would imagine, marriages between African men and Portuguese women were rare and, indeed, very much frowned upon.

This image of "racial toleration" was carefully cultivated and elevated to a philosophy of "lusotropicalism," whose main themes are summarized by Gerald Bender as follows:

> Given the unique cultural and racial background of metropolitan Portugal, Portuguese explorers and colonizers demonstrated a special ability—found among no other people in the world—to adapt to tropical lands and peoples. The Portuguese colonizer, basically poor and humble, did not have the exploitative motivations of his counter-part from the more industrialized countries in Europe. Consequently, he immediately entered into cordial relations with the non-European populations he met in the tropics.... The ultimate proof of the absence of racism among the Portuguese, however, is found in Brazil, whose large and socially prominent mestizo population is living testimony to the freedom of social and sexual inter-course between Portuguese and non-Europeans. Portuguese non-racism is also evidenced by the absence in Portuguese law of the racist legislation in South Africa and until recently in the United States barring non-whites from specific occupations, facilities, etc. Finally, any prejudice or discrimination in territories formerly or presently governed by Portugal can be traced to class but never color, prejudice.[14]

This was the ideology of Portuguese colonialism on paper as espoused by those who favored it. Historical evidence, however, suggests that the Portuguese saw themselves clearly as being superior to Africans. A Portuguese colonial administrator in the 1890s is reported to have referred to an African, whom he called the Negro, as "this big child—instinctively bad like all children—though docile and sincere," while the same colonial official argued in favor of Portugal instituting forced labor in its far-flung worldwide empire by saying that it was right for the state to force "these rude Negroes in Africa, these ignorant Pariahs in Asia, these half-witted savages from Oceania to work...."[15]

The consequence of this Portuguese social policy, over a period of time, was the emergence of a highly stratified social pyramid consisting of full-blooded Portuguese at the top, enjoying all the privileges and rights of Portuguese citizenship; a very tiny stratum of mestizos (mixed-race people) in the middle, who were entitled to only a few rights; and full-blooded African people at the bottom, who were extensively exploited and were subjected to all kinds of indignities and abuses. In Portuguese colonies, an African could be considered civilized only if he "could speak Portuguese, had divested himself of all tribal customs, and was regularly and gainfully employed."[16] Moreover, the African population was divided into two subgroups: *assimilados* (assimilated ones), who had basically adopted a Portuguese way of life as defined by Portuguese law, and *indigenas* (natives), the vast majority who had not given up all their culture, language, and way of life. If you happened to be an *indigena,* you were required to carry a pass at all times, you were likely to be drafted into labor camps either in the colonies or in South African mines, you or your children were excluded from attending government schools, you were subject to curfew hours after dark in certain towns and areas of the country, and you were segregated in many social facilities such as theaters and comfort amenities. In some parts of colonial Mozambique, the indigenas could open accounts in post office banks (government banks) but they could not withdraw their money without the permission of the local Portuguese colonial administrator. As more Portuguese immigrants arrived to take up residence in the colonies, the authorities found it harder and harder to distinguish between assimilados and Africans. Full-blown segregation became the order of the day. The assimilados found themselves subjected to the same indignities as the Africans.

The Belgian Mission

The king of tiny Belgium, Leopold II, managed to outmaneuver Portugal, France, Britain, and Germany (as well as the United States) into recognizing his claim to a huge chunk of Africa nearly ninety times the size of his own kingdom. His mission was to "civilize" the Africans. Patrice Lumumba, the first prime minister of the Democratic Republic of Congo, summarizes Belgium's colonial code number 29 as follows:

> Belgium's mission in the Congo is essentially a civilizing one. It has a two-fold aim. On the moral plane, it is to ensure the well-being of the native population and their development by the broadening of individual liberty, the steady relinquishment of polygamy, the development of private property and the support of institutions and undertakings promoting native education and giving the natives an understanding and appreciation of the advantages of civilisation. On the economic plane, Belgium's mission is to achieve the development of the colony for the benefit of the natives and, to this end, to work towards an increasingly complete organisation of the country which will strengthen order and peace and guarantee the protection and expansion of the various branches of economic activity: agriculture, commerce and industry.[17]

Indeed, those Africans in the Congo who had been educated in the mission schools were referred to as the *évolués*—"those who had 'evolved' from savagery to civilization."[18] To qualify as an évolué, an African had to have gone to school, exhibit good behavior, and be firmly opposed to such uncivilized practices as polygamy and witchcraft. These conditions were so vague and so indeterminate that when the scheme was introduced between 1948 and 1953, only 500 Congolese could be deemed to have risen to Belgian cultural standards.[19]

Despite the small number of Africans qualifying, the resident whites were still furiously opposed to any possibility of social equality with the Africans. The Belgian authorities then introduced yet another system, this time calling it *immatriculation*. Patrice Lumumba says that this second system entailed even more rigorous "standards" than the first one.[20] An applicant for the civilized status had to be "sufficiently educated and penetrated with European civilization and conform with it." To ascertain this, relatives and friends had to be interviewed and the applicant's house inspected. Lumumba says, "Every room in the house, from the living room, bedroom and kitchen to the bathroom, are explored from top to bottom, in order to uncover anything which is incompatible with the requirements of civilised life."[21]

Civilizing the African was just a pretext and a subterfuge. The real motive was profits and wealth. This is how Bill Freund describes the situation on the ground in the Congo:

> Nowhere in Africa was the regime of force so raw and dramatic as in the Congo Free State of Leopold II. King though he was, Leopold ran the Free state like a capitalist of the robber-baron era. The Leopoldine system had its roots in the king's pursuit of quick profits to create a capital base needed for large-scale investment, especially in transport. The forests of the Congo basin were rich in low-grade rubber, conveniently excluded from the free-trade provisions of the Berlin Conference, and rubber found a buoyant market in the West as the use of bicycles and then automobiles developed. It was rubber which, from the middle 1890s, made the Free State pay.[22]

The Democratic Republic of Congo provides a perfect example of a partnership involving the Catholic Church, the local colonial administration, and the mining companies exploiting the country's resources. There was virtually no accountability to anyone in Brussells for what was happening to the Africans. Social segregation was the norm, even for Africans presumably meeting European standards. Africans in employment were paid a fraction of what resident Belgians were earning. According to John Reader, "In 1955, for instance, more than one million Congolese were in paid employment, but their total remuneration barely exceeded the total paid to the 20,000 Belgians then working in the country—an average black- to-white wage ratio of 1 to 40."[23]

King Leopold's companies hired armed militia to go into the countryside and forcefully recruit workers for the rubber plantations. Africans who resisted were whipped or had their limbs chopped off. Severed hands were then brought to the recruiters' bosses as proof of their diligence in the recruitment exercise.[24]

What emerges from the foregoing discussion of the colonial mission as reflected in racial attitudes among the British, the French, the Portuguese, and the Belgians is that the colonizers had nothing but disdain for the African people and their culture and values. They all went to Africa with the avowed goal of transforming African people into imitation Europeans as they helped themselves to the resources in Africa. The French offered the promise of full membership in the French community if the African assented to complete acculturation. The British sought to "uplift" the African but without the promise of social equality with the British. The Portuguese went a step further in condoning or perhaps encouraging one-way miscegenation in the belief that to "change" an African required infusion of Portuguese ancestry, and thus an African with some Portuguese blood was inherently superior to one without, but obviously still not the social equal of a full-blooded Portuguese person. As for the Belgians, "despite fulfilling the conditions which had promised integration, the évolués were still denied access to the social and economic world of the Europeans. In the eyes of the Belgians, they were still Africans—black and inferior."[25]

COLONIAL ADMINISTRATIVE STYLES

To compare and contrast the styles of administration employed by colonial authorities in Africa makes it possible to see how each European power tried to tailor their style to their overall objectives in the colony. We have already discussed, broadly speaking, the political, cultural, and economic reasons for colonization. We now know that the French intended to turn Africans into French people once the process of colonization was completed. The acculturated Africans would then become part of the larger French community. The British wanted to "civilize" the African, but not to the point where the African might claim equality with the British (since that was impossible). The Portuguese envisioned a new society that would include assimilated Africans who preferably had Portuguese ancestry. Therefore, it would appear that the end product of these colonial experiences would be that Africans under French and Portuguese rule would become an integral part of the European communities. The Africans in the British areas would ultimately be left alone to run their own governments using ideas learned from the British. The Belgians really did not have a vision of what they wanted the Africans to look like, or what type of relationship they expected to have with them. The promise of integration made to the évolués, meaning the acculturated Africans, was never fulfilled. The Belgians seem to have counted on an indefinite stay.

When the Congolese people began to demand independence, the Belgians had no exit plan. Things disintegrated rather quickly. The handover to the Africans was done in haste. Within thirty days, the new government collapsed following an army mutiny, in which the soldiers were demanding better wages and to be led (commanded) by Congolese officers instead of Belgian officers. The U.S. involvement in the political chaos and Lumumba's murder are widely considered to have been based on American belief that Lumumba was a communist. The United States, therefore, provided extensive support to Lumumba's successor, General Mobutu Sese-Seko, who turned out to be one of Africa's most brutal and corrupt autocrats.

There is yet another vision for the colonized people, which was to see Africans as permanently inferior requiring the long-term tutelage of the European powers. This is the vision concretized by the white settlers of South Africa under the system of *apartheid*. Perhaps if the Germans had been in Africa longer, given what they did to others in Europe during the Third Reich, and considering the brutal manner in which they responded to anticolonial uprisings in South West Africa (now Namibia) and Tanganyika (now Tanzania), it is reasonable to surmise that they may have elected to confine Africans to permanent subjugation.

In any event, one can identify four administrative styles or approaches that were used by the colonial powers in Africa: indirect rule, long associated with the British; direct rule associated with France, Germany, and Portugal; company rule, closely linked to the Belgians; and finally, a hybrid approach which I'll call, indirect company rule, linked to Cecil John Rhodes' imperial efforts in southern Africa.

Indirect Rule

The British have always boasted that they went into Africa not to create black Britons, but rather to share their skills, their values, and their culture with a hope that someday African people would be able to run their own communities using the tools learned and acquired from the British. The British administrative style was more systematically formulated by an eminent colonial governor named Lord Frederick Lugard, who implemented it when he was governor-general of Nigeria at the turn of the century. Lugard called this style "indirect rule." Succinctly put, the approach involved identifying the local power structure: the kings, chiefs, or headmen so identified would then be invited, coerced, or bribed to become part of the colonial administrative structure while retaining considerable political power over the people in their own areas. In areas where "tribes" and "tribal" chiefs did not exist, the British created them. In fact in Tanganyika, where the Germans preceded the British, entirely new "chiefs" and "tribes" were created where none existed before. This is how "warrant chiefs" came to exist among the Ibos of Nigeria. In exchange for becoming part of the colonial structure, a chief was often given protection, a salary, a house, and numerous gifts. The chief was expected to enforce local ordinances, to collect taxes, to provide cheap labor if required, and to be accountable directly to the white (British) district officer or commissioner. The colony was governed by a governor who was appointed by the British government and reported to the British Colonial Office (headed by the colonial secretary, a member of the British Cabinet).[26]

The British always maintained that indirect rule was designed to protect and preserve African political systems, traditions, and cultures. But colonial powers found out rather early in the colonial game that the areas they seized were simply too large to be governed directly without the assistance of the indigenous people themselves. An African chief or king was certainly an important link between the African people and the colonial authorities. He understood his people's language and culture and could be counted on to transmit orders and directives. He was told that he could protect his own people's interests better by cooperating in this restricted power relationship. Moreover, in a place like Nigeria where there were powerful local rulers such as the emirs of the Muslim north, some accommodation had to be made to avoid protracted conflicts. Also by recognizing and offering to work with local leaders, not only did the cost of running the colonies remain low, it also became possible to raise revenue locally. It has been suggested that "indirect rule" was simply a necessity that the British somehow managed to turn into a virtue.

One significant political consequence of indirect rule was that it reinforced separate ethnic identities and stunted the development of a national or colonywide political consciousness. Indeed, the style served British colonial interests very well, permitting them to play ethnic groups against each other. Interethnic interaction through traditional trade unions or political organizations was severely restricted and discouraged. The British feared that national activities might lead to countrywide resistance against colonial rule. For obvious reasons, ethnic welfare societies were allowed and in some cases actively encouraged in urban areas. Welfare societies provided social services that colonial authorities were either unable or unwilling to provide. For example, these organizations helped settle down country folks who had migrated into cities to look for work and provided critical support networks for them. Social clubs also existed to provide opportunities for low-level African civil servants to meet, have (English) tea, and establish contacts and talk about things affecting them in a nice civil manner as the British would want. The Tanganyika African Association, the precursor of the nationalist movement the Tanganyika African National Union, began in this way. Meaningful political participation was not allowed; political discourse, so vital in any system but perhaps more so in one that was evolving, was not nurtured. It was, therefore, unrealistic for anyone to expect ethnic groups that had been played one against the other for so long to know suddenly how to forge one nation overnight when independence came. Incidences of interethnic political violence in former British colonies can be partly traced to indirect rule.

Belgium occupied Rwanda and Burundi in 1916. After World War I, the two colonies became a trust terrritory named Rwanda–Urundi under the League of Nations' mandate system. The Belgians found a strong kingdom politically dominated by the Tutsi people but consisting of the Hutu, who were a numerical majority, and the tiny community of the Twa people. The Tutsi and the Hutu shared the same culture and language. The arrangement was such that it was possible for the Hutu to rise within this society even to leadership positions. The Belgians coopted the Tutsi, convincing them that they were not only superior to the Hutus but actually different. This was an application of indirect rule at its worst. This cooptation led to the Hutus being openly discriminated against and created the animosity and hatred which manifested itself in horrific massacres in 1959, 1972, and 1984, and in the infamous genocide of 1994.

Direct Rule

The French, the Portuguese, the Germans, and the Belgians (in the Congo) exercised a highly centralized type of administration called "direct rule." This meant that European rule was imposed on the Africans regardless of the existing political relationships among the African people. The French empire was governed directly from Paris through the governor. The French did use African chiefs but, unlike in the British empire, these chiefs were appointed by French authorities, in large measure because of their support for French rule. They did not come from ruling families and, upon appointment, were not posted to their native regions. They did not hold power over any unit of the government; their powers were greatly diminished. The French, with few exceptions, did not attempt to preserve the uniqueness of the various African political institutions. Therefore, Africans were not Balkanized into "tribal" chiefdoms as those in the British areas had been.

At the turn of the twentieth century, the French federalized their empire, not politically but structurally. There were two federations: French West Africa and Equatorial Africa, each administered by a governor-general. French West Africa, based at Dakar (Senegal), consisted of eight colonies, officially called territories. These were Dahomey (now Benin), Mauritania, French Soudan (now Mali), Senegal, Guinea, Ivory Coast, Upper Volta (now Burkina Faso), and Niger. Each territory had a territorial assembly and was under the responsibility of a governor. Each territory was further divided into *cercles* (circles), each one being under an administrator, also called *Commandant de Cercle*. Some cercles were further broken down into subdivisions under a *Chef de Subdivision*. Equatorial Africa had four territories: Gabon, Middle Congo (now The Republic of Congo), Oubangi Chari (now Central African Republic), and Chad. The two federations had parallel structures except that in Equatorial Africa the territories became regions and the cercles became districts. After World War I, Togo and Cameroon had separate identities as (League of Nations) trust territories governed by French High Commissioners. All these officials were civil servants appointed by the French government. All laws emanated from Paris; measures enacted by the territorial assemblies had to be approved by the French national legislature in Paris. French direct rule had the effect of giving Africans from the empire the opportunity to work together across regions and ethnic groups. The long view was that the colonies would eventually become integral parts of France. Indeed, beginning from 1848, for a period of about eight years, one commune in Senegal was given the right to elect a representative to the French National Assembly. In the late 1880s, this "qualified franchise" was extended to another three communes. Few Africans elsewhere in the French empire enjoyed these many rights, and the serious implementation of the French assimilation policy flowed with the vagaries of French politics, with national debates raging as to whether this was the right thing to do. In fact the right to vote was always restricted to those Africans who were considered assimilated into French culture. Direct rule was not implemented uniformly across the empire. In the regions governed by more powerful rulers, like in Upper Volta where the Mossi people had strong chiefs or in northern Cameroon where the Moslem emirs were quite powerful, the French had to make serious political concessions and govern through the traditional rulers.

Interestingly, the result of this centralized administration was that the Africans were governed without any regard to existing ethnic stratification. The French imposed forced interaction and equal subjugation. Reinforcement of ethnic fragmentation did not occur. This is not to say that ethnic conflict did not or does not exist in French or Portuguese Africa. It is simply to suggest that it is less pronounced in former French colonies, but quite salient in former Portuguese-ruled ones.

Portugal's centralized administration was much harsher and stricter than that of the French. When Africans began to agitate for self-determination, the Portuguese response was to declare their colonies of Angola, Mozambique, Guinea-Bissau, and the islands of Cape Verde, São Tomé and Principe as "Overseas Portugal," as integral provinces of Portugal that just happened to be separated geographically from Portugal itself. The Portuguese had no intention of granting self-rule to their colonies. Like the French, they, too, at one time made a few Africans citizens of Portugal but the experiment did not last long and had to be refined. The Portuguese dictator Antonio de Oliveira Salazar, who ruled Portugal from 1932 to

1968, declared that Portugal and her colonies constituted "only one state, one territory, one population, one citizenship, and one government." As the previous discussion of Portuguese colonial policy clearly demonstrates, the impact of Portuguese colonialism alienated the majority of Africans and led them to reject Salazar's romantic view of Portugal's colonies.

German rule in Africa was the briefest of all colonial regimes, having begun in the late 1880s and terminated with the signing of the Treaty of Versailles in 1919, following the defeat of Germany in World War I. However, the German presence did not go unnoticed. Their colonial administration was highly centralized, with the German governors assisted by African subordinates and officers who had been handpicked without any regard to the traditional power relationships that may have existed in the area at the time. As already pointed out, the Germans created their own African assistants even in places where the Africans were not used to being governed by chiefs. The Germans, as latecomers into Africa, went into their colonies with the idea of economically exploiting the areas and maximizing their economic power as fast as possible. Military officers and private entrepreneurs were given power and responsibility, but their political ineptitude soon became evident when they encountered local resistance, which they suppressed harshly. In Tanzania, for instance, huge farms were set up in areas suitable for farming important cash crops like sisal, tea, coffee, and cotton. Forced labor was instituted to provide workers for these farms. Discontent, bitterness, and resistance ensued. A major uprising occurred in Tanganyika, which was put down with customary German precision, but at great cost in human lives. Other uprisings took place in another large German colonial holding in South West Africa, which were suppressed ruthlessly as well. Following the uprising in Tanganyika called the "Maji Maji Rebellion" (1905–1908), in which approximately 120,000 Africans were reported to have lost their lives, the Germans decided to introduce some reforms under a colonial policy they called "scientific colonialism." This fancy term referred to a policy that called for the setting up of a special colonial office in the German chancellor's office and promoting the idea that German colonization could be made acceptable to the Africans if German colonial administrators convinced the African people that they had something to gain from German colonization. To this end, the German government undertook several capital projects such as road and railroad building and trading centers. It was during this period of "scientific colonialism" that the main railroad was built running from Dar-es-Salaam (on the Indian Ocean coast) to Kigoma (along the shores of Lake Tanganyika). Urban settlements began to appear. Roads were laid. Brutality subsided; Africans were beginning to feel that the Germans meant well and that perhaps they (the Africans) should work with them. In 1914, World War I broke out in Europe and Germany was defeated. In losing that war, Germany also lost her colonial empire in Africa.

Company Rule

The Belgians are associated with probably the most brutal kind of colonial rule. Initially, the Congo Free State was established as a personal and private fief of King Leopold II of Belgium and not as an official colony. It had the glamorous name of the Congo Free State, but it was neither free nor a state in the real sense of the world. The king gave free rein to the Belgium businessmen to go in and exploit it. They had wide latitude in running the colony, with no accountability to anyone except the king, whose only interest seems to have been timely royalty payments. Exploitation was extensive and brutal; forced labor was rampant. Virtual slavery existed, as Africans who resisted being drafted to work or who did not work hard enough were flogged in public or had their hands and ears cut off. The treatment of Africans was so harsh that imperial powers themselves were forced to appeal to King Leopold to do something about the situation. As Lord Hailey put it, "If Belgium was to avoid further international pressure and the possibility of intervention by more powerful neighbouring powers, then clearly it was necessary for her to establish an administrative and judicial regime in the Congo which would obviate occurrences such as those which had brought the Free State under such hostile criticism."[27] African Americans, under the leadership of W. E. B. DuBois, also responded to reports of this brutality by raising the issue at the first Pan-African conference in 1919 and submitting petitions to Belgium urging that Africans be treated humanely.

A commission was appointed in 1904 to investigate conditions in the Congo and as a result of its findings, the Congo was annexed as a formal colony in 1908. Even then, the Belgians did not appear to have a coherent colonial policy. This lack of colonial vision, if you will, is attributable to the fact that the Belgians had not had the experience of governing colonies that the British or the French had. By 1919, the other colonial powers appeared to have been sufficiently impressed by what Belgium was doing to add Rwanda and Burundi to the Belgian empire as the League of Nations trust territories. What seems to have been put together was an administrative system involving a coalition of Belgian businessmen, administrators, and the clergy from the Catholic Church. The church ran the school system, which put major emphasis on religious education, rather than the kind of education that would have permitted Africans to play a greater role in the political affairs of their country in the future. The businessmen held sway in the administration of the colony even as they continued to mine Congo's plentiful minerals. This is the kind of rule that was given the term "company rule."

Belgian colonial rule saw massive transfers of wealth from the Democratic Republic of Congo to Belgium. Africans received only limited education, which would allow them to read the Bible, take orders efficiently from the missionaries, and function, at best, as clerks in the colonial bureaucracy. The Congolese were not prepared to assume control of their country once the Belgians left. When independence was granted in 1960, the Democratic Republic of Congo represented an interesting irony: it had a high literacy rate (in terms of the ability to read and write) due to missionary education, and yet the country had only one college graduate. The Democratic Republic of Congo exemplifies evangelical success for the missionaries; it enjoys the honor of being the most Roman Catholic country in Africa. The first Congolese priest was ordained in 1917 and the first bishop was consecrated in 1956. By the time the Belgians left in 1960, the Congolese boasted more than 600 priests throughout the country. The Democratic Republic of Congo also exemplifies colonial ineptitude; it was the least prepared for self-rule and continues to be among the worst governed and the poorest despite having one of the largest reserves of precious minerals on the continent.

Indirect Company Rule

Cecil John Rhodes, a British entrepreneur, after whom the famous scholarships to Oxford University are named, went to South Africa in the late 1800s. He had a long list of different personal and public goals to accomplish, the most ambitious of which was to extend British colonial rule from Cape Town to Cairo. He just about succeeded. Besides making a fortune by acquiring control over most of the world's diamonds and gold, Rhodes, in a period of just ten years from 1885 to 1895, had

> acquired two countries, Southern Rhodesia (now Zimbabwe) and Northern Rhodesia (now Zambia), that bore his name. He gave British protection to Botswana and Malawi, almost took Mozambique from the Portuguese and Shaba [a province of the Democratic Republic of Congo] from King Leopold of the Belgians, kept Lesotho independent, and prevented Paul Kruger's Afrikaner-dominated Transvaal from expanding far beyond its traditional borders.[28]

On arrival in southern Africa, after a brief and less-rewarding dalliance with growing cotton as a commercial crop, Rhodes got into mining, becoming extremely wealthy and acquiring enormous political power as prime minister of the Cape Province. In 1888, he decided to expand the British empire with hopes of duplicating the economic success that he had just had in South Africa. He sent several aides, led by his business partner, Charles Rudd, north to negotiate for some mineral rights with an African king by the name of Lobengula of the Ndebele people. There was a sense of urgency to this trip. There were other mining concession seekers in the area. Lobengula was a very powerful king. Rhodes felt that if he could get there first and obtain the mineral rights, the rest of that region would be easy to add to the British empire. Through trickery—by assuring the king that Rhodes and his associates were not interested in land but only in digging for gold—against an African king who could neither read nor write and who decided to trust his advisers, who included a prominent missionary, Rhodes' aides obtained an agreement, the Rudd Concession, granting him the right to mine in present-day Zimbabwe. This is what Rhodes promised to the Ndebele king and what he got in the Rudd Concession:

> The Rudd Concession begins with a promise to pay Lobengula £100 in British currency a month and to provide 1,000 Martini Henry breech loading rifles, together with 100,000 rounds of suitable ammunition. The first 500 of the rifles and 40,000 of the cartridges were to be delivered with reasonable dispatch, the remainder to be conveyed "so soon as the ... grantees shall have commenced to work mining machinery" within Lobengula's domain. Rudd also promised to place an armed steamboat on the Zambezi (or if Lobengula wanted it instead, £500). In exchange, the king assigned Rudd and company "the complete and exclusive charge over all metals and minerals situated and contained in my Kingdoms Principalities and dominions together with full power to do all things that they may deem necessary to win and procure the same and to hold and collect and enjoy the profits and revenue ... from ... metals and minerals." Lobengula also gave Rudd and his partners authority to exclude all others seeking land or prospecting privileges from his kingdom.[29]

Armed with the agreement, Rhodes set up a private company, the British South Africa Company, and applied for a royal charter. The charter gave him the right to administer the area comprising modern-day Zimbabwe, Zambia, and Malawi. In 1890, Rhodes' men set off for the area and on September 12, 1890, they hoisted the Union Jack in a town they named Salisbury (now Harare, the capital of Zimbabwe). Lobengula soon realized what had been done to him and to his country as white settlers started streaming in and seizing African lands to settle on. He attacked the new settlers in 1893 but was beaten badly. A bloodier and more widespread rebellion followed in 1896–1897, involving both the Ndebele people and the Shona (from whom the Ndebele had conquered the territory), but it, too, was crushed savagely. From about 1890 to 1923, the British South Africa Company set up a colonial administration—bureaucracy, police, and tax collection under his company but used the British model of indirect rule that has been discussed. There were powerful kingdoms, such as the Barotse in what is now Zambia, which were recognized as indigenous authorities by Rhodes and later given separate colonial identities as British protectorates. Political functionaries in the employ of the private company reported to the British Colonial Office as though they were government appointees. In 1923, the company colony of Rhodesia became a de facto self-governing colony, allowing the local white residents to run the colony without any interference from the Colonial Office in London. Local white settlers expected ultimately to be granted independence by the British in the same way that the whites in South Africa had been. It was even envisaged that a federal arrangement with South Africa might come about to include the other British colonies in the area, namely, Botswana, Lesotho, and Swaziland. Failing that, the white leaders in Zimbabwe certainly expected to rule over Malawi and Zambia. In the mid-1950s, a short-lived federation—called the Central African Federation—composed of Malawi, Zambia, and Zimbabwe was inauguarated, dominated by white authorities based in Zimbabwe. That development prompted the African nationalist movement in the federation to change their tactics, break up, and begin pressing for African rule for each country separately rather than for the whole federation.

THE ECONOMICS OF COLONIALISM

The specific economic policies and practices of the colonial powers lend strong credence to the economic theory of imperialism, namely, that colonization had everything to do with greed and very little, if at all, to do with race or religion. What we have tried to show is that there were other important dimensions to the phenomenon of colonialism, and that, moreover, there was a dynamic intercorrelation among the factors involved. The seven specific economic policies and practices that we are going to discuss are the following:

1. expropriation of land
2. exploitation of labor
3. the introduction of cash crops and the one-crop economy
4. unfair taxation
5. the introduction of immigrant labor from India
6. transfer of mineral wealth from Africa to Europe, and
7. the lack of industrialization.

Expropriation of Land

No one said it better than Lord Hailey when describing the importance of land to African people:

> It is not easy for those who know only the industrialized countries of the Western world to realize the significance of the position occupied by the land in the eyes of most of the peoples of Africa. Anthropologists have described the mystic bond which unites the African to the home of those ancestral spirits who continue, as he believes, to play an active part in

his daily life. Jurists point out that the tribal Chief derives his authority largely from the fact that he is in war the traditional defender of the lands of the tribe and in peace the arbiter of the differences which arise regarding their use.[30]

As already described in Chapter 2, land was communally owned. People exercised the right to use it and *not* to own it or dispose of it as they saw fit. It is this custom of communal ownership of land and the belief that land was not a commodity, or simply an economic factor of production that could be bought and sold, which made African people extremely sensitive to what the Europeans did once they gained control. What colonizers did was to determine the choicest land available and take it. The rationalization for taking the land was often based on the Western juridical idea that government has the right to take any land it wishes in the public interest. The government was not representative of the Africans and had not been set up by them; the colonial government simply took it upon itself that it was acting in the best interests of the "natives," whether the Africans knew it or not. Another reason given for taking African land was that the Africans had given it away through agreements or treaties. The interpretation of such treaties was the prerogative of the colonial government, regardless of what the African chiefs thought. In most of these cases, the chief thought he was granting the newcomers the right to use the land, *not* to own it or dispose of it. The third reason for grabbing African land was that it belonged to no one because when the colonizers arrived, no one was occupying it at the time. This interpretation was clearly unacceptable to Africans who, in most cases, may have used the land before and simply moved to another location to give the land time to renew itself. Whatever the official reason might have been, European appropriation of African land was ultimately based on the climate and the quality of the soil and on future prospects for farming the area.

In West Africa, due largely to an inhospitable climate, European immigration was not encouraged. For that reason, very little land was taken away from the Africans. In general, less than 0.5 percent of the land was taken away compared to much more in other parts of Africa. In Ghana, about 5 percent of land was taken from the African people due to the mining concessions. In Nigeria, the Royal Niger Company established large farms to produce coffee and palm oil. In east, central, and southern Africa, where some climates were more pleasant, some soils more fertile, and some environments more suitable for European settlement, colonial authorities encouraged white immigration. Incentives were provided in the form of free ninety-nine-year leases and low interest loans. Land acquired by colonial settlers ranged from a few hundred acres to hundreds of thousands of acres. Among the wealthiest entrepreneurs and British settlers with the largest landholdings in colonial Kenya, for instance, were Lord Delamere and Captain E. S. Grogan. Lord Delamere had been lured to Africa with an initial offer of 100,000 acres of land (ten times over the limit that had been set by the colonial administration) and Captain Grogan with 64,000 acres. Africans who had occupied those lands before the Europeans arrived were no longer allowed to hunt or fish on those lands, even if they were not being worked at the time. Trespassing ordinances were strictly enforced. Complaints sent to the colonial authorities in Europe by the affected Africans were ignored. Kenyatta was one of the Africans sent by his people to press the British government personally for the return of land to their rightful African (Kikuyu) owners. He lived in Britain from 1929 to 1946 during which time he married a British woman, studied at the London School of Economics, and lectured to British audiences on conditions in colonial Kenya, winning a lot of sympathy for the African cause among British liberals in the Labour Party and the Fabian Society. Nevertheless, he was totally unsuccessful in his mission to have the British government address the land issue. Upon returning to Kenya, despite his acknowledged position as the leader of the Kenyan people, he never was able to impose the moderate tone that had hitherto characterized the African movement in Kenya. As calls for African freedom increased and the nationalist movement grew in strength, the loss of land became the most serious grievance of the Kenyan people against colonial authorities.

Exploitation of Labor

It soon became clear that the settlers did not have adequate manpower to work the land and would have to decide on measures to generate the needed labor. Some Africans, realizing that they could not live off their land anymore, signed up to work for the white farmers; others moved into the burgeoning towns and trading centers to look for other types of work; yet others migrated elsewhere. Working conditions were horrendous. A publication in 1931 in Kenya reported that it was "accepted as a matter of course that farmers, planters and estate managers shall on occasion inflict corporal punishment, usually with a whip made of rhino hide ... for insolence, theft, desertion, laziness, breakages, or what not."[31] It was not uncommon for white farmers to guard their workers with rifles, firing in the air occasionally or at the workers' feet to terrorize them into working harder. Wages were extremely low, insufficient to make much difference in the lives of the Africans. Wages were determined exclusively by the farmers, later by the colonial governments completely dominated by the settlers themselves, and were based on the amount of work done. In patterns repeated by farm laborers everywhere, it often took a male worker, his wife, and children to complete the day's allotment of work. Only the male worker got paid. The payment was partly in cash and partly in food rations. Farmwork was not that attractive and shortages of labor persisted. Something had to be done. A labor policy was badly needed.

However, many Europeans settled in Africa were not enough to maximize the wealth extraction that the colonial authorities wanted. In a number of places, the British were able to use the existing indigenous landlords. Freund says,

> Where they appeared as obvious alternatives to settlers in certain parts of Africa, the colonial regimes dreamt of transforming native aristocracies into capitalist farmers and improving landlords. Such landlords had often been able to command tribute, tax and labour from a dominated population in the past.[32]

Zanzibar and Buganda provide good examples of such attempts by the British to coopt African landlords. At one time, for example, there were nearly 4,000 estates in the kingdom of Buganda owned by the Africans themselves, producing cotton for export. The export crop in Zanzibar was cloves.

Hut and Poll Tax

There were actually two reasons for introducing taxes in colonial Africa. One was to raise revenue to pay for the cost of running a government in the colonies and also for rudimentary services for the small settler communities. It was the policy of colonial powers that the colonies should shoulder an increasing share of the financial burden of running colonies, instead of having to rely on appropriations from the metropole. The need to generate local revenue grew even stronger following World War II, when European countries were nearly bankrupt from the war. The second reason was to coerce more Africans into the labor market. Even though colonial authorities argued that the imposition of taxes had nothing to do with trying to exploit African labor, that it was only for raising revenue, and that Africans had ample opportunity to refuse to work, the relationship between tax and the demands for labor cannot be denied. The tax had to be paid in European currency, and the only way one could obtain the currency was by joining the colonial labor force, either as a laborer on a European farm or as a worker for a business in town. The first type of tax to be introduced was the hut tax, levied on each hut found in a typical African homestead. In Kenya, the hut tax was introduced in 1901, about the same time in other parts of Africa. The hut tax yielded more workers, but not enough. There was quite a bit of resistance to the tax. It inflicted hardship on the Africans and was disruptive to their traditional way of life, depleting their traditional means of livelihood. The Maasai people in East Africa, who had a tremendous amount of wealth in their cattle, were forced to sell their livestock to obtain the cash to pay their taxes. Since the Africans knew that the money collected was not being used for their own benefit, in some communities, as a way of demonstrating their opposition to taxes, the people determined how much tax they had been assessed and sent only enough workers to earn the amount required to pay the tax and then quit. In response to this kind of resistance, the colonial authorities passed (in 1910, in Kenya) a poll tax, which was levied on each African male aged sixteen and older. There was much abuse in the collection of these taxes, as young men not older than sixteen, but judged so by African recruitment agents and unable to pay, would be hauled off to work camps for failure to pay the tax. The elders of homesteads were responsible for both the hut tax and poll tax. In Zaire and Portuguese colonies, the colonial authorities levied extra charges in an effort to use taxes to discourage men from having extra wives, but this disincentive seems not to have been successful. In any event, the net impact of the extra taxes was that more Africans signed up for work.

Labor Conscription

The labor shortage continued to plague the colonies from the turn of the century onward and especially between the two world wars. In East Africa, the end of World War I coincided with an increase in European immigrants. Many of the new arrivals were war veterans encouraged to settle in the colonies and awarded choice land for their sacrifices in the war. The new immigrants needed farm laborers. Existing industries and businesses needed workers to restart their operations after the war. The colonial government also wanted laborers to work on railroads, harbors, and other capital projects. Forced labor conscription, therefore, was initiated as government policy. Africans would be signed up by government labor bureaus that would send trucks into villages and towns. Labor recruits would then be transported many miles from their homes for periods ranging from a few months to a couple of years. Moreover, African chiefs and village headmen were enlisted to produce assigned quotas of workers. Thousands upon thousands of laborers were recruited in this way. For instance, every year between the 1920s and the 1950s, over 40,000 workers were forcibly recruited to work in Rhodesian mines. Conditions of work, as already described, were terrible, the pay was extremely poor, and many of the workers died from either work-related accidents or diseases contracted in the work camps. Davidson estimates that in the space of thirty three years between 1900 and 1933, about 30,000 African workers died in the Rhodesian mines.[33] All the European colonial powers employed forced labor, although there were laws on the books prohibiting it and from time to time questions would be raised about the issue of forcing Africans to work against their will. In the French empire, forced labor did not stop until after World War II. In the Portuguese empire, it continued right up to the time the Africans began to fight for their independence in the early 1960s.

Both in the case of tax and forced conscription, it was virtually impossible for the Africans to resist. If you did not pay your tax, you were picked up by the administrative police (who roamed villages looking for tax evaders), speedily convicted, and sentenced to hard labor, which meant that you would end up working on the same projects as those who had signed up. As convict labor, you did not get paid. If you tried evading conscription, you were harassed and hunted down by the labor bureau or the chief's police, determined to make sure that their chief's quota of conscript labor was met. When you were caught, your situation was that much worse for having tried to resist the order to sign up. Either way, you ended up providing the labor that was sought.

Again, there were all kinds of reasons adduced for forcing people to sign up for work. The rationalization was that Africans, deemed traditionally lazy, were being taught the value of hard work (even though the work did not benefit them directly), that it was right for the government to compel people to work on projects that were in the public interest such as roads, railroads, and other capital projects (again even though the people did not directly benefit). The chiefs played an important role in the forced labor draft. Labor conscription accelerated the African people's perception that the chiefs were part and parcel of the colonial establishment. Many of them were, more than ever before, alienated from their own people.

There were four main consequences of labor conscription that deserve mention. One was the disruption that the practice caused to Africans and their way of life. Able-bodied men were separated from their families for long periods of time. This was psychologically stressful, especially to the old men, women, and children left behind. Second, the draft meant that the most healthy of the workers in the village were often the ones taken to the labor camps. The result was a lack of productive manpower in the villages. Food production declined significantly. Famine resulted. Third, the conscripts were men. That meant that the camps were invariably all-men facilities much like the South African mine workers' hostels still are today. When many men were separated from their families for long periods of time, activities like prostitution and male homosexuality flourished. Prostitution near the labor camps meant that the little money that the workers made sometimes ended up being spent on beer or procuring the sexual favors of the women. Last, the labor draft served to alienate the chiefs from their own people, a development that eroded their authority, undermined traditional institutions and relationships, and proved problematical in later political development.

Cash Crops and One-Crop Economies

Because the whites were mainly interested in commercial crops to meet the industrial needs of their home countries, they introduced cash crops such as cocoa, coffee, sisal, tea, and cotton. West African countries like Ghana,

Ivory Coast, Nigeria, and Cameroon, which were suitable for growing coffee and cocoa, specialized in those crops. Uganda and Kenya grew coffee and cotton; Tanzania grew sisal and cotton. Countries like Ghana, Zaire, and the Rhodesias (i.e., Zambia and Zimbabwe) that had minerals were mined extensively. Vast amounts of land were devoted to cash crops. Two main points are worth noting here. First, cash crops were not food crops and food crops were neglected, with the result that famine began to occur in areas that had been previously self-sufficient in food production. Second, the specialization in cash crops meant that the colonial economy came to be based on a single crop or two crops, with serious consequences for the economy of Africa after colonization formally ended. To accentuate the exploitation, the Africans who wanted to join in the growing of the cash crops to benefit themselves found that they could not because they were not allowed to compete against the colonial settlers. Africans in Kenya, for instance, were not allowed to grow tea or coffee until the 1950s, when it had become obvious that the days of colonial rule were numbered. In West Africa, African farmers grew cash crops. Some prospered, especially those able to use laborers from the weaker and more fragmented ethnic groups. Many did not, particularly if they did not fill the quotas assigned. If one's quota for a current year could not be filled, one had a bigger quota to fill the following year. Some farmers used their own resources to buy crops from others in order to meet their assigned quota. They also encountered another obstacle: lack of credit. As Davidson says,

> ... even the most successful farmers often got into debt because their costs of production were not covered by the prices they were paid. Their debt was made worse by the general lack of any proper facilities for borrowing money from banks. Even the Gold Coast's (Ghana's) cocoa farmers, though producing most of the world's cocoa in those times, were often in debt, largely because they had no access to cheap credit.[34]

Finally, all the cash crops grown had to be exported to the "mother country," at a price that was set by the parastatal monopoly of the colonial government.

Prohibition of Inter-African Trade and Communications

Before colonization, Africans had been trading and bartering with each other. All inter-African trade came to an abrupt stop with the advent of the colonial era. Any trade was to be carried out only with the European powers. French colonies traded with France. British colonies with Britain; Portuguese colonies with Portugal, and so on. As we have already seen, African countries became producers of cash crops or minerals destined for European markets and factories. The skeletal infrastructure that was set up to service this trade was oriented toward Europe. All communications and banking facilities were integrated into those of the colonial power. It was impossible for two Africans who lived in two African towns separated by a colonial border to speak with each other directly on the phone. A phone call from Kilembe, Uganda, would have to go to London, England, then to Brussels, Belgium, and then to Kilembe in the Democratic Republic of Congo. And it would be prohibitively expensive. Money used was in European currencies and therefore not easily obtainable or exchangeable. The long-term consequence of this arrangement was that African countries and communities were cut off from each other. Even today, it is still easier to fly from Africa to Europe than between African countries. African economies were so intertwined with the economies of European colonial powers that, after independence, African states could not really trade with each other. All were producing primary products and not what other African countries needed. They could not trade with one another when they were producing the same agricultural products or mining minerals that they did not have the technology or the knowledge to process. It has taken more than thirty years for African states to begin to diversify their economies as well as their trading partners and to begin to change the communication facilities so that they can communicate directly with each other. The setting up of this dependent economic relationship may not have been a deliberate conspiracy to undermine the economic viability of independent African states, but the results show clearly that Europe did not have the Africans' interests in mind when they colonized them.

Immigrant Labor

As was alluded to earlier, European colonial powers continued to experience difficulties with African labor. Europeans thought that Africans were averse to hard work and that they were unable to adapt to the new social and economic order being introduced by the colonial powers. The British and the French did not fully realize the political significance of the African resistance to colonial labor policies. African behavior had nothing to do with sheer laziness. Indeed African people who were given opportunities to benefit significantly from the colonial economy, such as West African cocoa farmers, coffee growers in northern Tanzania, or cotton producers in Uganda, worked very hard and prospered. At any rate, the British, who controlled such a vast worldwide empire, decided to alleviate their labor problems in Africa by inviting contract laborers from the Asian subcontinent. Indians by the thousands were shipped into East Africa and southern Africa on contracts of up to ten years. Others came in on their own, sensing better times overseas than in their crowded homelands. They had heard of the successes of Indian merchants who had first come to the East African coast, around Mombasa and on the island of Zanzibar, from the early 1800s. Many of the Indians worked on construction jobs, as bus and train drivers, policemen, and civil servants.

When their contracts expired, some went back to India, but many elected to stay, and over the next forty to fifty years became beneficiaries of British favoritism. Economic incentives were provided in the form of loans. Because many of them were literate and skilled in business when they came, Indians found opportunities in Africa that they did not have back in their own country. They undoubtedly worked hard, but drew heavily upon cheap labor provided by Africans who, at the turn of the century, were beginning to flock to towns and trading centers. There was plenty of room for business expansion, and they did expand, setting up distribution centers and retail outlets in remote villages of the African countryside. Moreover, as migrant workers, Indians gave little trouble to the British. By being willing to perform some of the more unpleasant official tasks of running the colonies, the Indians helped insulate the British from direct contact with the Africans. The Indians' inward-looking cultural tendency to keep to themselves and to interact with Africans only in impersonal capacities as traders, employers, or government officials, their racist attitudes toward Africans (which were fed to them by Europeans), and their eventual control of the local economies in African countries tended to increase African resentment toward them. Later, when Africans began to agitate for independence, many Indians wavered when asked to join in the struggle. Those who joined, underwriting African publications in Kenya such as *Sauti ya Mwafrika* (The African Voice) and *Habari za Dunia* (World News)—so important in the mobilization of African opinion against colonial rule—were fully embraced by the African people.[35] Some Indians seemed openly to favor the status quo under British rule rather than submit to what they perceived as an uncertain future under untested African leadership.

The shipping of Indians to Africa had two important long-term effects that continue to reverberate across the African landscape. One is that Indians came to dominate the African countries' local economies to the extent that it was virtually impossible for Africans to break in. The Indians dominated the external and internal retail trade, they were favored by banks insofar as credit was concerned, and they enjoyed the support of the colonial government. In addition, most of their businesses were family-owned and, therefore, difficult to police or regulate. A very strong impression was created that the Indians did not care about the African people and were out only to exploit them as much as possible. Secondly, because many Indians did so well commercially under British rule and prospered, they seemed to equivocate on the issue of the struggle for independence. Africans accused Indians of being anti-African, of having favored colonialism, and of not having the African countries interests' at heart. The fact that many Indians opted for British (paper) citizenship, while continuing to reside in African countries, confirmed the Africans' worst suspicions about Indians. This simmering misunderstanding and mistrust between the two groups broke out into the open when, in the early 1970s, Idi Amin Dada (the former Ugandan dictator) chose to expel all Asians from Uganda, including those who had taken up Ugandan citizenship. Amin was wildly cheered by the African people for that decision. Tension persists between Indians and Africans to this day in countries like Kenya, Zambia, and Zimbabwe. In recent years, Indian Kenyans have become more active politically by running for parliament and gone into business partnerships with wealthy African Kenyans.

Lack of Industrialization

Finally, of the many plans that the colonial powers had for civilizing and modernizing Africa, none of them seem to have included modernization. Indeed, in light of our discussion of colonial practice, it would have been a contradiction in terms if industrialization had been actively pursued by the Europeans in Africa. Raw materials like coffee, cotton, and cocoa were badly needed for processing in the factories of Europe. This pattern of Africa producing raw materials to be processed in Europe, and then re-exporting finished products to Africa at prices that Africans could ill afford, has continued to characterize a substantial proportion of economic relations between Africa and Europe to this very day.

However, when it became clear following the end of World War II that colonial rule might be nearing its end, colonial powers began to think of ways to revitalize the economies of the colonies. Some African scholars have argued that this limited economic development was undertaken to persuade the new emerging leaders that colonization had benefited Africans and somehow to allow an amicable departure from Africa that would preserve colonial interests. This point will be discussed at some length in the subsequent chapter on decolonization and the struggle for independence.

COLONIAL RULE: DID THE AFRICANS BENEFIT?

As to whether colonization hurt or helped the African people is a subject both Africans and Europeans have very strong feelings about. It is an issue that will continue to engage the intellectual passions of scholars and may never be resolved fully. Much of the foregoing discussion on colonization focused on the negative side of the ledger. Let us summarize these points and then note in conclusion some of the positive contributions that colonization made to Africa.

On the negative side, the following points are salient and worth noting. There was massive exploitation of Africa in terms of resource depletion, labor exploitation, unfair taxation, lack of industrialization, the prohibition of inter-African trade, and the introduction of fragile dependent one-crop or one-mineral economies. The exacerbation of ethnic rivalries, which the British, especially, through the implementation of the colonial policy of "indirect rule," exploited in furthering colonial control, has continued to echo in post-independence conflicts in Africa. The alienation and undermining of traditional African authority patterns through the use of chiefs for colonial duties made the task of nation-building much more difficult. The creation of artificial boundaries has been the basis of much suffering in African states as political conflicts have flared up from time to time on account of territorial claims and counterclaims. The destruction of African culture and values through the imposition of alien religions and the relentless attack on African values mounted by mission schools contributed to a mentality of ennui and dependency and to the loss of confidence in themselves, their institutions, and their heritage. (The long-term consequence of self-hate is reflected and discussed in Franz Fanon's writings.) The denial of political participation to colonized Africans has retarded postcolonial political development, as the excessive use of force in addressing political problems has been carried over to the postcolonial period.

There are some political leaders who feel that on balance the Africans benefited from colonial experience. Interestingly, leaders of the two countries that were never formally colonized by Europe—the late Emperor Haile Selassie of Ethiopia and the late President William V. S. Tubman of Liberia—tried to explain away their countries' economic poverty by saying that they never benefited from colonization like other African countries. There are other leaders, notable among them, Ivory Coast's founding president, Felix Houphouet-Boigny, who feel that Africans ought to be grateful for having been colonized, because without colonization, Africa would still be backward in many areas of human endeavor.

Broadly speaking, there are five benefits of colonization that many scholars are likely to agree on. First is the introduction of Western medicine, which has made an incredible difference in the survival rates of the African population. In fact, the rapid growth of the African population began during the colonial era. Second, the introduction of formal education, anti-African as it might have been in so many countries, deserves mention in helping to broaden the Africans' outlook and to unlock the hidden potential of the African people. Both education and health care were provided by missionaries. Nearly all leaders who emerged after World War II to lead African colonies toward independence acquired their rhetorical and organizational skills from colonial education. Young political activists were able to challenge the status quo and to make demands for the restoration of African dignity and freedom by using political and moral ideas deeply rooted in Western education. Third, the small infrastructure that colonial authorities established became the foundation upon which new African leaders built their new national institutions. Roads, railroads, harbors, telephones, electric power, and water and sewerage systems were all built initially to service the white colonial community or to support the very small urban settlements. Africans acquired important skills by working for colonial bureaucracies. Later, their experience was important in helping to maintain these services during the often tumultuous period of political transition and afterwards. Fourth, the introduction of Islam and Christianity to African people greatly simplified African spirituality and created a new basis for Africans with diverse backgrounds to come together. Africans are a very spiritual people who believed in God and in life after death with ancestral spirits. It was unclear, however, what one needed to do in order to find salvation (defined as being one with God or being completely at peace after one died and passed on into the spirit world). The role of ancestral spirits was extremely significant and called for continual, elaborate rituals to pacify or supplicate them. This kind of spiritual heritage, while satisfying emotionally and spiritually, did, in many ways, stunt the development of rational thought and science.

Modern Christianity, despite its residual mysticism, was presented as a complete and self-contained package of rules and procedures. It defined in simple terms why human beings were created, the existence of eternal life after death, and how to live one's life on earth in such a way as to be assured of a wonderful life after death. Embracing one of these Christian denominations, in exchange for giving up their spiritual heritage and practice, the Africans freed themselves substantially from the uncertainties of daily sacrifices, rituals, and cleansing ceremonies that were traditionally required. The African was liberated from the belief that everything that happened to one in life was due entirely to the intervention of the spirits, a belief that required frequent consultation of the mediums in order to determine what one had to do to pacify those spirits and was also exceedingly fatalistic. Inherent in this liberation was the notion of individual salvation. Although these foreign religions required their adherents to evangelize and win more converts to their beliefs, ultimately the individual was saved or damned on the basis of what he or she did or did not do in following the doctrines of the various faiths. This individualism, of course, undermined the collective ethos and the social fabric of the African traditional community, yet it also made individual progress and personal growth possible. Christianity and Islam also created a new basis for community organization and networking. And these religious organizations worked to improve living conditions of people in many areas. They promoted literacy, health care, and self-help. They created a new basis for Africans to come together and assist one another as they had traditionally done.

Fifth, by imposing arbitrary boundaries on the African people, countries were created with the stroke of a pen. Colonization may have shortened considerably the process of state formation in some areas. In past eras, states were formed slowly and painfully, as powerful leaders waged wars and annexed their weaker neighbors. There is ample evidence of military annexations having occurred in Africa and certainly elsewhere in the world. Since independence, some African states—Somalia and Ethiopia, Kenya and Somalia, Libya and Chad, Morocco and Algeria—have fought with each other over inherited borders. There have been brutal civil wars in Nigeria, Sudan, Somalia, Sierra Leone, Liberia, Democratic Republic of Congo, and Côte d'Ivoire, to name a few. African leaders hesitate to put the issue of colonial borders on the agenda. It would open a Pandora's box. If further flare-ups do not occur—which does not seem likely at the moment (2008), given the escalating crises in Rwanda, Zimbabwe, Darfur, and Chad—thereby saving the African people more pain, suffering, and death, colonialism can claim some credit.

NOTES

1. Thomas Henriksen, "Portugal in Africa: A Noneconomic Interpretation," *African Studies Review,* Vol. XVI, No. 3 (December, 1973), p. 406.
2. Ali A. Mazrui, "European Exploration and Africa's Self-Discovery," *The Journal of Modern African Studies,* Vol. 7, No. 4 (1969), pp. 661–666.
3. Thomas Henriksen, "Portugal in Africa," p. 406.
4. Ibid.
5. Margery Perham, *The Colonial Reckoning* (New York: Alfred A. Knopf, 1962), p. 127.
6. Edward G. McGrath, *Is American Democracy Exportable?* (Beverly Hills, CA: The Glencoe Press, 1968), p. 50.
7. Ibid.
8. Ibid., p. 52.
9. Michael Crowder, *Senegal: A Study in French Assimilation Policy* (New York: Oxford University Press, 1962), p. 2.
10. Janet G. Vaillant, *Black, French, and African: A Life of Léopold Sédar Senghor* (Cambridge, MA: Harvard University Press, 1990), p. 53.
11. Michael Dutfield, *A Marriage of Incovenience: The Persecution of Ruth and Seretse Khama* (London: Unwin Hyman, 1990), p. 4.
12. Ibid., p. 44.
13. Frantz Fanon, *Toward the African Revolution* (New York: The Grove Press, 1967), pp. 17–27.
14. Gerald J. Bender, *Angola under the Portuguese: The Myth and the Reality* (Berkeley: University of California Press, 1978), p. 4.
15. Eduardo Mondlane, *The Struggle for Mozambique* (Baltimore, MD: Penguin Books, 1969), p. 37.
16. Ibid., p. 40.

17. Patrice Lumumba, *Congo, My Country* (London: Pall Mall Press, 1961), pp. 11–12.
18. John Reader, *Africa: A Biography of the Continent* (New York: Alfred Knopf, 1998), p. 633.
19. Ibid., p. 653.
20. Ibid.
21. Ibid.
22. Bill Freund, *The Making of Contemporary Africa: Development of African Society since 1800* (Bloomington, IN: Indiana University Press, 1984), pp. 115–116.
23. John Reader, *Africa*, p. 652.
24. Adam Hochschild, *King Leopold's Ghost: A Story of Greed, Terror, and Heroism in Colonial Africa* (New York: Mariner Books, 1999), especially ch. 8, "Where There Aren't No Ten Commandments," pp. 115–139.
25. John Reader, *Africa*, p. 654.
26. Lord Hailey, *An African Survey*, Revised 1956 (New York: Oxford University Press, 1957), p. 217.
27. Ibid.
28. Robert I. Rotberg, *The Founder: Cecil Rhodes and the Pursuit of Power* (New York: Oxford University Press, 1988), p. 7.
29. Ibid., p. 262.
30. Lord Hailey, *An African Survey*, p. 685.
31. R. M. A. van Zwanenberg, *Colonial Capitalism and Labor in Kenya 1919–1939* (Nairobi, Kenya: East African Literature Bureau, 1975), p. 69.
32. Bill Freund, *The Making of Contemporary Africa*, p. 125.
33. Basil Davidson, *Modern Africa*, 2nd Edition (New York: Longman, 1989), p. 17.
34. Ibid., p. 18.
35. Dana April Seidenberg, *Uhuru and the Kenyan Indians: The Role of a Minority in Kenya Politics* (New Delhi: Vikas Publishing House, 1983).

African Nationalism and the Struggle for Freedom

The British prime minister Harold Macmillan gave a famous speech to the all-white South African parliament in February 1960, in which he declared that there was a wind of African consciousness blowing across the African continent which Europeans in Europe and in the diaspora (i.e., the white settlers in Africa) must recognize for what it was. Macmillan was raising an intriguing point: If colonization was good for Africans as the Europeans had been contending all along, why then did some Africans have to take up arms to fight for their freedom? Where did this political consciousness come from?

INTRODUCTION

African nationalism is a subjective feeling of kinship or affinity shared by people of African descent. It is a feeling based on shared cultural norms, traditional institutions, racial heritage, and a common historical experience. One enduring historical experience shared by nearly all Africans was colonial oppression, discussed in the previous chapter. Along with this sense of shared identity is a collective desire to maintain one's own cultural, social, and political values independent of outside control.

It is worth stressing that African nationalism, like nationalism elsewhere in the world, is not new; it is as old as ancient times. In fact, in Africa, contrary to a common view in Western scholarship of Africa, African nationalism pre-dates colonialism. In the annals of African history, one finds coherent organized African communities with a very strong sense of identity, prepared to defend their territorial and cultural integrity against those who would want to destroy or undermine them. For instance, when the great African king Mansa Musa of Mali was on a pilgrimage to Mecca in 1324–1325, the Wolof people—who had been forcibly brought under the Mali kingdom—seized the opportunity to rebel against the Mali kingdom. The Wolof people were expressing a nationalism, a separate national identity and a desire to govern themselves in their own land. We also know that Africans did not passively accept European rule, which was alien and destructive of the African social order. The effective resistances put up against European colonization by the Ashanti people of Ghana, the Hehe of Tanzania, or the Zulus of South Africa suggest a very strong sense of national identity that was already in place—and a fierce determination not to succumb to any other authority but their own. The king of the Yao people in Tanzania had this to say to a German commander who had been sent to him to affirm the German colonial claim to his country in 1890:

> I have listened to your words but can find no reason why I should obey you—I would rather die first.... If it should be friendship that you desire, then I am ready for it, today and always; but to be your subject, that I cannot be.... If it should be war you desire, then I am ready, but never to be your subject.... I do not fall at your feet, for you are God's creature just as I am ... I am Sultan here in my land. You are Sultan there in yours. Yet listen, I do not say to you that you should obey me; for I know that you are a free man.... As for me, I will not come to you, and if you are strong enough, then come and fetch me.[1]

A Ghanaian king, Prempeh I of Asante, in the same tone, declined the British offer of protection—a euphemism for colonial control. He said that his kingdom wished to remain on friendly terms with all white people, and to do business with them, but he saw no reason why the Asante kingdom should ever commit itself to such a policy with the British government. The British took over the country anyway, the king was exiled for several years to an Indian Ocean island for noncooperation, and violent tensions between the Ashanti people and the British continued for ninety years, well into the beginning of the twentieth century. The king of the Mossi people of Burkina Faso told a French captain: "I know the whites wish to kill me in order to take my country, and yet you claim that they will help me to organize my country. But I find my country good just as it is. I have no need of them. I know what is necessary for me and what I want. I have my own merchants.... Also consider yourself fortunate that I do not order your head to be cut off. Go away now, and above all, never come back."[2] The French never went away and the Mossi lost their country. A leader of the Nama people in modern Namibia told the Germans: "The Lord has established various kingdoms in the world. Therefore I know and believe that it is no sin or crime that I should wish to remain the independent chief of my land and people."[3] The Germans were not impressed either. Westerners, for their own reasons, chose to call these groups "tribes," despite the fact that many of them were extremely large with well-structured social and political institutions. Ample evidence shows that these groups were nations occupying specific territories that they were willing to defend, if threatened or attacked. The sentiments expressed by the kings and leaders demonstrate nothing but nationalism by a people who wanted either such relations with foreigners as exist between equals or to be left alone.

Group sentiments that emerged in Eastern Europe following the collapse of communism are clearly manifestations of nationalism, not unlike what one would have seen in Africa on the eve of the European scramble for the continent. When the Soviet Union collapsed, its former republics split off, some of them facing internal conflicts as various groups sought to retreat into their linguistic or cultural enclaves. Yugoslavia disintegrated, throwing its people into a nasty civil war. Czechoslovakia divided in 1992 with agreement to split into two countries: the Czech Republic and Slovakia. What binds all these groups is a common heritage, based on religion, language, and historical experience. The historical experience of living under foreign hegemony or being governed by political parties thought to be manipulated by an outside power has been a potent driving force behind national secessionist attempts in Eastern Europe as well as in modern Africa.

MODERN AFRICAN NATIONALISM

After colonial rule had been firmly established, Africans continued to exhibit many forms of disaffection and resistance. Because Africa had been sliced into different colonies, as the resistance coalesced, organizations formed to protest various elements of colonial rule were often based on the territory under one colonial power (such as France, Britain, or Germany). Since it was virtually impossible for Africans to organize on a countrywide basis, regional or ethnic organizations became the most practical option. Because the colonizer was European and the colonized was African, such organizations came to be seen, particularly by outsiders, almost entirely in racial terms. It served the colonial powers' interests for them not only to play ethnic groups against one another but also to characterize the more militant or outspoken ones as being anti-white.

The Mau Mau uprising against British rule in Kenya is a perfect example of a movement that was presented in the Western media as an aimless, fanatically violent rebellion bent on killing and maiming any white person for the fun of it. Such a racial interpretation was simplistic and wrong. The goal of such an interpretation was to divorce the struggle from the legitimate grievances that undergirded it. As I have already pointed out, European colonizers had some racial motives for seizing African territories, but the Africans simply wanted their territories back and the freedom to live their lives as they saw fit. This surge in African nationalism was fueled by several catalytic factors besides the oppressive colonial experience itself: missionary churches, World Wars I and II, the ideology of Pan-Africanism, and the League of Nations/United Nations. Each of these factors will now be discussed.

Colonial Oppression

As was pointed out in the last chapter, colonization was mostly a negative, exploitative, and oppressive experience. Africans have bad memories of that experience, even though some may appear to have benefited materially. They were humiliated, their culture denigrated and distorted, and their land confiscated. European immigrants, who were encouraged to come to Africa as pioneer farmers and given large tracts of land to farm, forced Africans to provide cheap labor, which resulted in severe consequences for African communities. Large plantations were established for growing cash crops. How could anyone not expect Africans to resent this after a while? In fact, at the very beginning of colonial occupation, the African resistance took the form of armed revolt. The Temne and the Mende of Sierra Leone revolted against the hut tax. The Nama and the Herero people in Namibia revolted against German seizure of their land which, in turn, led to forced labor. In King Leopold's Congo, resistance to forced labor was so intense that labor recruiters were required to bring back with them severed human limbs and ears as proof that the Africans did not want to work virtually for free and were prepared to lose their limbs instead. These kinds of revolts were typical of "primary resistance," spontaneous and local uprisings. They were not militarily successful—for obvious reasons including the lack of a countrywide organizational base—and were brutally suppressed. Later, people adopted strategies that were more moderate and employed conventional means. Associations were formed for the purpose of addressing specific grievances: low wages, poor educational and health facilities, inadequate prices for cash crops grown by African farmers, lack of business opportunities, and absence of representation in local political councils. When these reforms were thwarted by colonial settlers who were loathe to spend any money on "natives," or to share any of their power with the Africans, or when the colonial officers in the metropole decided Africans were not yet ready for reforms, the Africans ultimately began to think about self-rule as their answer.

It has been suggested that the concept of political freedom was alien to the African people, that Africans were traditional and had no sense of democracy. African societies, to be sure, were collective societies in which the needs and rights of the communities as a whole preceded those of the individual. But collective ethos should not be equated to a lack of appreciation for personal freedom. As explained in Chapter 2, some African communities exercised a great deal of consultation in an atmosphere of unfettered debate and discussion. Leaders were chosen and held accountable for their actions. Those who resisted the wishes and demands of their people were often overthrown or replaced. In some societies, hereditary rule was permitted only so long as leaders performed according to standards accepted and sanctioned by their communities. When a leader was incompetent or betrayed the people's trust by being unfair or cruel, he was voted out and another leader chosen from a different house or family.

Missionary Churches

Christianity has been in Africa for a very long time, long before its proselytization brought European missionaries to Africa. The introduction of Christianity into Africa goes back to Roman times, when the Gospel writer Mark founded the Coptic Christian Church in Alexandria, as explained in Chapter 3. Islam became a far more widespread force from about the eighth century onward, aided by jihads (holy wars) against those who would resist conversion. Lucrative trade and immigration contributed to the Christian retreat into Ethiopia's highlands, where the Coptic Church survives to the present day.

The Catholic Church was introduced into Africa by the Portuguese in the late 1400s in Benin and was soon extended to Congo and Angola. At that time, Christian proselytizing seems to have been simply helpful in facilitating the establishment of Portuguese presence in Africa for commercial purposes. The African chiefs or kings that were approached also saw the political potential of using Christianity to unify their empires and strengthen their own positions. Richard Hull captures the mutuality of interests evident between the proselytizers and the traditional rulers as follows:

> Benin's Oba, or King, first encountered the Portuguese in 1486. European explorers were immediately impressed by the vastness of the empire, the strength of its rulers, and the possibility of transforming the state into a powerful Christian commercial [*sic*] ally. Benin, on the other hand, marvelled at the Portuguese items of trade such as modern weaponry and agricultural implements, fine cloth, and tales of a distant Portuguese empire. Both saw mutual advantages through the establishment of diplomatic relations....[4]

These relations between the Africans and the Portuguese (as explained in Chapter 3) later soured as the Portuguese began to pursue a more intrusive role in the internal political affairs of the kingdoms when they attempted to alter African customs such as polygyny (which allowed the king to maintain his power and influence by forming alliances). In other African countries, Christian missionaries either preceded the colonial takeovers or came in immediately after a country had been declared a colony. Colonial authorities found that Christianity had a pacifying effect on the African people, with its emphasis on spiritual matters over earthly affairs. Our lives in this world are so short, the missionaries would say, that it really does not matter what the colonial rulers do to us. What matters is what we do in preparation for the hereafter, for eternal life.

The Christian church also served to patch up the disintegrating African communities hit hard by colonial policy, without attacking the root causes of the disintegration. One such example was the devastating defeat suffered by Tanzanian people in the so-called Maji Maji Rebellion of 1905–1908. Africans chose to resist oppressive German colonialism. The Germans put down the revolt. When it was all over, 120,000 Africans had lost their lives. The destruction was so thorough that the Africans lost faith in their ancestral spirits also. They had been assured by their leaders that they would be duly protected by their ancestors in battle. In utter dismay and despondency, following their devastating defeat, most of these people turned to Christianity. The same phenomenon, the loss of faith in traditional religious institutions, is demonstrated in Sembene Ousmane's film *Emitai*, in which Africans in Senegal during World War II were forced "to volunteer" for the French Army and surrender their livelihood (rice) to the French colonial authorities. While the women hid the rice and were captured by French authorities and held hostage until they agreed to release the rice, their men, in hiding, were huddling together and making sacrifices to their ancestors and their gods, asking them to make sure that their livelihood would not be destroyed. Moreover, they believed that giving away the rice to the colonial authorities would be a serious violation of their social traditions. As the standoff continued, one by one the men began to falter in their faith. They began to wonder why, in this moment of critical need, their ancestral spirits would not come to their aid. Perhaps their gods were not true gods after all. Perhaps the doubts openly expressed by some of them may have incensed their gods, causing them to refuse to come to the people's rescue. The boycott collapsed. The men were held responsible for the rebellion and ultimately shot, despite having given in to French demands. Again here, as in the Tanzanian situation, Christianity offered solace in the face of a great national tragedy. The close symbiotic relationship between Christian missionaries and colonial authorities continued for the duration of colonial hegemony in Africa.

The catalytic role of the church in developing African nationalism arose from the education that the church schools provided in colonial Africa. In many African colonies, mission schools were the main educational institutions, and the expense of educating Africans was often borne entirely by the missions. In other colonies, the colonial government provided the funding, but the teaching staff and the curriculum were the responsibility of the missions.

Mission education had three modest goals: first, to provide the basic literacy that would enable Africans to absorb religious education and training and help in the spread of the Gospel; second, to impart the values of Western society, without which missionaries believed the Africans could not progress; and third, to raise the level of productivity of the African workers (both semiskilled and clerical) without necessarily empowering them sufficiently to challenge colonial rule. Mission education was, generally speaking, inadequate, especially in its emphasis on a religious education that Western society was already finding anachronistic. But, limited or flawed as it might have been, it was enough to whet the appetite of African people for more education and to pique their political consciousness. In central Kenya, for instance, the Kikuyu people were fascinated by the possibilities offered by a good education, but they were so dissatisfied with the missionary education provided by Anglican and Scottish missions that they began to found their own schools. African parents wanted the kind of education that would equip their children with more than just the ability to read the Bible and write in their own indigenous languages. They wanted their children to acquire the intellectual skills and language abilities necessary to fight for the land that had been taken away from their parents by European settlers and colonizers. Parents also wanted their children to succeed in the white man's world, the glimpse of which had been provided by colonial as well as missionary education. When colonial authorities restricted the number of African-run schools, some parents showed their defiance by keeping their children out of mission institutions.

Africans developed enormous respect for modern education. They believed, correctly, that colonial authorities were more likely to deal with an educated African spokesperson than one who was not. It helped a lot if an African emissary who was sent to plead the cause of his people happened also to be fluent in a relevant European language. In 1929, Jomo Kenyatta of Kenya was chosen by his people to go to England to present their grievances to British authorities. His people hoped that he would make a strong impression on the British and convince them that educated Africans, like himself, were not only ready to handle political responsibilities seriously but perhaps also able to run a government. During the long stay in England, Kenyatta studied at the University of London, producing *Facing Mount Kenya*, a book in which he not only interpreted Kikuyu life and culture to the Western world but also documented the cultural devastation that had occurred among the Kikuyu people at the hands of the colonial administration. Moreover, he made an impassioned case for his people's desire and right to regain their land and to govern themselves. In addition, he traveled all over Britain speaking to sympathetic British people willing to hear about colonial injustices in Kenya. Clearly, he contributed to the crystallization of British groups, such as the Fabian Society, as anticolonial organizations. These societies later not only lent their support to anticolonial organizations in the British empire but also contributed to the shifting opinion in Britain against continued colonialism. Kenyatta's rise to prominence and eventually to the leadership of Kenya was greatly assisted by his mastery of the English language.

Another African whose mastery and command of a European language became a pivotal factor in his political career was Léopold Sédar Senghor, the late first president of Senegal. Senghor was educated in Catholic mission schools in Senegal and later studied at the Sorbonne at the University of Paris. He rose through the ranks to become an important political figure in the French colonial system and, despite the intellectual controversy that attended his articulation of ideas such as negritude, he was a significant interpreter of African culture to the French-speaking world. Throughout his life, he enjoyed widespread respect and admiration as a philosopher, poet, and writer among French intellectuals and in the French-speaking world in general. In 1984, Senghor became the first African to be awarded membership in the exclusive French Academy. This is "the highest honor France can bestow on its statesmen and men [sic] of letters."[5]

Missionary education then had dual consequences for the Africans: it gave them skills with which to articulate their demands and question the legitimacy of colonial authorities; it also turned out to be a powerful medium of African acculturation of Western Christian (and political) values, values that the Africans very cleverly and ingeniously, to the utter surprise of his colonial master, incorporated into political debate over their struggles for freedom. As Ali Mazrui puts it, "The destruction of the 'pagan' African culture was naturally accompanied by attempts to replace it with *some* aspects of the English way of life. Next to making the boys and girls upright Christians, this was an important aim of the Christian educators."[6] He concludes that missionary education was perhaps far more successful at producing a new cultural African than a consistent Christian. The impact of the Christian church is evident all over the African continent.

The majority of the first generation of African leaders, among them Julius Nyerere (Tanzania), Jomo Kenyatta (Kenya), Léopold Senghor (Senegal), Kenneth Kaunda (Zambia), Nnamdi Azikiwe (Nigeria), and Hastings Kamuzu Banda (Malawi), were products of missionary education in their own countries. In South Africa, the Africans who organized the first nationwide political movement to address the needs of the Africans and to oppose the impending racist legislation being contemplated by the white minority government in 1912 were pastors. In Kenya, the independent schools that African religious leaders opened were quite political in terms of articulating the grievances of their people, as well as in combining local and Christian beliefs. Not surprisingly, the colonial government treated these schools as a very serious security risk.

Another sense in which the church influenced the growth of African nationalism was in the doctrine and content of its teachings. Christian doctrine stressed the spiritual kinship of people, the idea that all human beings, regardless of color and nationality, were God's children and equal in the eyes of God—therefore endowed with a right to treat each other, and to be regarded, with kindness and consideration. The church, however, failed to translate this doctrine into practice. It was contemptuous of Africans and their culture. It behaved as though it did not expect Africans to notice the contradiction between the benevolence of the doctrine and the virulence of the racism exhibited by some of the missionaries. In my thirteen years of missionary education in Africa, not once did I hear a priest or a monk utter a word of criticism of colonial rule. Indeed, student interest in political affairs and frequent discussion of political issues were frowned upon and often punished. The missionaries excluded the Africans from any meaningful role in running the churches. They maintained a discrete social distance from the Africans, interacting with them in a patronizing manner, and preaching the Gospel or teaching African school children simply as a job to do, not a sacred calling. Missionaries who had children, for instance, would send them abroad for education rather than to the same schools with African children. This may have been justified at the turn of the century when educational facilities in Africa were poor and primitive but not in the middle of the twentieth century. In eastern, central, and southern Africa, where European settlers had their own schools, the missionaries preferred to send their children to racially exclusive schools, never raising any moral objections to the existence of such segregated schools. Missionaries made few attempts to learn about and understand African traditions and values, although they wrote a great deal about Africans. They looked down upon African rituals, customs, and languages and, in some cases, deliberately attempted to destroy African institutions. Herskovits says,

> Other things being equal, Africans everywhere came to prefer schooling under secular auspices. One reason for this ... was that in lay schools they were less subjected to the continuous denigration of their own culture. In the mission schools, many aspects of African ways of life that continued to be highly esteemed, or were important for the functioning of society, particularly customs associated with sexual behavior and with marriage, fell under missionary disapprobation, and were attacked in the classroom.[7]

There was no attempt in such schools to consider points often raised in defense of certain African customs and rituals. When Africans, in defense of polygyny, pointed to the early Biblical tradition of polygamy, the missionaries responded simply by quoting the Church's dogma on monogamy as God's only sanctioned practice. When some sought to continue the veneration of their ancestral spirits along with Christian rituals, the missionaries threatened them with expulsion or excommunication from the church. Even the use of traditional music and dance in worship was severely discouraged as barbaric and heathen.

Except for scattered and isolated acts of defiance or opposition by a few missionaries toward forced labor or physical abuse of Africans, the churches, by and large, wanted Africans to believe that colonization was undertaken for the good of the Africans. They enunciated the "colonial purpose," whatever it was. Moreover, some missionaries served as apologists for colonial governments. For example, the Rev. Robert Moffat, a missionary in central Africa, is reported to have advised King Lobengula of the

Ndebele people to accept the Rudd Concession, even though he knew of Cecil Rhodes' ultimate imperial intentions to seize African lands north of the Limpopo River. Many Africans, of course, quietly endured this kind of treatment, believing that obedience, humility, and "turning the other cheek" were necessary for spiritual salvation. Others began to resent being treated like inferior human beings and decided that it was time to demand a voice in running religious institutions. They founded their own churches, separatist churches, where they could interpret the scriptures in ways that did not denigrate their cultures and their heritage and where the people could enjoy "religious self-expression." Such separatist churches included the Chilembwe church in Malawi, the Kimbangu and Kitawala churches in what is now called the Democratic Republic of Congo, and the Tembu church in South Africa. Colonialists called these churches "cults."

Dramatic examples of separatist Christian churches established with a clear political agenda are those that were built in central Kenya, having broken away from the Scottish and English missions. In addition to differences over doctrine, the Kenyans were concerned about colonial education in general:

> [Colonial education] was not designed to prepare young people for the service of their country. Instead, it was motivated by a desire to inculcate the values of the colonial society, and to train individuals for the service of the colonial state ...
>
> This meant that colonial education induced attitudes of human inequality, and, in practice, underpinned the domination of the weak by the strong especially in the economic field.[8]

Indeed, it came as no surprise at all, during the African uprising against the British known as the Mau Mau, that those schools run by the independent churches were singled out for punitive measures. They were accused of subversion, aiding and abetting Mau Mau "terrorism" and were closed down.

The anticlerical thread that runs through some African intellectual writing is attributable to this perception that Christian missions were anti-African and sympathetic to the colonial pillage of the African continent. Kofi Awoonor writes,

> The propagation of the Christian faith has always connoted the consolidation of imperial power. The Roman Emperor Justinian encouraged the Christianization of all African chiefs who sought his good will. He even bestowed investitures with robes and honorific titles for chiefs who embraced the Church. Religious propaganda was an essential aspect of imperial expansion, and the colonial powers had long grasped the important truth that it was cheaper in the long run to use the Bible than military power to secure distant dominions.[9]

The Christian church became an unwitting catalyst in the development of African nationalism by equipping the African intellectually to fight for his freedom and by presenting disparities between doctrine and practice in such a way as to arouse the African who expected equal and fair treatment after he was acculturated.

World Wars I and II

An African poet, Taban Lo Liyong, once said that Africans have three white men to thank for their political freedom and independence: Nietzsche, Hitler, and Marx; Nietzsche for contriving the notion of the superman, the master race; Hitler for trying to implement Nietzsche's idea in Germany with a view to extending it globally, thus setting off the most destructive war the world had ever witnessed; and Marx for raising the consciousness of the oppressed and colonized masses in Africa by universalizing the concept of economic exploitation of human beings.[10] Although Lo Liyong does not explicitly make the connection between African freedom and the three men, there is no denying the fact that both world wars had a tremendous impact on African nationalism in several important ways.

First of all, Africans were drafted to serve in both wars—a million of them in World War I and 2 million in World War II. The British alone were able to enlist about 700,000 Africans to fight on their side in World War II. The irony of using "unfree" Africans to fight against German imperialism and to die for the freedom of the allied countries was not lost on the African soldiers who saw military action in Europe, the Middle East, and Africa itself. They learned modern military skills in battle and demonstrated leadership abilities. Many of them performed acts of bravery and endurance that should have banished once and for all any racist notions that Africans, given a chance, could not measure up to Europeans. Once the war ended, African veterans felt that they had earned at least the right to be treated with respect. Basil Davidson quotes a Nigerian soldier who wrote home from India during the war:

> We all overseas soldiers are coming home with new ideas. We have been told what we fought for. That is 'freedom.' We want freedom, nothing but freedom.[11]

African veterans resented very much the lack of gratitude shown by their colonial masters. Many British veterans were rewarded for their part in saving Britain and her empire with generous pensions and offers of nearly free land in the colonies. The African soldiers were given handshakes and train tickets for the journey back home. They could keep their khaki uniforms and nothing else. These African soldiers, after returning home, were willing to use their new skills to assist nationalist movements fighting for freedom that were beginning to take shape in the colonies. Service in the colonial army made it possible for Africans from different regions of the same colony to meet and get to know one another, an important step in the breakdown of ethnic barriers and the development of shared identification with the country as a whole.

Beyond the military and leadership skills acquired, and the sharpening of contradictions inherent in colonized Africans fighting in wars to save their colonial masters from the tyranny of a fellow white man (Hitler), the two world wars had a very important psychological dimension. Because the conquest of Africa had been accomplished so thoroughly and so effectively, a myth of the white man's superiority and invincibility had developed. The white man, through his policy of racial segregation in the colonies and his harsh treatment of the "natives," had, in fact, nurtured this myth. He had behaved in Africa with impunity, as though there was nothing the African could do about it. The war experience changed all that, at least for the African soldiers who had fought side by side with the white man. The Africans noticed that, in war, the white man bled, cried, was scared, and, when shot, died just like anyone else. They also saw that he displayed a range of emotions and abilities that Africans knew they themselves had. It dawned on the African that beneath the skin, there was no difference between him and the European. In the words of the Zimbabwean nationalist Ndabaningi Sithole, "This discovery, for indeed it was an eye-opening discovery, had a revolutionizing psychological impact on the African."[12] From that point on, it would be impossible to convince the African that the European was some kind of "superman." African soldiers also heard about the spectacular military successes of the Japanese against the Russians; these exploits, of a presumably inferior non-European people, served to break the myth as well. The wars indeed helped fuel African nationalism.

On a personal level, this myth of white superiority was so embedded in my psyche that I was not even aware of it till I came to the United States. In Kenya, I had attended a racially segregated school for Africans. The European schools always did the best in national examinations followed by Asian schools. The African schools brought up the rear. It seems as though I had accepted the idea that Europeans were just naturally smarter than the other racial groups. During my first year in college in the United States, I took a freshman physics course in which I was the only black student. My white laboratory mate was not good in physics. I spent many hours helping him with laboratory exercises. I mentioned to a group of African students one evening that I was surprised at how slow this white student was. The African students broke out laughing. "What did you expect?" one of them asked. "They are just like us. Some of them are extremely bright, some of them are quite dumb." That is how my coming to the United States demythologized the white race for me. I now understand how racial segregation was used both in Kenya and elsewhere (especially in South Africa) to protect and perpetuate the myth of the inherent superiority of the white race. White people were afraid that if everyone were given an equal chance to compete or strive together, the myth simply could not hold together for long.

Finally, economic conditions deteriorated considerably in the colonies during and between the two world wars: high unemployment, accelerated rural–urban migration resulting in overcrowded cities, inadequate schools, and health facilities. All resources were diverted to the war effort, and Africans were coerced to produce more to feed Europe even as they were not producing enough to feed themselves. Africans were taxed more and forced labor became more widespread. European colonial powers were exhausted physically and economically after each world war. Thus, they were not willing or able to commit substantial resources to improving dire social and economic conditions in the African colonies. They were unwilling militarily to suppress nationalist movements that had been fuelled by the devastation of the war. After World War II, both Britain and France were looking for an honorable exit from Africa. Hitler, a man imbued with a racist ideology, determined to build a state of pure Aryans, precipitated World War II, and engaged his fellow Europeans to utter exhaustion in the most destructive and wasteful war the world had ever seen. It was certainly in this sense that poet Lo Liyong credited Hitler with helping to inspire the African struggle for independence.

Pan-Africanism

Three names often associated with Pan-Africanism are Henry Sylvester-Williams, W. E. B. DuBois, and Marcus Garvey. George Padmore gives credit to Sylvester-Williams, a West Indian barrister for originating the idea of Pan-Africanism, an ideology consisting of two key elements: the common heritage of people of African descent all over the world and the incumbency of African people to work for the interests and the well-being of one another everywhere. Sylvester-Williams, alarmed by the frantic extension of colonial rule all over Africa then underway and the racist treatment of Africans then living in London, decided to summon Africans to a meeting in 1900 to protest these actions to the British government and also to appeal to decent British people to do all they could "to protect the Africans from the depredations of the empire builders."[13] That meeting gave birth to the word "Pan-Africanism" to dramatize the need for them to work together to ameliorate conditions facing them as people of color. Shortly after the meeting, Sylvester-Williams returned to West Indies where he died within a year. The responsibility to continue the work begun by Sylvester-Williams then fell upon Dr. W. E. B. DuBois, an African American intellectual and political/social activist. It is ironic in a sense that a Pan-African movement, embodying the unity of all people of African descent, had its origins outside Africa, specifically in the United States and the Caribbean. DuBois felt that black people in the New World, in order to free themselves from racial discrimination and rampant racism, must reclaim their African roots and become proud of their heritage. He believed that people neither proud of who they are nor aware of where they came from could not successfully combat negative stereotypes being heaped upon them by other racial groups.

DuBois was moved to revive the Pan-African movement by two factors. One was the information coming out of Africa that showed that Africans were being severely mistreated for resisting colonial exploitation, especially in the Belgian Congo, where reports indicated that Africans refusing to sign up for labor were being physically tortured and mutilated. DuBois felt that something had to be done to stop this brutalization of Africans. The second factor was the need to seek some recognition for the important contributions that African veterans had made in World War I. Only European veterans were rewarded generously for their efforts, while the Africans who had fought valiantly and helped liberate German colonies were not honored in any way. Specifically, DuBois wanted the European powers to adopt a Charter of Human Rights for Africans as a reward for the sacrifices they had made during the war fighting for Allied powers. In 1919, a Pan-African conference, the first of five such conferences organized by DuBois, would not have been allowed to take place in Paris, had it not been for a prominent African Blaise Diagne of Senegal. The first African to serve in the French parliament Blaise Diagne used his influence with the French prime minister to secure permission for the conference to be held. The Allied powers, assembled to sign the Treaty of Versailles, were not sympathetic at all to such a large meeting of black people. The United States was afraid that DuBois might use the international forum to publicize lynchings of black people in the United States. The Europeans did not want any negative publicity associated with the brutal and repressive actions of their governments in African colonies. And none of the Allied powers wanted the sterling accomplishments of black soldiers highlighted by this gathering for fear of offending the white soldiers and the European public. This conference, and the next four that DuBois organized, influenced the growth of African nationalism in many significant ways.

DuBois was prophetic when he predicted in his 1903 book *The Souls of the Black Folk* that the major issue of the twentieth century was going to be one of race. Like most intellectuals, DuBois felt that prejudice and racism toward people of color was based on ignorance. So much negative and false theory had been written about Africans to justify colonization that most people in the Western world actually thought that Africans were worthless, had no past, and had made no contribution to human civilization. DuBois felt, therefore, that it was important for Westerners to be educated. He spent his life as a scholar-activist articulating issues that affected Africans globally.

It was unfortunate that in the United States the Pan-African movement was marked by intense and bitter rivalry between DuBois and Marcus

Garvey, despite agreement on the basic premise of their struggle (namely, that the lack of racial pride among black people was one key ingredient missing in the struggle for racial equality). Unlike DuBois, Garvey was a racial purist; he had deep disdain for blacks, like DuBois, who had a mixed racial heritage, and he felt that the best way to redress the tribulations of black people was to return to Africa. Unlike intellectuals who believed that all people were basically good and could be made to love others through education, Garvey was a doer. Using the slogan "Africa for the Africans at home and abroad," Garvey founded the Universal Negro Improvement Association (UNIA) in Jamaica in 1914 and moved it to the United States in 1916. He hoped that the UNIA would become a powerful mass movement with the goal of returning to Africa (to establish an African kingdom in Ethiopia that would rival in grandeur any white civilization that had ever existed). He started a series of business ventures (including a merchant ship), adopted a flag for the black race (red, black, and green), introduced an African national anthem set to martial music (that spoke of Ethiopia as the land of our forefathers, which our armies were poised to rush to liberate), and founded a newspaper, *The Negro World* (published in English, French, and Spanish). Garvey had charisma and commanded a huge following among black people in the United States as well as in Africa. He pressed the Allied powers to let him have the former German colonies in Africa so that he could show the world what black people were capable of doing. He was confident that the UNIA could develop the so-called mandated territories far better than the Europeans and South Africans (which had been granted a mandate for Namibia) ever could. If the Allies would not give him control over the mandated colonies, he insisted that he would have to oust them by force. Despite the obvious fact that Garvey did not have adequate military force to seize any part of Africa, his threats were enough to make sure that no imperial power ever permitted him to set foot on African soil. Under penalty of a huge fine and a long prison sentence, the *Negro World* was banned in much of Africa as a subversive document. His relationship with the U.S. black elite, who did not subscribe to his racial purism or political radicalism, continued to deteriorate. He was convicted of mail fraud in connection with his business activities and, after serving a short sentence, deported to his native Jamaica, where he was unable to reverse the rapidly declining fortunes of his organization. Despite his personal and legal difficulties in the United States and his eventual eclipse, Garvey is credited with psychologically rehabilitating the color "black," instilling in black people all over the world a keen awareness of their African roots and creating "a real feeling of international solidarity among Africans and persons of African stock."[14]

In the meantime, DuBois continued with his strategy of holding international conferences. The 1919 Pan-African conference concluded with a petition to the Allied powers to place the former German colonies under international supervision in order to prepare them for self-rule. The League did in fact adopt the mandate system, a measure that conformed to the spirit and intention of this petition. A resolution was also adopted demanding that European powers protect Africans from abuses of all sorts and set up a bureau under the League to make sure that legitimate demands of African people were being met. The Pan-African conference also demanded that education be provided, that "slavery," forced labor, and corporal punishment be outlawed, and that some form of political participation be permitted. These were moderate demands.

The 1921 Pan-African conference was conducted in three sessions held in London, Brussels, and Paris, respectively. The first session reiterated the same demands as the 1919 conference. However, this time, the demands were backed by an eloquent assertion concerning the inherent equality of human beings. This "Declaration to the World" delivered by the conference president, DuBois, is worth quoting at some length:

> The absolute equality of races, physical, political, and social, is the founding stone of world and human advancement. No one denies great differences of gift, capacity, and attainment, among individuals of all races, but the voice of science, religion, and practical politics is one in denying the God-appointed existence of super-races or of races naturally and inevitably and eternally inferior. That in the vast range of time, one group should in its industrial technique, or social organization, or spiritual vision, lag a few hundred years behind another, or forge fitfully ahead, or come to differ decidedly in thought, deed, and ideal, is proof of the essential richness and variety of human nature, rather than proof of the co-existence of demi-gods and apes in human form. The doctrine of racial equality does not interfere with individual liberty; rather it fulfils it. And of all the various criteria of which masses of men have in the past been prejudiced and classified, that of color of skin and the texture of the hair is surely the most adventitious and idiotic....[15]

The second session was moved to Brussels and immediately ran into controversy. The Belgian press alleged that the conference was communist inspired and that, if allowed to take place, it might incite the "ne'er-do-wells of the various tribes in the colony" (meaning, of course, the Africans in the Belgian-ruled Congo). The session was finally allowed to meet, albeit briefly, only to endorse the resolutions and statements already passed at the London session. The third session then moved on to Paris, where it was chaired by Monsieur Blaise Diagne of Senegal, attracting a large number of Africans from the French colonies. Here, once again, the demands for reforms were affirmed, and in addition, DuBois was chosen to present yet another petition to the League of Nations asking the League to look into the treatment of people of African descent the world over and to set up a mechanism for ameliorating their appalling conditions. These sessions were held in the capitals of three European countries with colonies in Africa in order to sensitize them to the situations prevailing in their colonies.

The 1923 Pan-African conference was held at a time when DuBois' rivalry with Marcus Garvey's organization was at its height. Attendance was much smaller than at the previous Pan-African conferences although the session in London was addressed by prominent British socialists like Lord Olivier and Professor Harold Laski. In addition to reiterating previous calls for colonial reforms, this session also called for due process (including jury trials) for Africans accused of crimes in the colonies and for an end to lynchings in the United States. Because of studies and reports indicating that forced labor and virtual slavery existed in Portuguese African colonies, DuBois and his colleagues decided to hold the second session of the 1923 conference in Lisbon. The hope was that the session might be able to link up with, and provide some support to, the few Africans who were studying in Portugal.

The 1927 Pan-African conference was held in New York. Several events of some significance to the black community were occurring at the time. First, Marcus Garvey's UNIP was near collapse and an end to the bitter and divisive rivalry between DuBois and Garvey was imminent. Second, the supreme ruler of the Ashanti people of Ghana King Prempeh I, who for years had been exiled to the Seychelles islands for refusing to cooperate with the British, had been allowed to return home. It lifted the morale of the conferees and added stature to the convention that the Ashanti king sent representatives to the New York meeting. Third, the imminent economic depression in the United States saw financial contributions to DuBois' work dwindle to a trickle. He had relied for financial support on the small but loyal African American middle class, which was soon threatened with economic ruin. Before the world community could recover from the Depression of 1929–1937, it was plunged yet into another major war. DuBois' desire to hold the next Pan-African conference on African soil had to be put off indefinitely, as economic conditions in Africa were even more grim than those in Europe or in the United States. Also, when the French government got wind of DuBois' plan, it adamantly opposed any such gathering being held in any of its colonies. It was not until 1945 that the next Pan-African conference could be held.

Elaborate preparations went into the 1945 Pan-African conference, to be held in Manchester, England. More Africans were involved in it than ever before, London being the center for a very large number of African students studying in Britain at the time. The conference committee was chaired by Dr. Peter Milliard (British Guiana) and T. R. Makonnen (British Guiana) was treasurer; George Padmore (West Indies) and Kwame Nkrumah (Ghana), political secretaries; Peter Abrahams (South Africa) was publicity secretary and Jomo Kenyatta (Kenya) was conference secretary. For the first time, African political parties, trade unions, youth leagues, and students' associations sent representatives. The roster of attendees included those representing the National Council of Nigeria and the Cameroons (NCNC), the Labour Party of Grenada (West Indies), the West Indies People's National Party, the Nigerian Youth Movement, the Nyasaland African Congress (Malawi), the African National Congress (ANC) of South Africa, and the Gold Coast Farmers' Association. The list of individual participants read like *Who is Who of the Black World,* and included, besides the conference planners, Wallace Johnson (Sierra Leone), Chief Obafemi Awolowo (Nigeria), Chief H. O. Davies (Nigeria), J. E. Taylor (Ghana), Dr. Hastings Banda (Malawi), Mrs. Amy Ashwood Garvey (then representing Jamaica Women's Movement), and Jaja Wachukwu (Nigeria). Some of these people went on to lead their own countries to independence. In general, the gathering was the largest and the most representative Pan-African conference ever held. It was a crowning achievement for DuBois, then universally acknowledged as the "Father of Pan-Africanism," who flew in from New York to convene it.

The deliberations of the conference were wide ranging in scope. Reports were presented on conditions of black people in Africa, the United States, the West Indies, and Britain. Some resolutions reaffirmed demands made by previous conferences but not yet implemented by the colonial powers; others expressed the solidarity of the people of African descent with other oppressed and colonized people, particularly the Vietnamese, Indonesians, and Indians who were, at the time, actively involved in their own freedom struggles. This Pan-African conference was important in several ways: As already noted, it was the best attended by Africans from the continent. Many of those who attended went on to lead their countries to independence, becoming presidents, prime ministers, or cabinet ministers. It marked the transformation of the Pan-African movement from a protest movement—seeking moderate reforms, including the right to form a trade union, to be paid a decent wage, to vote for representatives in local councils, to obtain health care and housing, and so on—to a "tool" of African nationalist movements fighting for self-rule. The idea of independence was echoed throughout all the discussions at the conference. Information was provided about other struggles elsewhere in the world that were being waged against the same colonial powers that Africans were facing, and the participants were able to draw some lessons that might be applied to the African struggles. The conference allowed Africans in attendance to develop ties and relationships among themselves that helped them later in organizing their people when they returned home. African activists who attended the conference said that they were inspired by the resolutions passed and encouraged by the moral support they received from each other.

When one looks at the first forty-five years of this century, one can identify three important objectives of Pan-Africanism, each coinciding with a specific time period. Pan-Africanism began as a protest movement against the racism endured by black people in the New World, slowly evolved into an instrument for waging an anticolonial struggle dedicated to bringing about African rule in Africa, and ended up as a dream or inspiration for African leaders and intellectuals who hoped that perhaps in the future, African states might be federated as the United States of Africa. Indeed, Pan-Africanism was the inspiration behind the efforts of Dr. Kwame Nkrumah, when, soon after becoming prime minister of the newly independent state of Ghana in 1957, he set about to convene in 1958 in Accra what might be called the sixth Pan-African conference. He called it the All-Africa People's Conference. It attracted new and more militant leaders like Patrice Lumumba of Congo and Tom Mboya of Kenya. The feeling at this meeting was buoyant. The question then was not whether all of Africa was going to be free, but how soon. In 1963, Nkrumah, Emperor Haile Selassie of Ethiopia, and Gamal Abdel Nasser of Egypt were instrumental in founding the Organization of African Unity (OAU), a meeting forum for all newly independent African nations. Many ideological obstacles had to be overcome. There were conservatives and radicals among independent African leaders; there were those who wanted a very strong organization that would be a foundation for a continental government and those who were interested only in a much weaker association of sovereign states. Major compromises had to be made and the OAU ended up being not quite the strong continental organization that some wanted, but certainly an important symbolic step toward the dream of a Pan-African unity.

Much has happened in the last forty years to dull the optimism about eventual unification of the African continent. The OAU remained a weak organization until it was replaced in 2001 by the African Union (AU). However, the dream of Pan-African unity lives on, at least in the rhetoric of African politicians and diplomats. In the end, the contribution of Pan-Africanism to the successful development of African nationalism and to the consciousness of people of African descent all over the world in helping them to secure a sense of connectedness with their African roots is quite significant.

The League of Nations and the United Nations

Following World War I, the world community was so shaken by the immense destruction wrought by that war that they decided to establish a new world organization to try to prevent the outbreak of another world war. The United States played a leadership role in founding the League of Nations although it never joined, a fact often mentioned as having contributed to the League's ineffectiveness and eventual demise. The League set up a mandate system under which colonies in Africa and elsewhere that had been governed by the losing World War I combatants, Germany and Turkey, could be transferred as mandates to victorious Allied powers. Such transfers were based on two conditions: that these mandated territories be administered with a view to their ultimately being granted independence, and that the European powers in charge of these mandated territories submit annual progress reports to the League as to what they were doing to prepare the territories for eventual self-rule. At that point, it was already being envisaged that German colonies such as Tanganyika, Togo, Cameroon, Namibia, Rwanda, and Burundi might be granted self-rule. Tanganyika, the western half of Togo, and the southwestern portion of Cameroon were mandated to Britain, however, while the eastern half of Togo and the eastern portion of Cameroon went to France. Rwanda and Burundi were mandated to Belgium, while South West Africa (whose name was later changed to Namibia) was mandated to South Africa. It was, therefore, only a matter of time before this idea of self-determination would be extended to the other colonies as well. In actual practice, the mandated territories were not governed much differently from other colonies, and there was no way for the League of Nations to force the mandate powers to pursue progressive policies.

That a major world war broke out within twenty years of the League's formation attests to the weakness of the League. The League's aims and principles were not articulated clearly enough and the League did not have the institutional mechanisms for resolving global conflicts (these shortcomings were later rectified in the United Nations Charter). The young Emperor Haile Selassie of Ethiopia was prophetic in his declaration at an emergency meeting of the League of Nations, following the unprovoked invasion of his country by Italy in 1936, when he said that a world body that seemed paralyzed to act in the face of such blatant aggression had failed miserably to justify its existence and was doomed to extinction. Three years after that statement, the war broke out in Europe as Germany undertook to conquer Europe and expand the Third Reich. In 1941, the United States was forced to join the war when the Japanese attacked Pearl Harbor. Four years after the United States entered the war, nearly 36 million people (soldiers and civilians included) had lost their lives, while Europe and the rest of the world had sustained untold physical destruction and economic ruin.

Just as it had happened after World War I, the world community was once again faced with the challenge of establishing a new world order that would try to prevent yet another conflagration on an even larger scale. Forty-six countries, including the United States, met in San Francisco and produced the founding charter of the United Nations Organization. The League's mandate system was transformed into the United Nations' trusteeship system, overseen by a Trusteeship Council. Italy subsequently lost her entire African empire, as Eritrea was given to Ethiopia, which annexed it. Italian Somaliland became a U.N. trust territory, and Libya was made "a self-governing kingdom" under the auspices of Great Britain.

The United Nations charter, in Article 62, directed its Economic and Social Council to "make recommendations for the purpose of promoting respect for, and observance of, human rights and fundamental freedoms for all."[16] In 1948, the United Nations approved a Universal Declaration of Human Rights, which spelled out an array of rights that all human beings are entitled to, regardless of their nationality or race. In Article 73, with respect to non-self-governing territories, the U.N. charter charged the relevant members of the world organization "to develop self-government, to take due account of the political aspirations of the peoples, and to assist them in the progressive development of their free political institutions, according to the particular circumstances of each territory and its peoples and their varying stages of advancement."[17] Despite the cynicism shown by some scholars toward the United Nations' emphasis on human rights, and the bitter controversy as to whether the United Nations had the right to demand from colonial powers periodic reports on the colonies, Articles 62 and 73 nevertheless represented an unequivocal moral and political statement to the effect that colonialism was, then as now, unacceptable in the international community and that all European colonies in Africa and Asia had the fundamental right to govern themselves.

The United Nations found itself being used increasingly by the emerging leadership of the independence movements in African colonies as a forum to press for their people's right to be free. Various U.N. agencies collected information on conditions in non-self-governing territories. The spokespersons of these countries used the forum provided by the United Nations to disseminate appropriate data and to ask for support. Socialist states like the Soviet Union, East Germany, and Czechoslovakia, ideologically opposed to colonialism and imperialism, and newly independent countries like India were more than willing to extend moral and material assistance to the African nationalist movements.

Even though the sentiment of national freedom was noble, the colonial powers were not entirely receptive to the notion. Portugal, for one, without any fear of disapprobation from her European allies, moved immediately to declare that her African colonies (Angola, Mozambique, Guinea-Bissau, and São Tomé and Principe) were not colonies but rather overseas provinces and, therefore, outside the purview of United Nations supervision. Nevertheless, through the United Nations, the international community went on record as condemning colonialism and offering support to those struggling for freedom. The United Nations has continued to be a catalyst in promoting independence, human rights, and literacy. It has provided hope to millions of working people by encouraging the adoption of progressive international labor legislation and by protecting the right of workers to form unions to improve their working conditions. The record of the United Nations in consistently opposing apartheid in South Africa and in helping newly independent African states to get on their feet is well known.

INDEPENDENCE MOVEMENTS

Much has been made of the fact that African nationalism was not quite like that of Europe because there were no states like those in Europe when colonization occurred. There are, however, many African groups with strong historical and social identities comparable to the ethnic and national groups of Europe. When colonial authorities drew boundaries, they did not pay any regard to the actual distributions of the various national peoples and ethnic communities; thus, the geographical entities that had been drawn to the convenience of the Europeans contained diversities of peoples. Ethnically homogeneous colonies were rare. What is important for our discussion, however, is that diverse African groups being governed by one colonial authority were able, through their leaders, to forge a sense of belonging to that geographical entity.

In political terms, African nationalism began to assert itself primarily after World War II. Organizations through which nationalism was channeled were varied and heterogeneous. William Tordoff identifies seven social/economic groups, each with its own factional interests to protect, yet willing to support initiatives directed toward securing greater political rights and even independence for the country.[18] These seven groups were as follows:

1. Professional groups, consisting of lawyers and doctors, who tended to be allied with wealthy merchants and contractors.
2. Teachers, clerks, and small merchants—or, in Marxian terms, the petty bourgeoisie—who were impatient with the status quo and eager to have the system transformed so that they could better themselves and perhaps help others as well.
3. The colonial bureaucracy, including Westernized Africans who were the immediate beneficiaries of the "Africanization" of top government positions when independence came.
4. The urban workers, interested in improving their wages and working conditions through trade unions (some of which were affiliated with emerging political parties, while others were not).
5. Small shopkeepers, petty traders, and hawkers who made up the "informal sector" of colonial economies.
6. Cash crop farmers, some of whom were wealthy, and all of whom constituted a powerful and important segment of Africans.
7. Peasant farmers, who toiled on their small farms in the country side and grew most of the food eaten in the country. Peasant concerns had to do with agriculture; they protested policies that controlled the market prices of their produce in urban markets, restricted ownership of cattle, or charged exorbitant fees for cattle dips.

"African nationalism was, therefore, composed of a number of different elements, representing sometimes interlocking, but often divergent, economic interests, which united temporarily in an anti-colonial 'struggle.'"[19]

The nationalist struggle was waged, in part, by religious associations, trade unions, and welfare organizations, as well as by political parties. In the case of religious associations, mission churches in Africa were closely identified with colonial rule from the very beginning. Many African church-goers broke away in order to be able to practice their customs: funeral rites, marriage celebrations, modes of dress, and so on. Early secession of churches occurred in Nigeria and South Africa as early as the 1890s. There were also Zionist churches that were founded by charismatic individuals who claimed to have received a divine calling to lead their people to spiritual and political salvation. They are analogous to present-day fundamentalist groups and were characterized by spontaneity and emotionalism. Examples of such churches were the Kimbangu and Kitawala churches in the Congo. In Kenya, there was the *Dini ya Musambwa* (Religion of the Spirits) founded by Elijah Masinde, which preached against colonial rule and attacked foreign religions as a deviation from the Africans' old and revered cultural ways. It campaigned for cultural authenticity and was strongly sympathetic to the Mau Mau uprising. Ironically, even after independence, Masinde did not relent in his attacks against the government, believing that Kenyatta's government was just as un-African as its colonial predecessor. Masinde spent a great deal of his life in detention until he died a few years ago.[20] As one can expect, leaders of radical religious movements were found to be equally threatening and jailed or executed.

Trade unions and welfare associations were formed as towns began to grow, particularly after World War II, and Africans in urban areas began to form associations to assist new arrivals from the rural areas with accommodations, jobs, spending money, and a supportive network of individuals from "home." In British colonies, these kinds of "tribal" associations, with parochial interests and regional bases, were encouraged because they met the needs that colonial authorities did not have the resources or the inclination to address. Trade unions also began to organize on a sectoral basis since they were not permitted to go "national" or to become political. Trade union leaders realized that without the strength of the numbers from a national base they would not be strong enough to improve the working conditions of their members. Moreover, the leaders of these organizations became a pool from which political organizations could draw. In some cases, the trade unions themselves became indistinguishable from nationalist movements. For instance, Tom Mboya of Kenya began his career as the head of the Local Government Workers' Union in Nairobi while also serving as an official of the Kenya African Union (KAU). KAU was banned during the Mau Mau uprising against the British. When Mboya was elected general-secretary of the Kenya Federation of Labor (KFL) in 1953, he attacked draconian colonial measures that included mass removals of African families from their homes, the practice of "collective punishment," and the introduction of the "kipande" (the pass book) for controlling the movement of Africans in the country. Tom Mboya's rise to the position of general-secretary of the Kenya African National Union (KANU), the party that led Kenya to independence in 1963, was a natural consequence of his extraordinary experience as a labor organizer and activist.

Sekou Toure of Guinea also began his political career as a trade unionist. As general-secretary of CGT-Guinee, he used African trade unions for political education and mass mobilization. During a long strike in 1953, he stressed that workers' unity was essential to any success and preached against "tribalism." Toure and his colleagues argued that "the trade union movement ... must integrate itself as the nationalist revolutionary and not as a reformist force within the context of other progressive forces. Its role in every instant is political."[21] Skills acquired in union organizing became critically important in Toure's rise to the top leadership of the of PDG (Parti Democratique de Guinee). In Nigeria, Morocco, Cameroon, and Zambia, trade unions wanted to maintain their autonomy and to concentrate on economic issues rather than to align themselves with political parties.

Many of these political parties began as interest groups composed of educated African civil servants, lawyers, doctors, and pastors often living in urban areas. They were originally moderate, reasonable, and interested only in limited reforms; they were not mass movements and did not try to supplant the colonial government. One of the earliest such groups was the Aborigines' Rights Protection Society founded in 1897, in Ghana, to ensure that the African people did not lose their rights to land. The National Congress of British West Africa, composed of educated Africans from the West African British colonies of Gold Coast (Ghana), Nigeria, Sierra Leone, and Gambia, wanted the right to vote extended to educated Africans. Its leader, a respected lawyer by the name of Casely Hayford, once said that "Our interests as a people are identical with those of the Empire."

Some political parties began as youth movements. A prime example would be the Nigerian Youth Movement, which began as the Lagos Youth Movement (LYM) in 1934, formed hastily by young people to protest the establishment of an African college in Lagos, which was to require the same amount of time in training, but would only issue diplomas instead of college degrees. It did not have a traditional affiliation with a British university, which meant that its education and diplomas would be considered inferior to those of other Nigerian schools. The LYM became the Nigerian Youth Movement, attracting support from all parts of Nigeria except the north and expanded its agenda to include protesting discriminatory legislation and pressing for the Africanization of the civil service. Dr. Nnamdi Azikiwe headed the Nigerian Youth Movement at one time, but political squabbles within the organization forced him to leave, taking with him some of the leaders to establish the National Council of Nigeria and the Cameroons in 1944. Another faction of the movement joined forces with Yoruba cultural groups to form an opposing party, the Action Group under the leadership of Obafemi Awolowo. Examples of other political parties that arose out of young people's clubs were the Rassemblement Democratique Africain (RDA) founded in 1946 in French West Africa, the United Gold Coast Convention founded in 1947 in Ghana, and the Northern Rhodesia African Congress formed in 1948.

The French believed that with assimilation, African peoples would ultimately remain within the larger French community of nations, under France's leadership. So they sponsored political parties in the colonies as chapters of the French national parties. For instance, the French Gaullist Party and the MRP (Movement Republicain Populaire) sponsored the Parti Republicain du Dahomey (in Benin in 1951), long after the French Socialist Party had established a chapter in Senegal (1936). It was through the auspices of French Socialists that Léopold Senghor worked his way through the political ranks to be a French deputy.

In British Africa, African organizations were allowed only if they were social/welfare committees or regional organizations. The British policy of "indirect rule" impeded the ability of Africans in the colonies to establish nationwide organizations or to be able to work with others outside their regions. When the NCNC began in 1944, it was as a federation of ethnic associations and social and literary clubs. In 1951, it was able to transform itself into a political party by admitting individual members. The NCNC was not able to make much impact in the northern or western regions of Nigeria, but instead became strongly identified with the Ibo people of Eastern Nigeria (under the leadership of Nnamdi Azikiwe). In western Nigeria, Chief Obafemi Awolowo combined parts of the Nigerian Youth Movement and a Yoruba cultural organization called Egbe Omo Oduduwa into a new political party called the Action Group (AG), which came to be identified almost entirely with the Yoruba people. In the northern part of Nigeria, a staunchly Muslim and conservative area, Abubakar Tafawa Balewa salvaged what was left of the Northern Elements Progressive Association and turned it into a Hausa cultural organization called the Northern People's Congress (NPC). When political support was secured from the powerful but conservative Muslim emirs such as the Sardauna of Sokoto, the NPC transformed itself into a political party. The colonial politics of Nigeria, from the early 1950s to the achievement of independence from Britain in 1960, was to be influenced by the existence of these three major political parties: the NCNC, the Action Group, and the NPC, each representing one of the three major ethnic groups of Nigeria.

In Tanzania, the Tanganyika African Association (TAA) was formed in 1929 as a discussion group, consisting of teachers and lower-level civil servants, who met often and shared their experiences and ideas. They were not permitted any political activity and did not get involved in politics until after World War II. In 1954, a young university graduate by the name of Julius Nyerere decided to transform the TAA into the Tanganyika African National Union (TANU), a mass political party prepared to address the rising demands of the African people and to press for independence. A couple of smaller parties were formed prior to Tanganyika becoming independent of Britain in 1961, but they were overwhelmed by TANU at the polls, and Nyerere became a persuasive and articulate political thinker; some of his ideas will be discussed in the next chapter.

In Kenya, in keeping with British practice of discouraging national organizations, a number of small regional tribal organizations were formed early in the century to protest specific colonial policies, but they found themselves targets of colonial repression. The Kavirondo Taxpayers' Welfare Association (KTWA) was formed in the 1920s by Africans from the western part of the country around Lake Victoria (comprising the Luo and Luhya) to protest unfair tax and land regulations, but they were banned by the colonial government because they chose to discuss their grievances publicly rather than simply go through official channels. There were also schisms within the organization due to ethnic and religious differences. The KTWA had a very short political life. Harry Thuku formed the Young Kikuyu Association in 1922 to protest the expropriation of Kikuyu land, before the authorities moved against him. He lost his job with the city of Nairobi and was subsequently detained and banished to a remote wilderness in the northern part of Kenya. The Young Kikuyu Association was soon succeeded by the Kikuyu Central Association (KCA), which later became the Kenya African Union, intended to be a territorywide organization both in its program and in its strident rhetoric of Kenyan nationalism; ultimately, due to effective colonial repression, the KAU never established a firm base outside the central region of the country. As the pace of political changes accelerated, especially following the emergence and suppression of the Mau Mau uprising, Tom Mboya, using his base as a trade unionist, established the People's Convention Party (PCP). The Kenya African National Union, which has dominated Kenya politics to this day, was formed in March 1960. Its support came mainly from the Kikuyu people in central province and from the Luo people in the western section of the country, around Lake Victoria. In June 1960, a number of smaller ethnic groups, fearing domination by the two largest groups (i.e., Kikuyus and Luos) and with material support from the small but economically influential white settler community, formed the Kenya African Democratic Union (KADU). The smaller ethnic groups were represented by the Kalenjin National Alliance, the Masai United Front, the Coast African People's Union, and the Kenya African People's Party. A far-reaching consequence of British colonial policy can be seen in the patchwork of political groups representing different ethnic groups coming together, toward the end of colonial rule, with very limited experience of having worked together at a national level.

Even though this was not articulated, it seems that the British had no intention of letting Africans eventually govern themselves in those colonies populated by significant numbers of British settlers. In South Africa, following a history of hostilities between the British government and the white settlers, power was ultimately transferred to the whites with no attempt to ensure constitutionally that the rights of the other racial groups in the country would be protected. In Southern Rhodesia, now Zimbabwe, the white settlers were given internal self-government in 1923, meaning that the colony was responsible for everything except defense and foreign affairs, which remained in the hands of the British government. In 1953, the British government assisted in the setting up of a federation of Zambia, Zimbabwe, and Malawi under the control of the white-minority colonizers. Five years later, the federation collapsed but the whites managed to retain their control of Zimbabwe and unilaterally to declare their independence from Britain in 1965. It took fifteen years of guerrilla warfare and thousands of lives for the Zimbabweans to pry their country from Rhodesia's white minority. In Kenya, the British settlers not only thoroughly dominated the country's politics but also heavily influenced British colonial policy toward Kenya.

CONCLUSIONS

Although the vast majority of African states achieved independence peacefully through negotiation, it nevertheless makes a lot of sense to refer to the process of transition from colonialism to independence as a struggle. Africans were never simply asked: When do you wish to become independent? They had to demand independence, they had to agitate for it. Many "agitators" went to jail; some of them were banished from their own countries for long periods of time. It used to be said that the surest path to becoming prime minister of an English-speaking African country was through jail. Indeed, Kenyatta (Kenya), Nkrumah (Ghana), Banda (Malawi), and many others served time in colonial jails before they became leaders of their own countries.

In the case of the Portuguese colonies, Portugal dealt with African demands for independence simply by annexing the colonies and declaring them "overseas" provinces of Portugal. The total refusal on the part of Portugal to entertain the thought that Africans were not Portuguese and might actually want to rule their own countries led the nationalists to launch protracted armed struggles.

Many factors mediated the struggle for independence: colonial educa-tion, the churches, ideas and expressions of support from individuals of African ancestry through the Pan-African movement, the exposure to the world through world wars, and, of course, the forum provided briefly by the League of Nations and later by the United Nations. It is interesting that the Christian church and colonial education, pivotal tools in the Europeans' "civilizing missions" in Africa, also inadvertently became the tools that the African would use in fighting for freedom. Despite the atomizing impact of the divide-and-rule policies employed by colonial authorities, which we described, it is remarkable indeed that African people were able to wage fairly unified movements. The struggle mirrored all the contradictions of African societies that existed before colonialism and which have persisted since independence.

In any event, more than forty years of independence show that winning freedom from European colonial powers was but the beginning of a long tortuous process of liberation, nation- and institution-building, consolidation, and economic development, a process which began with one-party systems and socialist economies and now, at the beginning of the twenty-first century, faces economic globalization and multiparty political systems. The next chapter takes a look at the first thirty years of African countries' experience as independent states.

NOTES

1. Boahen A. Adu, *African Perspectives on Colonialism* (Baltimore, MD: Johns Hopkins University Press, 1987), pp. 23–24.
2. Ibid., p. 25.
3. Ibid.
4. Richard W. Hull, *Modern Africa: Continuity and Change* (Englewood Cliffs, NJ: Prentice Hall, 1980), pp. 120–121.
5. Janet G. Vaillant, *Black, French, and African: A Life of Léopold Sédar Senghor* (Cambridge, MA: Harvard University Press, 1990), p. 1.
6. Ali A. Mazrui, *Political Values and the Educated Class in Africa* (Berkeley: University of California Press, 1978), p. 27.
7. Melville J. Herskovits, *The Human Factor in Changing Africa* (New York: Alfred A. Knopf, 1962), p. 247.
8. Julius K. Nyerere, "Education for Self-Reliance," in Julius K. Nyerere, ed., *Ujamaa: Essays on Socialism* (New York: Oxford University Press, 1968), pp. 44–45.
9. Kofi Awoonor, *The Breast of the Earth* (New York: NOK Publishers International, 1975), p. 21.
10. Author's conversations with Taban Lo Liyong at the University of Nairobi, summer, 1972.
11. Basil Davidson, *Modern Africa*, 2nd Edition (New York: Longman, 1989), p. 66.

12. Ndabaningi Sithole, *African Nationalism,* 2nd Edition (New York: Oxford University Press, 1968), p. 47.
13. George Padmore, *Pan-Africanism or Communism* (New York: Anchor Books, Doubleday, 1972), p. 96.
14. Esedebe P. Olisanwuche, *Pan-Africanism: The Idea and the Movement, 1776–1963* (Washington, DC: Howard University Press, 1982), p. 78.
15. George Padmore, *Pan-Africanism or Communism,* p. 108.
16. Harold K. Jacobson, *Networks of Interdependence: International Organization and the Global Political System,* 2nd Edition (New York: Alfred A. Knopf, 1984), p. 439.
17. Ibid., p. 441.
18. William Tordoff, *Government and Politics in Africa* (Bloomington, IN: Indiana University Press, 1984), pp. 51–52.
19. Ibid., p. 53.
20. Vincent G. Simiyu, *Elijah Masinde: A Biography* (Nairobi, Kenya: East African Educational Publishers, 1997), pp. 14–35.
21. Ioan Davies, *African Trade Unions* (Baltimore: Penguin Books, 1966), p. 88.

African Independence: The First Thirty Years

Kwame Nkrumah, first president of Ghana, is reported to have said: "First seek the political kingdom and the rest shall be added onto it." One can imagine, following the transfer of power, African leaders, in near panic, going, "Now what?" The first 30 years of African independence are a study in confusion and bewilderment in the face of mountains of inherited problems: fragmentation of identities, sky-high mass expectations of instant wealth, health, and education.

INTRODUCTION

The transfer of power by European colonialists—the actual handing over of political authority and control of the state's bureaucracies and resources to African nationalist leaders and parties—actually began in the early 1950s. This did not necessarily lead to changes in the political institutions that the Africans inherited or in the basic orientation of ordinary people toward the new leaders wielding authority and power over them. In the vast majority of cases, African leaders assumed roles and positions without altering the basic institutions and structures of the old colonial states. Worse yet, the constitutions under which the African leaders assumed power were negotiated between the nationalist leaders and the European colonial authorities without the consultation or the involvement of the citizens of the new country. Constitution making is one of the most important stages in the development of a nation-state. It is a process that allows the people to decide not only what form of government is appropriate for them but also what limits to place on that government and the exact nature of the relationship between the people and their government.

This chapter provides an overview, with examples, of the processes that led to the transfer of power following decolonization (1945–1965), the main issues and problems that Africans inherited along with self-government (1956–1965), the political and economic choices made by the leaders after independence, and an assessment of the first thirty years of independence.

The vast majority of African colonies experienced peaceful (i.e., negotiated) transfer of power to the African leaders. Those which underwent protracted and bloody armed struggles for national liberation include Algeria, Zimbabwe, Namibia, and the Portuguese colonies of Mozambique, Angola, Guinea-Bissau, and São Tomé and Principe. The African National Congress (ANC) of South Africa waged an armed struggle for nearly thirty years, but ultimately the white minority government decided to negotiate with the ANC and other anti-*apartheid* political groups for an all-inclusive democratic government. Eritrea, a former Italian colony, which had been annexed by Ethiopia after World War II, waged a relentless struggle to secede from Ethiopia. It won its freedom in 1993, following the disintegration of the Marxist government that overthrew the autocratic rule of Emperor Haile Selassie in 1976.

DECOLONIZATION AND THE TRANSFER OF POWER

The different colonial systems instituted by Europeans in Africa led to different processes of decolonization, but in both the British and French colonies of West Africa, the decolonization process took root and accelerated rapidly after World War II.

Centralization of Power

In modern Ghana, then known as the Gold Coast, a new constitution was promulgated in 1946. For the first time, Africans would have a majority of seats in the colony's legislature, and representatives from the Ashanti and northern regions and the British trust territory of Togo would serve on the British governor's Executive Council. In January 1948, massive riots occurred in the southern part of the colony, prompting the British government to appoint a Commission of Inquiry composed entirely of Africans. Believing that the underlying cause of the riots was popular frustration with colonial administration, the Commission decided to exceed its charge by suggesting a couple of constitutional changes. One suggestion was that the colony's legislature be enlarged and popularly elected and the second one was that the governor's Executive Council be turned into a Cabinet of Ministers, with Africans being given substantive policy responsibilities. The British accepted these suggestions and began to implement them gradually under a new 1951 constitution. The Executive Council was expanded to include eleven members, of whom three were British and eight Africans; six of the Africans had ministerial responsibilities.

In 1951, colonywide elections were held in which two political parties competed—the United Gold Coast Convention (UGCC, an older party led by Dr. J. B. Danquah) and the Convention People's Party (CPP), which had broken away from the UGCC and was then led by Kwame Nkrumah. The election was won handily by the CPP, and Nkrumah became Leader of Government Business in the legislature. In 1952, he was given the title of Prime Minister, and later he became head of what the British called internal self-government, meaning that Nkrumah's government was responsible for all state matters except defense and foreign affairs. The same year, the National Liberation Movement (NLM), representing the interests of the Asante (Ashanti) people and the north, was formed with the goal of retaining ethnic identities and regional autonomy after independence. The NLM strongly favored a federal constitution and the introduction of a second chamber of the legislature (a senate), which would increase their "clout" in independent Ghana. In the 1956 elections, held in preparation for the independence that had been promised for early 1957, the NLM was defeated at the polls. The CPP won the majority of seats in every part of the country except the north (the home base of the NLM). By 1957, the CPP was well on its way to exercising complete central political control over the whole of independent Ghana.

In 1957, following a tradition established since the nineteenth century for Canada, Australia, New Zealand, India, Burma, and other former British colonial possessions, Ghana became an independent dominion in the British Commonwealth (a loose association of former colonies that had become independent). The dominion of Ghana had a governor-general representing the queen of England as the titular head of state, but Nkrumah, as prime minister, became the head of government. Shortly afterward, Nkrumah successfully converted his position to that of executive president, following a precedent set in India, the first British colony to become independent after World War II. Later, Kenya, Uganda, Zambia, Malawi, and others followed a similar pattern. In Kenya, for instance, Jomo Kenyatta served as prime minister during the first year of independence under a regional (termed *majimbo* in Swahili) constitution, with a British governor-general; but the following year the constitution was amended, providing for a single legislative chamber and a powerful presidency in a highly centralized (unitary) political system.

This change from dominion status to republican status was a precursor to the kinds of autocratic personal rule that came to characterize so much of African political leadership since independence. Such trends toward centralization were rationalized on grounds that each African country needed to project its national identity and assert its sovereignty and independence by honoring its own head of state, not a foreign monarch, as the highest representative of the new nation. The creation of indigenous heads of state was an important first step in what turned out to be a long and difficult process of nation-building in independent Africa.

Regionalism and Separatism: Nigeria

The processes of decolonization and transfer of power in British Nigeria were somewhat more complicated due to its much higher degree of ethnic diversity (more than 300 different groups). Under British rule, the colony consisted of three regional units joined together in a loose federal system. The British colonial administration operated as though each of these three regions was a homogeneous area, which clearly it was not. While the north was dominated by the powerful Muslim emirs, there were also many non-Muslims there. Yoruba people constituted the majority population in the western region, but many people living in the delta and Benin were not Yoruba. Similarly, the Ibo region of eastern Nigeria included many non-Ibo people. Following the establishment of the British colony of Lagos in 1862, a nominated legislative council was set up. Under Governor Frederick Lugard, a Nigerian Council was formed in 1913–1914 to represent the southern and the northern regions of Nigeria, but it was only advisory and was not representative of the people. It was not until 1942 that reforms were initiated, providing for regional assemblies, and northerners were brought into the mainstream of colonial Nigerian political life. In 1946, new reforms in Nigeria's constitution resulted in an augmented legislative council whose members, this time, were nominated by "native authorities" in three designated regions of the country (North, West, and East). This series of constitutional reforms also created regional executive councils under the chairmanship of lieutenant governors. Criticisms of the 1946 constitution immediately surfaced and persisted—for example, that legislators were essentially nominated rather than directly elected, that the powers of the regional assemblies were vague, and that the relationship between the regional assemblies and the central legislature was not clearly spelled out. Following extensive consultations, a new constitution was promulgated in 1951.

Even under this new constitution, Nigerians continued to have trouble working together, since there was no national political party and no national agenda. Each regional group seemed intent on pursuing its own interests. Lord Hailey remarked thus:

> Opposition to British control had previously furnished the common link between the parties and the interests concerned, and with the approaching prospect of its removal the spirit of regional particularism, if not of separatism, grew all the more rapidly. It was impossible to secure unity among Ministers in the Central Government, or to carry out any common policy.[1]

Difficult negotiations followed during the 1950s, resulting in the eventual formation of a federation under a governor-general. Each region was headed by a governor and had an elected regional assembly. Each of the three major political parties continued to represent and control its own region: the National Council of Nigeria and the Cameroons (NCNC) administered the Eastern Region, the Action Group (AG) ran the Western Region, and the Northern People's Congress (NPC) held power in the

Northern Region. Common links between these three regions and parties remained fragile. Since 1960, the history of independent Nigeria has been a search for the means to establish and strengthen such linkages and create a strong Nigerian identity.

Regionalism and Separatism: East Africa

In Kenya, Uganda, and Tanganyika, where Lord Lugard's "indirect rule" policies guided British colonial policies, independence was preceded also by multiparty elections, although colonywide elections came much later in British East Africa than in Ghana or Nigeria. Decolonization processes in colonial Uganda—where several small but proud kingdoms (such as Bunyoro, Toro, and Nyankole) resented the special protection accorded the Kingdom of Buganda by the British during colonial days—were particularly bitter. When preparations began for African self-rule in Uganda, the *kabaka* (king) of Buganda fully expected to be accorded special treatment by the British. He vehemently resisted any suggestion that Buganda be incorporated into Uganda as a subordinate entity and threatened to secede from Uganda altogether. In the mid-1950s, the British sent him into exile in Britain for failing to cooperate with colonial authorities, but his exile served only to make the king an even greater hero among his people. Following the pre-independence elections of 1961, Milton Obote, head of the Uganda People's Congress (UPC), formed a hasty alliance with the king's monarchist party, the Kabaka Yekka (KY). Obote's UPC wanted a strong central government for independent Uganda, while the Kabaka Yekka was interested primarily in furthering the interests of the Buganda monarchy and the Baganda people as a separate, almost sovereign people. Following independence in 1962, Obote's compromise permitted the *kabaka* to retain his throne in Buganda and take on the added responsibility as nonexecutive president of the Republic of Uganda. Soon afterward, however, this marriage of convenience between UPC and KY began to flounder.

British colonial policies favoring Buganda had contributed to the persistence of separatist tendencies, which led, within a decade after independence, to a military takeover. Early in the colonial period, two counties that belonged to the kingdom of Bunyoro had been given to the Buganda kingdom as a reward for the latter's cooperation with the British. Despite repeated and energetic protests to England by the king of Bunyoro and active armed resistance by the residents of these "lost counties," the British chose not to return them to Bunyoro. During the constitutional conference that led to the transfer of power, a provision was inserted into the constitution transferring these counties to the central government, pending a referendum to determine if the people wanted to remain in Buganda, revert to Bunyoro, or become a separate district altogether. Residents in the two counties voted to return to their previous kingdom of Bunyoro. The *kabaka* of Buganda, in his official capacity as president of Uganda, had already set the stage for a major confrontation, latent with immense consequences for the country as a whole, by refusing to sign documents giving control of the lost counties to the central government until after the referendum. Moreover, the *kabaka* and his supporters began to complain that Obote, in his zealous attempt to strengthen the central government, was infringing upon Buganda's powers. Obote really never had intended to permit a federal system in Uganda. Like most of his contemporaries on the continent, he believed in a strong central government.

When Uganda's parliament voted to set up a commission to investigate charges of corruption against Prime Minister Obote, the minister of defense, and Deputy Commander of the Army Idi Amin, there were rumors that the *kabaka* had instigated this investigation in order to solicit outside help to overthrow Obote. In 1966, Obote quickly overthrew the king, had five members of his own cabinet arrested, and appointed himself executive president of the country. He also began drafting a new constitution, which outlawed all traditional kingdoms, made Uganda a unitary state, and reduced the Ugandan parliament to a "rubber stamp" (approving whatever Obote presented to it). Only a few years later, before he had laid out a clear direction of new national leadership, Obote himself, while out of the country to attend the Commonwealth summit in Singapore, was overthrown by the semiliterate man whom he had elevated to the top command of his military establishment: General Idi Amin Dada.

Decolonization in French Colonies

In French African territories, the decolonization process was somewhat different. France tried to implement its policy of assimilation under the constitutional reforms of 1946, which conferred French citizenship on all the people in its colonies, but the assimilation policy met with considerable resistance in North Africa and the island colony of Madagascar. Indeed, the Muslim people in North Africa had long resented the attempted destruction of their language and way of life through the imposition of French culture. By 1956, France had extended independence to Morocco and Tunisia, intensifying the determination of the Algerians eventually to rule themselves and weakening any arguments that would justify independence for Morocco and Tunisia but not for Algeria.

Thereafter, much debate ensued as to what to do with the French empire, especially in relation to the then recent humiliating loss in Indochina and the anticolonial rebellion in Algeria (1954–1962). When General Charles de Gaulle became president of France's Fifth Republic in 1958, he attempted to foster reconciliation in French colonial Africa and fashion a coherent policy. He called for a referendum in French colonies, including Algeria, to find out whether Africans wanted their countries to remain associated with France or to become independent nations. In the referendum, every French African colony (including Algeria) voted for de Gaulle's vision of a close-knit international French community led by France—except Guinea, which voted for outright independence. The French government reacted peevishly and punitively by severing ties with Guinea, withdrawing all French personnel and taking with them all their equipment including typewriters and telephones. The harsh treatment meted out to Guinea was an eloquent testimony to French paternalism. As Frantz Fanon might have said, Africans were loved only if they became French and did as the French told them to do. Nonetheless, de Gaulle's vision of continued French leadership in Africa was soon abandoned. By 1960, French colonial policy shifted toward favoring independence for all African colonies. Even their prize colony of Algeria was granted independence in 1962, after eight years of guerrilla warfare.

Some French Africans, particularly in Senegal, had voted regularly in French elections since 1848, and West Africa's first African deputy, Blaise Diagne, was elected to the French Assembly in 1914. After the 1946 constitutional reforms, other colonies began to send deputies to the French parliament as well as to territorial assemblies, and the political parties listed on ballots were headed by African leaders who had close connections with the French parties. In keeping with the French proportional representation system, Africans voted both for individual candidates and for parties. This experience meant that African parties in French colonial Africa were better organized, enjoyed greater political consensus in their own countries, and most were less ethnically fragmented than their counterparts in British colonial Africa. After World War II, Africans had been able to participate in colonial politics at three levels—in the French parliament in Paris, on the regional level in the colonies (i.e., in the federations of French West Africa and Equatorial Africa), and in individual colonies themselves. Thanks also to the French colonial administrative system of "direct rule," the power of traditional chiefs (a divisive element in British colonies) had been substantially undermined.

Despite the overwhelming "yes" vote in the 1958 referendum, the French government decided to amend its constitution in 1959 and allow its colonies to claim independence. The change was perhaps too abrupt, for not all African leaders wanted independence right away. Houphouet-Boigny of Ivory Coast wanted federation with France, believing that such an arrangement would ensure more rapid economic development for his people. France conducted negotiations with each country, and military and economic agreements were concluded to reward those nations that chose to remain within a modified French community (an association of French-speaking independent sovereign states somewhat analogous to the British Commonwealth). Close ties between the French ruling elite and their francophone African counterparts have continued to this day. These ties remain much stronger than those between the British political elite and independent anglophone African leadership.

PROBLEMS AT INDEPENDENCE

When African nationalist leaders and parties took over the reins of power at independence, they inherited serious problems that were to shape the subsequent course of politics on the continent. Among principal problems were people's high expectations for national development and prosperity, against the backdrop of seemingly intractable economic problems and territorial and ethnic divisions which were later to lead to political instability.

Popular Expectations

The high expectations of the African populace stemmed partly from the extravagant promises made by nationalist leaders in the process of competing for popular support. During election campaigns leading to independence, many politicians vowed to bring about dramatic changes in people's lives. They promised that once independence was achieved, nationalist parties would provide good jobs, decent houses, primary health care, and free universal education. In places like Kenya, with significant European settlers of visible affluence, Africans expected that when the Europeans fled the country—as many of them were widely expected to do—their houses and farms would be distributed to the people. Although there was much euphoria in the air, many people did not realize that there would not be enough houses or jobs to go around, nor would there be adequate funds to pay for the education and health care that so many people desperately needed. Kenya's political leaders failed to explain that even if the settlers chose to return to Europe, their property could not simply be seized for free distribution to the indigenous population. Such wholesale confiscation would not be legal or right and would not be tolerated either by the former colonial powers or by international institutions.

Disappointment set in as soon as the people discovered that their leaders could not deliver on all their promises. European lands, homes, and businesses that became available for sale were bought by Africans who had the money to buy them (professionals, successful businessmen, big farmers, and the politicians themselves). Jomo Kenyatta, Kenya's first prime minister, realized that land hunger, the primary grievance voiced over and over by the people in their long and bitter resistance against British colonialism, far exceeded available land and could not easily be satisfied. Indeed, during independence negotiations, the British government had been sure to protect the interests of British landowners in Kenya by insisting that the independent Kenyan government purchase that land at market prices. To sweeten the deal, loans were provided to the incoming government to enable it to purchase the land for distribution to landless peasants. Economic advisers (also provided by the British) told Kenyatta that there was not enough land to be given away and that it would not be economically prudent to take large European estates—often mechanized and very efficient—and break them up into small plots to give to landless peasants. The consequence of such redistribution, they warned, might be a drastic reduction in food production and agricultural productivity. As a result, Kenyatta took small portions of land from time to time and set them aside for redistribution. Whenever land redistribution was scheduled, he made certain that the occasion was fully publicized in the government-controlled media to show Kenyans that he was, in fact, fulfilling the promise made to landless peasants by the ruling party, the Kenya African National Union (KANU). In any event, such property issues were never resolved even within the ruling party (KANU), where radical politicians, led by Vice President Oginga Odinga, felt that the land agreement that Kenyatta had made with the British betrayed the interests of Kenyans who had lost their lands to white settlers. Odinga eventually broke with Kenyatta and KANU over this issue in 1966 and formed an opposition party called the Kenya People's Union (KPU). The assassination of Economics Minister Tom Mboya and the riots that followed in the wake of that killing in 1969 provided just the excuse the Kenyatta government needed to outlaw KPU and put Odinga in a long detention without trial.

Lack of Economic Development

The colonial era had left most Africans illiterate and most colonies dependent on exports of one or a small number of cash crops cultivated only in certain parts of each new state. In 1960, less than 20–25 percent of Africans could read or write. Countries such as Ethiopia and Somalia had literacy rates as low as 10–15 percent, while the Congo's was 40 percent—even though most of those who could read did not have the skills necessary for building a new country. Like other colonized Africans, the Congolese had been educated in mission schools, where the main goal of the missionaries was to enable the Congolese to read the Bible and perform religious work. By 1960, when the Belgians transferred power to Patrice Lumumba, the new country's first prime minister, there was reportedly only one qualified medical doctor in the country! The lack of a sufficiently educated citizenry meant that new leaders in independent Africa were faced with a dual challenge: locating resources to provide the education and training so desperately needed by the people and finding the skilled manpower necessary to help keep nascent infrastructures functioning effectively and productively. Dependence on European powers, the very powers the Africans had ostensibly freed themselves from, became unavoidable if the African national economies were to develop.

Beyond the issues of inadequate education, new African leaders faced even more compelling questions about what kind of education their people needed. Education in colonial days was geared toward the needs of European authorities. It justified colonial rule, inculcated foreign social values, alienated Africans from their own cultures, and prepared Africans for the kinds of jobs that newly independent nations were not yet ready to offer. At independence, African governments had to decide whether to continue with the type of education provided by mission schools and colonial governments or to initiate changes that might better serve their nations in the future. For most African countries, there was not sufficient time to consider such matters carefully, and they chose to defer the issue. One new country—Tanzania—however, decided to confront the educational issue directly. As its president, Julius Nyerere, indicated, "Only when we are clear about the kind of society we are trying to build can we design an educational service to serve our goals."[2] Having decided that African socialism, based on traditional values of cooperation and the extended family, was the most appropriate vision for the country's future development, Tanzanian leaders initiated the necessary changes in their educational system.

The national economies that African leaders inherited from the colonial era were often based on exporting agricultural commodities—such as coffee, cocoa, tea, groundnuts, sisal, or cotton—which served to enrich European economies, although a few African countries also exported minerals such as gold (from Ghana) and copper (from Zambia and the Democratic Republic of Congo). By the time of independence, almost all African countries had evolved economies that were extremely vulnerable and heavily dependent on the markets of former colonial powers; their exports earned the hard currency necessary to buy equipment and technology from industrialized countries of the West. Whether they exported crops, minerals, or both, newly independent African nations were incorporated into the international economy, to serve, as in colonial times, primarily the needs of Europeans. When Ghana, for instance, became independent in 1957, her economy was at about the same level as that of South Korea. In the 1990s, however, South Korea had achieved economic prosperity as a newly industrialized country, while Ghana had declined into one of the world's least developed countries.

The economic experience of independent African nations during the past thirty years has been rooted in their continued dependency on exporting agricultural commodities or minerals whose prices have fluctuated frequently on the world market. This has led to steadily declining terms of trade with advanced Western nations—even as such market prices and terms of trade have been determined by forces beyond the control of the Africans. Restructuring new national economies away from export-oriented primary commodities has been impeded since independence by the need to earn foreign exchange to provide vital services (e.g., health services and education) or to develop the infrastructure required for economic development. In any event, it became difficult for independent African nations to implement their development plans without knowing how much hard currency their exports were going to earn from one year to the next. It should be stated that official corruption, although it exists in varying degrees in poor and rich countries around the world, has had particularly deleterious effects on the ability of African governments to provide basic services to their people in education and health care and to maintain the weak infrastructure inherited from the colonial authorities.

In addition, the distribution of cash crop farming and mining previously had been laid out according to the needs of colonial powers or local settler communities, along the old lines of infrastructure (such as roads, railroads, telecommunications, and electric power). Thus, some areas in each colony were "more developed" at independence than others. After independence, there were often conflicts within each new country resulting from competition for scarce national resources, pitting the needs of the "less developed" areas against "more developed" ones. The consequences of this uneven development can still be seen in most African nations in terms of the distribution of the infrastructure and in wide disparities in the availability of education and health services.

Arbitrary Borders

New African nationalist leaders also faced the problems of artificial boundaries dividing their countries. Virtually every boundary in Africa splinters large ethnic groups between countries. The Maasai are divided between Kenya and Tanzania; the Hausa are scattered all over West Africa; the Somali are located in Ethiopia, Kenya, Djibouti, and Somalia; the Ewe are divided between Togo and Ghana; and the Bakongo can be found in the Democratic Republic of Congo, the Republic of Congo, and Angola. Given the existence of nearly 2,000 ethnic groups, each one with its own language, rituals, and social norms, no one, not even the Africans themselves, could have drawn perfect national boundaries on the African continent. However, splitting large ethnic groups into many different states or placing groups with a history of mutual hostilities together in a single country (as in Chad or Sudan) has contributed to the specter of irredentism and civil wars that has wasted scarce resources.

There have been destructive wars between Somalia, Kenya, and Ethiopia because the Somali people were divided by colonial boundaries (inherited by independent governments). Leaders in Somalia, during the first thirty years of independence, sought to unite all Somalis into one country by claiming the Ogaden province of Ethiopia, the northeastern province of Kenya, and all of Djibouti.

Some independent states have pursued vague historical claims to neighboring territories, as in Morocco's claim to all of Western Sahara and Libya's claim to the Aozou strip in northern Chad. Despite such continuing conflicts, independent African states have been extremely reluctant to seek a comprehensive review of African borders. Leaders feel that the question of national boundaries is a Pandora's box that could unleash endless claims and counterclaims. Africans are no different from other national groups in owing their primary allegiances to those who share their own language, religion, and culture. The challenge facing African nationalist leaders in this respect has been how to go about creating national loyalties to the new countries. This process has been time-consuming and painful and has been compromised by the contradictions of the rhetoric of African leaders and their tendency to favor their own ethnic groups.

Within each country's boundaries, interethnic fragmentation, sometimes referred to in domestic African political parlance as "tribalism," was most clearly inherited from Britain's colonial policy of "indirect rule." Indirect rule buttressed primordial loyalties to smaller kinship groups by strengthening the position of chiefs and incorporating them as "tribal" leaders into the colonial structure. Where "tribes" and "chiefs" did not exist, the British invented them and appointed "warrant chiefs" to administer these new entities. Most chiefs tended to limit their people's political vision; they were paid to collect taxes, recruit labor, and administer British laws among their "tribes." Nigerian nationalist chief Obafemi Awolowo has pointed out that "... indirect rule.... operated harshly to curb the articulateness of progressive Nigerians" and "individual freedom was severely limited" by chiefs.[3] It was unrealistic to expect that people who had been governed by British colonialists separately as "tribes," under the pretext of preserving their traditional values and institutions, would easily begin to cooperate with other ethnic groups in independent Africa. In colonial Nigeria, for instance, the Nigerian Youth Movement of the 1930s, with branches all over southern Nigeria, broke into two factions representing Yoruba and Ibo "tribal" interests, while northern Nigerians under the powerful Muslim emirs had no connection with the Youth Movement at all. In Kenya, meanwhile, political groups like the Kikuyu Central Association and the North Kavirondo Tax Payers Association also were ethnically based and were not permitted political links with groups outside their "tribes," and when they tried to work together, they were declared illegal and banned.

It is entirely possible that as full democratization comes to different independent African countries, some ethnic groups might begin to dream about creating separate states, and new micronationalisms may emerge. For instance, in the wake of concessions by former president, Kenneth Kaunda, to allow a multiparty system (1991), the Lozi people of western Zambia began agitating for a separate state of their own. The challenge of responding to the demands of micronationalists and "tribal" leaders, while also respecting citizens' democratic rights to speak out and assemble freely, will severely tax the capacity of independent African states not only to maintain their inherited territorial boundaries but also to establish democracy. We will return to this point in the next chapter when we talk about the struggle for democracy and free markets.

POLITICAL INSTABILITY

Many explanations have been offered for the pervasiveness of political instability and violence in independent Africa, including interethnic rivalry and economic competition for scarce economic resources. In addition, Claude Ake has pointed to political corruption and to the willingness of African politicians to use extreme measures to achieve their political goals and retain power. Political authority during colonial rule tended to nurture and reward sycophantic "native authorities" within hierarchical colonial systems where ultimate power usually rested with European governors. Since such authoritarian systems allowed no room for progressive African politicians, those who chose to become politically active were usually branded as "agitators." Such "agitators" were denied opportunities to participate legally and freely in political activities, and after World War II, their primary aim was to assume all political power from European colonial authorities. After independence, many leaders had no intention whatsoever of sharing that authority with anyone else; rather, they were afraid of what might happen to them if they ever lost possession of the reins of government.

Many African nationalist leaders, not having been exposed to the "democratic traditions" of their precolonial heritage or of the European metropoles, were determined not to share power or let anyone challenge them. In fact, the mass mobilization strategy employed by nationalist movements to appeal to rural peasants in their struggle for independence did not promote the give-and-take normally associated with open democratic politics. Generally speaking, nationalist parties and liberation movements were not democratic institutions; rather, they were tightly knit organizations dedicated to wresting political power from the colonial authorities.

Democratic politics is a "variable-sum game," in which the winner acquires only some of the power and is prepared to share it with others. African leaders often saw themselves as participants in a "zero-sum" game of politics, in which gains by one side are always made at the expense of the opposition. Independent African countries that inherited the British multiparty system (the "Westminster Model"), with a parliamentary opposition and an independent judiciary and civil service, have found that their ethnic and regional divisions have made it difficult to debate policy differences while also functioning cooperatively in national politics.

In many independent countries, minority or opposition parties were pressured into dissolving themselves and merging with governing parties. Kenya, for example, became independent in December 1963, under a two-party system, with Kenyatta's KANU in control of the government and the minority Kenya African Democratic Union (KADU) as an opposition party; but there was so much pressure and intimidation brought to bear on the opposition that only a year later, in utter frustration, opposition leaders decided to dissolve KADU and join KANU. In 1966, when important policy and ideological differences within KANU could not be resolved and Vice President Oginga Odinga resigned in order to form an opposition party—the Kenya People's Union—the KANU-led government reacted angrily and ordered new elections. KPU candidates were harassed, intimidated, and treated like traitors. The six KPU candidates who won in that by-election continued to be persecuted. Finally, in the widespread disturbances that occurred in the wake of the assassination of Economics Minister Tom Mboya, KANU government officials found a perfect excuse to proscribe the party and jail Odinga and his colleagues and supporters without trial. Thereafter, KANU's selective use of detention without trial against government critics made it unnecessary to legislate a one-party state. After Kenyatta died in 1978, his successor, Daniel arap Moi, continued the same pattern. In 1982, following an attempted coup d'etat, Moi welcomed a move by parliament to make Kenya a de jure one-party state. From then until 1991, it was illegal for anyone to criticize the one-party government or to suggest that other political parties be permitted to exist.

In South-Central Africa, Zambia and Zimbabwe offer parallel examples of how other dominant political parties have attempted to absorb or abolish opposition blocs. Zambia's Harry Nkumbula, head of the opposition African National Congress, was defeated at independence by Kenneth Kaunda's United National Independence Party (UNIP) and had to dissolve the ANC before he could join the UNIP-dominated government. In 1971, Kaunda's close friend and former vice-president, Simon Kapwepwe, formed the United Progressive Party (UPP). During the following year, UPP was also banned by the government, and Kapwepwe was detained without trial. Kaunda remained Zambia's president until 1991, when a strong pro-democracy movement forced him to recognize opposition parties, and he was defeated by trade union leader Frederick Chiluba in open elections.

Robert Mugabe, Zimbabwe's national leader since independence (1980), has stood against the continental pro-democracy movement of the early 1990s, seeking to impose one-party rule on his country. The bitter struggle between Robert Mugabe's Zimbabwe African National Union (ZANU) and Joshua Nkomo's Zimbabwe African People's Union (ZAPU)—who alternately acted as both allies and enemies during the long armed struggle against the white minority government of Ian Smith's Rhodesia (1965–1980)—also led to a forced merger after independence. Nkomo had not been allowed to function as a member of the opposition, while the ZANU-led government—the merger now referred to as ZANU-PF (ZANU-Patriotic Front)—often used excessive force in dealing with Zimbabweans who supported Nkomo. At one time, Nkomo himself had to flee abroad in fear for his life. As Mugabe's willingness to use deadly force in order to preserve his power escalated, Nkomo bought and stored arms and ammunition (in preparation, allegedly, for undertaking some kind of an armed bid for power). Even while Nkomo remained a senior minister in Mugabe's government, Mugabe continued to voice intentions of proclaiming a de jure one-party state (presumably to promote national unity in Zimbabwe). This proposal met with a great deal of resistance, both within his own party and in the country at large, forcing Mugabe to give up on the idea of imposing a one-party system on the country even though he believes to this day that Zimbabwe should be a one-party state.

Broadly speaking, then, new African countries and their leaders faced two problems at independence—one political and the other economic. Their political challenge was how to broaden their popular legitimacy while building cohesive national structures and ideologies. Their economic goal was to increase productivity, so as to improve the material well-being of ordinary African people who had experienced acute deprivation and poverty for so long during the colonial era.

POLICY CHOICES AFTER INDEPENDENCE

In confronting the various political and economic problems facing them during the years following independence, many African nationalist leaders sought to create "legitimacy" to generate unity and win support of all citizens in their new countries by initiating one-party states. Many also chose to pursue economic development actively by adopting various systems of African socialism (as opposed to the form of European capitalism they had experienced under colonial rule). Although one-party states and African socialism may have appeared to offer short-term solutions, in the long run these approaches actually created difficulties that continued to fester till the 1980s—difficulties that were reflected in the large numbers of military takeovers, civil wars, and refugees in independent Africa.

One-Party Systems

Many arguments have been advanced by African leaders as to why a one-party system was more suitable to independent African states than a multiparty system. African leaders have cited the ever-present danger of "tribalism," or what Eastern Europeans call "micronationalism." They have suggested that permitting more than one party would encourage people to form parties along "tribal" or micronational interests rather than national issues. It is indeed fair to say that much political conflict in Africa has sprung from demands for economic and political benefits being expressed in ethnic terms. As William Tordoff has written,

> Tribes or, more accurately, regional-linguistic groups ... were vehicles of symbolic expression of political and economic competition; in other words, "tribalism," which is as unsatisfactory a concept in political science as in social anthropology, was the idiom within which sectional competition took place. Sectional leaders fostered sectional identification by playing on the emotions of their followers to win support and votes.[4]

Claude Ake has suggested that such regional ethnic differences have often emerged from societies where "'blood ties' are the basis of social organization. In these communities, status is ascribed rather than achieved, primary groups dominate social interaction, and the development of secondary groups is at best rudimentary." Such social structures, inherited from the past, render "the social and political integration of members of different primary groups in the society slow and difficult."[5]

Thus, insistence on one party served a natural option by way of building new national identities and of combating tendencies for local leaders to create many competitive political parties based on family or regional-linguistic affiliation. African leaders also argued that political culture in Africa at the time of transition to independence was totally unsuited to multiparty systems or to "the carefully articulated pattern of parliamentary rule based on European examples."[6] This view was enunciated eloquently by Julius Nyerere:

> There can only be one reason for the formation of such parties [of opposition] in a country like ours—the desire to imitate the political structure of a totally dissimilar society. What is more, the desire to imitate where conditions are not suitable for imitation can easily lead us into trouble. To try and import the idea of a parliamentary opposition into Africa may very likely lead to violence—because the opposition parties will tend to be regarded as traitors by the majority of our people, or, at best, it will lead to the trivial manoeuvrings of "opposing" groups whose time is spent in the inflation of artificial differences into some semblance of reality for the sake of preserving democracy.[7]

Although such perceptions seemed reasonable, one-party states in independent Africa were increasingly challenged by pro-democracy movements, especially in the 1990s. One-party states, imposed on people in different countries without engaging any consultative mechanism to secure popular consent, have not fostered the national unity envisaged by nationalist leaders of the 1960s. Instead, many nationalist leaders used the specter of "tribalism" as an excuse to develop extremely autocratic systems, to stifle political discussion, to foster personality cults, and to ensure that they remained in office indefinitely. As Christian Potholm wrote with respect to Nkrumah's one-party rule in independent Ghana,

> Nkrumah took an essentially pluralistic society with a long history of individual freedom and personal achievement and attempted to rule it by increasingly arbitrary methods. He gradually outlawed all formal opposition, stifled dissent, and, by surrounding himself with a group of sycophants and expatriate white advisers, cut himself off from his people and ignored their increasing alienation from his regime. He did not attempt much political mobilization after independence and gener- ally disregarded the need to engage the people of Ghana politically. As a result, the CPP, formerly a true mass party, gradually withered away.[8]

As Nkrumah accrued more power, former allies and associates rose up to oppose him. He responded by enacting the Preventive Detention Act, which gave him the authority to detain, without trial or right of appeal, those who disagreed with him, and many prominent Ghanaian patriots like Dr. J. B. Danquah and Ako Adjei found themselves behind bars without due legal process. Establishing a security guard to protect himself and an extensive security network to spy on people suspected of disagreeing with his policies or opposing him, Nkrumah invited Soviet agents to help him run these elaborate security operations. He rigged a referendum submitted to the people, winning electoral support for the right of the president to hire and fire judges. Ali Mazrui, who described Nkrumah as a kind of Leninist czar, argues that he "destroyed the democracy in Ghana that he, more than any other man, had helped to create."[9] When he also took for himself the title of *Osagyefo* ("the Blessed Redeemer"), it seemed to some that Nkrumah also wanted to acquire magical powers to protect himself against political adversaries.[10] In any case, this title enhanced Nkrumah's sense of political invincibility and contributed to a personality cult. Mazrui concludes, "Nkrumah's czarist myths of splendor and sacred leadership might have served a purpose in Ghana's development. But Nkrumah carried it too far. He appeared to have become so obsessed with his own myths of grandeur that the whole organization of the Convention People's Party lost its inner efficiency."[11]

Under different circumstances, other newly independent African countries also established one-party governments. Independent Uganda, a quilt of four proud kingdoms and large ethnic groups, inherited from the British a federal structure that permitted considerable autonomy to different kingdoms. As mentioned previously, Milton Obote, Uganda's first prime minister, viewed the existence of such large political units in Uganda as a clear obstacle in his drive to attain a strong unitary government. Obote reneged on a political compromise to preserve the ceremonial post of president of Uganda for the *kabaka* of Buganda. He overthrew the king, suspended the constitution, abolished all the monarchies in the country, and took over the presidency of the country himself, transforming it into a powerful executive authority. In independent Zambia, the Barotse people had been governed as a protectorate called Barotseland, where their king (the *litunga*), his prime minister (the *ngambela*), and their advisers enjoyed significant autonomy and nursed hopes of leading their country toward separate statehood once the British left. However, Kaunda managed to co-opt this indigenous leadership into a centralized government with himself at the helm, making sure that many Barotse individuals held important posts both in the government and in the UNIP, the ruling party. Kaunda subsequently beat back efforts by other Zambians to form political groups by arbitrarily detaining and harrassing political opponents until 1991, when he was pressured into calling a genuinely competitive multiparty election—which he lost.

Similar trends have been apparent in Kenya, where the British crafted a federal constitution, based on *majimbo* (meaning "regions" in Swahili). KADU hoped a regional system would allay the concerns of smaller ethnic groups who feared the hegemony of Kenya's two largest ethnic blocs, the Kikuyu and the Luo of KANU. A year after independence, following the "voluntary dissolution" of KADU, Kenyatta's KANU government scrapped the "majimbo" constitution along with its elective regional assemblies. Kenya's original senate, composed of forty-one delegates (one from each district in the country at the time of independence), was merged with the lower house, thereby turning a bicameral parliament into a unicameral one. Kenyatta became executive president, the post of prime minister was abolished altogether, and local government reverted to the structures of colonial times (including district and provincial commissioners as well as "chiefs"). Local government authorities became extensions of Kenya's new central government, with wide discretionary powers to maintain "law and order." The arrest of Odinga and the banning of the KPU created a de facto one-party state in 1969, and the KANU government declared a de jure one-party state in 1982.

The same movement toward one-party rule occurred in independent francophone Africa, although one-party rule emerged there even before independence, beginning with the 1946 reforms that permitted colonized Africans to form political parties and vote in general elections. By 1962, when France had granted independence to all her former African colonies, many of these parties had become strong enough to overwhelm their opposition. This was the situation in Côte d'Ivoire (Ivory Coast), Guinea, and Mali. During decolonization (1948–1962), many French African nationalist leaders joined the Rassemblement Democratique Africain (RDA); each colony had an RDA chapter. Felix Houphouet-Boigny, who had been one of the founders of RDA, established the Parti Democratique de la Côte d'Ivoire (PDCI) as a chapter in Côte d'Ivoire. The PDCI initially took a somewhat radical stance toward France, even suffering some government repression, until it absorbed many smaller ethnic parties and eventually emerged as the dominant nationalist party in Côte d'Ivoire. After Houphouet-Boigny provided the support necessary for Guy Mollet to form a socialist government in France in 1956, elections were held in Côte d'Ivoire in 1957, in which the PDCI captured *all* sixty seats of their own new legislative assembly as well as the two Côte d'Ivoire seats in the French Assembly. In postwar Guinea, where Sekou Toure had begun his nationalist career as a militant trade unionist affiliated with the French Confederation Generale du Travail (CGT) and helped to form the Parti Democratique de Guinee (PDG) as a branch of the RDA, the PDG won fifty-six out of sixty seats for the local legislative assembly in 1957, overwhelming two smaller, ethnically based parties. In 1958, the PDG led Guinea in voting "no" in de Gaulle's referendum, asking if Africans wished to join an international

French "community." Guinea was the only French colony to have declined the invitation to join. Shortly afterward, the two smaller parties merged with Toure's PDG and a one-party state was born in independent Guinea. Like Nkrumah, President Sekou Toure abrogated to himself titles that led to a personality cult; in the government-controlled press, he was referred to as the "Faithful and Supreme Servant of the People," the "Doctor of Revolutionary Sciences," and the "Liberator of Oppressed Peoples." Similar stories of one-party states, with different particulars, could be told about Senegal, Mali, Cameroon, and most other independent francophone African countries.

African Socialism

At the time of independence, new African leadership sought to establish economic systems and institutions that would develop their national economies and transform people's lives for the better. Because colonial capitalism had drained their resources and left their people destitute, many African leaders turned to newly formulated policies. People's thirst for education and their desperate need for medical care to heal common maladies were overwhelming, and popular expectations that promises made by nationalist politicians would be fulfilled were dauntingly high. The decolonization period had not provided enough time for African nationalists to think specifically about what kinds of economic systems they wanted to build or about how they could best achieve economic growth; it was much easier to campaign against colonialism than to figure out the complexities of how to promote self-sustaining national economies in the modern world.

African societies and economies had been changed by the colonial experience in ways that people and their leaders were only beginning to appreciate fully. The choice facing Africans was not between reviving "traditional" economic systems that existed before the colonizers came and maintaining economic systems molded by the colonial presence. The traditional systems had changed dramatically, and the colonial systems had failed to develop African economies. African nationalist leaders themselves had gone through colonial educational systems and had become exposed to, or acculturated by, Western political and social ideas. They coveted the material way of life they had seen Europeans enjoying, either as settlers in Africa or in their own countries in Europe. However, in their desire to assert their autonomy and distance themselves from colonial policies as much as they could, new nationalist leaders attempted to combine elements of socialist theory and "traditional" African values into different policies—what they called African socialism. The goal of these ideologies was to build nations in which there would be a high degree of social and economic equality, where lands that had been expropriated from Africans would either be restored to the original owners or given to those who were prepared to work them for the benefit of all.

Philosophical debates raged during the 1960s over the exact meaning of African socialism. Were there indeed different kinds of socialism, or just one "scientific" socialism, which had been first and fully articulated by Karl Marx himself? Was it possible for African societies, with no clearly defined social and economic classes, and only a minimum of modern industrial technology, to move directly into modern socialist production without first passing through a capitalist stage of economic development? Did African leaders understand enough about existing socialist societies in Eastern Europe and China to emulate them successfully? Would it be possible for African countries to adopt socialism while also maintaining close relations with Western powers?

Despite their uncertainty about the answers to such questions, most African nationalist leaders professed to institute economic policies based on their various notions of African socialism. The concept was not only fashionable, but it also seemed to be the best economic ideology for fostering a radical restructuring of African colonial economies, and its underlying moral precepts were compellingly attractive. Socialist countries had not been involved in colonial oppression of the Africans; most of them openly came to the Africans' aid during their struggles for independence, so it made ample sense to look to them for help. Many African nationalist leaders equated capitalism with the negative and exploitative experience of colonial rule. They feared that pursuing a capitalist development path would exacerbate social and political inequalities, thus spawning political conflict.

A number of independent African governments declared that they were pursuing socialist policies when, in fact, they were not. Kenyatta's KANU-led government professed to be socialist and even produced a sessional paper entitled *African Socialism and Its Application to Planning in Kenya*. This paper was vague as to what African socialism meant. It raised many economic and political questions, suggesting that the KANU government was not sure what needed to be done to implement socialism or what a socialist Kenya would look like. On closer examination, the national economic policies established by KANU were neither African nor socialist, since Kenyatta and Economics Minister Tom Mboya had decided to continue with the economic system inherited from the British. Before he was assassinated in July 1969, Mboya himself admitted that he thought socialist policies would lead to poverty. He asserted that what Africans needed were economic policies that encouraged the production of commodities that would earn foreign currency, improve the national economy, and raise the living standards of the people. Mboya quipped that socialism meant equal distribution of wealth, not equal distribution of poverty, and that a nation could not distribute wealth without first creating it.

Of the many African leaders who set out to build new national economies by pursuing policies reflecting African socialism, Julius Nyerere of Tanzania, Kwame Nkrumah of Ghana, Sekou Toure of Guinea, and Léopold Senghor of Senegal are the most notable.

Tanzania

Although each of these leaders developed different ideologies that they described as African socialism, Julius Nyerere's concept of *Ujamaa* (Kiswahili for "familyhood" or "extended family") was most clearly and concretely translated into both policy and ideology (especially between 1967 and 1973). During the first year of Tanzania's independence, Nyerere set forth the broad outlines of *Ujamaa*, which he described as "the basis of African socialism." He assumed that each African country would develop its own kind of African socialism, a version that was best suited to its unique historical, social, and political conditions. Nyerere argued that before colonization, Tanzanian people lived in extended family networks that embraced a collective ethic, in which all shared their resources, owned some land in common, and worked in their lands cooperatively in order to provide for the needs of the entire community. Taking some "oratorical license," he declared that there had been no class divisions; all were workers, and no one exploited anyone. To drive his ideological point home, Nyerere quoted a Swahili proverb: *Mgeni siku mbili, siku ya tatu, mpe jembe* ("Treat your guest as a guest for two days, on the third day, give him a hoe"). As he wrote in 1962,

> One of the most socialistic achievements of our society was the sense of security it gave to its members, and the universal hospitality on which they could rely.... the basis of this great socialistic achievement was this: that is was taken for granted that every member of society—barring only the children and the infirm—contributed his fair share of effort towards the production of its wealth. Not only was the capitalistic, or the landed exploiter, unknown to traditional African society, but we did not have that other form of modern parasite—the loiterer, or idler, who accepts the hospitality of society as his "right" but gives nothing in return! Capitalistic exploitation was impossible. Loitering was an unthinkable disgrace.[12]

Conceding that no traditional African society enjoyed complete economic equality, he nonetheless argued that historically those who had greater resources helped their communities in times of need—such as during famines or disasters, when they shared freely with others. This egalitarian, pre-colonial Tanzania, Nyerere believed, was interrupted by the imposition of a new colonial order beginning in the 1890s. Because Tanzanian society under colonial rule remained mostly rural, preindustrial, and underdeveloped—with plenty of land and labor and no overwhelming indigenous class interests, and with its people still living in kinship groups— Nyerere was certain that it was entirely possible to build a new kind of socialist society in modern Tanzania. In 1962, he argued as follows:

> The foundation and the objective of African Socialism is the extended family. The true African Socialist does not look on one class of men as his brethren and another as his natural enemies.... He rather regards *all* men as his brethren—as members of his ever extending family. That is why the first article of TANU's Creed is: *Binadamu wote in ndugu zangu, na Afrika ni moja.* If this had been originally put in English, it could have been: "I believe in Human Brotherhood and in the Unity of Africa."
>   *"Ujamaa,"* then, or, "Familyhood," describes our socialism. It is opposed to capitalism, which seeks to build a happy society on the basis of the exploitation of man by man; and it is equally opposed to doctrinaire socialism which seeks to build its happy society on a philosophy of inevitable conflict between man and man.[13]

More concretely defined in the Arusha Declaration (1967), Nyerere's *Ujamaa* policies sought to attain the following goals:

1. Complete human equality and the absence of economic classes with wide disparities in income and benefits.
2. Political democracy in which individuals would be allowed to vote in open elections for candidates of their choice, and in which anyone, within certain rules, could run for elective office at the local, regional, or national level.
3. Just and fair wages for work performed.
4. The eradication of all forms of exploitation and the prevention of accumulation of wealth incompatible with the nature of a classless society.
5. Public ownership of the economy, that is, all firms, factories, industries were to be owned by the state in order to advance economic justice for everyone.
6. Respect for a certain amount of private property such as personal belongings and household goods, so long as the amount was not enough to give the owner undue influence or the ability to exploit other people.
7. Basic political freedoms of speech, association, movement, and worship, *within the context of law.*[14]

Nyerere's was a genuine attempt to establish a new society in independent Tanzania that would draw from the highest principles its old order, and traditional cultures had to offer as ethical guidelines for modern development.

Politically, Nyerere established a one-party democracy. The only parties opposing TANU in the pre-independence elections (1958–1961) based their platforms on "racialism" (which, like "tribalism," Nyerere and TANU tried to eradicate in independent Tanzania) and won no seats. The procedures for picking candidates for parliamentary election were relatively open. To run for parliament, one had to be a member of the party (open to all Tanzanian citizens) and obtain at least twenty-five signatures of party members in the constituency that the aspiring candidate wanted to represent. Thereafter, the TANU District Conference Committee interviewed the applicants and voted to select two or three official candidates for parliament in each constituency. Since the parliamentary elections of 1965, subsequent national elections (held every five years) have been quite competitive, resulting in considerable turnovers in the membership of parliament and among cabinet ministers—especially those found to be out of touch with constituents or corrupt in their duties. There was some restriction of discussion during campaigns: Candidates were forbidden to appeal to ethnic, religious, or regional sentiments. Discussion of other issues, however, was wide ranging enough to earn Tanzania a well-deserved reputation as a functioning one-party democracy.

After mainland Tanganyika (independent in 1961) joined the island of Zanzibar (which became independent in 1963) to form a federal United Republic of Tanzania (1964), Zanzibar was ruled by the Afro-Shirazi Party (the only legitimate party on the islands), while TANU ran the government of mainland Tanganyika. In 1977, after painstaking negotiations and long preparations, the two parties merged to form the Chama cha Mapinduzi (CCM or the Revolutionary Party). The CCM severely restricted party membership and trained party members to become government functionaries. Prior to the merger of the two political parties in 1977, executive party organs were fairly representative of Tanzanian society as a whole—including the National Union of Tanzanian Workers (NUTA), the National Women's Organization (UWT), the Cooperative Union of Tanzania (CUT), the TANU Youth League (TYL), and the Tanzania Parents Association (TAPA), together with the universities, the Association of Chambers of Commerce, and most regional constituencies.

Implementation of *Ujamaa* called for the state to play a very strong role in developing the country's rural economy. As Nyerere himself put it, Tanzania was "a rural society where improvement will depend largely upon the efforts of the people in agriculture and in village development."[15] Since Tanzania had ample land and labor but little capital, agricultural production would be the first target for national development. *Ujamaa* villages, established by peasant families, would work with producer cooperatives, practicing cooperative labor and community decision making. Between 1967 and 1973, the function of the national government was simply to provide guidance and support for the creation of such villages. According to the Leadership Code of the Arusha Declaration, party and government leaders could not hold stock in a private company, be a member of the board of directors of a private company, have more than one source of income, or be a landlord. After 1967, government and party officials increasingly became central planners and parastatal (quasi-governmental) bureaucrats with responsibility for regulating the production, distribution, and marketing of cash crops such as coffee, tea, and sisal.

During the mid-1970s, however, government and party officials moved beyond providing guidance and support for *Ujamaa* villages. Beginning in 1974, officials supervised mass movements of rural Tanzanians away from ancestral homes and into new "development villages" that were better served with roads and other infrastructure. There was widespread resistance against this "villagization" policy. Rural Tanzanians were closely attached to their ancestral land, and new development villages were located on roads far away from the most productive fields. When CCM bureaucrats came into these new villages to supervise development policies, they were auto-cratic, commanding villagers to comply with their directives. Local people resented being moved and ordered about, and rural productivity began to fall off during the late 1970s.

Meanwhile, Tanzania's social service sector, financed chiefly through foreign aid, especially from Scandinavian countries—grew immensely in rural areas. The country's educational system (thoroughly reformed in 1967) grew especially fast, so that by 1980 more than 90 percent of Tanzania's school-age children were attending classes regularly. Adult education classes had also helped to raise Tanzania's literacy rate above 80 percent, making it one of the highest in all of Africa. Free medical dispensaries and clean water supplies were made available to many rural people, for the first time, in new development villages, and the income ratio between the highest government salaries and the minimum wage was reduced to 6:1. Nonetheless, falling productivity among peasants generated less national income and made it impossible for Tanzania to continue supporting its social service sector.

The national economy began to stagnate as inefficient parastatal agencies replaced locally based producer cooperatives and transport services. By the 1980s, Tanzania's national economy was experiencing negative growth. Bureaucrats became more entrenched and corrupt. Inflation soared as the national currency lost value. Little business was conducted through official channels, and public morale plummeted. Unable to repay the interest on foreign aid loans from the 1980s, Tanzania could not even borrow enough money to maintain ongoing development projects in the 1980s, much less to expand development. Hardworking peasants, no longer in control of their own economic lives, resented party and government officials who earned much more, lived better than they did, and continued to order them about.

Tanzanians, whose national army successfully repelled an invasion by Ugandan dictator Idi Amin and pushed him out of Uganda altogether in 1979, were unable to meet the 500 million dollar cost of the war. Even as

OPEC oil prices soared, Nyerere refused to accept the Structural Adjustment Programs (SAPs) imposed on Tanzania by the World Bank and donor agencies. SAPs were conditions that had to be met by poor countries in order for them to reschedule their debts and to qualify for additional foreign aid. Realizing that his economic policies had led independent Tanzania into bankruptcy, Nyerere resigned as president in 1985 in order to make it possible for his successor, Ali Hassan Mwinyi, to accept and implement the SAP reforms required by the international financial institutions.

Ghana

Whereas Nyerere believed that traditional African societies were classless and that a new type of socialist development based on African values and traditions was feasible, Kwame Nkrumah of independent Ghana did not think there was such a thing as African socialism. Influenced heavily by European Marxists, Nkrumah argued that African societies had always had classes and class interests:

> Today, the phrase "African socialism" seems to espouse the view that the traditional African society was a classless society imbued with the spirit of humanism and to express a nostalgia for that spirit. Such a conception of socialism makes a fetish of the communal African society. But an idyllic, African classless society (in which there were no rich and no poor) enjoying a drugged serenity is certainly a facile simplification; there is no historical or even anthropological evidence for any such society. I am afraid the realities of African society were somewhat more sordid. All available evidence from the history of Africa, up to the eve of the European colonization, shows that African society was neither classless nor devoid of a social hierarchy.... Colonialism deserves to be blamed for many evils in Africa, but surely it was not preceded by an African Golden Age or paradise. A return to the pre-colonial African society is evidently not worthy of the ingenuity and efforts of our people.[16]

In the early years of his political leadership in Ghana (called the Gold Coast by the British colonialists), Nkrumah stressed common elements in African society for the purpose of unifying an independent Ghana. But the racism and discrimination he had encountered in the United States when he was going to college, coupled with exposure to the radical ideas of Pan-Africanists Marcus Garvey, George Padmore, W. E. B. DuBois, and C. L. R. James, convinced him that precolonial African societies had classes and that traditionally based class interests had been reinforced during the colonial era. From 1961 until 1966, when his CPP government was overthrown, Nkrumah attempted to implement Marxist–Leninist policies under the rubric of African socialism. Neither his rhetoric nor his policies were as coherently and concretely articulated as those of Julius Nyerere. As T. C. McCaskie has observed,

Until the early 1960s, the CPP stood for a rather ill-defined mixture of ideas: nationalism, a very vague "socialism," and nebulous conceptions of "Africanity" and of solidarity with other developing countries. These concepts underwent considerable refinement in the early period. Pan-Africanist ideas, together with an ill-defined "African socialism," were welded together into an ideology called "Nkrumahism." The Pan-African component was fostered by Nkrumah himself in practical ways; he sponsored the first of a series of conferences on the subject in Accra in 1958. "Socialism" was refined from a number of considerations. It was, in one sense, the logical extension of "state" nationalism—the idea that the state's power should be used to Africanize the leading sectors of the economy. It was also a response by Nkrumah, among other African leaders, to what he viewed as a serious escalation of Western neocolonialist adventurism in the former Belgian Congo in 1960.[17]

A few years before his death, writing from Guinea where he had taken refuge following his overthrow, Nkrumah wrote most openly and angrily as a revolutionary Marxist, advocating armed struggle to bring about socialism and the complete disengagement of African economies from the Western capitalist system and "neocolonial" dependency.

During the socialist phase of his leadership in independent Ghana, Nkrumah saw the CPP as a mass party and the country's only legitimate political organization—although it appears that there was very little mass participation in it. Political opponents were harshly dealt with, and the secret police made sure that any threats to Nkrumah's power were removed. National leaders who survived under Nkrumah's version of African socialism did so by acting like sycophants. Nkrumah played individuals and factions against each other to keep them off balance and exploit their insecurity. He undermined the integrity of the military by creating a separate presidential guard and consistently favoring it over the regular military establishment. In the process, Nkrumah became isolated from his own people and greatly antagonized the military and leaders of other important national institutions.

Economically, Nkrumah chose not to nationalize key industries, an approach normally favored by doctrinaire socialists. In fact, in the early 1960s, he signed an agreement with an American firm to build an aluminum factory using electricity produced by the hydroelectric plant on the Volta Dam. He tried, without success, to attract foreign investment by establishing an industrial park at Tema.[18] He created parastatals—state enterprises in partnership with foreign-based companies. State agencies were set up to manage and market the production of cash crops such as cocoa. Cocoa-growing farmers were forced to sell their produce to state agencies at prices that were much lower than those in the international marketplace. Ghana's cocoa production began to suffer as more farmers decided that growing it as a cash crop was no longer lucrative. At independence (1957),

Nkrumah inherited the healthiest economy in West Africa and was able to spend freely on projects he felt were important for advancing national and Pan-Africanist linkages. He hosted an important All-Africa People's Conference in 1958, for which he built expensive conference facilities. In the same year, he extended considerable financial aid to Guinea following that country's economically disastrous break with France. Using American aid, he financed the construction of a massive hydroelectric plant on the Volta River, an ambitious but very expensive project that Ghana needed but could neither afford nor use efficiently. Meanwhile, as the international market price of cocoa was declining, Nkrumah began to borrow heavily from abroad. After 1961, Nkrumah's vociferous anti-imperialist rhetoric further alarmed Western countries, whose aid he continued to seek. By 1965, when he sought more than $2 billion in financial aid from Western nations, not one was willing to help. By the time that Nkrumah was overthrown in February 1966, the Ghanaian economy was bankrupt and the price of cocoa was at its lowest level ever.

Guinea

Another African socialist leader whose ideology was mostly derived from Marxist thought was Guinea's Sekou Toure, who began his political career as a trade unionist. While he believed in a communal Africa much like Nyerere described, he also felt that class interests and class exploitation had arisen in Guinea during colonial times, citing African chiefs as an example of a greedy and oppressive class that had been strengthened by French colonialism. Once such oppressive classes were eliminated, Toure was certain that a return to the classless communal past was both possible and highly desirable. He was also committed to a one-party state. From the time of independent Guinea's first constitution in 1958, Toure's PDG was the only legal party in the country. At that time, the PDG was truly a mass party, with nearly one half of Guinean adults holding membership in it. Membership assessments were automatically deducted from the pay of all union workers and sent to the party treasury. Initially, Toure was reluctant to follow strict Marxist–Leninist principles, which his more radical colleagues in the PDG urged him to do. He talked about African socialism as "communocracy," in terms not unlike Nyerere's *Ujamaa*. By 1968, however, he had instituted Marxism–Leninism and established about 8,000 Local Revolutionary Powers (PRLs), with branches in virtually all Guinean villages. Ideally, these PRLs were to broaden the base of party democracy and involve people at the grassroots level, where they would be consulted in all decisions affecting their lives. In practice, however, the PRLs simply created a large layer of party functionaries—close to 300,000 of them altogether—who benefited from dues and proceeds remitted by Guinea's citizens. These PRLs brought Toure's PDG party no closer to ordinary people, since decision making was still centralized within PDG's National Political Bureau, presided over by Toure himself.

Because Toure was the only French African nationalist leader to campaign defiantly against Charles de Gaulle's referendum in 1958 and prevail, he earned the respect and admiration of leftist intellectuals and other militant nationalists throughout Africa. Unfortunately, Guinea's "no" vote piqued de Gaulle's pride, and the French left Guinea abruptly. Faced with the daunting task of having to build an entirely new infrastructure under deplorable economic conditions, Toure spent most of the 1960s trying to stay in power. Maintaining state security became the principal goal of the PDG, and power became centralized under PDG rule, alarming many Guineans. Toure became increasingly intolerant of any criticism and launched attacks against political opponents. Detention without trial became a *modus operandi* for dealing with critics of the government. As many as one-third of the Guinean people fled into neighboring countries, and there were widespread reports of torture in Guinean jails. Diallo Telli, a Guinean national and the first secretary-general of the (continental) Organization of African Unity (OAU), was starved to death in detention because he did not fully support Toure. Given Telli's international stature, Toure feared that Telli might become the focus of strong domestic opposition.

In terms of economic development, Sekou Toure initially relied on technical assistance from the Soviet Union and China. The Soviets helped Guineans with the mining of bauxite, whereas the Chinese taught Guineans new techniques of growing rice. Toure's government nationalized banking, insurance, and manufacturing and collectivized agriculture. Collectivization was resisted by peasants, who continued to spend more time tending their small private plots than working on large state farms. Guinea's food production fell drastically, necessitating the purchase of food imports and leaving little or no money for economic development and investment. By 1979, Toure began to soften his hard-line Marxist posture toward Western countries. He made state visits to France and the United States urging private companies to consider investing in Guinea. By the time he died in 1984, Sekou Toure had abandoned much of his Marxist rhetoric and many of his African socialist policies.

Senegal

Léopold Senghor, another West African socialist, articulated a unique ideological vision that informed the kind of socialism he advocated and tried to implement in Senegal. During the 1930s and 1940s, Senghor was instrumental in developing the concept of "negritude" (blackness). This was a reaction to European racism toward Africans in Europe and the Europeans' continuing assertions that Africans were an inferior people who had no history and who had not made any significant contribution to world civilization. Negritude was an affirmation of the inherent worth and dignity of people of African descent. Like the West Indian poet Aime Cesaire, Senghor reacted to European assertions of African inferiority by arguing that the worth of Africans lay principally in their being an emotional, experiential, and humanistic people—as opposed to Europeans, who were mechanistic, rational, and calculating. As life in Europe had become dehumanizing, Senghor argued, the contribution of Africans to the world community of the future would be their ability to humanize it and provide an antithesis to the alienation and spiritual emptiness of modern Western life. "Negritude" as an intellectual movement never quite caught on in English-speaking Africa, partly because African intellectuals disagreed with its precept that Africans were less rational and with the implicit corollary that they were less intelligent than Europeans. Wole Soyinka, Nigeria's Nobel laureate in Literature (1986), dismissed the whole concept of negritude by saying, "Negritude is rather silly. After all, a tiger does not spend his time going around expressing his tigertude." Moreover, there was the feeling that "negritude" was an elitist ideology contrived by Africans who had become acculturated into French culture and who viewed Africans and African culture through European eyes.

As president of Senegal (1960–1980), Senghor claimed that his ideas on negritude went beyond a simple affirmation of the inherent worth of African people, arguing that negritude was a basis on which to develop African socialism. As a socialist, but not a Marxist, he asserted that precolonial African societies were community based and classless, and he sought to reclaim the kinds of economic democracy and spiritual freedom that had undergirded those traditional values. In seeking to implement African socialism in independent Senegal, Senghor believed that his challenge was not to end exploitation of man by man, but to prevent it from spreading, for he conceded that capitalism already existed in colonial Senegal and could not be eliminated simply by government decree. He felt that capitalist values would wither away as African socialism flourished in independent Senegal and that although Senegalese development would require foreign capital and technology, it would not dominate African peasant life. He continued to retain close ties with former French rulers while attempting to build national unity and economic development by advocating community-based African socialism.

African Capitalism

In the 1960s, as their leaders were forging new economic systems, most African countries found it fashionable to assert that they were pursuing a form of African socialism. They believed that socialism would ensure that African workers benefited from their labor and would restore fairness and justice. However, in practice, many of these countries practiced capitalism (free-market systems) or some variation of mixed economies. Kenya was one nation that opted for capitalism while insisting that it was really practicing African socialism.

As mentioned earlier, in 1965, the Kenyan government issued a sessional paper titled *African Socialism and Its Application to Planning in Kenya.* This document asserted that "our country would develop on the basis of the concepts and philosophy of Democratic African Socialism. We rejected both Western Capitalism and Eastern Communism and chose for ourselves a policy of positive non-alignment."[19] Even though this statement may indicate some confusion between economic policy and foreign policy, it is clear that Jomo Kenyatta, Kenya's first president, had no intention of drastically restructuring Kenyan society. The process of linking Kenya's economy with Western capitalism began in the late nineteenth century, when the British East African Company established itself as the governing authority in what later became a British colony. By the time Kenya was declared a Crown colony in 1920, tens of thousands of British settlers had been lured to Kenya by the prospect of being given huge farms. Through taxation and labor conscription, Africans had been forced to join the monetized economy as laborers or peasant farmers growing cash crops for the export market. The settlers were extremely powerful in the colony of Kenya and managed to attract multinational corporations, such as Brooke Bond (which built large tea estates), Bata Shoe Company, and Lonrho. The settlers and the multinational corporations found allies among Asian merchants and African entrepreneurs. By 1963, the Kenyan economy had been successfully incorporated into the Western capitalist economy. Any attempt to restructure it would have meant taking away the power enjoyed not only by white settlers but also by Asian merchants and African professionals, and they would have resisted it vigorously.

Unlike socialist countries, which invariably sought to seize "commanding heights of the economy," Kenya chose not to nationalize industry. At the outset, Kenyatta and his colleagues knew that nationalization would surely frighten away foreign investors and speed up the transfer of funds abroad by Asians and British settlers. So the government embarked on a deliberate policy to lure foreign speculators by assuring them that their investments would be secure. Appropriate legislation was passed extending attractive terms to companies that chose to stay and invest in Kenya. Emphasis was placed on the Africanization of the economy. This simply meant that as British expatriates left, their positions would be taken over by Kenyans of African descent with appropriate education, capital, and skills. The government also initiated measures to acquire companies from foreigners willing to sell them or to provide incentives for African entrepreneurs to become business people. So as to give the fledgling African businesses a chance, Asians—whether Kenyan citizens or residents with British passports—were restricted as to where they could set up businesses or even which commodities they could trade in.[20] Kenyatta decided against a large-scale return of real estate to landless peasants whose property had been taken away by colonial settlers. Expatriate advisers told Kenyatta that agricultural productivity would suffer greatly if a lot of land, which had previously been farmed mechanically with high productivity, was subdivided into small parcels and given out to peasants free or at concessionary prices. For political reasons, some land was purchased by the government and given to landless peasants, but the bulk of it was left to their owners to sell to whomever had the money to buy it.

On behalf of the government, quasi-governmental agencies, such as the Kenya Tea Development Corporation, the Kenya Tourist Development Authority, and the Coffee Board of Kenya, took over sectors of the economy previously dominated by foreign firms. In some instances, the parastatal agencies went into partnership with foreign companies.

These agencies were established for several reasons. One was effectively to transfer ownership of the Kenyan economy from foreign monopolies to Kenyan national control. The second was to facilitate investment in areas that had desperate human needs but not a high enough profit value to attract the private sector. This is true in the case of education, health care, housing, and transportation. Market demands alone are not enough to generate economic development in poor countries. The state must invest in education and social services to provide citizens with skills that would get them jobs. It must also build an infrastructure (roads, communications) upon which economic growth can take place. Unfortunately, the quasi-governmental agencies became inefficient and corrupt, thereby attracting the attention of foreign aid donors and international financial institutions for SAPs. The problem was not excessive government planning but rather the politicization of the parastatals themselves. Political leaders began to use these agencies to create make-believe jobs as productivity declined, and it became necessary to subsidize them with public funds in order to keep them functioning. Instead of contributing to economic growth, these parastatals became a major drain on the country's treasury.

Kenya's capitalist orientation was buttressed by extremely heavy reliance on Western advice and aid. Indeed, even the sessional paper on African socialism[21] was reportedly written by an expatriate adviser in the ministry of economic planning. A key assumption in the economic development plan was reliance on direct assistance from Western industrialized countries. Assistance was provided in the form of highly skilled people, soft loans extended at low interest rates with long grace periods, budgetary grants, and regular loans at commercial bank rates. Highly skilled technocrats began to arrive in large numbers. These people were almost always paid from foreign aid funds and soft loans—raising an interesting question as to whether aid money paid to the nationals of the donor countries was really benefiting the poor country or the donor country itself.

If through nonalignment Kenya intended to come up with a unique, African form of economic system, it was not successful. Kenya was nonaligned only in rhetoric and in its membership in the nonaligned movement, but certainly not in terms of its economic and political relationships. In the cold war and in the extent and intensity of its diplomatic and international activities, Kenya was clearly on the side of the West. Groups within Kenya that showed any sympathy for socialism or that advocated strong ties with the East were ruthlessly suppressed.

WHAT WENT WRONG IN INDEPENDENT AFRICA?

The assertion was made at the beginning of this discussion that African leaders faced two major challenges when they took over the reins of power in their countries: to create strong unified nation-states, where perhaps none existed, and to improve the material conditions of their people by establishing productive economic systems that would help ordinary people realize their hopes and dreams of better lives in the future, after all the deprivation and neglect of the colonial era. These challenges meant that after all the psychological euphoria of having "won" independence subsided, these leaders had to show concrete results.

One-Party Systems

In the political realm, African leaders, at independence, tried to mold unified nations out of the many ethnic groups in each country, some of which had maintained distinct institutions and identities throughout the colonial era. Having hammered out independence constitutions in European capitals, these leaders did not go back to the drawing board after independence and engage their citizens in a constitution-making exercise, during which serious national discussion might have occurred as to the type of the national political system the people wanted, what the development priorities might have been, and what sacrifices were going to have to be made and by which segments of society. It was a mistake that African countries did not go through this important "national" experience. They would have learned a great deal about each other that they didn't know before. They would have built a vision for their future together. Thinking that they were building cohesive nations, many leaders chose to make a change in the constitutions they had, in effect, inherited and leave the rest virtually intact: they established one-party systems with severe limits on basic political freedoms, without which democracy could not take root or thrive. The leaders assumed that African people needed a very strong central government. They assumed that leaders, by definition, knew everything and did not need to consult the people about anything. They assumed that Africans had no social or political differences since they were all black and had been equally oppressed under colonial rule. And they assumed that multiparty systems would somehow undermine national leadership and encourage these putatively "artificial" regional, religious, or ethnic differences to get out of hand. As it turned out, with highly centralized governments, local government officials were reduced to acting as agents of the national government in maintaining law and order and transmitting government directives from the top to the citizens at the bottom. Powerful single parties, staffed with people who lived off membership payments— collected often forcibly from ordinary men and women—tried to make certain that there were no challenges to their control of state power.

Personality Cults

There were deliberate attempts to create personality cults around political leaders with highly embellished titles—the worst examples are perhaps Nkrumah's self-bestowed title of "Osagyefo," meaning the "Redeemer" and Toure's "Doctor of Revolutionary Sciences." In any event, whether the title was "Mwalimu" (for Tanzania's Nyerere) or "Mzee" (for Kenya's Kenyatta), the intent was to convey the image of an all-knowing, all-powerful, benevolent leader—clearly above the law, above reproach, and without a peer—who must be obeyed without question. If anyone had doubt that it's important to have "a vision," Africa is proof that countries led by individuals who have no vision are simply stuck. Such countries are governed ad hoc, plodding day by day from one unbalanced budget to the next. In such countries, decision-making processes are routinely improvised. The leaders normally have no idea where they intend to lead their countries in the future, never try to make the case for why the many ethnic/culture groups in the country need one another, or what kind of society they would like to have achieved by the end of their term in office. Indeed, none of these leaders contemplated ever being out of office. African leaders could have used the euphoria of independence and the goodwill generated then to forge ways of addressing historical grievances among people thrown together by colonial fate, managing and mediating differences, and resolving conflicts, some of which were foreseen in the early stages of independence. These opportunities were lost.

Coups d'etat and Civil Wars

The major consequence has been that the African continent has experienced more military coups than any other, the latest one occurred in Mauritania in August 2005 as President Taya was attending the funeral of King Faud of Saudi Arabia. More than half of African states have had military regimes since independence, and many have endured long civil wars, and several, like the Sudan and the Democratic Republic of Congo, continue to do so.

The Nigerian civil war (1967–1970), for instance, came about when the Ibo people of the southeast sought to secede from Nigeria, then under a military government, in order to create their own Republic of Biafra. This secession followed the killing of thousands of Ibo people in the north; this slaughter was prompted by an earlier military coup (1966), during which Ibo army officers had killed a popular prime minister from the north. During the Biafran War, up to 2 million Ibo lives were lost.

Civil war has also been going on intermittently in the Sudan since 1960, resulting in the deaths of more than a million people. The northern Sudanese, without regard for the traditions of their southern neighbors, have sought to impose Islamic law on their southern compatriots who do not wish to become Muslims. The southern Sudanese have not demanded a separate state; they only wish to live either as Christians or according to their traditional customs. Several cease-fires, established when regional autonomy was recognized in the south, collapsed whenever northern Sudanese leadership attempted to establish Islam as an official state religion and ideology. To compound this religious intolerance, the southerners continue to be subjected to unspeakable brutality, including slavery, the buying and selling of mostly southern children by northerners, a practice that suggests that northerners do not regard southerners as equal human beings. The crisis in Darfur, western Sudan, in which militias armed by the Sudanese government have attacked and killed innocent civilians, raped women, and burned their villages, has exposed the institutional racism toward the dark-skinned Sudanese. Estimates of the dead range as high as a half million. More than 300,000 people have been rendered homeless.

The civil wars following independence sent more Mozambicans and Angolans to their deaths than all their protracted liberation struggles against Portuguese colonial rule combined. Political chaos and economic misery have gone hand in hand in Africa, as elsewhere, and war-torn nations that used to feed themselves have been reduced to waiting for handouts from international relief agencies.

The long-term dictator of what used to be called Zaire General Mobutu Sese Seko was finally ousted, in May 1997, by Laurent-Desire Kabila, who, himself, after a very brief three-year tenure, having failed to unite his diverse country, was killed by his own soldiers and replaced by his young son, Joseph Kabila. The elder Kabila renamed the country the Democratic Republic of Congo. The curse of mineral wealth that lies beneath the Congo attracted neighboring states which made matters worse. Rwanda and Uganda supported insurgents, while Angola and Zimbabwe supported Kabila's government. Initial mediation efforts, first by the late Julius Nyerere (the first president of Tanzania) and later by Nelson Mandela (first president of a democratic South Africa) were not successful. Subsequent talks, sponsored by the United Nations produced a shaky truce, in spite of which foreign armies have never completely left the Congo, especially the resource-rich eastern region of it.[22]

Wars over national boundaries involving Somalia, Ethiopia, Morocco, Algeria, Libya, and Chad have led to armed struggles between Africans living in different countries. Murderous dictatorships in independent Uganda, Central African Republic, and Equatorial Guinea have collectively also cost millions of lives. Even countries without obvious racial/ethnic/ linguistic differences such as Somalia, Rwanda, and Burundi have disintegrated with tremendous losses of human life, for the most part because the leaders lacked a vision to find ways of addressing grievances and issues of differences before conflicts actually broke out. There is nothing of lasting national value to show for the many years of Mohamed Syad Barre's rule in Somalia from 1969 to 1990. During long wars for national liberation and their aftermaths, millions of other Africans in Algeria, Mozambique, Angola, and elsewhere died. Such wars have inevitably resulted in economic devastation.

Refugees

Since independence, Africa's refugee populations have steadily grown. Of the more than 14 million refugees worldwide in 1988, nearly one-third of them were to be found in fifteen African countries. If one were to include internal refugees—people forced to leave their homes because of civil wars or government repression but who remain within their national boundaries— Africa accounts for more than half of all refugees worldwide.[23]

Centralized Economies

Economically, independent African governments established a variety of forms of African socialism or state capitalism. In any case, development imperatives made it seem logical that governments should guide and control their new national economies and most established quasi-governmental corporations called parastatal agencies. These parastatals oversaw the production and marketing of cash crops, most of which had been introduced during colonial times and were to remain Africa's chief earners of hard currency. Parastatals bought these cash crops from the farmers—often at low prices that thwarted incentives to increase production—and sold them abroad for higher world market prices. Although the income that governments gained in this way was supposed to augment the national treasury and underwrite development projects, many government agencies were run inefficiently. They did not provide essential extension services promised to farmers, who were often paid for their crops only after unconscionably long delays. Parastatal agencies, created ostensibly to augment the national treasuries on behalf of the public, were instead directed by politicians to hire more employees than necessary, did not earn profits, and required annual subsidies from the national treasury to stay in business. Appointments to the parastatal agencies were based on political connections rather than professional qualifications of the appointees. Compensation paid to managers of these parastatals reflected the appointees' political clout (in terms of proximity to the president of the country) rather than the performance of the agency. Corruption became the order of the day. This is what was implied in the statement made earlier that African governments were run ad hoc, from budget to budget with no thought as to the long-term viability of the countries' economies.

International Debt

By the 1980s, it was clear that government corporations were weakening Africa's national economies and severely diminishing any earlier hopes of fostering reasonable economic growth and prosperity. Their economic predicament was exacerbated by adverse international economic conditions and commodity prices, sharp increases in the cost of importing oil from OPEC nations, and concomitant recessions in Western industrialized countries as well as in Africa. To stay financially solvent, African governments had grown dependent on foreign aid and loans from the World Bank and the International Monetary Fund, Western countries, and the United Nations. During the 1970s, the loans extended to African countries began to accumulate alarmingly. By the end of the 1980s, the debts comprised, on average, 87 percent of the countries' gross national product or 47 percent of their exports.[24] According to a U.N. report, "between 1970 and 2002, African countries received some $540 billion in loans, paid back close to $550 billion in principal and interest, and still held debt of $295 billion at the end of 2002."[25] Massive international debt has continued to be a major obstacle to economic development in Africa, as most countries find themselves spending meager earnings of hard currency to pay back the interest on their debts. In addition, many of independent Africa's national economies have been devastated by warfare.

Corruption

A point worth mentioning is corruption, which is now pervasive throughout much of Africa, destined to get worse unless something is done. Surely, when economies are stagnant and people are having a hard time making a living, the temptation is extremely high among civil servants to expect or demand payment for performing a task for which they are already being paid. The connection between poverty and corruption cannot be overstated, particularly in this era of global communications in which people all over the world are amply aware of how much they lack compared to the people in the more affluent countries. The other reason for corruption is based on the expectation of people in public office to take care of people from their areas, beginning with members of their families and then those of their ethnic group, without regard to merit. There has been no attempt to find the right balance between support for meritocracy, as a good value in a heterogeneous society, and loyalty to one's relatives in the extended family, also regarded as a good value in tradition-rich Africa. Even though most people understand why corruption exists, it is important for there to be a national discussion and debate, not the kind of debate in which everyone condemns corruption as a terrible thing that is corroding national morality and a sense of fairness, but one in which rules are drawn up to prevent corruption from generating bitterness among citizens of different groups and creating a vicious circle in which each generation of leaders seems bound to repeat what their predecessors did. A leader with a vision can initiate national discussion on such an issue and demonstrate by example how to go about creating a society in which merit is an important component of equity and fair play.

HIV/AIDS

The scourge of the pandemic of AIDS has been catastrophic for the Africans living below the Sahara Desert. It is mentioned here because of the enormity of the disease in Africa and the consequent impact it has had on the economic and social development of the continent. According to the United Nations, in its 2007 report, of the 33 million people worldwide living with HIV, the virus that causes AIDS, 22 million (about 67 percent) of them are in sub-Saharan Africa, an area that contains slightly over 10 percent of the world population. Nearly 2 million children under the age of fifteen years are infected with the virus. Indeed, worldwide, 90 percent of the children with HIV are African children.[26] Because of poverty, lack of education, poor planning, conditions attached to U.S. aid to teach only abstinence (without mentioning safe sex), and certain cultural practices, Africans have been unable to deal with the pandemic effectively. When U.S. president Barack Obama came into office in January 2009, he immediately lifted the restrictions imposed on American aid to fight HIV/AIDS epidemic.

It's been said that in the mid-1950s, when African governments began to gain independence, their level of economic development was the same as that of Asian countries such as Taiwan, South Korea, and Singapore that are now emerging as newly industrializing countries (NICs). Africa is still at the bottom of the economic pile. Bad economic and political choices and decisions, economic mismanagement, corruption, lack of vision on the part of the leaders, and lack of open political discourse and accountability explain Africa's sad story.

THE GAINS OF INDEPENDENCE

It would not be entirely fair, however, to present current African conditions as inexorably hopeless; indeed, many African nations have accomplished much since achieving self-rule during the 1950s and 1960s. A new sense of nationhood has taken root in most African countries. More and more Africans have come to identify themselves as citizens of their new countries, and African leaders have taken responsibility for development policies, some of which have proved useful. There have been major accomplishments in overcoming micronationalism and illiteracy, even in multiethnic states in which people speak many different languages and identify with diverse kinship or religious groups. In the early 1990s, tightly controlled political systems and economic centralization—along with tendencies for governments to resort to force in order to impose order—began to give way to pro-democracy and free-market policies. This process is the subject of the next chapter.

Economically speaking, there have been impressive successes in countries like Egypt, Botswana, Kenya, Gabon, Nigeria, and others. Independent African governments have expanded such national infrastructures as communications facilities, hard-surfaced roads, rail transport, rural health centers, schools, and universities. Indeed, it has been noted that "the growth of education in Africa over recent decades has been phenomenal by any standard, and rates of school attendance have often increased by several thousand percent."[27] Although three of every five Africans still live in the countryside, cities have grown immensely since independence, and many have become national or regional business centers. In the postcolonial years, Africa's annual population increase has been higher than that of any other continent, and traditional attitudes favoring large families still persist. As populations have grown and fertile land has become scarcer, more Africans have left the social safety of their rural homes in search of employment in urban areas. Children born to wage earners in urban areas represent more mouths to feed from inadequate fixed or declining incomes, although rural children still provide needed labor on farms. Greater availability of modern medicine since independence has contributed to dramatic reductions in infant mortality rates, although these rates remain high compared to those of other parts of the world. Family planning is increasingly coming to the attention of government officials as an important component of development policy. Today, more Africans have seen improvements in their material lives than ever before, even as numbers of those experiencing famine and poverty have gone up. Despite impressive advances in such fields as education and health care, however, Africa as a whole has remained the world's poorest continent—beginning with European colonial rule a century ago and continuing in independent Africa today.

NOTES

1. Lord Hailey, *An African Survey*, Revised 1956 (New York: Oxford University Press, 1957), p. 311.
2. Julius K. Nyerere, "Education for Self-Reliance," in Julius K. Nyerere,ed., *Ujamaa: Essays on Socialism* (New York: Oxford University Press, 1968), pp. 44–75.
3. Chief Obafemi Awolowo, "Early Political Organization in Nigeria," in Wilfred Cartey and Martin Kilson, eds., *The Africa Reader: Independent Africa* (New York: Vintage Books, 1970), p. 80.
4. William Tordoff, *Government and Politics in Africa* (Bloomington, IN: Indiana University Press, 1984), pp. 81–82.
5. Claude Ake, "Explaining Political Instability in New States," *Journal of Modern African Studies*, Vol. 11, No. 3 (1973), p. 354.
6. Basil Davidson, *Which Way Africa*, 3rd Edition (New York: Penguin Books, 1973), p. 112.
7. Ibid., pp. 113–114.
8. Christian Potholm, *The Theory and Practice of African Politics* (Englewood Cliffs, NJ: Prentice Hall, 1979), pp. 52–53.
9. Ali A. Mazrui and Michael Tidy, *Nationalism and New States in Africa* (Nairobi, Kenya: Heinemann, 1984), p. 61.
10. Christian Potholm, *The Theory and Practice of African Politics*, p. 116.
11. Ali A. Mazrui and Michael Tidy, *Nationalism and New States in Africa*, p. 61.
12. Julius K. Nyerere, "Ujamaa—The Basis of African Socialism," in Julius K. Nyerere, ed., *Ujamaa: Essays on Socialism* (New York: Oxford University Press, 1968), p. 5.
13. Ibid., pp. 11–12.
14. Julius K. Nyerere, "The Arusha Declaration," in Julius K. Nyerere, ed., *Ujamaa: Essays on Socialism* (New York: Oxford University Press, 1968), p. 13.
15. Julius K. Nyerere, "Education for Self-Reliance," p. 52.
16. Kwame Nkrumah, "African Socialism Revisited," in Wilfred Cartey and Martin Kilson, eds., *The Africa Reader: Independent Africa* (New York: Vintage Books, 1970), pp. 202–203.
17. Tom C. McCaskie, "Ghana: Recent History," in Synge, R. and McCaskie, T. C., eds., *Africa South of the Sahara 1990–1991* (London: Europa Publications, 1990), p. 507.
18. Colin Legum, *Africa Since Independence* (Bloomington, IN: Indiana University Press, 1999), p. 23.
19. Government of Kenya, *African Socialism and Its Application to Planning in Kenya* (Nairobi: Government Printer, 1965), p. i.
20. Colin Leys, *Underdevelopment in Kenya: The Political Economy of Neocolonialism, 1964–1971* (Berkeley: University of California Press, 1974), p. 151.
21. Government of Kenya, *African Socialism and Its Application to Planning in Kenya*.
22. Martin Meredith, *The Fate of Africa: From the Hopes of Freedom to the Heart of Despair, a History of 50 Years of Independence* (New York: Public Affairs, 2005), pp. 539–544.

23. McColm R. Bruce, "The World's Unwanted," *The Wall Street Journal*, Vol. 23 (September 28, 1989), p. A22.

24. Africa Recovery Unit, *African Debt: The Case for Debt Relief* (New York: United Nations, 1992).

25. http://www.africafocus.org/docs04/debt0410.php. Accessed on May 30, 2006.

26. 2006 Report on the global AIDS epidemic, www.unaids.org/en. Accessed on May 8, 2009.

27. Donald G. Morrison, Robert C. Mitchell, and John N. Paden, eds., *Black Africa: A Comparative Handbook*, 2nd Edition (New York: Paragon House, 1989), p. 87.

The African Struggle for Democracy and Free Markets

Prime Minister Margaret Thatcher and President Ronald Reagan were the harbingers of the Structural Adjustment Programs (SAPs) as a transition to free-market capitalism and democracy. Were these two leaders, the IMF, and the World Bank truly interested in the development and prosperity of Africa?

INTRODUCTION

The veteran South African journalist Colin Legum has characterized the years 1939 to 1970 as an era of romanticism in modern African history.[1] The choice of 1939 is deliberate. It was the year World War II began, and with it, the realization that the great war in Europe, among European powers, was going to have profound repercussions for Africa as well. Indeed in Chapter 5, I suggested that World War II was a catalyst in the rise of African nationalism for two major reasons. First, African soldiers who were drafted to fight in the war acquired leadership skills, had their political consciousness raised, and were not prepared to return to their own countries as second-class citizens. Many of them became active in nationalist movements, especially in West Africa. Second, by the end of the war, European colonizers had begun to see the writing on the wall and to realize that their days in Africa as colonial masters were numbered. In response, they initiated a few reforms such as allowing trade unions and political parties to be formed and setting up elected legislatures. For the first time ever, in many countries, Africans were being allowed to run for seats in nascent legislatures to represent African masses. There was great optimism in the air about the future. With political freedom on the horizon, African politicians thought that life was going to be much better for the average African.

Legum refers to the years 1970–1985 as the years of disillusionment.[2] This is the period during which political and economic experiments, which we have already discussed, were tried: the one-party system and variations of centrally planned economies popularly referred to as socialist economies. We now know that these experiments were dismal failures.

Legum thinks that a period of realism began in 1988.[3] Actually, by 1988, many African leaders under enormous pressure from Western governments and international monetary institutions were already admitting that their countries' economies had failed. Promises of prosperity and better lives made to the people had not been kept, and many of these leaders were looking for new ways to revive their economies.

Political realism for Africans has meant for most of them going back to the drawing board to determine for sure what went wrong. In the twenty-seven-year period between 1966 and 1993, no less than sixty-three military coups had occurred on the African continent, not to mention civil wars and wars of national liberation in places such as Zimbabwe, Namibia, South Africa, and the former Portuguese colonies of Angola, Mozambique, and Guinea-Bissau.[4] The soldiers who wrested power in military coups from inept civilian authorities themselves had no clue as to what democracy was all about. Violence and repression were rife in most of these military regimes. Thousands of people either were displaced internally or fled their countries to safe havens in neighboring countries or to Europe and North America. Despite commanding a preponderance of force, these military dictators could not even make the trains run on time. Their performance in office in terms of protecting their people, delivering basic services, or maintaining the infrastructure was as bad as or worse than that of the civilian regimes they had replaced.

THE STRUGGLE FOR DEMOCRACY

Talk of reforming African political and economic systems began in earnest with the coming to power of Prime Minister Margaret Thatcher (1979–1990) of Great Britain and President Ronald Reagan (1983–1991) of the United States.

Questions about the ability of African states to make it on their own after independence have been raised from the time the European colonial states started handing over power to the African elites. As already indicated, African leaders have been searching for winning formulas ever since. Centralized economies and one-party states have failed to deliver prosperity and democracy that the African people fought for and which their leaders promised them. The fall of socialist systems in Eastern Europe, the dismal performance of African economies, and the aggressive salesmanship of the Western democratic and free-market ideas all contributed to the courage of the African people to speak out against dictatorships in their own countries. People's political demands were quite modest: lifting restrictions on freedom of assembly and speech; freeing political prisoners (almost all of whom were jailed without due process); eliminating corruption in the electoral process (much of it having to do with rigging ballots or stuffing ballot boxes, etc.); and permitting other political parties to contest in elections.

Different African states responded to these demands in a variety of positive or negative ways. Some, like Benin, the Gambia, Mauritius, Senegal, and Zimbabwe, permitted competitive elections in which more than one political party contested for parliamentary seats. Benin chose to democratize by holding a national conference, which methodically guided the country toward democratic elections. The irony of the exercise in Benin was that a former president, Mathieu Kérékou, a previously self-declared Marxist, ended up being elected president, but a president whose powers were greatly curtailed by the new constitution.[5] In other countries such as Kenya, the Democratic Republic of Congo (formerly Zaire), and Cameroon, the leaders strenuously resisted calls for reform.

KENYA: FLIRTING WITH DEMOCRACY

In an attempt to mollify international opinion, President Moi of Kenya released political prisoners and held hearings around the country, chaired by his vice-president, to determine the types of reforms people wanted. A report was submitted but Moi refused to release it to the public, arguing that Kenyans were not yet ready for full democracy and that a multiparty system would revive "tribalism." Moi stalled for time and continued to alarm the public with warnings that a repeat of ethnic cleansing that occurred in 1992 might happen again. The president could not suppress the people's yearning for basic democratic freedoms. Moi did, however, accede to two reforms: the reinstitution of the secret ballot in primary elections and the restoration of an independent judiciary. The secret ballot had been scrapped prior to the 1988 general elections in favor of voters queuing publicly behind their candidates' portraits during the so-called nomination process. The candidate attracting more than 70 percent of those queuing was declared the winner. Many voters, afraid to queue behind candidates not favored by the Moi government were, in effect, disenfranchised. The independence of the judiciary had been taken away soon after Moi became president, when parliament, always supine and ever obliging to the president, gave him the power to appoint and fire judges. Now some judges, except those of the High Court and the Appeals Court are still being appointed by a Judicial Service Commission and have security of tenure.

In Kenya, Moi reluctantly recognized other political parties but, taking advantage of divisions within the opposition parties and with some rigging, he managed to win the general elections of December 1992. The government continued to intimidate and harass its opponents, although the press was somewhat freer than before. In June 1997, Moi responded with force, killing scores of people during political demonstrations. He still maintained that Kenyans were not yet ready for democracy. Nevertheless, churches and political and other civil society groups continued to press for and won some constitutional reforms, the most important of which limited the president to two five-year terms beginning from 1992. When the next elections were held in December 1997, Moi won another term, but by then, it was clear that this would be his last term. Efforts by the president's supporters in parliament to extend the terms of office to three were not successful. In December 2002, fourteen of the more than twenty opposition parties formed a coalition called the National Rainbow Coalition (NARC), which won a little over 62 percent of the vote.[6] Heading the NARC ticket for the presidency of Kenya was Mwai Kibaki, a veteran politician who had served as finance minister under the first president of Kenya, Jomo Kenyatta, and as vice-president under Daniel arap Moi, Kenyatta's successor.

Electing a coalition government did not mean that democracy had come to Kenya. The transition to democracy had just begun. The government was not able to deliver a new constitution to the people. It had promised that it would do so within the first 100 days of its new administration. A Constitution of Kenya Committee, chaired by a Kenyan law professor, Yashpal Ghai, drafted a constitution, which was discussed and amended at a national constitutional conference. Instead of the document being submitted directly to the voters, in a referendum, for an up or down vote, parliament decided to amend it, restoring to the presidency the extensive powers that had been taken away. This and other changes infuriated and polarized the voters into two camps, using fruit symbols for their slogans. The banana symbol represented those in favor of the parliament-amended constitution; the orange symbol represented those opposed to the draft document. As expected, there were ethnic/tribal overtones to the debate. When votes were counted, the draft constitution was defeated and the NARC coalition collapsed. There is little doubt that the failure of the Kibaki government to deliver a new constitution became one of the most hotly discussed issues during the general election held on December 27, 2007.

The government also promised to attack corruption, even going so far as to appoint an anticorruption czar reporting directly to the president. In less than two years, the anticorruption czar fled to Britain and later released a report suggesting that the government had not been really serious about ridding the country of corruption. He disclosed that he had told the president about the hurdles he was encountering in his work and the president had done nothing about it. A number of scandals involving theft of large sums of money came to light and were subjects of heated debate in the elections in 2007.[7] To muddy the waters even more, reports began to appear showing that Kibaki's cabinet and senior officers in the government were mostly members of the president's ethnic group. The feeling by other Kenyans, therefore, was that Kibaki was running, not a Kenyan government but, a Kikuyu government. When the elections were held and the Kenya Electoral Commission took three days to announce the winner, people suspected that extensive rigging had occurred. President Kibaki was declared the winner, even though his particular party christened Party of National Unity (PNU) and its allies were losing badly their bid for seats in the single chamber legislature. Election observers, especially those from the European Union (EU), said that the electoral process had not been transparent. Public reaction was swift and intense. What began as public anger at election fraud soon irrationally turned into a huge ethnic conflict as Kikuyu people, anywhere in the country, were presumed to have supported the president and, therefore, subjected to severe attacks by members of other ethnic groups such as Luos, Kalenjins, Luhyas, who allied themselves with the opposition Orange Democratic Movement (ODM). By the time, order was restored and negotiations between PNU and ODM were under way, thanks to the diplomatic skills of former U.N. Secretary-General Kofi Annan, 1,500 Kenyans had lost their lives and more than 300,000 were displaced (i.e., had become refugees in their own country). The Freedom House organization of New York rated Kenya in 2011 as being only Partly Free or Partly Democratic.[8]

MUGABE: "ZIMBABWE BELONGS TO ME"

Robert G. Mugabe, the eight-four-year-old dictator of Zimbabwe, who has been in power since 1980, had shown flashes of extreme intolerance when he faced an uprising in Matabeleland in 1983–1984 in support of Mugabe's political rival, Joshua Nkomo. International reaction to the massacres in Matabeleland was somewhat muted due to Mugabe's tenacious conduct of the guerrilla war that brought down the white minority government of Ian Smith. Mugabe was hailed as a national hero and admired internationally. In 1987, he became executive president of the country. The office of prime minister was then abolished. Despite his popularity at that time, parliament refused to accept his demand for a one-party state. Mugabe became increasingly repressive as his political party, ZANU-PF, won more and more seats. Sanctions have been imposed on Zimbabwe. The people of Zimbabwe have endured starvation and government-directed violence. Mugabe continued to argue that the Western world is out to recolonize his country. In one press conference, he declared that Zimbabwe belongs to him and that the West just better get used to the idea. It's believed that he was reelected in 2002 through rigging. Then as in the elections of 2008, his opponent was Morgan Tsvangarai, a former trade unionist. Mugabe has already indicated that he is going to run for reelection in 2012.

DEMOCRATIC REPUBLIC OF CONGO

In Congo, President Mobutu initially raised hopes by promising a multiparty system. When university students continued to hold demonstrations and to demand more political concessions from his government, Mobutu unleashed savage military force on them, and many students were killed. The reform process remained stalled in Congo until November 1996, when a guerrilla group by the name of the Alliance of Democratic Forces for the Liberation of the Congo began an armed campaign to dislodge Mobutu from power. In less than seven months of the campaign, the rebels, with covert support from Uganda and Rwanda, had captured more than two-thirds of the country. Mobutu's government had the support of Zimbabwe, Angola, and Namibia. Despite that support, Mobutu's thirty-two-year brutal and corruption-ridden dictatorship came to an ignominious end in May 1997 when Mobutu himself fled into exile (in Morocco) and rebel leader Laurent-Desire Kabila triumphantly rode into Kinshasa where he was installed as president of the newly renamed Democratic Republic of Congo. Kabila failed to end what was then clearly a civil war that had cost the country 2 million lives. He himself was murdered in January 2001 by one of his own security men. The elder Kabila was succeeded by his son, Joseph Kabila, then only twenty-nine years old. The younger Kabila proved to be politically more shrewd than his father, vowing to work for peace and to end the civil war. He signed a peace accord with other Congolese political parties and armed rebel groups in 2002 under South African mediation and was eager to hold free and democratic elections to enhance his government's legitimacy. Although late by the peace accord's timetable, the first democratic elections since 1960 were held on July 30, 2006. There were thirty-two candidates running for the presidency and 9,000 candidates vying for the 500 seats in the national assembly (the lower house of the national legislature). Kabila got more votes than any of his opponents but not enough to avoid a run-off election in October 2006 in which there were only two candidates: Jean-Pierre Bemba of the Movement for the Liberation of the Congo (MLC) and Joseph Kabila on the People's Party for Reconstruction and Development (PPRD) ticket. Kabila won the runoff. His party also won 40 percent of the seats in the national assembly, again, the largest block of seats, but not enough to form a government in 2007 without the support of some opposition parties.[9] To make matters worse, fighting continues in eastern Congo as Rwandan soldiers reportedly pursue the Hutu militia hiding out in refugee camps to which Rwandans have fled for their lives. The killings continue. In the meantime, foreign businessmen continue to flock into the Congo looking for lucrative deals, even as Western countries weigh the risks of getting deeply involved in what is turning out to be a difficult transition to a post-Mobutu era.

General elections were held in the Democratic Republic of Congo in November 2011. Joseph Kabila was declared the winner after a runoff.

In the first ballot, there were eleven candidates running for president. There were irregularities which called into question the legitimacy of the election. There is no evidence that things are going to get better in the near future.

CAMEROON: PAUL BIYA'S DEMOCRACY

Cameroon has the unique distinction in Africa of having two European languages—French and English—as the official languages of the country. The United Republic of Cameroon was formed when the British sector and the French sector were unified in 1961. The first president, Ahmadou Ahidjo, was autocratic in the tradition of the first generation of African heads of state and presided over a one-party system under the Cameroon National Union. In 1982, Ahidjo, believing that he was in poor health, unexpectedly resigned and was succeeded by his prime minister, Paul Biya. Biya came to power promising democracy and transparency, but conflicts with Ahidjo, who had retained the chairmanship of the ruling party, may have put him into a corner. Ahidjo was forced into exile, then tried in absentia and convicted of attempting to overthrow the government. Ahidjo's supporters in the Presidential Guard staged an unsuccessful uprising against Biya. As a result of the coup attempt, Biya became more and more repressive—despite changing the ruling party's name to the Cameroon National Democratic Movement (CNMD)—and has governed Cameroon in the same autocratic manner of his predecessor. Enormous political pressure forced him to permit political opposition, but he has used state apparati—state-controlled media and an elaborate security network—to win reelections in 1992, 1997, 2002, and 2007. A brief war with Nigeria in 1994 and 1996 over the disputed Bakassi peninsula in the Gulf of Guinea, thought to have rich oil deposits, provided further excuse to deploy the military and use it repressively against political adversaries.[10] Freedom House rated Cameroon in 2010 as being Not Free.[11]

In spite of resistance to progressive change by the likes of Cameroon, Congo, Zimbabwe, and Kenya, reform is occurring, albeit slowly. Schraeder identifies four different ways by which transition to democracy has occurred.[12] First, some countries have reformed their political systems by making the electoral process more competitive, permitting the formation of more political parties and the freedom to campaign for public support. Although Schraeder cites South Africa as an example of a country that democratized through elections, it cannot be forgotten that an armed struggle had been waged since the early 1960s and that political groups had nearly paralyzed the country through nonviolent demonstrations and strikes. These actions, which had unprecedented international support, led to intense negotiations over several years for the release of Nelson Mandela from prison in February 1990. Following further intensive negotiations, the white minority government agreed to hold elections, in which, for the first time ever, all South Africans of every race could vote. Those elections, held in April 1994 and won by the African National Congress (ANC), paved the way for Nelson Mandela to become the first African to lead a democratic South Africa.

The second method by which the transition occurred is the one that was employed by the leaders in Benin. First, against a backdrop of mass demonstrations and strikes by workers in urban centers, a national conference of a broad spectrum of leaders met in a crisis mode. The conference managed to reduce the powers of the president, transformed itself into an interim legislature, and conducted new elections which ushered in a new president and a newly elected legislature.

The third method is called "guided democratization" and is characterized by a leader imposing democracy on the country. Former president Jerry Rawlings of Ghana fits this model. As a young flight lieutenant, he overthrew the government initially in 1979, put on trial two former military officers who had ruled the country from 1972 to 1979—Col. Ignatius Acheampong and General Frederick Akuffo. They were convicted of looting the country's treasury and oppressing the people and promptly executed. He then organized elections in which a civilian candidate—Hilla Limann—was elected. Two years later, he decided that Limann had been too weak a president, who had failed to improve economic and political conditions in the country. Limann was overthrown. Once again, Rawlings took over the government. This time, he took the time to outlaw the existing political parties, to have a new constitution drafted, to legalize political parties once again, to permit a freer press, and even to create an independent human rights commission. He cast off his military uniform, civilianized himself, and ran for the presidency of the country in the new elections which he organized. To no one's surprise, he won. A real seed for democracy may have been planted when he voluntarily stepped down in the year 2002 after serving the two four-year terms stipulated in the constitution he helped write. The Freedom House organization has rated Ghana since 2003 as being Democratic or Free. Rawlings' successor, John Kufuor, served two terms and, in 2008, was succeeded peacefully by John Atta Mills. Democracy appears to have finally taken root in Ghana.[13]

The last reform method is called a "co-opted" transition.[14] In a co-opted transition, the leaders normally accede to popular demands for democracy by preemptively allowing new political parties to be formed. For tactical reasons, "snap" elections are then called. In this way, the opposition parties do not have enough time or adequate resources to mount a credible challenge to the party in power. The media and the military are usually still under the firm control of the governing party. A good example of a co-opted transition is provided by the response of the founding president of Côte d'Ivoire, Felix Houphouët-Boigny, in 1990. Faced with popular pressure to liberalize the political system, he moved quickly to do just that, won the election that year, and claimed credit for introducing democracy to his country. This co-opted transition did not hold. More than eighteen years later, Côte d'Ivoire is torn in a near civil war between the north and the south and is one of nineteen African countries considered Not Free by the Freedom House.[15]

There are several organizations which have been tracking political reforms taking place in Africa since the campaign for democracy began in the late 1980s. Each organization has its own scheme for determining not only what type of political system exists but also the stages of transition to democracy and the degrees of commitment to democracy. In the second edition of this text, the author relied on the work of the Carter Center at Emory University to categorize African states. In this edition, Freedom House (to which repeated references have already been made), has refined its rating scheme to a degree that would command wide consensus among Africa scholars.

Freedom House is an organization that has been publishing surveys of the state of freedom around the world since the early 1970s. It uses two broad categories of freedom: political rights and civil liberties. In the organization's words,

> Political rights enable people to participate freely in the political process including through the right to vote, compete for public office, and elect representatives who have a decisive impact on public policies and are accountable to the electorate. Civil liberties allow for the freedoms of expression and belief, associational and organizational rights, rule of law, and personal autonomy without interference from the state.[16]

Freedom House asserts that its view of freedom is not culture-bound and relies largely on standards derived from the Universal Declaration of Human Rights.[17] It rates countries on ten political rights questions and fifteen civil liberties questions and then comes up with a composite score of 1 through 7, "with 1 representing the highest and 7 the lowest level of freedom. Each pair of political rights and civil liberties is averaged to determine the overall status of being "Free," "Partly Free," or "Not Free." These terms may be used interchangeably with "Democratic," "Partly Democratic," and "Not Democratic."

In addition to these terms, Freedom House assigns the designation of electoral democracy to states which have competitive, multiparty political systems, universal adult suffrage for all citizens, regularly contested elections engendering the secret ballot and without massive voter fraud, and significant access of major political parties to the voters through the media and open political campaigning.[18] The determining factor is the degree to which the last major presidential or legislative election held in the country was competitive. This explains the designation of Liberia, for instance, as an electoral democracy, although the country emerged from a murderous dictatorship only in 2003 when Charles Taylor was persuaded to go into exile in Nigeria. He is now on trial at the Hague on charges of crimes against humanity not only in Liberia but also in neighboring Sierra Leone, where he supplied arms to the RUF (Revolutionary United Front), notorious for cutting off the limbs of civilians, whom they believed not to support them. An interim government assumed control. Elections were held in November 2005 and Mrs. Ellen Johnson Sirleaf, a Harvard-educated economist, emerged victorious, becoming, in January 2006, the first female elected president on the African continent.

Table 7.1 shows the "comparative measures of freedom" of the fifty-three independent African states. Nine are classified as free or democratic, twenty-four as partly democratic, and twenty as being not free.

TABLE 7.1

Independent African Countries: Comparative Measures of Freed

Free	Partly Free	Not Free
Benin	Burkina Faso	Algeria
Botswana	Burundi	Angola
Cape Verde	Central African Republic	Cameroon
Ghana	Comoros	Chad
Mali	Djibouti	Congo, Republic of
Mauritius	The Gambia	Congo-DR
Namibia	Guinea-Bissau	Côte d'Ivoire
São Tomé and Principe	Lesotho	Egypt
South Africa	Liberia	Eritrea
	Madagascar	Ethiopia
	Malawi	Gabon
	Mauritania	Guinea
	Morocco	Libya
	Mozambique	Rwanda
	Niger	Somalia
	Nigeria	Sudan
	Senegal	Swaziland
	Seychelles	Tunisia
	Sierra Leone	Zimbabwe
	Somaliland (unrecognized)	
	Tanzania	
	Togo	
	Uganda	
	Zambia	

Source: Drawn from http://www.freedomhouse.org/template.cfm?page=415&year=2011. Accessed December 15, 2011.

ECONOMIC REFORMS

When Reagan first ran for president of the United States, the world was experiencing a serious economic recession. Reagan began his presidency by questioning the assumptions undergirding the aid flow from the industrialized countries of the West to the developing countries of Africa. In retrospect, the international situation was just right for this man with a cause: to proselytize the blessings of the free enterprise system. He intended to release the energies of the free market on the U.S. economy. Reagan promised again and again to get the government off the backs of hardworking Americans so they could reap the full benefits of their labor with as few government regulations as possible. In time, this was a cause that he would try to sell to the rest of the world as well. (Whether Reagan actually achieved his goals of reducing government and deregulating the economy is an issue that will continue to be debated in American politics for some time to come.) What we are interested in, however, is the impact of his rhetoric and his presidential actions on the behavior of African countries that were regular recipients of American aid.

A series of conferences were held early in 1981 heralding a shift in the way industrialized nations had been assisting the poor countries of the world. Until then, especially in the wake of a report by the Brandt Commission on the world economic crisis facing poor countries in the 1980s—the report was issued in 1980 under the title *North-South: A Program for Survival*— the international consensus had been that wealthy countries in the north had reaped benefits not by exploiting poor countries but by trading with and obtaining raw materials from them. A subsequent report by the same commission, issued three years later, *Common Crisis: North-South, Cooperation for World Recovery*, recommended a series of reforms that included providing more direct aid to poor countries, opening up markets in rich states (at prices that were both fair and sufficient to lift the lives of people in these countries out of poverty) and reforming international financial and economic institutions. In any event, in 1981, a major north–south conference was held at Cancún, Mexico. The southern delegation comprised a cross-section of countries ranging from economically impoverished states like Bangladesh and Tanzania to resource-rich ones like Saudi Arabia and Venezuela. The others, including the host country of Mexico, were China, India, the former Yugoslavia, the Philippines, Nigeria, Côte d'Ivoire, Guyana, Algeria, and Brazil. The industrialized nations represented were the G-7 countries (the United States, Great Britain, Germany, France, Italy, Japan, and Canada), together with Austria and Sweden.[19] At that conference, the poor countries made four basic demands: a larger share of manufacturing industries to be located within their borders; better prices for their exports to the wealthier states; lower protectionist tariffs against goods, especially agricultural products from poor countries; and greater access to international capital for investments. A final communiqué, in a language typical of diplomatic compromise, expressed some sympathy for the economic predicament of countries in the south and reaffirmed the prognosis of economists that the situation in the poor countries was a serious one requiring immediate action. Reagan, a sworn disciple of free markets, was, however, not keen to support these demands, reasonable as they might have sounded to everyone else. His heart lay in selling the "magic of the marketplace." He believed that poor nations "simply want a policy of take away from the haves and deliver to the havenots."[20]

After Cancún, the U.S. Agency for International Development confirmed that the United States was opposed to any restructuring of the world economy along the lines envisaged in the demands of the Third World countries, particularly the demands for better prices for their goods and access to development capital. According to Reagan, there was nothing wrong with the international economic system. It had worked quite well for the industrialized world, so why would it not work equally well for poor countries? The problem lay with the economies of the poor countries: these needed restructuring. This perception was not new. Indeed, industrialized countries shared that view. Reagan was perhaps the first modern American president to decide to force other countries to emulate the American system.

The U.S. Agency for International Development began to target its aid to countries that had agreed to use the free market as the main approach to spurring development.[21] The World Bank, an institution in which the United States wields nearly one-fourth of the voting power, accelerated its program designed to restructure Third World economies to make them more efficient. Preconditions for World Bank loans included:

1. Balanced government budgets
2. Cuts in social spending, especially for health care and education
3. Deep cuts in a variety of subsidies, particularly food subsidies so common in the cities and towns of Africa
4. More concessions from poor countries to multinational corporations in order to entice them to invest in African countries
5. Allowing currency exchange rates to find their own level rather than setting them officially, so as to stem the loss of hard currency to the poor countries through the black market
6. Selling off parastatal (i.e., quasi-governmental) agencies that were unprofitable and, therefore, not contributing revenue to the government as intended
7. Reducing bloated government payrolls through retrenchment.

Some of these measures were already being implemented before Reagan became president. The Lome Convention, for instance, issued a series of agreements signed in 1976 between a number of African, Caribbean, and Pacific countries and several European states to improve trade terms for the poor countries. Reagan's ideologically vociferous advocacy of the "magic of the free market" simply accelerated the adoption of the reforms. Reluctantly and at great pains, African governments began to come to terms with the possibility that direct transfers of resources to poor countries in the form of aid were going to diminish and, instead, more difficult terms were going to be attached to any future aid. The last twenty years have seen massive efforts directed toward restructuring the economies of poor countries.

Results have been inconclusive. What we know is that the so-called Structural Adjustment Programs promoted in African countries exacerbated people's suffering. The poor and rural peasants in these countries bore the brunt of restructuring efforts. Without government subsidies, prices for food, fuel, and other necessities skyrocketed. Workers were declared redundant and thrown out of work. Migrations to the cities increased greatly. Demonstrations and strikes were rife in many African countries against the hardships resulting from mandated reforms. Governments in Gabon, Cameroon, Côte d'Ivoire, and elsewhere were rendered weaker by these actions.

Let us now turn our attention to a couple of major initiatives that have been established since the failure of SAPs. At the beginning of the new millennium, the world's governments—189 of them—meeting at the United Nations, signed a Millennium Declaration whose cornerstone was to attack poverty. In the words of the declaration, the international community was committing itself "to free our fellow men, women, and children from the abject and dehumanizing conditions of extreme poverty." The declaration contained specific goals called the Millennium Development Goals (MDGs). These goals were to:

1. Eradicate extreme poverty and hunger
2. Achieve universal primary education
3. Promote gender equality and empower women
4. Reduce child mortality
5. Improve maternal health
6. Combat HIV/AIDS, malaria, and other diseases
7. Ensure environmental sustainability
8. Develop a global partnership for development

The international community even set a deadline—the year 2015—by which they hoped poverty, at least, would have been reduced by one half and child deaths and infectious diseases would have been eradicated or significantly reduced.[22]

As of 2011, with four years remaining to the deadline, how have the African countries been doing? Well, it looks like the target date will be missed. According to a comprehensive report on the MDGs prepared by agencies affiliated with the United Nations,[23] this is how Africa is fairing in trying to achieve each goal:

1. In trying to eradicate extreme poverty and hunger, Africans have experienced setbacks since 1990. The report admits that a huge

number of people are "chronically hungry in sub-Saharan Africa." Indeed, "during the 1990s, extreme poverty dropped in much of Asia, fell slowly in Latin America, changed little in Northern Africa and Western Asia, and rose and then started to decline in transition economies (i.e., the highly centralized economies of former communist states). But in sub-Saharan Africa, which already had the highest poverty rates in the world, the situation deteriorated further and millions more fell into deep poverty."[24] In short, Africans are getting poorer. Why such extreme poverty in Africa?[25] Well, the straight and simple answer is that the Africans don't have the money. They don't have the money because they don't have jobs. They don't have jobs because none are being created. Peasant farmers who till the land don't produce enough to have a surplus to sell and earn some money.[26] As if things were not bad enough, HIV/AIDS has had a devastating impact, killing people in large numbers, most of them in their prime. Natural disasters like drought and floods and "unnatural" ones like armed political conflicts have exacerbated the situation, displacing people from their homes and turning them into refugees in their own countries.[27]

2. With respect to the second MDG of providing universal primary education to every child, some African countries have made some progress; however, compared to the rest of the world, Africa still comes in dead last. Over one-third of Africa's children don't have access to education. In five African countries, less than half of the children are able to find places in school.[28] Some of the factors which correlate with poverty do also explain the barriers to education for young people. Children from poor families cannot afford to go to school. They have to work to help support their families. If their countries are at war, many children are displaced from their homes and, therefore, cannot go to school because there are no schools in refugee camps. Moreover, the high mortality rates arising from AIDS mean that some children have to drop out of school to care for their younger siblings, have no one to care for them, or simply because they have no teachers. The report says, for instance, that in 1999 nearly 1 million children lost their teachers to AIDS.[29]

3. What about promoting gender equality and empowering women? The data show that many African countries have narrowed the gap between boys and girls when it comes to access to education. But again, where poverty is severe, many parents would rather send their sons than daughters to school. The importance of educating girls cannot be overstressed. Empowering women is imperative to developing a country. It is a waste of a half of a country's human talent not to educate young women. A wise person once said, "When you educate a man, you educate an individual, but when you educate a woman, you educate a family." One area which offers some hope for the future is

politics. African women are now being represented in their national legislatures in greater numbers than ever before. In Africa, 14 percent of seats in national legislatures are held by women. The world average is 16 percent. It is a measure of some success that between 1990 and 2005, the representation of women in African parliaments doubled, rising from 7 to 14 percent. Africans can be proud of the fact that the tiny country of Rwanda, which experienced one of the worst genocides of modern times, boasts the highest female representation in its legislature: 53 percent. Nine African countries—Burundi, Djibouti, Eritrea, Morocco, Mozambique, Namibia, South Africa, Tunisia, and Uganda—have constitutional provisions reserving a certain number of seats for women.[30]

4. The fourth MDG is to reduce child mortality rates. Again, Africa leads the world in child mortality. The average infant mortality rate for Africa in 2011 is 74 deaths per 1,000 live births. The world average is forty-four.[31] Diseases which account for half of the deaths of children under the age of five years are pneumonia, diarrhea, malaria, measles, and AIDS. Malnutrition, so intimately linked to poverty, contributes nearly half of the deaths.[32]

5. The fifth goal is to improve maternal health. The aim here is to reduce by three-fourths, between 1990 and 2015, the rate of death of women in childbirth. Africa leads the world in maternal mortality rates with more than a half of the countries registering over 550 deaths per 100,000 live births. Another way to measure the risk of pregnancy to African mothers is to note that "the chances of dying during pregnancy or childbirth over a lifetime are as high as 1 in 16 in sub-Saharan Africa, compared with 1 in 3,800 in the developed world."[33]

6. The sixth goal is to combat AIDS, malaria, and other diseases. AIDS is the number-one killer of Africans, followed by malaria and tuberculosis.[34] Malaria appears most prevalent in the world's poorest countries. Tuberculosis, once thought to have been eliminated, has made a comeback, thanks to the HIV and AIDS. The statistics don't even begin to capture the extent of the devastation of AIDS on African societies. A little more than a tenth of the world's population resides in Africa south of the Sahara and yet they make up nearly two-thirds of all people with HIV. Two million of those with HIV are children under the age of fifteen. Put it another way, nine out of ten children with HIV are in sub-Saharan Africa.[35] At the end of 2005, 1 percent of the world's adult population had HIV/AIDS. For Africa that statistic was 5 percent of all adults, and in sub-Saharan Africa, 6 percent of the adults had the virus. There are tremendous variations in infection rates, ranging from 0.1 percent in Tunisia to 33.5 percent in Swaziland.[36]

Robert Guest put it more bluntly:

> In several countries in southern and eastern Africa, a fifth or more of adults carry the virus. That does not mean that a fifth of the population of these countries will die of AIDS. It is worse than that. Almost all those who are now infected will die in the next ten years, but before they die they will infect others. In Botswana, the worst-hit nation, more than a third of adults carry the virus. The former president of Botswana, Festus Mogae, lamented in 2001 that unless the epidemic was reversed, his country faced 'blank extinction.' [37] He was not exaggerating.

7. With respect to environmental sustainability, there are a number of salient issues to be considered. One is preserving the forests, which are being lost at an alarming rate, especially in poor countries which depend on wood and charcoal for fuel. Other issues include providing access to drinking water, installing basic sanitation facilities to minimize pollution which makes people sick in the first place, and improving life in the slums which can be found in all large cities in Africa and elsewhere in the Third World. Sub-Saharan Africa ranks third (after South and East Asia) in the number of people living in slums. Most African countries cannot cope with the influx of people from rural areas in search of better lives in the cities. Egypt, Senegal, and South Africa are among the few African countries undertaking measures (provision of potable water, electricity, and basic sanitation) to improve life in slum areas. [38]

8. The last goal is to forge global partnerships in efforts to confront the problems discussed earlier. These partnerships are to involve NGOs, corporations, government agencies, and international organizations. Partnerships are appropriate and important vehicles by which to attack Africa's enormous challenges. Aid is obviously critical because all the goals mentioned will require money in order to be accomplished. NGOs are crucial in generating financial resources. External debt has, for years, severely handicapped African countries in their drive for economic development. A report by the U.N. Conference on Trade and Development (UNCTAD) indicated that between 1970 and 2002, Africa received 540 billion dollars in loans, but paid back 550 billion dollars in principal and interest. At the end of 2002, Africa still owed 295 billion. The numbers are worse for the poorest of the poor in sub-Saharan Africa. There is a net outflow of cash from a continent that is extremely poor. Not all of this indebtedness can be blamed on corruption. The debt situation grew worse when SAPs were in full force and when African governments were being scrutinized by the World Bank and the IMF. [39] Debt forgiveness is, therefore, critical. The current policy of trying to forgive debts owed only by the poorest of the poor is not adequate.

African countries also need access to markets in the well-developed countries. Free trade should not be a one-way transaction, should not favor the rich trading partners, and should not be considered a gift to poor countries. It is still the case that when it comes to free trade, more developed countries tend to do better than poor ones. It is actually in the long-term interests of the wealthier countries—for instance, in reducing illegal immigration—to have economic relationships which enable the poor countries to prosper.

Pharmaceutical companies are vital partners in the fight against HIV/AIDS not only by lowering the price of antiretroviral drugs but also by allowing the manufacture of generic versions once the patents have expired.

A careful analysis of the MDGs casts doubt on the probability that these goals will be achieved in the time frame postulated by the international community. Moreover, no one anticipated the worldwide economic recession of 2008–2009 and the monetary crisis confronting European countries as the year 2011 comes to a close. No one knows for sure when this crisis will end and how much damage will be inflicted on the fragile economies of African countries.

NEPAD

The second initiative that is worth a mention is the New Partnership for Africa's Development—known by its acronym NEPAD. NEPAD is described as a vision and strategic framework for Africa's renewal. This is a purely African initiative which arose from discussions in the continental Organization of African Unity (OAU)—which no longer exists—when five countries were asked to come up with "an integrated socio-economic development framework for Africa."[40] It was timed to coincide with the founding of the African Union, which will be discussed in the next chapter. The five countries charged with producing the historic document were Algeria, Egypt, Nigeria, Senegal, and South Africa. It is interesting to note that the five include the most populous (Nigeria) and the wealthiest (South Africa).

The NEPAD document is more detailed than the United Nations' MDG. The introductory statement in the document sets the tone thus:

> This *New Partnership for Africa's Development* is a pledge by African leaders, based on a common vision and a firm and shared conviction, that they have a pressing duty to eradicate poverty and to place their countries, both individually and collectively, on a path of sustainable growth and development and, at the same time, to participate actively in the world economy and body politic. The program is anchored on the determination of Africans to extricate themselves and the continent from the malaise of underdevelopment and exclusion in a globalizing world.

The document represents a vision of where the African leaders want to take their countries; an appeal to the African people to move away from a mind-set of dependency to one of confidence and efficacy; a recognition that peace, security, and democratic governance are a *sine qua non* for any lasting economic development; setting the priorities of improving the infrastructure, investing in its people and reversing the brain drain so that the continent's best and brightest do not migrate to wealthier countries; protecting its environment; preserving its culture (especially those aspects which represent "indigenous knowledge"); harnessing technology; and establishing mutually beneficial partnerships with international organizations and more developed countries.

Although the NEPAD Declaration sounds bold and courageous and was launched with a great deal of fanfare, early reaction by veteran observers of Africa is that not much is likely to change on the continent any time soon. Armed conflicts persist. The genocide in Darfur, Sudan, persists. The 7,000 African Union peace-keeping troops are no match for the Sudanese government-backed militia. The Sudanese government refuses to abide by the terms of the peace-keeping operations which would enable them to really monitor the cease-fire that was signed between the rebel groups in Darfur and the government. Moreover, the African Union does not have the money to keep the troops in the Sudan much longer.[42]

Famines are prevalent, almost endemic. African states have been unable to do anything to stop the catastrophe unfolding in Zimbabwe, whose economy has collapsed and currency rendered worthless and where a cholera outbreak had killed nearly 1,000 people toward the end of 2008 and 60,000 new cases of cholera were being predicted by international agencies. "Why the catastrophe," one might ask. The answer is President Robert Mugabe, who appears to have lost the last election, but refused to concede defeat. It is clear from his behavior during the ongoing crisis that Mugabe had no intention of leaving office, even if he lost the election. Despite prodding by former South African president Thabo Mbeki, who tried to mediate the conflict between Mugabe and the opposition, Mugabe has not negotiated in good faith to share power in a coalition government. Cholera continues to pick its helpless victims, and Zimbabweans continue to stream out of the country into South Africa in search of food, drinkable water, and medicine.

There is no evidence that corruption is declining sufficiently in countries like Nigeria, Kenya, Zimbabwe, and others, which are listed every year by Transparency International among the most corrupt countries in the world.

Furthermore, the NEPAD initiative contains the same flaws that have crippled other initiatives. The document is tilted toward the elite, it employs a top-down approach, it does not provide for popular participation, it appears to exclude civil society organizations, which have proliferated in large numbers on the continent, and it is based on the false premise that corrupt leaders can be trusted to reform themselves and to champion transparency.[43]

CONCLUSIONS

Tables 7.1, 7.2, and 7.3 show that African countries, by and large, have responded positively to calls for change. Whereas in 1988, only two African states were judged by the Freedom House to be free or democratic, since 2002, eleven are now considered to be free. Table 7.2 shows that twenty-three countries are considered electoral democracies although, in twelve of them, there are still enough deficiencies for the countries to be characterized only as partly free. Even in those countries which are partly free, but have a very vocal press and freedom of speech, it is hard to imagine their going back to the autocratic past. The genie of freedom is out of the bottle. Many leaders believe that democracy is a good thing, even if they insist that their countries may not be ready for it. Many African countries are now getting ready to go through the second round of multiparty elections. An important beginning has been made, and it is only a beginning. The notion of people choosing leaders through a competitive process is taking root, the press is freer now than ever before, Africans can now speak their minds more freely than before, and there is a proliferation of political parties and movements being formed. But democracy is much more than competitive elections and the freedom to form more political parties. The values that sustain democracy have to infuse the political process and inform the Africans' ability to negotiate their differences, whatever those differences happen to be.

It is true also that the collapse of communism had a salutary effect on political developments in Africa. The collapse deprived

▶ TABLE 7.2

African Electoral Democracies

Free	Partly Free
1. Benin	1. Burundi
2. Botswana	2. Central African Republic
3. Cape Verde	3. Comoros
4. Ghana	4. Kenya
5. Lesotho	5. Liberia
6. Mali	6. Madagascar
7. Mauritius	7. Malawi
8. Namibia	8. Mozambique
9. São Tomé and Principe	9. Niger
10. Senegal	10. Nigeria
11. South Africa	11. Seychelles
	12. Sierra Leone

Source: Extrapolated from data in Table 7.1.

TABLE 7.3

Progress toward Democracy

Measure of Democracy/Freedom	Year 1988 No. (%)	2002 No. (%)	2008 No. (%)
Free	2 (4)	11 (21)	11 (21)
Partly Free	16 (31)	22 (41)	23 (43)
Not Free	33 (65)	20 (38)	19 (36)
Total	51 (100)	53 (100)	53 (100)

Sources: The numbers for the years 1988 and 2002 are extrapolated from Peter J. Schraeder, *African Politics and Society*, 2nd edition, p. 231. The numbers for the year 2008 are drawn from www.freedomhouse.org/template.cfm?page=415&year=2008.

African authoritarian regimes of models to emulate. The other countries realized that this "second wind of change," like the first one that a former British prime minister spoke about in 1960, could not be stopped and that the leaders might as well welcome it or be swept aside by it, with the real possibility of losing power.

The relationship between politics and economics is much clearer now than it was at the time of independence over forty years ago, when defeating colonialism was treated perhaps as the only issue and a panacea to the many problems that people faced at that time. We now know that economic reforms without the freedom that comes from democracy can only lead eventually to recidivism, repression, and inability to deal with national issues. We also know that abject poverty makes democracy harder to sustain and nurture and invites the possibility of populist but autocratic leaders emerging again with false promises of prosperity and freedom.

Africans themselves are going to have to take the lead in changing their systems and improving their lives. They cannot sit on the sidelines and be spectators. Years of sympathetic words from the West at international forums, years of foreign aid of all kinds, and decades of expert advice from expatriates have not lifted Africans out of poverty. As Richard Sandbrook argues with respect to economic reform,

> Africans must look to domestic responses to their crisis. The realities of the international economy and the immensity of the problems confronting the people compel this conclusion. Of course, the international order does need reform. But we must recognize Africa's limited economic power—and thus its limited capacity to force or benefit from a new international order.[44]

Sandbrook identifies three strategies for reforming African economies:

1. *An end to relying on the state as the chief planner and mover.*
The record of African states since independence shows not only that the state has been grossly inefficient but also that it has been riddled with corruption and decision making designed to serve vested interests rather than the country as a whole. Recent experiences in Ghana, Uganda, and Congo-DR—to mention only three countries severely devastated in the 1970s and 1980s by internal political conflict and economic mismanagement—prove that local communities can do a lot on their own without waiting for the almighty state to take care of them. In those three countries, local initiatives led to the expansion of the so-called informal sector. With the collapse of the monetary sector, people in rural areas abandoned cash crops grown to earn foreign currency in favor of growing food and raising cattle and other animals. Urban dwellers found that they could not live on their wages and salaries, so they retreated to rural areas to try to live off their farms. Local crafts people began producing things—through recycling discarded material such as used tires, metal containers, and the like. Many of those things such as utensils, implements, and furniture that previously had to be purchased from modern shops, which had probably imported them from abroad thus depleting foreign reserves which might have gone instead for acquiring things that truly could not be produced locally.

2. *Utilizing the free market.* As pointed out earlier, the free market was touted by Reagan, Thatcher, and other Western leaders as the savior of ailing African economies. The adoption of this strategy would result in shrinking the size of government and diminishing its regulatory responsibilities. Indeed, the free market would energize the self-reliance implicit in the informal sector. The sizable resources that used to go to finance the bureaucracy would now go toward providing the type of incentives just described.

3. *Rehabilitating the state.* This essentially means streamlining the state and making it more efficient. The state would be responsible for building the infrastructure (roads, street lights, telecommunications, water, and sewer systems); providing essential services in health care and education; collecting taxes efficiently and fairly; setting exchange rates at realistic levels that accurately reflect the health of the economy; and making sure that people working for the government are paid at rates in line with the cost of living. This would discourage corruption, which is by no means unique to Africa, but is certainly more pervasive than in more economically developed areas. Poorly paid bureaucrats tend to make up for the shortfall in their remuneration by extorting money for services that they are hired to provide in the first place.

And because they are so badly paid, they display a conspicuous lack of enthusiasm in their work. To quote Sandbrook: "Bureaucracy that works is part of a process of increasing secularization, organizational complexity, economic development and literacy."[45]

Obviously, the three strategies would work best if they were accompanied by or carried out in a climate of democratic reforms discussed earlier.

NOTES

1. Colin Legum, *Africa since Independence* (Bloomington, IN: Indiana University Press, 1999), p. 1.
2. Ibid., p. 30.
3. Ibid., p. 50.
4. Ibid., pp. 31–32.
5. Peter J. Schraeder, *African Politics and Society: A Mosaic in Transformation*, 2nd Edition (Belmont, CA: Wadsworth/Thomson Learning, 2004), pp. 226–233.
6. http://africanelections.tripod.com/ke.html. Accessed May 27, 2010.
7. "Map of Freedom 2006," http://www.freedomhouse.org. Accessed September 15, 2008. Accessed December 2, 2011.
8. http://www.bbcnews.com.
9. http://www.africafocus.org/docs11/drc1111.php. Accessed December 13, 2011.
10. "Country Profile: Cameroon," http://newsvote.bbc.co.uk. Accessed August 24, 2006.
11. http://www.freedomhouse.org/uploads/special_report/99.pdf. Accessed December 1, 2011.
12. Peter J. Schraeder, *African Politics and Society*, pp. 226–233.
13. http://www.bbcnews.com.
14. Peter J. Schraeder, *African Politics and Society*, p. 231.
15. http://www.freedomhouse.org/uploads.special_report/99.pdf. Accessed December 1, 2011.
16. http://www.freedomhouse.org/template.cfm?page=15.
17. Ibid.
18. Ibid.
19. http://newsvote.bbc.co.uk. Accessed on August 17, 2006.
20. Alan F. Matthews, "World North-South Issues at the Cancún Conference," in Chau T. Phau, ed., *World Politics 1982/83,* Annual Editions (Guildford, CT: Dushkin Publishing Group, 1982), p. 111.
21. Ibid., p. 112.
22. http://www.un.org/millenniumgoals. Accessed August 19, 2006.
23. Organizations involved in the preparation of the Millennium Development Goals status report include: ILO, FAO, UNESCO, WHO, the World Bank, the IMF, the International Telecommunications Union, the U.N. Economic Commissions on Africa (ECA) and Europe (ECE), the U.N. Economic and Social Commissions on Latin America and the Caribbean, Asia and the Pacific, and Western Asia; the Joint U.N. Programme on HIV/AIDS; UNICEF; UNCTAD, the U.N. Development Fund for Women, UNDP; UNEP, the U.N. Framework

Convention on Climate Change, UNHCR, UN Human Settlements Programme, UN Population Fund, Inter-Parliamentary Union, OECD, and WTO. *Source*: http://unstats.un.org/unsd/mi.

24. "The MDGs Report 2005," http://unstats.un.org/unsd/mi/pdf/MDG%20Book.pdf. Accessed December, 15 2011.

25. http://unstats.un.org/unsd/mi/pdf/MDG%20Book.pdf. Accessed December 15, 2011. Poverty is defined in terms of the proportion of people living on less than $1 a day. See "Introduction: Why Is Africa so Poor?" in Robert Guest, ed., *The Shackled Continent: Power, Corruption, and African Lives* (Washington, DC: Smithsonian Books, 2004), pp. 4–27.

26. Ibid., p. 7.

27. Ibid., p. 9.

28. Ibid., p. 10.

29. Ibid., p. 11.

30. Ibid., p. 17.

31. *2011 World Population Data Sheet* (Washington, DC: Population Reference Bureau, 2011).

32. http://unstats.un.org/unsd/mi/pdf/MDG%20Book.pdf, p. 18.

33. Ibid., p. 22.

34. Ibid., p. 26.

35. *2006 Report on the Global AIDS Epidemic* (Geneva: UNAIDS, 2006), p. 15. http://www.unaids.org. Accessed November 29, 2011.

36. *2006 World Population Data Sheet* (Washington, DC: Population Reference Bureau, 2006), p. 5.

37. "Sex and Death," in Robert Guest, ed., *The Shackled Continent*, p. 90.

38. http://unstats.un.org/unsd/mi/pdf/MDG%20Book.pdf, p. 34.

39. AfricaFocus Bulletin (October 2004), http://www.unctad.org.

40. http://www.nepad.org/2005/files/home.php. Accessed December 15, 2011.

41. http://www.nepad.org/history. Accessed 15 December 2011.

42. Lydia Polgreen, "With Little Authority, African Union Struggles with Its Mission in Darfur," *New York Times*, September 9, 2006.

43. Michael F. Lofchie, A Review of Ian Taylor, *NEPAD: Toward Africa's Development or Another False Start* (Boulder, CO: Lynne Reinner, 2005) in *Africa Today*, Vol. 52, No. 4 (Summer, 2006), pp. 144–145.

44. Richard Sandbrook, *The Politics of Africa's Economic Stagnation* (New York: Cambridge University Press, 1985), p. 148.

45. Ibid., p. 155

Africa in World Affairs

What has Africa, with 53 members in the United Nations contributed to the world community? How have Africans fared both in keeping the peace on the continent and using their resources and numbers in the United Nations to demand a voice on the world stage for the numerous hurdles they still face in addressing poverty, deadly conflict, disease and famine?

INTRODUCTION

For much of modern history, Africa, with its many states, has not been a major player on the world stage. If anything, the African continent has been the target of the actions of other countries in the international system. Major contact in the fifteenth century between Africa and the outside world ushered in an era of slavery, which was soon followed by a period of imperialism. Both conditions, consequences of Africa's small, fragmented, and technologically backward societies, had extraordinary effects on African societies, effects that can be seen in the behavior of African countries toward other nations.

In Chapter 4, we established that besides coming to Africa to discover and learn about the "Dark Continent" and convert "heathen" Africans to Christianity, Europeans also wanted to claim land there, in the form of colonies and dependent territories, for their rulers. Why did European countries regard empires as so desirable? There were a couple of significant reasons, of course. Colonies had strategic value: Colonized people provided large reservoirs of manpower for use in major wars that European powers were involved in at that time or might get entangled in later, and colonial territories provided a strategic advantage to the imperial powers by virtue of their location. The Strait of Gibraltar (the gateway to the Atlantic Ocean from the Mediterranean Sea), the Cape of Good Hope (at the southern tip of the African continent), and the Horn of Africa are examples of such strategically desirable areas. Egypt became important, for example, following the building of the Suez Canal connecting the Indian subcontinent and Europe. Another reason is that imperial possessions conferred status and prestige. Having an empire allowed a European country to exercise power and influence in geographic areas many times its own size. The feeling was heady. As Naomi Chazan and her colleagues have asserted in reference to France: "The African Empire was one of the great exploits of French history. Especially since 1830, when an expeditionary force set foot in Algeria, Africa has loomed very large in the French imagination and world view."[1] One might add that the sense of the French people about themselves was greatly augmented by their imperial conquests.

Colonization created instant states in Africa and ensured their complete incorporation into Western economies by the time they became independent. Africa's pattern of international relations bears an imprint of that colonial experience. Relationships between France and Britain and their respective former colonies in Africa remain close and exist in the form of loose associations—the French Community and the (British) Commonwealth of Nations—maintained through a set of foreign aid agreements, military pacts, and close personal relationships between African and European political leaders. At the zenith of the colonial era, France and Britain together controlled nearly three-fourths of the African continent. As the colonial era came to a close, most of the economies in the colonies were owned and controlled by the European powers. It was, therefore, to be expected that colonial powers might try to maintain a "neocolonial" presence in their former colonies, not so much to help the newly independent countries, as they insisted, but to safeguard their property and investments, of which they had many.

This is not to say that since independence there has been no friction between Africans and their former European colonial masters. Indeed, British relations with her former colonies were severely tested by a series of crises that either began or intensified in the 1960s. During the Nigerian civil war, a highly divisive conflict that lasted from 1967 to 1970, Britain came under harsh criticism for choosing to side with, and provide arms to, the Nigerian federal government against the breakaway state of Biafra. Britain's equivocation in recognizing political rights of Africans in its colony of Rhodesia led the tiny white minority there (less than 5 percent of the population at the time), which had politically dominated the self-governing colony since 1923, to unilaterally declare independence from Britain in 1965. Britain's response was tepid, limited to imposing economic sanctions against the illegal minority regime. Africans wanted a military intervention, arguing that a unilateral declaration of independence was nothing more than a rebellion against the British Crown. Sanctions helped weaken the illegal regime but could not bring it down. The African people in Rhodesia reacted by waging a bloody and costly, but ultimately a successful fifteen-year armed struggle. Britain was held responsible both for the destruction resulting from the guerrilla war and for the intransigence of the white minority leaders, who refused to negotiate with the African leaders of the military campaign for freedom. The long African struggle against apartheid in South Africa in the face of Britain's substantial economic involvement there saw sharp disagreements aired during Commonwealth summit meetings. This was a difficult period in the relations between Britain and African countries. Sometimes it looked as though the Commonwealth might come apart.

The French have not had smooth sailing either. The French pulled out of Guinea abruptly in 1958 when Guinea voted to go its own way in Charles de Gaulle's famous referendum asking France's African colonies to choose between independence and continued (dependent) association with France. France's punitive reaction against Guinea was supposed to serve as a lesson to other countries who might be tempted to bite the French hand that fed them. France's abrupt departure ignited U.S.–Soviet rivalry in Guinea, and Guinea turned to the former Soviet Union for assistance. For many years, the French were accused of callousness in testing their nuclear weapons in the West African desert in total disregard of the well-being of the African people or their sovereignty. They were also accused of maintaining strong contacts with, and helping to prop up, autocratic regimes, such as the Central African Republic, with no regard for the suffering of the African people.

These difficulties aside, former colonies in Africa continued to interact with their recent masters more frequently than with each other or with other countries. It is impossible, therefore, to discuss the role of African states in the world without considering how that role is mediated by their colonial experience and postcolonial relationships.

When African states became independent, they hoped to use the international stage to accomplish four things: first, to consolidate their positions as sovereign independent states; second, to mediate the ideological conflict between the capitalist West and the socialist/communist East through a policy of "positive nonalignment"; third, to harness resources from the international community for their pressing development needs; and fourth, because of their own difficult colonial experience, to help champion the cause of peace and understanding among different races and nations. African political leaders seemed unaware of and, therefore, unprepared for the response of the industrialized world and the former colonial powers to this new world crowded with African states ready to assert themselves and eager to play an important role. Europeans had not lost their empires willingly. Some of them were fretting over this loss and over the sudden change in their international status. Portugal, for one, in the face of nationalist fervor sweeping the continent and demands for independence by her own subject peoples in the mid-1950s, had attempted to preempt the African struggle by declaring that Mozambique, Angola, Cape Verde and Guinea-Bissau, and the islands of São Tomé and Principe were not colonies at all, but rather overseas provinces—and therefore integral parts—of Portugal and that it was redundant to speak of these areas becoming independent. The stage was thus set for a costly and brutal armed struggle. Moreover, the former Soviet Union, which had been kept out of colonial Africa, was getting ready to vie for a foothold on the continent. Anti-imperialist and socialist, the Soviet Union presented itself to the newly independent states as a more appropriate model for rapid economic development and social progress than the West. Once again, African states did not seem to have a coherent way to respond to the ideological rivalry looming on the horizon between the West and the East, between the United States and the Soviet Union. All these developments were bound to make the international stage a very tumultuous place to be and to exacerbate the dilemma between the need for national self-identity and the practical necessity to maintain some sort of ties with former colonial masters.

The following pages will provide an account of the impact of this ideological rivalry on African states, their decision to join the Non-Aligned Movement (NAM), the role played by the Organization of African Unity (OAU), how the United States and the former Soviet Union shaped the behavior of African states both outside the continent and within it, and a brief summary of the new institutions of the African Union, formed in 2001 to replace the OAU.

THE COLD WAR

During the cold war, a period marked by intense ideological rivalry between the United States and the former Soviet Union, whatever the Africans did was seen by outsiders through the prism of that conflict, in terms of the global strategic interests of the two superpowers. It became difficult for African leaders freely to devise economic or political programs that were best suited to their needs. And because African states needed infusions of material resources from the more developed countries in the West, African leaders felt compelled to favor one side over the other, either ideologically or in terms of specific policy or material concessions. Somalia is one such country. From 1968 to 1977, for strategic reasons, it maintained close relations with the Soviet Union, culminating in a friendship treaty in 1974.[2] When the Soviets failed to help the Somali regime pursue its foreign policy of "Greater Somalia," it turned to the West.

In other instances, the help given wasn't quite what was needed or asked for, but rather what served the interests of the donor states themselves. For example, aid might be given to improve agricultural production in some African country, but with the condition that the money be used to purchase advanced agricultural equipment from the donor country. The donor country benefits by increasing sales of agricultural technology, which the recipient country may not yet be quite ready to use effectively. And the transaction goes on record as aid for the poor country.

In many African states, internal politics were influenced by the cold war, as the United States or the Soviet Union supported political factions that were closer to their ideological positions or able and willing to promote superpower interests. The public feud in Kenya in the 1960s between two leading politicians, Tom Mboya (assassinated in 1968) and Oginga Odinga (first vice-president of Kenya and father of the current prime minister of Kenya), was a classic example of a furious political feud by proxy. Mboya played the lackey of the Americans with an extensive network of private and governmental contacts in the United States, while Odinga successfully solicited Soviet assistance for political and economic projects in Kenya.[3] Repression in Kenya (as indeed in other countries such as the Democratic Republic of Congo, Somalia, and Sudan) was defended by political leaders on grounds that restrictions were necessary to combat subversive communism. Repression, corruption, and mismanagement were often condoned by aid donors in the West so long as the recipient states were considered bulwarks against the spread of communism.

Jean Kirkpatrick, an intellectual proponent of the so-called Reagan revolution, who later served as U.S. ambassador to the United Nations, contrived a distinction between regimes that were characterized as totalitarian and those that were referred to as authoritarian. According to Kirkpatrick, self-avowed Marxist states were totalitarian and therefore totally inimical to American interests, whereas right-wing, anticommunist—but equally repressive states—such as the Democratic Republic of Congo under General Mobutu, Central America's Nicaragua under Anastasio Somoza, and the apartheid-era South Africa under white minority rule, were authoritarian and therefore worthy of American support. In her own words,

> Authoritarian governments—traditional and modern—have many faults and one significant virtue: their power is limited and where the power of government is limited, the damage it can do is limited also. So is its duration in office. Authoritarian systems do not destroy all alternative power bases in a society. The persistence of dispersed economic and social power renders those regimes less repressive than a totalitarian system and provides the bases for their eventual transformation. Totalitarian regimes, to the contrary, in claiming a monopoly of power over all institutions, eliminate competitive, alternative elites. This is the reason history provides not one but numerous examples of the evolution of authoritarian regimes into democracies (not only Spain and Portugal, but Venezuela, Peru, Ecuador, Bangladesh, among others) and no example of the democratic transformation of totalitarian regimes.[4]

The logic here—which time has proved to be false—is that authoritarian governments could change; totalitarian ones could not. Cyrus Vance, former U.S. Secretary of State under President Jimmy Carter, in an article highly critical of Kirkpatrick's support of repressive governments, paraphrased it even more succinctly. He said that Kirkpatrick, in effect, meant that "anti-communist autocracies tolerate social inequalities, brutality, and poverty while revolutionary (read: Marxist) autocracies create them."[5] Hers was a valiant, albeit a pretentious and perhaps cynical, attempt to convince public opinion in the United States that political repression in the Congo was somehow much different from repression in Guinea, because one occurred in a right-wing regime and the other in a self-styled Marxist state. Indeed, some African governments were subverted by the United States merely because they were Marxists, not necessarily because they were hostile to American interests.[6] Fortunately, events around the world in the past twenty years have proved Kirkpatrick totally wrong. Previously totalitarian regimes in Eastern Europe are in the process of being transformed into democracies—hence the term "transitional democracies"—and the human rights dimension in U.S. foreign policy continues to make it possible for the United States to exercise some constructive influence in the changes taking place in those countries. Unfortunately, however, until the early 1990s, Kirkpatrick's views continued to shape policy in Washington toward such countries as Angola and Mozambique, where the United States provided financial assistance to rebel groups like UNITA (it's Portuguese acronym for the National Union for Total Independence of Angola) in Angola and RENAMO in Mozambique. The consequence of such assistance was to enable the brutal rebel groups to inflict untold suffering on civilians and to raise the level of conflicts into civil wars. Both Mozambique and Angola, despite their avowal of Marxism, continued to express a willingness to establish a closer relationship with the United States. They not only moderated their economic policy to favor American interests but also showed a desire to talk to their political opponents. The Democratic Republic of Congo continued to receive American support, despite the end of the cold war and despite only half-hearted promises of imminent democratization.[7]

THE NON-ALIGNED MOVEMENT

The groundwork and the ideological basis for the NAM are said to have been laid in 1955 at an Afro-Asian conference in Bandung, Indonesia, hosted by President Sukarno of Indonesia and attended by President Josip Broz Tito of Yugoslavia, President Gamal Abdel Nasser of Egypt, and Prime Minister Jawaharlal Nehru of India, who became the principal figures in the movement. The NAM itself was not formally launched until 1961 in Belgrade, Yugoslavia.[8] Having emerged out of colonial tutelage or from the ashes of World War II, the new countries wanted to band together in order to promote their interests and to make important contributions to the world community. Sensing that the rivalry between the United States and the former Soviet Union for influence in the Third World was going to become more contentious, these new states hoped to use their numbers to mediate between the two leading nuclear powers, while guarding their newly won independence.

To this end, nonaligned countries protested aboveground nuclear testing in Africa and elsewhere in the Third World. They also took courageous stands against the dumping of toxic and nuclear waste on African soil and the shipping of experimental, untested drugs into Africa for use on African people. They issued communiqués and statements on conflicts made worse by the involvement of superpowers in such places as Nicaragua, Cambodia, and El Salvador and protested the arming of both sides in the ten-year (1980–1990) Iran–Iraq war. In addition, they championed the cause of liberation movements that had not yet succeeded in freeing their countries from colonialism. Observer status was accorded to liberation movements such as SWAPO (the South West African People's Organization of Namibia), the Patriotic Front of Zimbabwe, and the Palestine Liberation Organization (PLO) to voice their grievances and seek support for their cause. Further, nonaligned countries resolved to work for the establishment of a new international economic order in which wealthier countries might be persuaded or pressured to extend unconditional aid to the new poorer states and to improve terms of trade for poor countries, so that these countries can obtain better prices for their agricultural and mineral exports. They hoped that in the new international economic order, they would finally be allowed to participate in all the major political and economic organizations of the United Nations as equal partners and gain greater access to technology and education in the industrialized countries.

Because of strong opposition from industrialized countries, the new international economic order has not come to fruition, but the NAM made it possible for another grouping, the South-South Commission, organized by the late former president Julius Nyerere of Tanzania, with the hope of promoting self-reliance among poor countries and exploring ways they might be able to help themselves without the traditional reliance on rich countries. The African states, which eventually constituted half of all nations in the NAM, began to play a very strong and decisive role in the movement. Indeed, after the founding meeting, the next three summit meetings were held in Africa, during which time the group's focus successfully shifted toward the anticolonial struggle in Angola, Mozambique, Namibia, Rhodesia (now called Zimbabwe), and South Africa. The movement can also be credited with having helped to establish the Group of 77, the primary world forum for addressing issues of trade, economic development, and inequality among nations of the world. The Group of 77, now numbering around 120 countries, was instrumental in the formation of the United Nations Conference on Trade and Development (UNCTAD), an important arm of the United Nations that has spearheaded a number of agreements dealing with trade, primary commodities, and aid between industrialized nations and poor countries. Finally, it can be argued that the NAM inspired the inclusion in the OAU charter—chapter III—of a principle requiring its members to adhere to international nonalignment.

Without a doubt, the NAM succeeded in providing a forum for airing political and economic issues important to its members. It successfully advanced the right of colonized and oppressed people to be free. Virtually all of Africa is now free of colonial rule. South Africa, the last bastion of white supremacy in Africa, abandoned apartheid, its white leaders entering into negotiations with the African National Congress and other civil and labor groups. Nelson Mandela was freed from jail and went on to become the country's first African president following the historic elections of 1994, in which all South Africans of all races were allowed to vote.

On the other side of the ledger, the NAM found the larger goal of transforming the world economy elusive for several reasons. First, the international political system and the world economy were designed by Western countries for their own benefit and could not be dismantled without fierce resistance from the industrialized countries. The NAM remains dissatisfied with the level of participation its members have been able to achieve. Moreover, they found out not only that relations between Western nations and governments of poor countries were intricate and extensive but also that multinational corporations based in the rich countries represented multiple fronts, by which Western penetration and control of the poor countries' economies were maintained. Given such relations, poor countries risked economic, financial, and even military ruin by standing up to them. Furthermore, the persistence of such relations tended to compromise the credibility of the NAM and to undermine their attempts to change the international system. Hence, the dependent relationships already in place became nearly an insurmountable hurdle, and the policies pursued by international organizations to restructure African economies continued to reflect policy prescriptions of the industrialized countries, with little regard for the devastating impact on the peoples of the poor countries. Nuclear proliferation and the later emergence of Japan as an economic giant introduced both political and economic multipolarity in the world system, which undermined the assumptions upon which bipolar dynamics were based. It was much easier to target the United States and the Soviet Union in pursuit of justice or peace than to confront so many other actors.

The NAM continues to exist. A hundred and sixteen countries belong to it, including nearly all of the African countries. It held its fourteenth summit meeting in Havana, Cuba, in September 2006. The chair of the movement from 2006 to 2009 was the Cuban ambassador to the United Nations.

In light of the collapse of the Soviet Union and other communist governments, NAM now finds itself at a crossroads, a movement in search of a focus. Some members have urged that its name be changed, while others want it to become an international organization, with its own secretariat and headquarters. Still others feel that since its economic aims are so close to those of the Group of 77, perhaps it could simply join that body and cease to exist as a separate entity altogether. (Many of its members already belong to the Group of 77.) In spite of the triumph, for now, of the idea of free-market economies, the gap between poor and rich countries remains alarmingly high and shows every sign of getting worse in the future. Political conflict in poor countries will continue to attract intervention from Western countries, most probably in the form of arms supplies or peace-keeping efforts. Extreme poverty will continue to tempt these countries, for example, to accept payments for allowing toxic waste to be dumped on their territory.

Nick Childs concludes, "And, against the background of international economic upheaval, the movement is confronted with the reality that a grouping which is numerically strong, but which represents predominantly poorer states, has much less influence than, for example, the Group of Seven leading industrial countries."[9] In any case, poor countries will continue to need an extra voice in the NAM to address issues of poverty and famine and to press for more favorable economic breaks in the form of debt relief, commodity price stabilization, or loans from wealthier countries and international lending institutions.

THE ORGANIZATION OF AFRICAN UNITY

From 1963 to 2002, the OAU was the primary continental political organization in Africa. All independent African states belonged to it. South Africa was admitted in May 1994 as the fifty-third member following historic elections in April 1994, which saw Nelson Mandela sworn in as the first black president of South Africa. The OAU was a natural outcome of the end of colonial rule in Africa. African leaders sought to fashion an institution that would represent them on the world stage and through which they could fight for the things they wanted. Security was clearly an important factor, since the departure of the colonial powers had left a security vacuum. Some of the African countries were worried about their own internal stability and wanted an organization that could assist them in dealing with threats to that stability.

Although the desire to have a regional organization might have been natural, the process of forming one was not at all easy. To underscore the impact of systemic factors on African countries, several factions emerged in the course of negotiations and discussions that led to the formation of the OAU. Ghana, with the support of Guinea and Liberia, pressed for a much stronger political union, arguing that without it, African states could not wield enough influence to play a significant role on the world stage. Nigeria objected to the idea of a political union, saying that, while such a union was a desirable political goal for African nations, it was premature to expect new states to give up their newly acquired sovereignty so soon after becoming independent. Nigerians urged that a political union be allowed to evolve gradually and not be rushed. They echoed the feelings of many other states by asserting that a great deal of work remained to be done domestically to prepare the groundwork for such a union.

In the case of Africa, the daunting task of molding national identities out of many ethnic groups, of state-building, and of consolidating power had just begun. Tanzania thought that regional organizations already in place, such as the East African High Commission—linking Kenya, Uganda, and Tanzania in well-coordinated services such as transportation, weather forecasting, currency, education, and others—and several francophone regional organizations, might be used as building blocks of an eventual political union. The years 1960–1962 saw larger and stronger factions emerge within the community of African states. One example was the Brazzaville-Monrovia Group, made up of approximately twenty states; it was very conservative, pro-France, afraid of the radicalism of Ghana's Kwame Nkrumah and Guinea's Sekou Toure, and unsympathetic to the troubles of another young radical leader, Patrice Lumumba, the new prime minister of the Congo. Emerging in opposition to the Brazzaville-Monrovia Group was the Casablanca Group, which embraced Lumumba, supported Morocco's claim to Mauritania, recognized Algeria's armed struggle for independence from France, and favored a stronger continental union. Moreover, the Casablanca Group's support for a continental union seemed to be driven by individual needs and interests. Orwa asserts,

> Morocco wanted support for its opposition to Mauritania's independence and admission to the United Nations. Nasser [of Egypt] saw the group as a chance of increasing Egyptian influence in Africa and to gain the support of African states against Israel. For Sekou Toure the enlarged group provided a badly needed political support against France and the former French colonies that had ostracized him for refusing to remain within France's sphere of influence. To Modibo Keita [of Mali] and Nkrumah the group offered a forum for projecting a collective African view on the Congo crisis and for advancing the idea of a union of African states.[10]

Ultimately and certainly not unexpectedly, the African states failed to agree on a stronger union. The OAU was founded in 1963 in Addis Ababa, Ethiopia, where it maintained its headquarters. Its final charter—drawn from and preceded by several charters named after the cities in which they were drafted (i.e., the Casablanca charter, the Monrovia charter, and the Lagos charter)—was, in fact, a compromise document that fell far short of what Nkrumah and his radical colleagues wanted. The African states were simply not ready for a political union. They did not fully trust Nkrumah, who did not conceal his ambition to be the first president of a United States of Africa, and they were not prepared to surrender any of their sovereignty or disrupt the special relationships they had nurtured between themselves and their former colonial masters, especially Britain and France.

The purposes of the OAU as enshrined in Article II of the charter were as follows:

a. to promote the unity and solidarity of the African states;
b. to co-ordinate and intensify their co-operation and efforts to achieve a better life for the peoples of Africa;
c. to defend their sovereignty, their territorial integrity, and independence;
d. to eradicate all forms of colonialism from Africa; and
e. to promote international co-operation, having due regard to the Charter of the United Nations and the Declaration of Human Rights.[11]

The OAU also bound its members to adhere to the following principles:

1. the sovereign equality of all Member States;
2. non-interference in the internal affairs of States;
3. respect for the sovereignty and territorial integrity of each State and for its inalienable right to independent existence;
4. peaceful settlement of disputes by negotiation, mediation, conciliation, or arbitration;
5. unreserved condemnation, in all its forms, of political assassination as well as of subversive activities on the part of neighboring States or any other States;
6. absolute dedication to the total emancipation of the African territories which are still dependent; and
7. affirmation of a policy of non-alignment with regard to all blocs.[12]

The OAU headquarters consisted of four central institutions. The first one was the Assembly of the Heads of State and Government, which met annually to discuss policy and deal with specific issues that needed to be handled at the highest level of the organization. The Assembly was "the supreme organ of the organization," with the authority to create and abolish all agencies connected with the OAU.

The second institution was the Council of Ministers, made up of foreign ministers of the member states, who met at least twice a year, one of the meetings usually devoted to the preparation of the annual summit meeting. The Council was responsible to the Assembly and was supposed to take up issues referred to it by the Assembly as well as to figure out the implementation of decisions made by the Assembly. The OAU charter also charged the Council with coordinating inter-African cooperation in a variety of fields.

The third central body was the General Secretariat, the administrative arm of the organization, directed by a general-secretary, who was assisted by several assistant secretaries-general. This body implemented directives from the Assembly of Heads of State and Government and the Council of Ministers.

Finally, there was the Commission of Mediation, Conciliation, and Arbitration, which was guided by a separate document known as a protocol. The Commission was established to concretize the pledge of African states to settle all their disputes by peaceful means. The Commission consisted of twenty-one members, elected by the Assembly from a list of professionally qualified individuals whose names had been recommended by African governments to the secretariat. They served for five years and were eligible for reelection by the Assembly, if nominated.

The OAU charter also established the following five specialized commissions: Economic and Social Affairs; Educational and Cultural Affairs; Health, Sanitation, and Nutrition; Defense; and Scientific, Technical, and Research Affairs. Members of these commissions were government ministers responsible for the portfolios covered by the commissions.

Finally, a very special structure was formed to address the one issue on which there was perhaps the highest consensus and about which Africans were very emotional: the liberation of the African continent from colonialism and racism. This body was called the Coordinating Committee for the Liberation of Africa, had its own secretariat, and was based in Tanzania to be close to the liberation movements. Its job was to oversee the implementation of a coherent African policy toward the liberation struggle in Zimbabwe (then called Rhodesia), Namibia, the Portuguese colonies of Mozambique, Angola, Guinea-Bissau, Principe and São Tomé, and white minority—ruled South Africa. The Coordinating Committee set up a liberation fund to receive contributions from African states for distribution among liberation movements recognized by the OAU. In addition, the Committee canvassed for more support for the struggle both within Africa and internationally, helped to mediate conflicts and raise morale among freedom fighters, and provided a forum to keep the issue of freedom on the world's agenda. With the end of apartheid in South Africa, the Committee was finally dismantled in 1995.

By adhering to noninterference in the internal affairs of each member state, respecting each other's territorial integrity, and discouraging subversion against neighbors, the OAU was, in effect, affirming the territorial and political status quo inherited by African leaders. Unfortunately, the principle left very little room, if any, for the kind of involvement that might have been called for in trying to shape or nudge the states into a stronger political union—or even in trying to discourage the kind of internal oppression and tyranny that occurred in Uganda and the Central African Republic and is currently going on in the Darfur region of Sudan and in Equatorial Guinea. Indeed, the controversies engulfing the OAU during summit meetings pertained to charges and countercharges of harboring dissidents from neighboring countries or plots to overthrow unfriendly governments.

Over the years, the OAU did not live up to the noble promises enshrined in its charter or envisaged by its founders. Yet most observers would agree that the existence of the OAU was a good thing. The organization represented the best hope of Africans trying to deal with their problems by themselves instead of relying on outsiders. It certainly has gained some visibility for the continent at international forums and in the United Nations. It has helped to keep a lid on potentially explosive issues by, for instance, vowing to keep the old colonial borders rather than redraw them. The OAU also was credited with maintaining a unified stance on the issue of eradicating racism and colonialism from the continent. From 1980 to the end of the century, the OAU focused its attention on human rights. A human rights charter was drawn up and ratified by the majority of the countries. This was a considerable achievement. Much discussion has been directed toward the high number of stateless persons on the continent, with a view to assisting refugees better and treating them more humanely. The OAU has come up with several ideas on the long-term economic survival of the continent. The HIV/AIDS epidemic has been discussed openly, and public education campaigns have been initiated to slow down the spread of the disease, which, in Africa, is spread mostly through heterosexual contact. And following the collapse of socialist regimes in Eastern Europe and increasing demands for democratization, the OAU attempted to spearhead the discussion of political reforms at the continental level. An analysis of the struggle for political and economic reforms is the subject of Chapter 7.

On the negative side, there were many disappointments. To begin with, the organization did not enjoy the full confidence and support of the member states. At any given time, as many as three-fourths of the members were behind in their dues payment. In 1992, for example, $30 million was owed to the organization, an amount equal to that year's budget.[13] Attendance at summit meetings was often poor, with as few as ten heads of state showing up and the rest of the delegates being foreign ministers or prime ministers. African heads of state have been far more eager to attend other international meetings than their own. For reasons of protecting sovereignty, African nations had been reluctant to use the mediation mechanisms provided in the charter. The office of the secretary-general was deliberately designed to be weak so as not to diminish the importance of the chairman of the OAU. The secretary-general had no authority to speak for the organization or the continent.[14] He was seen simply as an international civil servant whose major function was to carry out the orders of various committees of the organization and not initiate any policies or speak for the OAU.

Moreover, the tradition of rotating summit meetings of the organization with a new chairman elected every year, usually the president of the country in which the summit was being held, created problems. Some presidents threatened to boycott the summit because they did not like the host who was slated to become the organization's chairman. The tenures of President Ahmadou Ahidjo of Cameroon, Idi Amin Dada of Uganda, and Col. Mengistu Haile Mariam of Ethiopia were controversial indeed and nearly tore the organization apart. The practice of having a different spokesperson for the organization every year meant that there was no continuity or consistency in the organization's voice. Each head of state brought a different style and emphasis to the position and sometimes, if he was a controversial figure, confusion and discord, which the organization could ill afford. Also the practice of holding summit meetings in a different country each year proved too costly for some nations that were tempted to host a summit meeting as a way of showcasing their country to the rest of the world. Allocating money to the summits in the face of more pressing demands produced unrest of huge proportions, often with tragic consequences. Liberia's uneasy stability was broken when President Tolbert decided to host the summit meeting in 1979. In order to raise funds for such an undertaking, the government decided to reduce subsidies on food staples, thereby causing food prices to rise. Riots followed in the streets of Monrovia, which were quelled ruthlessly. The summit meeting took place, but the demonstrations and the repression that followed set off a chain of events that ended in the military overthrow of the Liberian government and the assassination of Tolbert himself in 1980, before his term as the chief spokesperson of the OAU ended.[15]

Summit meetings led to civil unrest in other countries as well. In Sierra Leone, students organized demonstrations and workers went on strike because of the enormous expense—about $200 million—of hosting the summit meeting in 1980. That the unrest in Sierra Leone did not reach the destructive level it did in Liberia may have been due, in part, to the economic rescue mounted at the last minute by Algeria, which donated fifty Mercedes-Benz cars, 500 tons of gas, and food and cash for the summit meeting. In 1981, the summit in Nairobi, Kenya, was preceded by increased military security to repressive levels and the closure of the University of Nairobi to prevent demonstrations that had been planned to protest against the government policy of detaining political dissidents without trial.[16] This was all unnecessary because the organization's permanent headquarters in Addis Ababa could easily have been made the permanent summit venue. And for the purpose of educating the African people as to the work of their continent's organization, the OAU's council and commission meetings, which did not require such enormous expenses and elaborate preparations, could occasionally be scheduled in other African countries. Following the disaster of 1982, when the OAU summit scheduled to take place in Tripoli, Libya, could not muster a quorum, the OAU reverted for the next eight years to the practice of convening its summit meetings in Addis Ababa. In 1991, Nigeria hosted the summit at its new federal capital of Abuja. In 1992, the OAU met in Dakar, Senegal. The OAU summit venues from the time it was founded until its dissolution are listed in Table 8.1

As stated before, the charter provides arbitration and mediation as a way of resolving conflicts and disagreements among African states. African

TABLE 8.1

African Summit Meetings: OAU/AU, 1963–2006

Year	Summit	Venue/Host	Chairman
1963	Founding Summit	Addis Ababa, Ethiopia	Emp. H. Selassie, hon. pres.
1964	1st Summit	Cairo, Egypt	Pres. Gamal Nasser
1965	2nd Summit	Accra, Ghana	Pres. Kwame Nkrumah
1966	3rd Summit	Addis Ababa, Ethiopia	Emp. Haile Selassie
1967	4th Summit	Kinshasa, Zaire	Pres. Mobutu Seseseko
1968	5th Summit	Algiers, Algeria	Pres. H. Boumedienne
1969	6th Summit	Addis Ababa, Ethiopia	Pres. A. Ahidjo of Cameroon
1970	7th Summit	Addis Ababa, Ethiopia	Pres. K. Kaunda of Zambia
1971	8th Summit	Addis Ababa, Ethiopia	Pres. O. Daddah of Mauritania
1972	9th Summit	Rabat, Morocco	King Hassan II
1973	10th Summit	Addis Ababa, Ethiopia	Pres. Y. Gowon of Nigeria
1974	11th Summit	Mogadishu, Somalia	Pres. Syad Barre
1975	12th Summit	Kampala, Uganda	Pres. Idi Amin Dada
1976	13th Summit	Port Louis, Mauritius	Prime Min. Sir S. Ramgoolan
1977	14th Summit	Libreville, Gabon	Pres. Omar Bongo
1978	15th Summit	Khartoum, Sudan	Pres. M. Numeiri
1979	16th Summit	Monrovia, Liberia	Pres. William Tolbert
1980	17th Summit	Freetown, Sierra Leone	Pres. Siaka Stevens
1981	18th Summit	Nairobi, Kenya	Pres. Daniel arap Moi
1982	No Quorum	Tripoli, Libya	Pres. Daniel arap Moi
1983	19th Summit	Addis Ababa, Ethiopia	Col. Mengistu H. Mariam
1984	20th Summit	Addis Ababa, Ethiopia	Pres. J. Nyerere of Tanzania
1985	21st Summit	Addis Ababa, Ethiopia	Pres. Abdou Diouf of Senegal
1986	22nd Summit	Addis Ababa, Ethiopia	Pres. Sassou-Nguesso of Congo Republic
1987	23rd Summit	Addis Ababa, Ethiopia	Pres. K. Kaunda of Zambia
1988	24th Summit	Addis Ababa, Ethiopia	Pres. M. Traore of Mali
1989	25th Summit	Addis Ababa, Ethiopia	Pres. H. Mubarak of Egypt
1990	26th Summit	Addis Ababa, Ethiopia	Pres. Y. Museveni of Uganda
1991	27th Summit	Abuja, Nigeria	Pres. I. Babangida

(continued)

TABLE 8.1 (CONTINUED)

Year	Summit	Venue/Host	Chairman
1992	28th Summit	Dakar, Senegal	Pres. Abdou Diouf
1993	29th Summit	Cairo, Egypt	Pres. H. Mubarak
1994	30th Summit	Tunis, Tunisia	Pres. Zine Ben Ali
1995	31st Summit	Addis Ababa, Ethiopia	Pres. Meles Zenawi
1996	32nd Summit	Yaoundé, Cameroon	Pres. Paul Biya
1997	33rd Summit	Harare, Zimbabwe	Pres. Robert Mugabe
1998	34th Summit	Ouagadougou, Burkina Faso	Pres. Blaise Campaore
1999	35th Summit	Algiers, Algeria	Pres. Abdel Aziz Bouteflika
2000	36th Summit	Lome, Togo	Pres. Eyadema
2001	37th Summit	Lusaka, Zambia	Pres. Frederick Chiluba
2002	38th & Last OAU Summit	Durban, South Africa	Pres. Thabo Mbeki

Source: Compiled from *Africa Contemporary Record: Annual Survey & Documents*, 1968–1982; *Facts on File*, various issues; and *Keesing's Record of World Events* (formerly *Keesing's Contemporary Archives*), various issues; *Africa News*, Vol. 38, No. 6 (April 26–May 8, 1993), p. 11; *Africa Research Bulletin*, Political, Social & Cultural Series, Vol. 31, No. 6 (1994); Vol. 32, No. 6 (1995); Vol. 33, No. 7 (1996); www.africa-union.org.

countries, however, have been reluctant to use arbitration, which would involve submitting cases to a panel of experts and having to abide by their decision. African states seem to regard arbitration as impinging on their national sovereignty by requiring them to abide by decisions made by another body. I suspect that because of this perception, force continues to be the preferred choice of dealing with contentious issues. Only when force is unsuccessful or the warring parties are exhausted has there been an attempt to use mediation. But the kind of mediation sought most often has been a high-risk one, involving heads of state rather than their expert emissaries. Unfortunately, when heads of state fail to resolve issues, they tend to view failure in personal terms and, sometimes, to carry grudges against their colleagues. The reverberations of such failures often spill into other conflicts, thus making their resolution more complicated and more difficult to achieve.

THE AFRICAN UNION

The idea to form a stronger continental organization than the OAU was born at an extraordinary session of the OAU Heads of State and Governments in September 1999. The African leaders felt that they needed an organization that would help them achieve the following three goals: (1) accelerate the process of political, social, and economic integration of the continent; (2) have a stronger entity that would play a more effective role in the emerging global economy; and (3) mitigate the consequences of globalization, which they thought might hit weak developing economies harder than industrialized economies. The birth of the African Union (AU) occurred in stages. The OAU summit of 2000 in Lomé (Togo) adopted the Constitutive Act of the Union, which is basically the AU charter. The summit the following year (2001) in Lusaka (Zambia) set down the specific guidelines for implementation.

The last summit of the OAU was held in Addis Ababa (Ethiopia) in July 2002 for the heads of state and government to congratulate themselves on the foundation laid by the OAU to enable them to establish the AU and to effect the transfer of the infrastructure of the OAU to the new organization. The feeling among OAU members was that a foundation for a stronger group had, in fact, been laid by the OAU going as far back as 1980, when the OAU issued the Lagos Plan of Action urging African states to adopt self-reliant development. The OAU was praised for passing the African Charter on Human and People's Rights (1981), the Priority Program for Economic Recovery (1985), the Declaration on the Political and Socio-Economic Situation in Africa (1990), the Charter on Popular Participation (1990), the Abuja Treaty of 1991, advocating the formation of an African Economic Community in stages using a regional approach and, finally, the Mechanism for Conflict Prevention, Management, and Resolution (1993).

The first AU summit was held in Durban (South Africa) in July 2002 under the chairmanship of Thabo Mbeki, then-president of South Africa. There have since been ten ordinary-session summits and several extraordinary-session summits: one on poverty alleviation in Africa and another one on U.N. reform. The sixth summit in January 2006 met in Khartoum, Sudan. Normally the president of the host country serves as the chair of the AU summit, but during the sixth summit, Sudan's bid to have its president, Omar El-Bashir, chair the AU summit was scuttled by two events: the conflict in Darfur, which has killed more than 300,000 black Sudanese and produced more than 2 million refugees and the refusal by Sudan to allow U.N. soldiers to assume peace-keeping duties alongside the AU soldiers.

Objectives of the African Union

Whereas Article II of the OAU charter had five objectives of the organization, the AU lists fourteen objectives. They are as follows:

1. To achieve greater unity between African states
2. To defend the sovereignty, territorial integrity, and independence of the African states
3. To accelerate political and socio-economic integration of the continent
4. To promote and defend African positions on issues vital to Africa

5. To encourage international cooperation in keeping with the U.N. charter and the Human Rights Charter
6. To promote peace, security, and stability of Africa
7. To promote democracy, popular participation, and good governance in Africa
8. To uphold the African Charter on human and people's rights
9. To enable Africans to be effective in global economic and international negotiations
10. To promote sustainable development
11. To raise the people's living standards
12. To coordinate and harmonize the different economic regional communities for the eventual attainment of integration
13. To promote research in science and technology, and
14. To work with other countries and organizations to eradicate diseases and promote good health among Africans.

Organs of the African Union

There are eight key institutions of the AU and eight specialized technical committees. A brief summary of the eight institutions follows:

1. The Assembly of Heads of State and Governments, required to meet annually and in limited or extraordinary sessions, if necessary, is where the ultimate authority of the AU rests.
2. The Executive Council of Ministers, whose main responsibility is to prepare the summits' agenda. This is the same function as in the old OAU.
3. The African Union Commission. This is the Secretariat, the main administrative arm of the AU. It consists of a chairperson, a deputy chairperson and eight commissioners, and senior staffers. The first regular chairperson of the Commission, elected in 2004, is Alpha Omar Konare, a former president of Mali. Each commissioner is in charge of each of the following portfolios: peace and security; political affairs; infrastructure and energy; social affairs; human resources, science, and technology; trade and industry; rural economy and agriculture; and economic affairs.
4. Permanent Representatives' Committee. This is composed of ambassadors from AU member states who are accredited to the AU. Their function is to prepare the work of the Executive Council of Ministers.
5. The Peace and Security Council
6. The Pan-African Parliament
7. The Economic, Social, and Cultural Council, and
8. The Court of Justice.

Financial Institutions of the AU

There are three: the African Central Bank, the African Monetary Fund, and the African Investment Bank. The functions of these institutions have yet to be spelled out.

An important departure from previous practice is the Peace and Security Council. The OAU charter bound its members to adhere to a principle of noninterference in the internal affairs of member states. This principle made it virtually impossible for the OAU to act to prevent murderous regimes of past African dictators like Uganda's Idi Amin Dada, Zaire's (now the Democratic Republic of Congo's) Mobutu Sese-Seko, and Central African Republic's Jean-Bedel Bokassa. African leaders could do to their own people virtually anything they wanted with utter impunity. Article 4 of the AU charter, however, "allows the AU to intervene in a member state in what are called 'grave circumstances'—where there have been war crimes, genocide or crimes against humanity."[17] Indeed, it is under Article 4 that the AU deployed 2,000 troops in Darfur, Sudan, to protect thousands of refugees who were being attacked by the Sudanese government-armed militia called "the janjaweed." So far, since 2003, nearly 350,000 people in Darfur have lost their lives and close to 3 million have been displaced from their homes and are now refugees either in their own country or in refugee camps in neighboring Chad and Central African Republic. Without sufficient funds, personnel, or equipment, the AU mission has not been successful. Efforts have been stepped up to persuade a reluctant Sudanese government to permit a U.N. force to protect the refugees and enforce a cease-fire. A recent indictment of the Sudanese president, Omar El-Bashir, by the Prosecutor of the International Criminal Court (ICC) for genocide, murder, and crimes against humanity is part of that pressure. The irony of the indictment is that the AU is asking ICC and the U.N. not to move hastily to enforce the indictment by trying to arrest the Sudanese president. So much for progress toward ending government-sanctioned brutality and impunity toward its own people!

The AU appears paralyzed to take any action to save the people of Zimbabwe, who are dying of brutality inflicted by the security forces loyal to President Robert Mugabe, who rigged the 2008 presidential elections in order to stay in power and has made life intolerable for supporters of the opposition Movement for Democratic Change (MDC). The country was also in the throes of an epidemic of cholera, a virulent but curable disease. According to the World Health Organization report in 2008, nearly 1,500 people had already died of cholera and another 26,500 were infected.[18] The economy has collapsed, most hospitals have closed for lack of money to buy drugs, there is widespread famine, Zimbabweans who can, are fleeing to South Africa. Despite this level of unspeakable suffering, the president of Zimbabwe is so detached from reality that he has publicly declared that there is no cholera epidemic in the country and has vowed "never, never, to surrender, because Zimbabwe is mine."[19] Very few African leaders have criticized President Mugabe. The AU managed to wrest an agreement for Mugabe to share power with MDC, whose leader now holds the post of prime minister. The coalition is fragile, the killings have subsided, but Mugabe remains very much the supreme leader. The conclusion to be drawn from this brief narrative is that the Africans still lack the capacity to protect their people from incompetent or autocratic leaders or the moral courage to criticize them.

THE UNITED STATES AND AFRICA

The United States, unlike Britain and France, had no colonies in Africa, but it did have a long-standing relationship with Liberia going back to the founding of that country by freed African American slaves in the 1840s. Indeed, the city of Monrovia is named after the fifth U.S. president, James Monroe. The Liberian flag is patterned after the American flag, and Liberia uses the American dollar as its unit of currency.

From the very beginning, the United States sought to follow the lead of Great Britain, its close ally and a leading colonial power in Africa. After World War II and into the 1950s, when signs pointed to the beginning of the end of colonial rule, the United States made no serious attempt to know Africa, to get acquainted with its emerging leaders, especially radical ones like Kwame Nkrumah of Ghana, or to learn about the issues and problems these countries were going to face in the near future. The most telling evidence of this lackadaisical approach to Africa was when the United States chose to abstain on a crucial vote in the United Nations on the U.N. Declaration on the Granting of Independence to Colonial Countries and Peoples.[20] The U.N. Declaration meant a great deal to African countries and offered an opportunity for the United States to demonstrate some understanding of African sensitivities and show some sympathy for African resentment against colonial rule. Both African leaders and their allies in the Third World were quite surprised by this American action.

The election of John F. Kennedy as president in 1960 signaled a major change in the American position toward Africa. The cold war was well under way. Americans were wary of Soviet moves in Africa, fearing that American and Western interests might be harmed by such moves. Kennedy was worried about what he detected as a tendency toward communism on the part of young African leaders. He expressed the hope that African nationalism would triumph over communism, but he knew that hope alone would not protect Western interests. He also felt that Britain was on the retreat from a strong political role in Africa. He created the Bureau of African Affairs within the State Department to craft a coherent

U.S. policy toward sub-Saharan Africa and appointed G. Mennen Williams, a liberal governor of Michigan as the bureau's first assistant secretary of state. (The northern part of Africa was put in a different category with Asia and handled by a different bureau.) The goal of the Africa bureau was to tone down the anti-Western rhetoric of the new leaders like Nkrumah and Nnamdi Azikiwe (of Nigeria), to facilitate an orderly transition from colonialism to independence, and to protect Western strategic and economic interests. The means to achieve those goals was to court and support moderate and reformist leaders like Jomo Kenyatta of Kenya and Mobutu—who had taken over Congo-Kinshasa (then renamed it Zaire until he was overthrown in 1990 when the new leaders yet again changed the name to the Democratic Republic of Congo)—following the murder of its first leader, Patrice Lumumba.

During the 1960s, the Vietnam War sapped much of America's energy, and American action in Africa was generally aimed at winning the cold war rather than addressing African problems. The U.S. consistently sided with Western countries against African interests. They backed the British stand on Rhodesia and voted against a U.N. resolution condemning Britain's failure to topple the illegal government in Rhodesia. The Americans sent one-half billion dollars worth of military equipment to Portugal in the latter's struggle with freedom fighters in Mozambique and Angola. They maintained extensive economic, political, and military relations with South Africa, arguing that whites in southern Africa were there to stay (true) and so much in control that change was possible only through dealing with them (and appeasing them).

In the early 1970s, support for the status quo at the expense of core African interests continued, but by the time Carter became president of the United States, Kissinger under Nixon and Ford had begun to tilt toward majority rule in Zimbabwe and Namibia—although showing much more sensitivity toward the anxieties of the white minority than the needs of the African people. Carter's presidency heralded almost a revolutionary shift in U.S. policy toward Africa.[21] Carter was highly moralistic in his foreign policy announcements, anchoring American policy on human rights. He felt that for too long, the United States had not tried to reconcile its moral principles (which he felt had a universal appeal) with its activities abroad and its relationships with other countries. He reached out to Africa through his appointment of Andrew Young, an African American, as ambassador to the United Nations. He pursued increased cultural and economic ties with large states like Nigeria (which also happened to be a major supplier of crude oil to the United States) and dedicated himself to eventual African rule in Namibia, Zimbabwe, and South Africa. Andrew Young was centrally involved—and was quite effective because of his rapport with African leaders—in the British-brokered negotiations among warring factions in Zimbabwe that produced a settlement leading to Zimbabwe's independence in April 1980.

When Ronald Reagan became president in 1981, some things could not be reversed. The struggle in the southern part of Africa had progressed too far. The United States could not renounce the human rights dimension of U.S. foreign policy. However, the emphasis changed to cold war themes. Reagan's appointee as Assistant Secretary of State at the Bureau of African Affairs, Chester Crocker began to stress the importance to American strategic interests of limiting Soviet influence on the continent. Even conflicts in southern Africa had to be addressed, because they represented a vacuum created by the Europeans' lack of interest in Africa and, therefore, an opportunity for the Soviets to solidify their advantage. American aid was to be tied to the extent to which Africans supported American interests.

Deliberately, Reagan linked the settlement of the Namibian conflict to the withdrawal of Cuban troops in Angola. These forces had been invited by the Angolan government in the mid-1970s to assist the MPLA (one of the three main liberation movements in Angola) in its war against UNITA (the second of the Angolan liberation movements, which leaned to the right) following the abrupt departure of the Portuguese. Reagan believed that Cuban troops in Angola were sent there in response to Soviet request, as an extension of Soviet policy in Angola rather than as Cuba's own foreign policy initiative in support of a beleaguered ally. A policy of constructive engagement was inaugurated by the Reagan administration, to the dismay of Americans opposed to apartheid, who felt that such a policy might mislead supporters of white supremacy into thinking that the American public supported the white power structure in Africa.

Following strong public pressure, Reagan imposed mild sanctions. Congress voted much stronger economic and military sanctions, which Reagan vetoed. The veto was overturned by Congress. With economic sanctions in place, isolation of South Africa from international sports complete, chaos in the country's cities and townships rampant, and the armed struggle being waged by the ANC from the neighboring states—popularly referred to as frontline states—the white minority power structure knew that its days were numbered. It became prudent to seek a way out of the conundrum through negotiation. By the time Reagan left office, serious discussions were going on between South African government and various black groups within the country, the ANC had been unbanned, and rumors were rife not only that secret discussions were going on but also that the world's most famous political prisoner and the most likely first black president of South Africa—Nelson Mandela—might soon be freed from prison.

It is difficult to characterize President Bill Clinton's foreign policy during his administration (1993–2001) and this is not the most appropriate place to critique it. Clinton's National Security Adviser, Anthony Lake, in a major policy speech during the first year of Clinton's presidency, suggested that "the successor to a doctrine of containment (of communism) must be a strategy of...enlargement of the world's free community of market democracies."[22] As it so often happens, events in the world normally do not conform to doctrine or policy. Clinton's administration was confronted with the challenge, not of enlarging market democracies in Africa, but stemming the civil war so that starving civilians might get international relief in Somalia and wavering whether or not to intervene in Rwanda where it knew full well that mass killings on the scale of a genocide were taking place. In a period of 100 days beginning in April 1994, more than 800,000 Tutsis and their Hutu sympathizers were killed by the Hutu dissidents. The same month, a happier revolution was taking elsewhere: South Africa was conducting the first democratic elections in which all South Africans of all races and colors were voting and electing Nelson Mandela as their first African president.

THE SOVIET UNION AND AFRICA

Much of the literature on Soviet policy toward Africa tends to be woefully biased, casting the former Soviet Union as the main villain in the contemporary international system and in Africa against which the United States had to be vigilant at all times. The truth is that both the United States and the Soviet Union were superpowers who were keen to shape the international system according to their ideologies, ideologies that they felt had universal appeal. As the two superpowers competed to influence and win friends among African countries, the interests of the African countries in which much of this rivalry was played out were secondary. The Soviet Union had always felt that it played a very significant role in the defeat of the Axis powers in World War II and had actually contributed to the end of the colonial empire worldwide. Indeed, as Ali Mazrui has observed, "Lenin bequeathed to the colonized peoples of the world a theory of imperialism ..."[23] As the war ended and old animosities between the Americans and the Soviets resurfaced, and as the anticolonial struggles picked up momentum—having been fueled in part by the war experience—Soviet thinkers began to emphasize the centrality of Marxist ideas in those struggles. A Soviet scholar once said,

> A complete and final victory of a colonial revolution is possible only under the direction of the proletariat ... Only the working class leading the national front of all the anti-imperialist forces is capable of carrying out a consistent struggle for independence.[24]

In the course of the struggle for independence and afterward, African leaders were certainly receptive to new ideas, initiatives, and offers of help for reconstructing their societies. They were curious about Soviet claims that communist societies were better models for the new countries of Africa than the West. The Soviets stressed the fact that they had never colonized African countries and that African countries could not progress if they stayed within the Western orbit. Some African leaders were familiar with Marxist ideology and had even employed Marxist rhetoric in mobilizing their own people for the independence struggle. Some of these leaders had been prosecuted for advocating independence for their countries. Many of them, while appreciative of Soviet willingness to help, did not want to trade one master for another, even if the new master claimed to understand imperial oppression. They thought of ways to befriend the Soviet Union without getting entangled in the rivalry between the superpowers. The NAM was established in an attempt to resolve the ideological dilemma, to permit new countries to participate fully in international affairs, and to take stands on issues vital to them—and there were many such issues—without undue pressure from the superpowers.

The Soviet Union's initial venture into Africa occurred in the early 1950s, when it signed an arms deal with Egypt, whose president, Gamal Abdul Nasser, was leading a Pan-Arab campaign against Israel on behalf of Palestinians. It also maintained steady contact with the Algerian Front for National Liberation, which, from 1954 to 1962, successfully fought to drive France out of Algeria. Other contacts followed, involving Guinea, Ghana, and Mali in the late 1950s. The Soviet Union was eager to demonstrate the vitality of its revolutionary ideology.

There were bound to be problems, and these arose quite early in the relationship between Africans and the Soviets. For one thing, the Soviets were not really familiar with Africa.[25] They did not know the languages, the cultures, and the prevailing economic and political conditions of the continent. It was not going to be easy to convince African leaders to adopt Soviet-style Marxism. There were too many contradictions. There was no national bourgeoisie in African countries to speak of. There was not a proletariat either. There were many ethnic groups, living very traditional lives, tied to local leaders, and sustained by a variety of beliefs and practices going back centuries. Many of these groups had been subjected to cultural influences from missionaries, colonial settlers, and commercial entrepreneurs. The political leaders, though curious about Marxism, were individuals who came from groups that had somehow benefited from colonial rule—they were well-educated and acculturated in Western schools; some had cultivated a taste for the Western lifestyle, but were very conservative and very nationalistic, with their own ideas of what they wanted done to develop their countries. Some of these leaders were already beginning to sense that no country had so far been transformed successfully from a poor peasant country into an industrial socialist one and that the Stalinist approach in the Soviet Union, which had catapulted the country into a great power but at an enormous human cost, was probably not applicable to Africa.

Other forces and events complicated the situation in Africa for the Soviets. The Chinese were in the process of bolting out of Soviet control and beginning to assert themselves as far better models for African countries than the Soviets were. The Chinese reminded Africans that they, too, were non-European—unlike the Soviets who were basically European—that they had suffered imperial incursions by the West, and that their society was more comparable to African societies. Indeed, the theory of guerrilla warfare, refined and synthesized by the founder of modern China, Mao Ze Dong, was far more cognizant of traditional culture, and therefore more applicable to Africa, than Lenin's experience as a leader of revolutionary Bolsheviks. Moreover, having just won independence, African leaders were reluctant to relinquish this new power or take orders from anyone. They were faced with the daunting challenge of building new nation-states and consolidating their fragile power bases through single nationalistic parties.

The Soviets began to appreciate the bewildering complexity of the leaders, societies, and political groups in the new African states. Early in the 1960s, they developed the concept of the "state of national democracy" in order to accept the rather different development process being adopted by Guinea, Ghana, and Mali[26] and to justify having to work with all kinds of African national groups not reflected in Marxist thinking. The "state of national democracy" was defined as:

> A state which consistently upholds its political and economic independence, fights against imperialism and its military blocs, against military bases on its territory; a state which fights against the new forms of colonialism and the penetration of imperialist capital; a state in which the people are ensured broad democratic rights and freedoms ... the opportunity to work for the enactment of an agrarian reform and other domestic and social changes, and for participation in shaping government policy.[27]

The state of national democracy was conceived to be a transitional stage leading toward "socialism." Barely a year later, this concept was revised again to endorse what was called "socialism of the national type." Despite grave doubts about the kind of socialism Ghana, Guinea, and Mali were promoting, Soviet policy formulators constructed this new model of socialism, one that was not quite scientific but purportedly drew on a variety of African traditions and historical experiences. This quick, not-so-well-thought-out revisionism may have been occasioned by the aggressive initiative of the Chinese government to gain a foothold in Africa. But in the long run, the Soviets experienced one setback after another as their allies were overthrown or economic policies failed to lift the countries out of poverty. Ghana's Nkrumah was driven from power in 1966, Mali's Keita was ousted in 1969, and Guinea lapsed into vicious political repression. The economies of all three countries stagnated. The Soviets had aid programs in many other countries including Kenya, Tanzania, and Uganda, but these programs were inefficiently run and inadequate. Not enough resources were transferred to ameliorate the appalling economic conditions of these African countries.

In the military sphere, there is no doubt that the Soviets made a tremendous impact. They supported practically all of the liberation movements in southern Africa and the former Portuguese colonies.

Such support was consistent with their belief in their revolutionary past and commitment to the eradication of political oppression and exploitation wherever they existed. They also viewed the liberation struggles as the basic building blocks of future alliances with the Soviet Union. The victories of liberation movements in Mozambique, Angola, Guinea-Bissau, and Zimbabwe would not have been realized without substantial Soviet material and logistical support.

In some countries with revolutionary potential, the Soviets found themselves caught up on the losing side of disastrous civil wars. This was clearly the case when the Soviets supported the *Simba* rebels in the Congo. When *Simba* rebels held some Belgian missionaries hostage, Western intervention, led by the United States and Belgium, was massive and swift, resulting in conservative, pro-Western domestic political forces prevailing. President Mobutu enjoyed Western support over the years, despite leading one of the most corrupt and repressive governments in Africa. Also, when General Mohammed Siad Barre toppled the Somali government in 1969, the Soviets were quick to extend help. The relationship thrived, culminating in the signing of a friendship treaty in 1974. The new radical government in Somalia had grandiose plans to reclaim areas in Ethiopia and Kenya that were inhabited by people of Somali origin, and they needed military hardware from the Soviets for this effort. Somalia is strategically located in what is known as the Horn of Africa, close to the explosive Middle East. The Soviets needed a foothold there and were glad finally to get one so as to keep an eye on the United States. The United States, on the other hand, had been for a long time comfortably ensconced in Ethiopia, where they had set up huge communication facilities in Asmara in the northern part of the country. Conservative emperor Haile Selassie could always count on American support. The Soviets armed Somalia generously until 1974, when Selassie was overthrown by a group of extremely radical young airforce lieutenants. As the conflict between Somalia and Ethiopia escalated, Somalia hoped that its alliance with the Soviets would secure for them the weapons they needed to wage a successful war against Ethiopia and capture their "lost" territories. The Soviets, for their part, hoped to mediate that conflict. As it turned out, they could not be in both countries and remain impartial in the rapidly escalating conflict. They failed miserably to mediate. Because Col. Mengistu Haile Mariam and his colleagues in Ethiopia sounded like committed Marxist revolutionaries, determined to transform their economically backward feudal empire into a modern socialist state, the Soviet Union decided that Mengistu and his fellow officers were a better bet than the Somalis and decided to back them fully. Predictably, the Somali government threw the Soviets out in 1977. With enormous amounts of military hardware supplied by the Soviets, Ethiopia defeated Somalia resoundingly, destroying Barre's military machine. Barre fled for his life and eventually died in exile in Zimbabwe. The country he left behind disintegrated into a totally failed state.

Another high-profile involvement by the Soviet Union in Africa was in Angola, where a Marxist liberation movement, the Popular Movement for the Liberation of Angola, was locked in a three-way struggle to secure control of the country following the sudden departure of the Portuguese colonial authorities. Africans had waged a liberation struggle in Angola from the early 1960s. There were three main African groups, all ethnically based. After a long war, which precipitated a coup in Portugal itself in 1974, Portugal tried but failed to unite the three groups or to merge the three guerrilla armies into one national military force. As a result, there was no coordinated international response to mediate the incipient civil war. Different outside groups intervened on behalf of the side they supported. Troops from Zaire (now, Democratic Republic of Congo) intervened for the FNLA, the Chinese sent military trainers to help UNITA, the South Africans weighed in on the side of either UNITA or FNLA, and the Soviets sent large shipments of arms to help the MPLA. Extra help came from Cuba in the form of troops. Although most observers in the West saw the Cubans as nothing more than an extension of Soviet policy, the relationship between the MPLA and Cuba went back many years. The Cubans were responding independently to requests for assistance from the MPLA and would probably have contributed troops even if the Soviets had not been around. It became much more efficient to coordinate Soviet and Cuban assistance together. The West responded to MPLA victory by continuing to fund UNITA, until changes in the Soviet Union forced negotiations that led to the Cuban withdrawal from Angola. After many years of protracted negotiations involving the United Nations, the MPLA government, UNITA, and several African heads of state acting as mediators, elections were held in Angola in September 1992 which were won by MPLA. UNITA rejected the results of those elections arguing that they were rigged and resumed the fighting which continued intermittently into 1997. Until he was killed by government forces in 2002, UNITA's Jonas Savimbi continued to raise one objection after another against joining a government of national unity and reconciliation which he and the other revolutionary leaders had agreed upon earlier.

Mikhail Gorbachev's assumption of power in the former Soviet Union in 1985 was a turning point in relations between the USSR and African countries. When Gorbachev became the leader of the Soviet Union, he was shocked to discover that the Soviet economy was in far worse shape than he could ever have imagined. The Soviet empire—in the form of allies in the Warsaw Treaty Organization, Marxist states abroad, and radical regimes in the Third World—was draining the Soviet economy.[28] The Soviet Union was paying almost 80 percent of the cost of the Warsaw Pact, pouring about $20 billion into the economy of Eastern Europe in direct aid as well as subsidizing oil and natural gas. This state of affairs could not go on forever. There was no way that the Soviet economy could ever prosper without a fundamental change not only in the Soviet economy itself but also in its economic relationships with dependent countries around the world. Gorbachev had to do something about it. He decided that the key to reducing the cost of the Soviet empire was to make fundamental changes in Soviet society, including reductions in the Soviet military and disengagement from some of the obligations inherent in maintaining an empire. Domestically, Gorbachev embarked on a dual policy of *glasnost* and *perestroika*.[29] *Glasnost* would permit freedom of speech so that people could speak openly on issues and problems facing the country and share their ideas on possible solutions. *Perestroika* would entail the restructuring of the massive, centrally controlled Soviet economy. Initially, Gorbachev, perhaps not only the best-educated Soviet leader since the revolution but also one totally schooled in the political culture of the country, thought that he could liberalize the system without abandoning the thoughts of Marx and Lenin.[30] The situation was stalemated due to very stiff domestic resistance until an unsuccessful coup occurred on August 18, 1991, following which Gorbachev was forced to resign. His position was taken over by Boris Yeltsin. The Soviet Union disintegrated. The three Baltic states of Estonia, Latvia, and Lithuania were the first to become independent states and to join the United Nations. A looser federation was formed called the Commonwealth of Independent States, with Russia and nine other republics, but it collapsed. Ethnic conflicts continue to beset former Soviet republics such as Armenia, Azerbaijan, Tajikistan, and Georgia.

Internationally, Gorbachev's impact was just as great and dramatic. He withdrew Soviet forces from Afghanistan, allowed Soviet allies in Eastern Europe to decide on the kinds of political and economic systems they wanted, and began to nudge Third World friends toward resolving long-standing conflicts whose enormous cost had been underwritten all these years by the Soviet Union. Ethiopia and Angola, both heavily dependent on the Soviet Union for arms and money, began to explore ways of ending their costly civil wars. The Marxist dictatorship in Ethiopia, having agreed to exploratory negotiations with the rebels in Eritrea, collapsed. The former strongman Mengistu Haile Mariam now lives in comfortable exile in Zimbabwe. The former Marxist MPLA government in Angola concluded a peace accord with the Western-supported UNITA movement and held free elections in September 1992, which were monitored by international observers. The MPLA won the elections. UNITA refused to accept the outcome, charging that serious election irregularities rendered the election illegitimate; they resumed the fighting. Another peace accord was reached in 1994, following which the U.N. sent in peacekeepers. UNITA continued to violate the peace agreement till 2002, when the leader of UNITA, Jonas Savimbi, was killed in a battle with government soldiers. The civil war ended then, although there is a small rebel movement in Cabinda province, an enclave in the southwestern corner of the Republic of Congo, completely detached from Angola. The rebel group claims that although most of the oil is pumped from Cabinda, people in the enclave have not benefited from the revenue. In any event, the scale of the fighting has declined drastically from when UNITA was waging a full-scale war. Angola remains one of the poorest countries in Africa. There is plenty of rebuilding of the country to be done. The countryside is also littered with mines from the civil war, which continue to maim civilians.

CONCLUSIONS

African states entered statehood with tremendous disadvantages, as explained in this book. Yet the leaders were determined to secure their place in the family of nations and assert their rights as independent states. The international stage was provided by such forums as the United Nations and its agencies, the Non-Aligned Movement, and regional organizations like the Organization of African Unity and the African Union. Through their participation in these organizations, they have earned their legitimacy. They were able to reorient discussion at the United Nations toward issues that mattered to them the most: issues such as self-determination, racism, and economic inequality. Some of the agencies formed under the U.N. rubric, such as the United Nations Conference on Trade and Development (UNCTAD) and the United Nations Development Program (UNDP), were a consequence of sustained pressure by African and other poor countries on Western countries to assume some of the responsibility of assisting poor countries through multilateral agencies to get out of poverty. There is no doubt that some African countries benefited from the international rivalry between the former Soviet Union and the United States.

Domestic challenges facing Africa proved even more formidable. Needs of power consolidation and nation-building meant that many African leaders would try to dispense with the fragile structures they had inherited from the colonial authorities in the waning days of colonial rule. As African countries continued to grapple with domestic problems and experimented with different models of development, nothing seemed to work well. Instability and repression increased; so did economic problems. Moreover, the economic gap between African countries and Western industrialized nations only got wider. Even those countries in a position to exploit the cold war found themselves being used as pawns. The Horn of Africa is a good example of this.

Things seem to have come full circle, with the fall of Eastern Europe, the liberation of Namibia, and the abolition of legal and constitutional apartheid in South Africa. Indeed, even the African summits have changed their agenda from talking about racism and self-determination to economic problems—erasing the $260 billion debt is a key issue—human rights and democratic reforms, the environment (to try to slow down the process of desertification and the disposal of toxic waste from industrialized countries), and regional security.

As these problems persist, there is real danger of Africa being marginalized now that the cold war is over. A number of scholars have already suggested that Africa is about to enter a period of "benign neglect" as major powers turn to their own internal problems or seek to help the newly freed communist states of Eastern Europe. There is also the feeling that after nearly four decades of foreign aid, the level of poverty in sub-Saharan Africa is almost nearly as bad as it was forty years ago, and that, according to an American aid official, "pouring substantially more foreign money into the region (i.e., Africa) would do no good whatsoever."[31] But as Gilbert Khadiagala argues persuasively, "The real danger of marginalization for Africa comes from the interdependence component of the new order. The coalescence of extra-African world into regional integration schemes promises to reduce Africa's already diminishing capacity to participate in world trade."[32]

In the much-altered international environment of the twenty-first century, there is a great deal of evidence that Africa is still being driven by events outside its control. If Africans can adapt well, assume control of the democratization process now taking place in their own countries, and push for regional approaches to long-standing economic and security concerns, then perhaps the new world order will not see the increased marginalization of Africa that is feared by some scholars.

Fortunately, there is already some evidence that Africans have begun to come up with ideas of their own on the most pressing problems facing the continent. Four serious efforts merit mention. The African alternative framework to the structural adjustment programs initiated by the World Bank originated with the U.N. Economic Commission for Africa in 1989, directed at that time by a Nigerian economist, Adebayo Adedeji.[33] It is a candid look at what is wrong with the African economies, what the African economies must adjust to in order to meet the needs of the people, the effects of the World Bank–mandated adjustment programs that have resulted in much suffering for the average African without any commensurate improvement in the economic performance of the countries, and some hard-nosed recommendations for the long-term and short-term development of African economies. The second effort, a meeting convened in Tanzania in 1990, brought together Africans from a variety of organizations, governmental and nongovernmental. The conference was called "out of concern for the serious deterioration in the human and economic conditions in Africa in the decade of the 1980s, the recognition of the lack of progress in achieving popular participation and the lack of full appreciation of the role popular participation plays in the process of recovery and development …"[34] What emerged out of that conference was something called: an African Charter for Popular Participation in Development and Transformation, endorsing democratic reforms as a necessary condition for economic recovery. The third effort is the Kampala Document, a result of a meeting sponsored by the African Leadership Forum.[35] The forum is the brainchild of former Nigerian president, Olusegun Obasanjo, who believes that Africans must begin to develop the kind of imaginative and competent leadership that will prepare their countries for the challenges of the twenty-first century. The Kampala Document dealt with security issues, stability, development, and cooperation, very broadly defined. The fourth effort was, the New Economic Partnership for African Development (NEPAD), discussed in Chapter 7.

The success of political change so far in so many countries in Africa that only a few years ago would not have been judged ready or even capable of change offers ample reason for hope and optimism. The euphoria that accompanied transition to independence is gone. Now there is only the realization that to make the dream of peace and prosperity come true, everyone is going to have to work very hard, and that Africans themselves are going to have to take charge of their lives in the way they have not been called upon to do. The era of the second liberation of Africa, internationally and domestically, may, indeed, have just begun.

NOTES

1. Naomi Chazan, Robert Mortimer, John Ravenhill, and Donald Rothchild, *Politics and Society in Contemporary Africa,* 2nd Edition (Boulder, CO: Lynne Reiner Publishers, 1991), p. 379.
2. Joseph L. Nogee and Robert H. Donaldson, *Soviet Foreign Policy since World War II* (New York: Pergamon Press, 1983), p. 182.
3. Zaki Laidi, *The Super-powers and Africa: The Constraints of a Rivalry, 1960–1990* (Chicago: University of Chicago Press, 1990), p. 9.
4. Jean Kirkpatrick, "Human Rights and American Foreign Policy," in Chau T. Phau, ed., *World Politics 82/83,* Annual Editions (Guildford, CT: Dushkin Publishing Group, 1982), pp. 16–19.
5. Cyrus Vance, "The Human Rights Imperative," in John T. Rourke, ed., *Taking Sides,* 3rd Edition (Guildford, CT: Dushkin Publishing Group, 1991), p. 235.
6. William Attwood, *The Reds and the Blacks: A Personal Adventure* (New York: Harper & Row, 1967).
7. Ted Galen Carpenter, "The U.S. and Third World Dictatorships: A Case for Benign Detachment," in Jeffrey M. Elliott, ed., *Third World,* Annual Editions (Guildford, CT: Dushkin Publishing Group, 1991), pp. 123–127.

8. A. W. Singham, ed., *The Nonaligned Movement in World Politics* (Westport, CT: Lawrence Hill & Co., 1977).

9. "Non-Aligned: For What, Against What?" http://news.bbc.co.uk/2/hi/162711. stm.

10. Olatunde J. C. B. Ojo, D. K. Orwa, and C. M. B. Utete, *Africa's International Relations* (London: Longman, 1985), p. 78.

11. Thomas A. Imobighe, *The OAU, African Defence and Security* (Owerri, Benin: Adena Publishers, 1989), p. 136.

12. Ibid., p. 136.

13. *Keesing's Record of World Events,* Vol. 38, No. 8, p. 38992.

14. See B. David Meyers, "The O.A.U.'s Administrative Secretary-General," *International Organization,* Vol. 30, No. 3 (Summer, 1976), pp. 509–520.

15. Vincent B. Khapoya, "The Politics and the Political Economy of OAU Summitry," paper presented at the annual meeting of the African Studies Association, Washington, DC, November 4–7, 1982.

16. Ibid.

17. Corrine A. A. Packer and Donald Rukare, "The New African Union and Its Constitutive Act," *American Journal of International Law,* Vol. 96, No. 2 (April, 2002), pp. 279–365.

18. http://news.bbc.co.uk. Accessed December 27, 2008.

19. Ibid.

20. Donald Rothchild, "U.S. Policy Styles in Africa," in Kenneth A. Oye, Donald Rothchild, and Robert J. Lieber, eds., *Eagle Entangled: U.S. Foreign Policy in a Complex World* (New York: Longman, 1979), pp. 307–309.

21. Donald Rothchild and John Ravenhill, "Subordinating African Issues to Global Logic: Reagan Confronts Political Complexity," in Kenneth Oye, Robert J. Lieber, and Donald Rothchild, eds., *Eagle Resurgent? The Reagan Era in American Foreign Policy* (Boston: Little, Brown & Company, 1987), pp. 398–400.

22. Richard N. Haas, "Fatal Distraction: Bill Cinton's Foreign Policy," *Foreign Policy,* No. 108 (Fall, 1997), p. 113.

23. Ali A. Mazrui, "The USSR and China as Models of Innovation," in A. A. Mazrui, ed., *Political Values and the Educated Class in Africa* (Berkeley: University of California Press, 1978), p. 170.

24. Joseph L. Nogee and Robert H. Donaldson, *Soviet Foreign Policy since World War II,* p. 132.

25. Robert Legvold, *Soviet Policy in West Africa* (Cambridge: Harvard University Press, 1970), pp. 1–2.

26. Ibid., p. 113.

27. Joseph L. Nogee and Robert H. Donaldson, *Soviet Foreign Policy since World War II,* p. 135.

28. Nick Eberstadt and Tom Ricks, "The Cost of Pax Sovietica," in Chau T. Phau, ed., *World Politics 1982/83,* Annual Editions (Guildford, CT: Dushkin Publishing Group, 1982), pp. 42–47.

29. Michael G. Roskin, *Countries and Concepts,* 3rd Edition (Englewood Cliffs, NJ: Prentice Hall, 1989), pp. 243, 265.

30. Ibid., p. 223.

31. Richard J. Barnet, "But What about Africa? On the Global Economy's Lost Continent," *Harper's Magazine,* Vol. 280, No. 1680 (May, 1990), p. 45.

32. Gilbert M. Khadiagala, "Thoughts on Africa and the New World Order," *The Round Table* Vol. 324, No. 3 (1992), p. 442.

33. William Minter, ed., *Africa's Problems... African Initiatives* (Washington, DC: Africa Policy Information Center, 1992), p. 9.

34. Ibid., p. 25.

35. Ibid., p. 35.

INDEX

Note: page references with *t* and *illus* notation refer to a table as well as illustration on that page respectively.